The Justices of the Peace, 1679–1760

The Justices of the Peace, 1679–1760

Norma Landau

UNIVERSITY OF CALIFORNIA PRESS
Berkeley · Los Angeles · London

University of California Press
Berkeley and Los Angeles, California
University of California Press, Ltd.
London, England

1 2 3 4 5 6 7 8 9

Library of Congress Cataloging in Publication Data

Landau, Norma.
The justices of the peace, 1679–1760.

Bibliography: p.
Includes index.
1. Justices of the peace—England—History.
I. Title.
KD8309.L36 1984 347.42'016 82-23760
ISBN 0-520-04623-4 344.20716

To My Parents

Contents

PART FOUR: THE IMAGE OF THE BENCH

APPENDICES

Tables and Illustrations

TEXT TABLES

APPENDIX TABLES

APPENDIX FIGURE

MAP

Acknowledgments

I am very glad that I have this opportunity to thank those who helped me in the writing of this book. As a graduate student, I received fellowships from the Canada Council and the University of California at Berkeley. A summer Fellowship from the National Endowment for the Humanities, a grant-in-aid from the American Philosophical Society, and a Junior Faculty Fellowship from the University of California at Davis enabled me to continue my research in England. I enjoyed doing that research, in part because of the interest and assistance of the librarians and archivists of the manuscript collections cited in the bibliography. I am especially indebted to Dr. Felix Hull and his staff at the Kent Archives Office, Mr. L. R. A. Grove of the Maidstone Museum, and the late Mr. George Lawrence of the Sevenoaks Public Library.

I am grateful to those who have permitted me to consult and quote from their manuscripts and manuscripts in their keeping: Lady Ravensdale, Lady Monson, Lady Anne Bentinck, the Duke of Marlborough, the Marquess of Bath, Lord Sackville, Sir Michael Culme-Seymour, Mr. C. S. Davis, Charrington and Company, the Deputy Keeper of the Records, Public Record Office of Northern Ireland, the Keeper of Western Manuscripts, Bodleian Library, and the archivists of the Hampshire Record Office, the Hertfordshire Record Office, the Gloucestershire Record Office, the Lincolnshire Archives Office, and the Kent Archives Office. Mr. E. L. C. Mullins and Professor B. Henning kindly allowed me to examine the biographies of members of later Stuart Parliaments being prepared for publication by the

History of Parliament Trust. I also wish to thank Professor F. M. L. Thompson, editor of the *Bulletin of the Institute of Historical Research,* for permitting me to reproduce portions of an article by Dr. L. K. J. Glassey and myself, which appeared in the *Bulletin* in 1972.

As I write this, I realize how fortunate I have been in my friends, colleagues, and teachers. Doing research in English documents while working in North America poses some peculiar problems. Dr. Scott Waugh, Dr. Roger Knight, and Mr. Michael Collinge took time from their own researches to locate documents and send me information. My sister, Reva Landau, both copied documents in the British Library and recruited her friends to stamp headings on hundreds of cards so that I could concisely record information on Kent's justices. I very much appreciate her forbearance and good humour.

It was my very good fortune to take undergraduate courses from Professor John M. Beattie at the University of Toronto. Professor Beattie's lectures aroused my interest in eighteenth century England, and his subsequent advice and encouragement stimulated my research. As a graduate student, I studied at the University of California at Berkeley, where I found in Professor Thomas G. Barnes a scholar eager to impart his knowledge of English law and local government. The comments of Professors Walter Woodfill, David Spring, D.C. Moore, Daniel Calhoun, and William Hagen assisted me in transforming early versions of my manuscript into a book. This book began as a doctoral dissertation written under the direction of Professor Sheldon Rothblatt of the University of California at Berkeley. As Professor Rothblatt talked to me about history, encouraged me in my work, criticized my manuscript, and worried about his University, I learned from him the meaning of scholarship. For his guidance, aid, and example, I am very grateful.

N. L.

Davis, California
October, 1982

Note on Style and Abbreviations

All dates in the body of the text retain Old Style dating for day and month, but the year is changed to New Style. All dates in the footnotes are given as they appear in the source cited, but if the New Style year differs from that of the Old Style, the New Style year is added in brackets. All names in the body of the text are given their modern spelling, but names in the footnotes are given as they appear in the source cited. All quotations are given as they appear in the original, except ampersands which are replaced by "and."

The following abbreviations are used:

Abbott	Abbott collection of parliamentary papers in the British Library
Add. MSS	Additional Manuscripts
A.O.	Archives Office
B.L.	British Library
B.I.H.R.	*Bulletin of the Institute of Historical Research*
CSPD	*Calendar of State Papers Domestic*
HMC	*Publications of the Historical Manuscripts Commission*
P.R.O.	Public Record Office
R.O.	Record Office

Introduction

This book is about the later Stuart and early Hanoverian commission of the peace, an institution which contemporaries regarded as peculiarly English and therefore both guardian and representative of English liberty. Members of the commission were justices of the peace, and their commission established the justices as both magistrates and local governors of the county for which they were commissioned. On the Continent, commentators noted, sovereigns entrusted magistracy to salaried functionaries who took office "that they may eat Bread" and governed those whom they have never seen before. In England, magistracy rested upon unpaid justices of the peace, men of "ample Fortunes" who administered the communities in which they resided.[1] So the justices were the premier exemplars of two traditions of government which the English considered unique to their island: the practice of self-government at the king's command and acceptance of responsibility by the elite. On the Continent, the elite fled from their estates, preferring the pleasures of the court to the burdens of local leadership. In England, the elite accepted the obligations inherent in their social status. Their mansions dominated the English countryside, not city streets, and their rural residence proclaimed their determination to minister to the communities nourished by their lands.

The justices' beneficence may be disputed, but their importance to an understanding of both English government and social structure is unquestionable. Of all the European landed elites, only the English

1. T. Barlow, *The Justice of Peace: A Treatise Containing the Power and Duty of that Magistrate* (London, 1745), pp. vii–viii.

captured the central government. Only in England did the state not develop into an entity separate from the elite and in conflict with it. In England the landed elite monopolized government, and the justices therefore embodied the peculiarly English union of social and official power. With their Glorious Revolution English landowners indubitably established their dominance of government. At no time, therefore, were the justices more powerful than in the century and a half following the Glorious Revolution.

So powerful were the justices that they were virtually independent, and it is their independence which makes the justices fascinating. Neither the central government nor Parliament told them what to do, closely supervised their activity, or even insured that they act at all. Therefore, the justices' activity is an unusually direct reflection of their motivation. They did what they did because they wanted to do it and thought they should do it. By examining the justices' activities, we can discover what England's local governors thought was important in government. By examining their conduct, we can discover how they thought a governor should behave. And by examining their decisions as to whether they should act at all, we can discover what rewards the justices derived from office. Examination of the justices therefore involves discussion of the ideals, structures, and inducements inherent in English local government which propelled the English elite to assume their distinctive role as paternal rulers.

Unfortunately, the label 'paternal ruler' is more evocative than analytic. Indeed, it so stimulates our imagination that it may summon up visions of all who exercise authority in a fatherly manner—those who exercise authority in the household or workshop, for example. This book employs a narrower definition of the term: paternal rulers here are those who exercise official powers of government, and references to paternalism are restricted to the fatherly activities and attitudes of governors when they act as governors. Even this restriction of the term does not altogether clarify its meaning, for there may be as many varieties of paternal ruler as there are roles for fathers. Like fathers, paternal rulers exercise authority within a hierarchic structure, and their official powers are but a portion of those powers which society considers appropriate to those in their station. Like fathers, paternal rulers are involved in the affairs of those over whom they exercise authority. And, like fathers, paternal rulers express attachment to and concern for those they govern. The label 'paternal ruler' emphasizes the involvement of a member of the elite in the concerns of a community composed of his inferiors, but it does so at the expense of camouflaging the variety of attitudes, activities, and roles which might be regarded as paternalist. Two paternal rulers might exercise authority in different manners; their concern for their inferiors might be expressed in different fashions; the degree and nature of their involvement with their communities might differ; and so might the inducements which impel them to assume their paternalist roles.

As the forms in which a paternal ruler might appear are so various, I begin by sketching two different stereotypes of the paternal ruler. Both stereotypes can be used to describe the eighteenth-century justice. Both stereotypes are also rooted in contemporary usage, for we are apt to describe as paternal two somewhat different types of activity: (1) action by a superior which the community desires for defence of its interests but which can be executed only by a person endowed with uncommon powers; and (2) action by a superior which the superior realizes will benefit the community, though the community may not be mature enough to appreciate the wisdom of such action. The first demands a leader so affected by the condition of his inferiors that he instantly springs to their defence; the second, a leader sufficiently distanced from the community to discern its contours and its path. The first type of paternalist is so closely tied to his community that he might be regarded as its patriarch. As the second type does not think he is immediately affected by decisions which affect his inferiors, he can compliment himself upon the disinterested judgment which allows him to provide patrician leadership to a plebeian community.[2] While self-interest motivates the patriarchal paternalist, the patrician paternalist can claim the virtue of altruism. As the patriarchal paternalist is so bound to his community that its condition affects his interest, he may define his community primarily in terms of those of its members whose condition most immediately affects his. Since the patrician paternalist is sufficiently distanced from his community that he does not think he is immediately affected by the condition of any group within it, he may be more apt to think in terms of the community of all his inferiors. Because the patriarchal paternalist is so intimately tied to his community, he is likely to base his identity and claim to leadership on his status in the locality. In contrast, the patrician paternalist is more

2. I have borrowed the label 'patrician' from E. P. Thompson, "Patrician Society, Plebeian Culture," *Journal of Social History* 7 (1974), and "Eighteenth-century English society: class struggle without class," *Social History* 3 (1978), esp. n. 25. Both articles also comment upon paternalism.

likely to think of his identity within a national context; he derives his identity not from the acknowledgment paid him by the inferiors of his neighbourhood, but instead from his superior culture, a culture he shares with others in the nation and which enables members of his group to decide what is best for the communities in which they live.

It might be possible to write a history of the commission of the peace from its inception to the present in terms of struggle over which of these two forms of paternalism it should embody. The violence characteristic of the late mediaeval elite may make them unlikely paternalists. Nonetheless, the debate on the commission which preoccupied late mediaeval Parliaments was that of local versus national power: Were the justices to be emissaries of the sovereign, imposing the central government's definition of order, or representatives of the shire, administering government in the interests of the local elite? While the sovereign retained control over the appointment of justices, from the Elizabethan period onward those appointed to the bench were gentry possessed of local power and eminence, and the central government could not insure enforcement of its directives when the justices did not choose to enforce them. Given the central government's reliance upon local gentry, the tension between local and national perspectives in the administration of local government could be resolved only if local gentry distanced themselves from their localities and adopted a national perspective. During the sixteenth and seventeenth centuries, many tendencies encouraged this transformation in gentry culture—the attractions exerted by the court and London, humanist education at the universities, legal education at the Inns of Court, conflict between various forms of Protestantism, to cite only the most obvious.[3] Nonetheless, it was not until the late eighteenth century that both the national government and the justices countenanced economic hardships in a locality in the interests of furthering the national economy.[4] By the first half of the nineteenth century, paternalists were proclaiming their belief in the self-regulating laws of

3. For a depiction of the seventeenth-century gentry as "brokers" between the localities and national culture, see C. Holmes, *Seventeenth-Century Lincolnshire, History of Lincolnshire,* vol. 7 (Lincoln, 1980), pp. 64–87. For a synthesis of the literature on the gentry, see G. E. Mingay, *The Gentry* (London, 1976). For the eighteenth-century gentry, see *idem, English Landed Society in the Eighteenth Century* (London, 1963).

4. E. P. Thompson, "The Moral Economy of the English Crowd in the Eighteenth Century," *Past and Present* 50 (1971): 83, 85–88, 129–131, 136; E. F. Genovese, "The Many Faces of Moral Economy: A Contribution to a Debate," *Past and Present* 58 (1973): 165–168.

society, while governing plebeians with whom they were unacquainted.[5] It was in the eighteenth century that the patrician, more distanced, variety of paternalism became a notable feature of judicial government.

Because both patriarchal and patrician paternalists graced the eighteenth-century bench, the eighteenth-century justice remains our model of the quintessential justice. For the quintessential justice embodies both the patriarchal and patrician paternalist—both the local father who symbolizes the community and responds to its immediate needs, and the more Victorian and distant paterfamilias whose rule accords with the just but impersonal laws of nature. As the evolution of the justices' image of themselves suggests, in the eighteenth century the new judicial role was assimilated within the old.

The creation of stereotypes inevitably results in crude contrasts and the erection of ahistorical watersheds. That after 1760 the county bench began to produce county leaders interested in reform of county administration and of the manners of the populace has been interpreted as evidence of the rise of a new sense of social responsibility among the later Hanoverian elite, and of the moral lassitude of their predecessors.[6] The same phenomenon might be presented as evidence of the contrast between two modes of paternalist rule. But alterations in behaviour are rarely swift or complete. Undoubtedly patriarchal concepts of rule influenced later Hanoverian justices. So, too, patrician rule did not suddenly appear in the late eighteenth century. Between 1679 and 1760 changes in concepts of magistracy, in the composition of the bench, in the justices' relations to the governed, and in the structure of politics and local administration were engendering a local government fit for patrician rulers. In examining the justices of later Stuart and early Hanoverian England this book depicts a crucial stage in the self-transformation of England's most autonomous local patriarchs into administrators for the nation.

As paternal rulers, the justices epitomized the virtues of both English social structure and English government. Some of the greatest of

5. D. Roberts, *Paternalism in Early Victorian England* (New Brunswick, N.J., 1979), pp. 41, 271.

6. S. and B. Webb, *English Local Government from the Revolution to the Municipal Corporations Act,* vol. 1, *The Parish and the County* (London, 1906), pp. 364–372. That later Hanoverian justices were increasingly apt to sentence violators of the game laws might also be indicative of a new mode of rule, a mode which supplanted patriarchal involvement with the governed by patrician adherence to an abstract code of justice; see P. B. Munsche, *Gentlemen and Poachers: The English Game Laws 1671–1831* (Cambridge, 1981), pp. 100–101.

the historians of England have analysed the structure of eighteenth-century local government, the nature of its politics, and the mode of rule adopted by its elite. Their analyses provide the framework for this study.

1. THE STRUCTURE OF LOCAL GOVERNMENT

Were it not for the work of Sidney and Beatrice Webb it would be impossible to produce a concise description of the structure of eighteenth-century local government. The powers of the eighteenth-century justice had been defined by at least five centuries of statutes, and five centuries of statutes can produce an amazing number of anomalies, exceptions, oddities, and red herrings, not to mention a rather confusing allocation of power. The Webbs carefully detailed the organization of local government in the century following the Glorious Revolution, and their analysis emphasized both the justices' autonomy and their activity as administrators of local government.

The justices had not originally been either autonomous or administrators. The justices' office descends from that of the keepers of the peace who were entrusted by the sovereign's commission with, among other duties, the task of assuring that both charges of criminal behaviour and the alleged criminals themselves be brought before the sovereign's judges. In the fourteenth century the justices truly became justices, for they acquired the power to hear and determine criminal cases. This they did at their court of Quarter Sessions, the quarterly assembly of all the justices of the county. From the mid-fourteenth century these judicial officers gradually acquired administrative authority. Later Plantaganet justices exercised powers to regulate the economy—to set wages, to prevent forestalling and engrossing, to enforce statutes on weights and measures. Under the Tudors and early Stuarts the justices' administrative burden increased. Now justices supervised parish government. Most important of their numerous new duties was superintendance of highway maintenance and of the collection and distribution of rates to relieve the poor. For these functions the county commission subdivided into smaller and yet more local meetings, meetings which became the foundation of petty sessions. Meanwhile the justices were acquiring new powers of summary jurisdiction over minor offences. Statute allocated jurisdiction over some offences to one justice and over others to two. By the late seventeenth century the justice was both a judicial and an administrative officer:

he insured that alleged miscreants appeared to answer for their offences; sitting either in or out of Quarter Sessions, he heard and determined charges of all but the most major offences; he supervised parish government; and he administered county government.

While they were acquiring increasing judicial and administrative powers, the justices also gradually acquired a near monopoly of local judicial and administrative authority. Other local courts had competed with those of the Plantaganet justices. In 1461, Parliament ordained that criminal charges laid before hundred courts—the public courts of justice inherited from Anglo-Saxon times—be forwarded to the justices in Quarter Sessions. Private courts, both manorial and leet, had exercised powers concurrent with those of Quarter Sessions over a variety of offences and public nuisances. By the early seventeenth century many of these courts had disappeared; by the late seventeenth century most were either nonexistent or insignificant. No local court now contested the justices' local rule.

Early Stuart justices may have been undisputed rulers of the county, but unlike their successors they could not claim autonomy. Star Chamber, the judicial arm of the Privy Council, exercised the power immediately to punish an erring justice. Star Chamber was abolished in 1641. The early Stuart Privy Council, the supreme administrative body of the realm, issued directives to the justices. After the Glorious Revolution, a Privy Council directive was a rare signal of emergency—of war, threat of invasion, or danger from an unusually infectious disease. The central government's remaining instrument of control was the judges. Twice a year the judges presided at each county's Assizes. At Assizes the judges heard those criminal cases with which the justices could not or chose not to deal. At Assizes the judges determined disputes about rights to property (justices never had the power to hear or determine property cases). At Assizes the judges instructed the justices in the niceties of the law and, in cooperation with the justices, issued orders on local administration. And, either at Assizes or at their courts at Westminster, the judges heard appeals from the justices' orders and judgments, and even cases brought against the justices themselves. By the eighteenth century the judges' supervision of the justices had also declined. The command that the justices attend Assizes was more honoured in the breach than in the observance. Few orders on county administration emanated from Assizes. Rarely were justices' judgments or orders appealed to the higher courts, and even more infrequently were charges brought against a justice for misconduct in office. By the early eighteenth century, then, the justices' autonomy was established and the legal structure of their government determined. No directive from the central goverment—no Privy Council order, no parliamentary act, no judge's decision—would cause a major alteration in either their powers or the structure of their courts for over one hundred years.

Perhaps because they were Fabians and twentieth-century dirigistes, the Webbs were most interested in the formal administrative structure of rule—structure as determined by Privy Council orders, acts of Parliament, and orders of Quarter Sessions. Since the Webbs wished to examine change in the formal structure of local government and the ideological and administrative determinants of that change, they focused on the late eighteenth and early nineteenth centuries, emphasizing those orders of Quarter Sessions which inaugurated the era of efficiently administered, centrally directed, and bureaucratically based local government. As the formal powers and organization of the justices hardly altered between the Glorious and American Revolutions, the Webbs' work portrays the early Hanoverian justices as lackadaisical and their government as static. Nonetheless, it was the later Stuart and early Hanoverian justices who elaborated the administrative framework prerequisite for the reforms in local government which so fascinated the Webbs.

Change in local government occurred in the later Stuart and early Hanoverian eras, though it was not change in local government's formal structure. In contrast to the Webbs, this book examines the informal structure of the justices' rule: their development of institutions whose work is not reflected in formal orders of Quarter Sessions or acts of Parliament; their behaviour in office; their use of their powers; and their assumptions about the rewards and nature of their office. A brief discussion of petty sessions may illustrate both informal structure and its change. Because the Webbs relied on the formal records of Quarter Sessions, they thought petty sessions had been introduced into rural counties during the last third of the eighteenth century. As petty sessions wielded those powers assigned by statute to any two justices of the county, the Webbs considered petty sessions an institution which introduced rational order into the anarchic administrative structure of local government, an institutional expression of the justices' administrative enlightenment. In fact, marginal notations in Quarter Sessions' records and the records of petty sessions—which were not available to the Webbs—reveal that petty sessions were flourishing in the early eighteenth century, acquiring an extra-legal monopoly over many of the powers allocated by statute to two justices, and altering the relation between the justices and those they governed. For the justice as familiar patriarch of his neighbourhood, petty sessions substituted the justice as one of a group of governors. The justices, not Parliament or the central government, built petty sessions, and their elaboration of this institution underlines the interplay between change in administrative structure and change in the elite's conduct and concept of rule.

The development of petty sessions likewise illuminates the interplay between the justices' perception of the rewards of their office and their elaboration of their institutions. The rewards of judicial office were unofficial, informal—influence over the inhabitants of a neighbourhood. Because the justices wielded administrative power, their orders affected the tax burden borne by their communities. As many taxpayers were voters, judicial office endowed its tenants with political influence. So, change in the justices' assessment of the nature of politics affected change in local administration. The rise of party in the later Stuart era gave impetus for the consolidation of petty sessions, while the decline of party strife in the mid-eighteenth century encouraged the emergence of justices interested in administrative structure and its reform. While the Webbs' analysis of the formal structure of local government therefore provides the indispensable foundation for a study of the justices, examination of the informal structure of rule suggests that administration cannot be examined in a vacuum. Changes in the justices' administration were related to the justices' non-administrative concerns, politics not least among them.

2. THE STRUCTURE OF POLITICS

There are two related reasons for incorporating an examination of politics in a study of the justices: justices influenced the votes cast by the electorate; because justices wielded political influence and because judicial office was an honour bestowed by the central government, ministries manipulated the composition of the peace. The sovereign's ministers wished to place their allies upon the bench and to exclude their opponents. Therefore an analysis of the composition of the commission is also an analysis of the structure of the political alliances made by England's local elites.

Analysis of the structure of politics leads ineluctably to the debate about party, for 'party' was a contentious word in later Stuart and early Hanoverian England. In sober analyses and vituperant polemic, men condemned party and praised it, asserted that party had vanished and testified to its persistence, claimed that party was based on principle and denied that distinction between political ideologies could produce a realistic description of English politics. Modern historians still engage in that debate, for their assertions about party have to be based on an analysis of political structure, and analyses of political structure engender conclusions about the ideals and behaviour of the political nation which engendered parliamentary democracy.

Modern debate about the political structure of eighteenth-century England centers on the work of Sir Lewis Namier. Namier examined the structure of politics at the accession of George III and argued that by 1761 English politics was not party politics. Rather than voting according to the dictates of political ideology, both the electorate and members of Parliament responded to the more mundane influence of family and professional ties and the patronage networks of both the aristocracy and the central government. In Namier's view, the structure of parliamentary politics at the accession of George III is most accurately described by categorizing members of Parliament in groups as defined by the ambition of their members: politicians who sought office, civil servants and pensioners who wanted jobs and emoluments from the national government, and independent country gentlemen who prized the prestige of a parliamentary seat. Namier's argument therefore denies that ideology influenced political behaviour; indeed, his own ideology argued that ideology should not influence political behaviour.[7]

While English historians have been reluctant to adopt the view that ideology either does not or should not affect politics, Namier's analysis of political structure has proved to be unusually persuasive. Some historians of seventeenth-century England have extended Namier's conclusions to suggest that the major political division of that century was between the Court—those who had access to the plums at the disposal of the national government, and the Country—those who did not have such access. That both seventeenth- and eighteenth-century politics can be analysed in terms of patronage networks has suggested that the private connections of English gentle-

7. Sir L. Namier, *England in the Age of the American Revolution,* 2nd ed. (London, 1961); *idem, The Structure of Politics at the Accession of George III,* 2nd ed. (London, 1957).

men provided the adamantine structure on which politics was based, and that the impetus for the political activity of England's gentlemen was undiluted self-interest.

Namier framed his argument so as to counter the Whig school of historiography. The Whigs both averred that eighteenth-century English politics can best be analysed in terms of struggle between parties and emphasized the benefits which politicians' adherence to political principle confers upon the nation. As Burke declared, party is "a body of men united for promoting by their joint endeavours the national interest upon some particular principle in which they all are agreed." Ideally, adherence to principle assists political participants in forming groups which are more cohesive, effective, and altruistic than those based upon private self-interest. So, the Whig school found early Hanoverian politics particularly distasteful, for despite the presence of party Walpole and his followers acted in their own self-interest, while the Tories were unable to discover principles suited to the promotion of the nation's welfare.

The Whig school could insist that party was present in mid-eighteenth century England because in at least two earlier periods struggle between parties had dominated English politics. Modern research has confirmed that on both occasions party struggle incorporated but was not restricted to the conflict between Court and Country. Party first appeared in the late 1670s, when a group libelled as Whigs battled a group slandered as Tories over the exclusion of the future James II from the line of those entitled to inherit the throne. Likewise, in Anne's reign conflict between Whigs and Tories again structured English politics. In both periods, the parties elaborated principles relevant to national concerns and attempted to enact laws based on their principles. In both periods there is impressive evidence of party organization and in Anne's reign impressive evidence of party cohesion.[8] The extent to which the parties subsumed Court and Country in the period between the Exclusion crisis and the accession of Anne is a matter of current debate, and whether party existed at all in the seven decades following Anne's death has been the subject of considerable and heated argument.

The problem of analysing party in the periods which currently generate debate is complicated by change in the nature of the Whig

8. J. R. Jones, *The First Whigs: The Politics of the Exclusion Crisis* (London, 1961); G. Holmes, *British Politics in the Age of Anne* (London, 1967); W. A. Speck, *Tory and Whig: The Struggle in the Constituencies 1701–1715* (London, 1970).

and Tory parties themselves. During the Exclusion crisis the Whigs had attracted Country adherents, while Court supporters—including the king—carried the Tory banner. After the Glorious Revolution and especially after 1693, the parties found their actual position at odds with their ideological stance on the conflict between Court and Country. Since the Whigs now possessed office, it behooved their leaders to use the government patronage they had once despised. Tories, on the other hand, no longer dispensed the good things of English political life, and their supporters had to choose between Tory principle and the attractions of the Court.[9] By Anne's accession, the Tory party endorsed Country principle and drew Country supporters, while the Whigs were more closely aligned with the Court. Because of the confusion caused by this realignment, it has been suggested that there were four relatively independent political groups in William's reign: Whig and Tory, Court and Country.[10]

Likewise, in the reigns of the first two Hanoverians change in political circumstance again altered the parties' situation. The Whigs obtained office and they remained in office for at least seventy years. The first two Hanoverian monarchs very much preferred alliance with the Whigs to reliance on the Tories. Consequently, anyone possessed by a compulsive appetite for national office—that is, every politician—had to call himself a Whig. Since by 1761 combat for office was a struggle between Whig politicians, Namier could declare that politics should be analysed without reference to party. Instead factions, relatively incohesive groups motivated not by principle but simply by the desire to gain power, fought for office.

While there is general agreement that by 1761 the politics of party had been superseded by the politics of faction, there is less agreement about the timing of this transition. Did party politics disappear shortly after the accession of George I, or did it slowly fade away? As party politics entailed struggle between two parties, answers to questions about the survival of party politics center upon the fate of the Tories. If, as has been contended, the Tory party soon vanished as an effective political force, then the structure of early Hanoverian politics was not that of struggle between two parties.[11] If, on the other hand, the

9. J. H. Plumb, *The Growth of Political Stability in England, 1675–1725* (London, 1967).

10. D. Rubini, *Court and Country 1688–1702* (London, 1967); see also H. Horwitz, *Parliament, Policy and Politics in the Reign of William III* (Manchester, 1977).

11. G. Holmes, "Harley, St. John and the Death of the Tory Party," in *Britain after the Glorious Revolution*, ed. G. Holmes (London, 1969).

Tories continued to pose a threat to Whig supremacy, then the political struggles of early Hanoverian England were less factious and symbolize more serious disputes about power and government than has been supposed.

Until very recently, there has been relatively little examination of early Hanoverian party, in part because the era's parliamentary politics has proven singularly impermeable to analysis of political structure.[12] While there are several criteria for determining whether a parliamentary group is a party or a faction, the criterion which most allows an historian to discern the nature of parliamentary alliances rests on analysis of the behaviour of members of a parliamentary group when they have an opportunity to gain office. Since members of a faction are motivated by self-interest, they abandon both their erstwhile principles and colleagues for the rewards of office. In contrast, party members accept office only when they can do so without renouncing either colleagues or principles. As several groups struggled for and attained office under George III, their behaviour can be analysed and these analyses debated. But, under the first two Hanoverians a handful of Whig politicians so monopolized office that few politicians had to choose between office and adherence to colleagues and principles. Since the Tories were given little opportunity to exhibit the stigmata of party behaviour, and since the difficulties of finding evidence of united Tory activity were compounded by the Tories' propensity for prudential destruction of their papers, it has generally been assumed that the Tory party disintegrated shortly after the accession of George I.[13] New examination of the Tories in early Hanoverian Parliaments has now revealed that they functioned as a party. Indeed, it is contended that the Tories survived as a parliamentary party into the reign of George III.[14] The debate about party, a debate begun in the eighteenth century, continues still.

12. See, however, A. S. Foord, *His Majesty's Opposition 1714–1830* (Oxford, 1964); B. W. Hill, *The Growth of Parliamentary Parties 1689–1742* (London, 1976); W. A. Speck, *Stability and Strife: England 1714–1760* (Cambridge, Mass., 1979); and J. B. Owen, *The Rise of the Pelhams* (London, 1957).

13. For a summary of work on and opinion about early Hanoverian party, see W. A. Speck, "Whigs and Tories dim their glories: English political parties under the first two Georges;" G. Holmes, "Colloquy on chapter 3;" and J. Cannon, "Final discussion" in *The Whig Ascendancy,* ed. J. Cannon (London, 1981).

14. L. Colley, "The Loyal Brotherhood and the Cocoa Tree: The London Organization of the Tory Party, 1727–1760," *Historical Journal* 20 (1977); L. Colley, *In Defiance of Oligarchy: The Tory Party 1714–1760* (Cambridge, 1982); see also J. C. D. Clark, "A General Theory of Party, Opposition and Government, 1688–1832," *Historical Journal* 23 (1980), and "The Decline of Party, 1740–60," *English Historical Review* 93 (1978).

A study of the justices provides another perspective from which to view the phenomenon of party, for the composition of the commission of the peace reflected the structure within which England's local elites forged their political alliances. Many personages attempted to influence decisions on the composition of a county's bench: the county's Lord Lieutenant, its custos rotulorum (keeper of the county's judicial rolls and therefore nominally head of the county's commission), members of Parliament, and county magnates. Nonetheless, ultimate responsibility for both the appointment and dismissal of justices rested with the Lord Chancellor. As Lord Chancellors were politicians, skilled in assessment of the nature of political alliances, it is not surprising that appointments and dismissals of justices map the changing contours of later Stuart and early Hanoverian politics. Examination of the composition of the local bench reveals the chronology of the rise, persistence, and partial disintegration of party.

Even more important, examination of the justices presents politics within a new and wider framework. Investigations of English politics have usually focused on Parliament, and it is not clear whether parliamentary conflict magnified, minimized, or even reflected divisions among the political nation. The justices' involvement in party struggle proves that minor members of the elite played an active role in national politics. Country gentlemen lived in the provinces, but their horizons were by no means provincial. Connected by party to both parliamentary leaders and the elites of other counties, engrossed by national as well as local issues, early eighteenth-century country gentlemen were self-conscious members of a national governing elite. Party therefore generated change in the local elites' assumptions about the structure of English society. For when party struggle diminished, the governed found that their rulers were not merely eminent individuals possessed of power over a neighbourhood; instead they now confronted a united ruling social stratum.

3. THE JUSTICES' MODE OF RULE

As the foregoing suggests, the justices took advantage of the potential inherent in changes in the structure of politics and the informal structure of rule for alteration of their image. During the reigns of the later Stuarts and early Hanoverians they gradually modified the model of the local governor that they presented to the public. The image which the justices presented to the populace was an important component of their rule, for the very manner in which they displayed themselves conveyed a message to those they governed. As E. P. Thompson has suggested, communication between governors and governed in eighteenth-century England can be characterized as participatory theatre. The governed informed their rulers of their expectations not through written demands or formal negotiations, but in street parades, riots, and finely graded exhibitions of deference which served as signals of their ideals.[15] Likewise, both the composition and conduct of the bench informed the governed of their rulers' notion of the appropriate relation between governors and governed. By the mid-eighteenth century, the gentry justice typical of late seventeenth-century England was joined on the bench by the gentleman proto-bureaucrat. The gentry justice was patriarch of his neighbourhood because he possessed an interest in that neighbourhood; the gentleman justice possessed little interest but was intrigued by administration. Together they faced the populace; together they symbolized union among the rulers' social strata and fundamental agreement across the rulers' disintegrating party barriers; together they elaborated a governmental structure which both moulded the rulers into a more cohesive group and distanced the rulers from the ruled. While it would be an exaggeration to characterize change in the justices' behaviour as indicative of the making of the ruling class, the justices' alteration of the image they presented to the public does nonetheless indicate the emergence of a new mode of rule—a mode of rule which replaced government by the gentry as eminent individuals with government by the rulers as a group, and which remodelled patriarchal involvement in the neighbourhood into patrician concern for the condition of Englishmen.

Inevitably, modification of the image which justices presented to the public involved modification of the justices' own model of the ideal justice. When the justices appraised their refurbished image, they found it plausible to emphasize their altruism and their disinterested service—both virtues which had always been implicit in the judicial model, but which had not heretofore been so apparent. Exercise of both virtues demands that the rulers be somewhat distanced from their communities. Only a justice who does not possess an interest in his neighbourhood can claim to be disinterested. Only when many justices find the rewards of office too trifling to assume its burdens—only when many justices cannot or do not want to use office markedly to increase their influence in their communities—can active justices preen themselves on their altruistic public service. Since

15. See Thompson's articles in nn. 2 and 4 above.

the justices enacted the elite's view of its role and personified government for the populace, the justices' modification of their image has had a profound impact on English concepts of conduct appropriate to governmental office. The ideal civil servant and the ideal colonial governor are both altruistic and disinterested, as was the ideal Victorian member of Parliament.

This book begins in the era of the Glorious Revolution, when party first appeared and local government had attained a definitive formal structure. It ends at the accession of George III, just before the emergence of the political groups which begat modern parties and of the administrative reformers who altered the activities of local government. Both administrative and political historians have characterized the early Hanoverian era as one of the more corrupt and stagnant in English history. As the justices' new image suggests, the allegedly more praiseworthy administrative structures and concepts of responsible behaviour attributed to later elites were manufactured by the rulers of early Hanoverian England.

Therefore, this book is organized so as to emphasize the justices' view of their office. Chapter I examines the manner in which justices used their powers to assume the leadership of their neighbourhoods and so influence voters, while chapter II focuses on the justices' use of their courts to disseminate political propaganda. The next three chapters trace the interaction between change in the nature and ideology of the parties and change in the concept and composition of the local bench. Analysis of the relation between political structure and the commissions of the peace can be based upon national records, but detailed investigation of the actions of county government must be based upon county records. So, chapters VI through VIII analyse changes in the activities of Kent's justices and in the administrative structure of their rule. The final three chapters describe the justices' subtle modifications of their behaviour and image, modifications which echo alterations in the structure of politics and administration. Chapter IX examines changes in the justices' presentation of themselves as a group of governors; chapter X examines changes in the image of the justice inherent in the composition of both Kent's bench and its active bench; and chapter XI examines changes in the legal model of the model justice. In depicting the osmosis of the older role of the gentry justice with that of the newer role of the gentleman justice, this book illuminates the paradoxical evolution of the somewhat contradictory standards by which governors were and still are judged.

PART ONE

The Justices' Influence

CHAPTER ONE

The Uses of Justice

"Emolumentum justiciae magnum est."

Three or four Parsons, three or four Squires,
Three or four Lawyers, three or four Lyars,
Three or four Parishes bringing Appeals,
Three or four Hands, three or four Seals,
Three or four Bastards, three or four Whores,
Tag, Rag, and Bobtail, three or four Scores;
Three or four Bulls, three or four Cows,
Three or four Orders, three or four Bows,
Three or four Statutes not understood,
Three or four Paupers praying for Food,
Three or four Roads that never were mended,
Three or four Scolds,—and the Sessions is ended.[1]

So a mid-eighteenth century satirist extended the literary conception of the pastoral to a depiction of a country Quarter Sessions. In the artificial world of the pastoral, whether set in the classical Italy of ordered nature and happy shepherds, or the England of hedged meadow and simple folk, change and conflict are remarkable only by their absence. Government loses its political connotations and becomes mere administration—the settlement of petty disputes, the supervision of the expenditure of the few shillings in the parish funds, and the regulation of matters so minor as to be ludicrous.

The impression that local government was mere administration, that it dealt in a routine manner with matters that did not involve serious conflict, is reinforced by the setting in which it was conducted.

1. From the *Ladies Magazine* for Dec. 15, 1750, quoted in R. Robson, *The Attorney in the Eighteenth Century* (Cambridge, 1959), p. 107n.

The justices of the peace governed England's counties, and the justices governed in and through courts of law. Despite Thomas Hobbes, the inhabitants of English-speaking countries usually do not characterize the pronouncements of law courts as the determination of right by might. English law's reliance on custom and precedent camouflages conflict, for legal decisions are framed in forms and language which affirm the continuance of traditional order. Since much of eighteenth-century local government consisted of administrative decisions promulgated in courts of law, the justices' government seems the placid exercise of sanctified routine for settling trivial matters.

Because the justices' administrative decisions seem to deal with minor matters, because their administration took the form of legal orders, and because the justices possessed, literally, hundreds of powers, the importance of their administrative powers has been slighted. The justices' administrative decisions may appear innocuous, but only if it is assumed that administration is the routine decision of trivial matters. The taxpayers of eighteenth-century England would not have considered the justices' administrative concerns trivial, nor their decisions entirely routine. Almost all of the justices' administrative decisions affected the taxes paid by the inhabitants of one or more parishes. As taxpayers had reason to be grateful to a justice whose decisions decreased their taxes, his administrative powers therefore enabled a justice to maintain and expand his interest.

Interest: in the eighteenth century it was a "magical" word.[2] Its peculiar charm was that it adumbrated without precisely defining both the influence which members of the elite might exercise over their inferiors and the bonds which linked members of the elite to inferiors whom they influenced. Because of its very imprecision, it exactly described the nexus of social relations of a hierarchical society whose laws emphasized the rights of the individual while its elite exercised—indeed almost monopolized—social, economic, and political power. The elite's wealth, especially their landed wealth, and their ties to government enabled them to affect the condition of their inferiors. Some of their inferiors wanted to be installed as tenants on the elite's lands; others wanted jobs for their offspring in the elite's households and in the service of government; artisans and shopkeepers hoped to acquire the elite's patronage; some communities benefitted from the elite's benefactions; other communities solicited a member of the elite

2. G. S. Holmes, *British Politics in the Age of Anne* (London, 1967), p. 25.

to obtain parliamentary acts which protected their economy. Those whom a member of the elite so served were regarded as in his interest. They were receptive to his influence, and legitimately so. As one expert practitioner of politics explained: "Service is obligation, obligation implies return."[3]

The elite's opportunities to serve their inferiors created a bond between them, and this bond too was comprehended by 'interest.' In eighteenth-century usage, 'interest' bore connotations of physical and moral involvement.[4] A gentleman was interested—involved—in the fortunes of his following. Their welfare affected his, for their condition advertised his importance, attracting or deterring others from joining his following. This was the aspect of interest which judicial office highlighted, for judicial office enabled gentlemen to protect their adherents and attack adherents of opposing interests. Though few of their substantial neighbours were at any time subject to the justices' powers under the criminal law, all taxpayers were affected by their administrative decisions, for their administrative decisions determined which parish—and sometimes which taxpayer—would have to pay more taxes and which less. Since their administrative decisions revealed who among the justices was able to protect his adherents, the justices' administrative decisions were the final verdicts on struggles between members of the elite endeavouring to maintain their influence over taxpayers.

In emphasizing the justices' administrative powers, the foregoing description of the justices is somewhat at odds with a more standard and more immediately entrancing portrait. Emphasis is usually placed upon those of the justices' powers which allowed them to intervene directly in the lives of the poor. A justice could order that a vagrant be whipped or a poor person given poor relief. A justice could be a petty tyrant or a benevolent ruler: he could be a Squire Western or a Squire Allworthy. Emphasis upon those powers which allowed the justice directly to affect the lives of some individuals enhances the image of the justice as virtually autonomous ruler, free to establish whatever rule he willed in the little kingdom which was his parish. Accordingly, depictions of the justice usually focus on his power to decide whether the least eminent inhabitants of his neighbourhood

3. Speech of George Bubb Doddington in 1754, quoted in W. Holdsworth, *The History of English Law,* vol. 10 (London, 1938), p. 578.

4. S. I. Tucker, *Protean Shapes: A Study in Eighteenth Century Vocabulary and Usage* (London, 1967), pp. 210–212.

would be aided or punished, and then proceed to list the justice's more humdrum administrative responsibilities. Power may corrupt, but it nonetheless fascinates the observer. The more absolute the power, the greater the fascination.

Those who wield power may have a different viewpoint. They may be more fascinated by those powers which yield them the most satisfaction. Possession of arbitrary power over the poor can doubtless be quite satisfying, but, if dominance be regarded as the prime requisite for satisfaction, surely dominance over a larger and more substantial community than the poor yields even greater satisfaction. By emphasizing those powers which allowed the justice to rule the poor, the traditional depiction of the justice posits that the justice was most interested in domination while avoiding presentation of those powers which enabled him to assume the leadership of his neighbourhood. The justices themselves had a less restricted view of their rule. They used their powers to maintain and increase their interests, and their success was attested by the behaviour of their neighbours at elections, for elections were the ultimate contest of interests. In early eighteenth-century Kent, the justices set the pattern for the voting behaviour of their neighbours. That judicial office augmented their ability to influence the electorate is evident in the behaviour of voters residing near newly appointed justices: these voters were markedly more responsive to the persuasions of a gentleman when he became a justice than they had been when he was a mere landowner.[5] Since justices manipulated their powers so as to extend their interests, it seems logical to suggest that justices derived considerable satisfaction from their positions as leaders of interests. Indeed, it may not be unduly cynical to suggest that the powers they most valued were those which enabled them to build an interest.

The justices' attention to interest therefore provides an analytic framework for analysing their powers which reflects the justices' own view of their office. The justices possessed so many powers, wielded in so great a variety of structures, that it has been difficult to categorize them. Statute allocated some powers to one justice acting alone, others to two justices, and still others to the justices of the county meeting at Quarter Sessions. Nor does this list exhaust the structures for judicial rule: when a justice sat on the grand jury at Assizes he might pro-

5. N. Landau, "Independence, Deference, and Voter Participation: The Behavior of the Electorate in Early-Eighteenth-Century Kent," *Historical Journal* 22 (1979): 572–579.

nounce on some matters which were also cognizable at Quarter Sessions. Examination of the extent to which the justices used their powers within each of these structures so as to maintain their interests emphasizes the importance of their administrative decisions. Somewhat paradoxically, emphasis on administration does not negate the traditional presentation of the justice as ruler of his parish. Instead, it enhances it. For while the traditional portrait delineates the justice as local ruler by focusing on his power to dominate the poor, attention to the justices' administrative decisions reveals the manner in which justices protected or attacked their more substantial neighbours. Because the justices' administrative decisions affected taxpayers, and because many taxpayers were voters—the stuff of interest—justices found administration interesting. Because he wielded power over both the poor and the taxpayer, a justice could regard himself as leader of an entire community.

1. THE SINGLE JUSTICE

The single justice's powers of summary conviction have long been regarded as the insignia of eighteenth-century judicial rule. In truth, these powers are impressive. One justice, acting in and for the county for which he was commissioned, could order a vagrant whipped, or the imprisonment of those aiding smugglers; at harvest time he could put those who refused to labour in the stocks; at all times he could command the distraint of goods for nonpayment of fines and the imprisonment of those who did not have money or goods sufficient to pay fines. He could fine a fair proportion of the community: the idle, lewd, and disorderly; those who uttered profane oaths, who conducted their business or assembled to play sports on Sunday, who stole wood or pulled down hedges, or who hunted or possessed guns, greyhounds, snares and nets for hunting and fishing but did not possess the requisite legal qualification. He could fine bakers for selling bread at less than the weight fixed by law, carters who placed more horses in harness than the law allowed, hawkers who did not have a license, workers in cotton, flax, hemp, wool, or iron who stole material from employers, etc., etc., etc. The catalogue seems endless and indicative of powers sufficiently varied and decisions sufficiently arbitrary to insure dominance of a neighbourhood. Nonetheless, a list of the single justice's powers of summary conviction still excludes one of his most potent weapons: his power to demand that a person enter into a recognizance.

A recognizance is a bond in which the person bound promises to act in a specified manner on pains of forfeiting a specified sum of money to the sovereign. The recognizance in itself constituted a minor punishment. Those whom the justices bound usually both had to pay a small fee and to appear at Quarter Sessions or Assizes, an appearance which might involve a troublesome and expensive journey. Justices wielded two varieties of recognizance over miscreants. The first, the recognizance of the peace, obliged the person bound to keep the peace. The justice could demand this recognizance only after he had received complaint from an individual that he feared injury from another. The justice had greater opportunity to exercise his discretion in the demand of the second type of recognizance, that of good behaviour. If the justice had reason to believe that an individual might be a rioter, quarrelsome, idle, disorderly, lewd, likely to commit homicide or robbery, the father of a bastard, or a miscreant, he could demand that the individual enter into a recognizance of good behaviour, and the justice did not have to await receipt of a complaint from an aggrieved party before making the demand. If an individual refused to enter into a recognizance or had neither sufficient property nor sureties of sufficient property to enter into a recognizance—and both the sum specified in the recognizance and the judgment of adequacy of property and sureties were left to the discretion of the justice—the justice could commit him to jail, there to await delivery by due course of law. So potent was the mere threat of demand of a recognizance that it could be alleged that justices used it for their personal advantage. One Welsh justice was said to have compelled people to work for him by binding those who refused in recognizances of good behaviour. He was also said to have collected "exorbitant fees" from one bound in a recognizance in return for neglecting to certify the recognizance to Quarter Sessions, an omission which spared the person bound a journey to the court.[6]

The powers of the single justice therefore appear impressive, but not all contemporaries were overawed. It was the opinion of some that the power to convict summarily affected only "*Vagabonds, Hedge-Stealers,* and other *disorderly Persons* who are known to live by pilfering."[7] Likewise, only those on the lower rungs of the social ladder were likely to be bound in recognizances to keep the peace and to

6. B.L., Add. MSS 35600, f. 32.
7. *The Craftsman,* Appendix to no. 355, April 21, 1733, p. 225.

be of good behaviour. Doubtless, a justice was gratified by his power to preserve the peace in his immediate vicinity, but his ability to harass the lower orders did not of itself endow him with influence. After all, vagabonds, hedge-stealers, and most of England's lower orders did not vote.

Indeed, it could be argued that the single justice's power to dominate the lower orders endowed him with influence because a justice's treatment of the poor indirectly affected his more substantial neighbours. A justice's use of his powers of summary conviction could bolster his neighbour's authority. When a gentlemen in a nearby parish complained to Sir Edward Filmer, J.P., that three labourers had engaged in drunken brawls and uttered disrespectful remarks, Filmer sentenced the three to six hours exhibition in the parish stocks with pots hung round their necks. The gentleman was pleased to report that the punishment had quelled disorder in his parish, and noted that he preferred Filmer's choice of the stocks to a sentence condemning the labourers to the house of correction: it was a "busy time" and the labourers were "very much wanted in the Turnip Ground."[8] Conversely, a justice's treatment of the less powerful residents of an area could affront even the mighty. The mighty proved their might by protecting their adherents, and a magnate's interest might extend even to the lowly. Let a justice but bind servants or tenants of a member of Parliament to keep the peace, and he would receive that dignitary's indignant protest.[9] Similarly, a justice's refusal to render aid might endanger a magnate's property. Near Lord Fermanagh lived a justice who both stated that Fermanagh's hedges had been erected illegally and refused to fine an alehousekeeper who had pulled down a hedge. According to Fermanagh, the justice had "given all the Encouragement possible" to the inhabitants of the area to destroy his hedges. As Fermanagh remarked, this justice had always challenged the power of his lordly estate.[10] It was the justice's duty to use his power to preserve the peace, but the law also allowed the justice to use his discretion to determine in whose interest the peace would be kept.

8. Kent A.O., U120/O11, J. Hardy to Filmer, July 31, 1752; examination of J. Hardy, July 6, 1752, and of J. Pope, July 7, 1752; warrants of July 6 and 7, 1752, against R. and J. Holland and W. Barrington; see also Rob. Mann to Filmer, Dec. 19, 1749.

9. *HMC, Cowper*, vol. 2, pp. 394–395, Sir Henry Avery to Thomas Coke (1699).

10. Lady Margaret Maria Verney, *Verney Letters of the Eighteenth Century from the Manuscripts at Claydon House* (London, 1930), vol. 2, pp. 210–211, Lord Fermanagh to Earl Verney, Aug. 7, 1745.

Though the single justice could use his power to maintain his interest and protect or vex the interests of others, almost all the powers allotted to the single justice directly affected only the least substantial inhabitants of his vicinity. The laws which gave him power, laws made by England's gentlemen, did not allow him sole authority over more important matters and persons. Without the cooperation of neighbouring justices, no justice could rule even his own parish. William Brockman was the owner of the mansion of Beachborough in the parish of Newington in the county of Kent; he was heir to the family which had dominated Newington since the sixteenth century; he had been a member of Parliament; and, like his father before him, he was a justice of the peace. Yet William Brockman was unable to close an alehouse in his own parish. According to law, an alehouse could be suppressed by order of two justices. The justice nearest Brockman would not help him. Two justices farther away, in another petty sessional division, at first seemed more amenable; but after three months of manoeuver and negotiation they still hesitated. As Brockman noted, they acknowledged that the alehouse ought to be suppressed, but "They would have me de novo to renew the whole proceedings at the next Sessions, Alledging Scruples, foreign, I take it, to the Case as to their owne Acting therein and in the Division, where they do not reside. . . ." Brockman needed a judicial ally. But he was a Whig, and all of the recalcitrant justices were Tories. Eventually, he found two more kindred spirits—one a Whig justice who resided in a neighbouring petty sessional division, and the second a justice who resided in Brockman's division and maintained his neutrality amidst party struggle. The Whig joined with Brockman in suppressing the alehouse. The alehousekeeper managed to obtain another licence. So, Brockman and the neutral justice issued a warrant to take down the alehousekeeper's sign. The warrant was never executed. Shortly after they had issued the warrant the justices learned that the Tory government had provided a new commission of the peace for the county, a commission which removed Brockman's Whig ally from the bench. As the neutral justice now advised, to persist would be "labouring otherwise against the Pricks."[11] Because Brock-

11. B.L., Add. MSS 42587, f. 244, W. Honywood to Brockman, Apr. 19, 1710; f. 248, Same to Same, May 12, 1710; f. 244v, Brockman to Honywood, May 9, 1710; Add. MSS 42588, f. 16, H. Aucher to Brockman, Thursday the 16th; f. 16v, Brockman to Corbett, Apr. 20, 1713; f. 27, Brockman to Sir H. Aucher, June 13, 1713; ff. 27v–28, Brockman's memorandum; ff. 29–30, T. Marsh to Brockman, June 19, 1713; f. 37, Tho. Morris to Brockman, Aug. 16, 1713; Add. MSS 42598, pp. 101, 102, 104.

man could not obtain the aid of another justice, his parish continued to sport the sign of the Chequer.

Some justices found these restrictions upon their single power irksome. Richard, Lord Willoughby de Broke, persuaded himself that he alone could license alehouses even though a mean-spirited law insisted that all licences be signed by two justices. De Broke let it be known that, if anyone had been refused a licence by the other justices, he had only to apply to his lordship. De Broke's eccentricities produced other anomalies. Claiming that a cleric had incited a gravedigger to attack a de Broke servant, he ordered that the cleric be taken into custody. Unfortunately for de Broke, the cleric's brother was one of the county's justices. Justices in the county responded by demanding that this uncooperative aristocrat be removed from the bench. While de Broke acted, they stated, "it will be improper for any Gentleman to act in the Commission of the peace for this part of the County." Willoughby de Broke was struck from the commission.[12] His judgment clouded by delusions of grandeur, de Broke had over-estimated both the extent of his interest and the powers of a single justice. A single justice could use his powers to fortify his interest in his vicinity. Successful preservation and extension of that interest demanded the acquiescence of neighbouring justices whose authority and interests had also to be respected.

2. PETTY SESSIONS

While the law allotted the single justice considerable power over those accused of crime, the majority of administrative powers bestowed upon the justices were vested in the 'double justice'–i.e., two justices acting together. As the law entrusted the surveillance of parish government, the appointment of overseers of the poor and the surveyors of highways, the approval of parish accounts, and the licensing of alehouses to two justices, the double justice controlled parish affairs. Every justice was almost automatically appointed to the commissions of the land and window taxes.[13] As assessments to the parish poor and

12. B.L., Add. MSS 35585, ff. 66–67, 69–70, warrants and mittimus dated June 11, 1742; f. 71, Carrick and Willoughby de Broke to Mr. Landen; Add. MSS 35601, ff. 63–64, W. Cotton to the Hon. Mr. Justice Parker, June 19, 1742; P.R.O., C234/34, July 26, 1742.

13. 43 George III c.48 belatedly recognized the inevitable appointment of justices to the land tax commission. It provided that a justice could act as land tax commissioner even if he was not listed as a commissioner in the land tax act.

highway rates had to be ratified by two justices,[14] and three commissioners of the land tax and two commissioners of the window tax constituted a court of appeal for their respective amercements, the justices of the peace determined the total amount of direct taxation to be paid by every person of property. Two justices could, under certain restrictions, determine the amount of small tithes owed an impropriator, and under less restraint adjudge cases brought against Quakers for nonpayment of great and small tithes and church rates. Therefore, two or three justices acting together made almost all the administrative decisions which immediately affected a gentleman's property, the parish which he wished to dominate, and his interest. The power of the double justice was therefore the crucial power in local government.

Obviously, justices had to associate with each other to exercise the power of the double justice, and a justice would usually associate with other justices of his 'division.' The division had emerged in the late sixteenth and early seventeenth centuries when justices had divided their counties into smaller areas and assigned the justices of each area responsibility for those chores which required the consultation of small groups of justices. By the eighteenth century, many of these informal meetings had acquired a more formal character. Regular meetings of a division's justices were known as petty sessions. Despite the importance of the power of the double justice, neither the division—the geographical framework for the exercise of that power, nor petty sessions—the institutional framework for the exercise of that power, were legally defined.

The law specified neither the number of divisions in a county nor the geographical boundaries of a division. Legal regulation of the structures within which justices could exercise their double power was likewise less than stringent. Petty sessions was a term unknown to law. Some acts simply allocated authority in a matter to two justices. Other acts insisted that the two justices be of the neighbourhood, or of the division; a few went so far as to decree that the power conferred by these acts on two justices be exercised in a specific meeting of the justices of the division; and all such limitations were less restrictive than they appeared. According to the judges of England, those statutory phrases allotting any power to a justice or justices of a division were "merely directory," merely indicative of the tribunal which might most conveniently deal with a

14. County rates were usually paid from funds gathered in the poor rate.

matter. In fact and in law, any justice could act anywhere in the county for which he was commissioned.[15] Probably that power of the double justice which was most hedged about by specific legal restriction was the licensing of alehouses. According to 2 George II c.28 and 26 George II c. 13, alehouses had to be licensed at a general meeting of the justices of the division held on or within twenty days of September 1, and alehouses could be licensed only at such a meeting. Nonetheless, in 1789 it was thought reasonable to object to the appointment of two country clerics to the Lancashire commission because "by acting together [they] may have it in their power to thwart in particular cases (as in that of licensing public Houses, etc.) the patriotic Acts of even a petit Sessions. . . ."[16] The division, then, was the creation of justices acting together, and any group of two or more justices could assume the powers of petty sessions.

Though influence over the exercise of the powers of the double justice was crucial to the maintenance of an interest, the framework within which these powers were exercised was at once structured and elastic. The degree of monopoly of a division's government enjoyed by a division's justices was determined by the assessment of each justice in the county of the limits appropriate for the use of his power in the circumstances of the moment. William Brockman, unable to gain support in his own division for his campaign against his parish's alehouse, and so unattractive an ally that he could not persuade justices elsewhere in the county to interfere in the government of his division, was confronted by a group of hostile divisional justices who exercised an effective monopoly over his division's government. Other justices might find these affairs better ordered. Ensconced in divisions whose petty sessions usually supported their endeavours, and so sufficiently powerful in their neighbourhoods to attract extra-divisional allies, these justices could exploit both the monopoly of local government usually exercised by their petty sessions and the opportunity afforded by law to evade that monopoly. Such a justice was John Toke, of Godinton in Kent.

John Toke, Esq., twice a member of Parliament for East Grinsted in Sussex, heir of Sir Nicholas Toke, J.P., who was in turn heir of Nicholas Toke, "the Captain," J.P. and by his fifth marriage son-in-law of the Earl of Winchilsea, resided at Godinton, Great Chart, in the

15. W. Paley, *The Law and Practice of Summary Convictions on Penal Statutes by Justices of the Peace* (London, 1814), p. 8.

16. B.L., Add. MSS 38446, f. 332, T. Russell to [Lord Hawkesbury], Sept. 17, 1789.

Ashford division of Kent. The Toke family had lived in Kent from time beyond the records of Englishmen, and Godinton had come into their possession by marriage in the fifteenth century. In the seventeenth century, the Captain had converted an impressive Kentish hall house into a mansion worthy of a member of the Kentish gentry. The expansion of Godinton, the introduction of a staircase that attempted to be grand, the addition of a Great Chamber panelled with figures illustrating the military drill of an Elizabethan manual at arms, the erection of chimney pieces of Bethersden marble carved with a multitude of moving creatures: all testify to the family's new position in society. With prosperity and the acquisition of gentility came yet more property. In the 1730s, the Toke estate included, besides Godinton and its adjacent farms in Great Chart and Hothfield, lands in the parishes of Benenden, Bethersden, Bonnington, Kenardington, Kingsnorth, and Shadoxhurst:[17] all but two in the Ashford division.

The justices of the Ashford division met at Ashford, the major market town on the road from London through Maidstone to Hythe. The division was, literally, pastoral. The sheep and cattle dotting the southern slopes of the North Downs and the rolling lands of the Weald sustained the fortunes of its governors. In the late 1730s, eight justices were listed as active in the government of the division.[18] Each possessed a residence and estate impressive enough to survive the depredations of both house-wrecker and modern taxation. The residences of Toke's associates are, like his, marked as important edifices on the most recent one-inch ordnance survey and all but one are shown to be surrounded by an ornamental park. The exception, the Derings' seat in Pluckley, is shown as emparked on a map of 1769.[19]

According to the only surviving record of Ashford petty sessions in the 1730s, a record both informal and incomplete, three of this group of eight justices never or hardly ever attended petty sessions. These three justices all lived near the division's northern border, and of the two Whigs among them, at least one found a neighbouring petty sessions more congenial. Control of the division's petty sessions rested with the five justices living in the mid and southern portions of the division, within eight miles of Ashford: John Sawbridge, heir of the

17. E. Lodge, ed., *British Academy. Records of Social and Economic History, The Account Books of a Kentish Estate* (London, 1927), pp. xix–xxii, xxvi–xxvii.

18. The list of active justices is in Kent A.O., Q/SB 1748. The list was probably made in 1737 or 1738.

19. J. Andrews, A. Drury, and W. Herbert, *A Topographical Map of the County of Kent* (London, 1769).

director of the South Sea Company who had purchased the Olantigh estate in Wye and father of the John Sawbridge whose participation in City politics as a Tory radical led to his association with Wilkes and Tooke; Thomas Broadnax May Knight, M.P., whose last two names commemorate his inheritance of impressive estates, including his place of residence, Godmersham, which he built in 1732—a plain but huge Palladian mansion that later in the century would receive Jane Austen when she visited her rich relations; Sir Edward Dering, Bart., member of Parliament, heir to a family claiming pre-Conquest eminence in Kent and owner of Surrenden Dering in Pluckley; John Toke of Godinton: prominent Tories all.[20]

The fifth member of the Ashford quinquumvirate was Sir Wyndham Knatchbull, Bart., premier descendant of the family seated at Mersham-le-Hatch since 1485, son and heir of Sir Edward—M.P. for Kent, father of the baronet who would employ Adam to erect an even more impressive residence at Mersham, and brother to Sir Edward Knatchbull, M.P. for Kent in the 1760s. Sir Wyndham's father had converted from Tory to Whig in the mid-1720s and had thereupon desisted from further attempts to retain his Kentish seat. Instead, he had in 1727 been brought into Parliament as the representative of a government borough. Unlike his judicial colleagues, Sir Wyndham Knatchbull was a Whig, a friend and correspondent of Lord Chancellor Hardwicke, and an ally of the Duke of Dorset whose son stood for knight of the shire as a government candidate in 1734. Surrounded as he was by proponents of Kentish Toryism, it is not surprising that Sir Wyndham chose to spend his winters in London, enjoying the congenial company of the fashionable and powerful. At other seasons, he was to be found at Mersham, where he wrote his "Account of such Sessions and Sittings as I have been at, since my acting as a Justice of the Peace, A. 1734."

Sir Wyndham's "Account" is unique. Almost all our knowledge of eighteenth-century Quarter and petty sessions is based upon formal records—the beautifully inscribed books enshrining the orders of Quarter Sessions, and the more hastily written notes of petty sessions' clerks, listing the documents issued by petty sessions. These records

20. A. N.. Newman, "Elections in Kent and its Parliamentary Representation, 1713–1754" (D.Phil. thesis, Oxford University, 1957), pp. 123, 181; R. Sedgwick, ed., *History of Parliament, The House of Commons 1715–1754* (London, 1970), vol. 2, *sub* Thomas May; Kent A.O., U269/C148/7, Thomas Hales to the Duke of Dorset, Sept. 26, 1733.

omit the judicial debates which reflect the struggles for power that precipitated the requests for these orders and documents. Sir Wyndham is less laconic. There he sat at Ashford petty sessions, the sole Whig justice in the heartland of Kentish Toryism, observing the judicial schemes of Sir Edward Dering, Tory candidate for knight of the shire in 1734, and of Dering's campaign manager, John Toke.[21] Toke lived about two miles north of Ashford, and as Knatchbull lived four miles southeast of Ashford, Toke was the justice nearest Knatchbull and so was the justice whose activities were most likely to affect Knatchbull's interest. Both proximity and political antagonism probably explain why Toke is the only justice upon whose activities Knatchbull comments. As Knatchbull recounts the judicial contretemps produced by Toke's manoeuvers, we can see the way in which an aggressive justice could use both the power of the double justice and the elastic framework for that power to enlarge his interest. Toke was especially interested in manipulation of the double justices' powers over taxation.

Obviously any justice would be delighted if he were able simultaneously to decrease his own taxes and increase his influence. Toke saw a way to do just that. He both resided and had property in Great Chart, and in association with two nonjudicial land tax commissioners, he ratified a schedule of assessments to the land tax which increased the assessment of the parish rector, and thereby decreased the assessment of every other landowner in the parish, including that of Toke himself.[22] Naturally the rector protested. In August 1739, he appeared at the joint meeting of the Ashford division's petty sessions and land tax commissioners seeking a reduction in his assessment. In a magnificent piece of contorted reasoning, Toke argued that the section of the land tax act which provided for appeals actually prohibited appeals in a great number of cases, including the rector's. Dering sided with Toke. Knatchbull and Knight disagreed. As the justices were equally divided, and as the nonjudicial land tax commissioners present were not asked to give their vote, the result was a stalemate. The rector was advised to take the advice of counsel and appear at the next meeting.

At the next meeting, the rector's counsel argued successfully for the rector's right to appeal. So, Toke now had to explain why the new

21. Kent A.O., U269/C148/1, John Toke to the Duke of Dorset, Aug. 15, 1733.

22. Parliament determined the total amount of land tax levied on each county; the land tax commissioners determined the total amount levied on a parish. Though, in theory, the commissioners could annually alter the portion of the county's land tax paid by each parish, by mid-century they were adhering to an apportionment hallowed by precedent.

assessment was more equitable than the old. He was equal to the task. When the rector averred that his living was over-assessed, Toke offered to find him a tenant who would rent his house and tithes at the amount assessed. One justice asked the rector if he thought any in the parish were under-assessed. The rector instanced the farmer of one estate, but Toke countered that the estate was now let at less rent than it had been formerly. As no one knew the present rent of the farm, Toke was again victor in the skirmish. The battle continued, but Knatchbull was not there to chronicle it. Autumn had arrived and it was time to depart for London.

In June 1740, Knatchbull once again returned to pastoral peace, to Mersham, and to Ashford petty sessions. Once again he had the fortune to witness the *rector of Great Chart* v. *Toke*. This time, the rector appeared armed with the accounts of receipts from his living. As they proved, the new assessment had not overrated the rector. Nonetheless, the new assessment did undervalue the estates of all the other landowners in the parish. So, Toke and the rector agreed to a compromise. The rector's assessment was decreased, but it was still higher than it had been before the contested assessment of 1739. Therefore, the assessments of all the other landowners in Great Chart were lower than they had been before 1739. The parishioners of Great Chart had good reason to acknowledge Toke as their patron. So did the rector. At the last moment, Toke arranged for an additional reduction in the rector's assessment.[23] By reconciling the rector to his influence, Toke secured to himself a parish united and universally thankful for reduction in its taxes, a parish that would most readily follow the leadership of John Toke.

Great Chart was undoubtedly a prize, but any gentleman who wished to establish a considerable interest would have to influence a populace more numerous than that inhabiting one or two of Kent's rural parishes. Of all the justices in his division, Toke lived nearest Ashford—the most populous town in the Ashford division, one of the three most populous towns subject to the jurisdiction of the justices in south Kent, a town which in 1663 already boasted 267 households.[24] There lay before Toke's door the fairest prospect of extending his interest.

The domination of Ashford would require a strategy somewhat

23. Kent A.O., U951/O4, pp. 56–57, 60–62, 64–65.
24. D. C. Coleman, "The Economy of Kent under the Later Stuarts, 1660–1714" (Ph.D. thesis, University of London, 1951), pp. 9, 398, 402.

more sophisticated than the simple manipulation of the land tax which proved so successful in Great Chart. In so populous a town there were bound to be several factions, and a justice bent on conquest would have to ally with the most powerful. Toke did. He chose to become the patron of both Ashford's vicar and its overseers. Since both the vicar and overseers were important members of the parish vestry, Toke influenced those who administered parish government. Since the vicar also had weekly opportunity to advise the assembled parish—advice which might well include a homily on politics—Toke's strategy was, as usual, based on a keen assessment of the structure of local power. Once again, his tactic was manipulation of tax assessments. This time he chose to alter assessments to the poor rate.

Toke's management of Ashford's affairs first came to the attention of the county in July 1737, when three of Ashford's inhabitants appealed to Quarter Sessions against an assessment to the poor rate. Knatchbull thought there were grounds for the appeal; the rate had been ratified in a "clandestine" manner: Toke had signed the rate and also secured the signature of a Tory justice on the northern border of the division, a justice who rarely travelled to Ashford even for so congenial a gathering as petty sessions. Ashford's vicar must have held a different opinion of the assessment. The vicar was not assessed at all, nor were eleven other inhabitants of Ashford. Quarter Sessions ordered that both the vicar and the eleven inhabitants be assessed, but Toke had just begun to fight.

Toke now rejected a new list of assessees presented by the parish officers and insisted that the additional names be appended to the old assessment schedule. The officers added the names to the old schedule and brought both the new and old schedules to Ashford petty sessions, where Knatchbull and Knight were the only justices present. Knatchbull refused to sign the old schedule. Only the new, he maintained, was valid. And so Knatchbull persuaded Knight to sign the new schedule. Possibly these manoeuvers over choice of schedules were merely symbolic—an attempt to prevent Toke from raising his standard over Ashford. More probably, the schedules differed in a more material fashion, for within six months the same three citizens of Ashford were once again appealing to Quarter Sessions against the assessment for Ashford's poor rate. This time they contended that the assessment of the vicar considerably under-estimated his prosperity. Toke managed to have the appeal respited, but finally in July 1738, the vicar capitulated. He would accept the assessment proposed by his opponents, an assessment 333 percent greater than his present assessment. Whether Toke's manoeuvers had decreased the taxes paid by his supporters cannot be determined. It is not unlikely that the vicar and eleven inhabitants were still under-assessed; it is indubitable that they regarded Toke as their champion.

Certainly, the vicar's capitulation did not spell the end of Toke's dominance of Ashford, for at that same Quarter Sessions he demonstrated his power to its citizenry. The three obstreperous townsmen had also appealed to Quarter Sessions against the accounts of Ashford's overseers. The accounts included a charge for the legal defence of those Ashford assessments which had underrated the vicar. Toke had ratified these accounts, and the second judicial signator was a justice who, Knatchbull noted, lived "quite out of the Division." Nonetheless, Toke was able to convince a bare majority of the justices at Quarter Sessions that "the Overseers were Trustees for the Parish, and therefore were, if any difficulty arose, obliged to defend the Parish Sesses." Knatchbull viewed the matter in a different light: "A most monstrous piece of injustice, and nothing to be said in excuse of it. The true question at bottom was, whether or no the Parish shou'd beer [bear] Mr. Toke's charges in carrying on a Lawsuit against the Parish."[25] Ashford had to pay for contesting Toke's influence. Indeed, even Knatchbull's own parish contributed to the support of one of Toke's clients: Toke manipulated the powers of the double justice so as to enable the highway surveyor in Knatchbull's parish to spend parish funds on the surveyor's private road.[26]

To a modern observer, it might appear that only a few of the double justices' administrative powers could be wielded so as to affect the pockets of voters. Justices might manipulate tax assessments or abet the petty peculation of parish officials. But surely their ability to influence was limited to their supervision of the assessment and expenditure of taxes? To eighteenth-century voters and taxpayers, such a description of the influence inherent in the administrative powers of the double justice would seem unduly restrictive. Almost every administrative matter brought to a justice's attention presented opportunity for an interested response because almost every administrative decision affected the tax burden borne by a parish. Even a seemingly abstruse decision on the settlement of a pauper could immediately

25. Kent A.O., U951/O4, pp. 30–32, 42–44; Q/SO E6; Q/SMa E5.
26. Kent A.O., U951/O4, pp. 17–20, 29.

affect any parishioner wealthy enough to be assessed to the poor rate. So, both country gentlemen and aristocrats displayed a seemingly inordinate concern over the details of settlement cases and solicited the aid of friendly justices in the protection of purse and parish.[27] The influence inherent in the adjudication of the settlement of paupers was not lost upon John Toke.

In fact, Toke's adjudication of a settlement case made him the centre of a legal *cause célèbre* which ultimately necessitated deliberations by both the judges of King's Bench and Parliament. The case revolved around a perfectly routine decision, a decision allocated by statute to the double justice. Toke and another justice determined that a pauper was not settled in Great Chart, where he currently resided, but in Kennington, and they issued an order that the pauper be removed from Great Chart to Kennington, there to be provided for. The order was appealed to Quarter Sessions and thence appealed to King's Bench, which quashed it for the same reason as had Quarter Sessions—namely, that as Toke was a resident of Great Chart and chargeable to its poor rate, he was an interested party to the case: his own taxes were affected by his decision. In making the decision Toke was acting as a judge, and judges should be disinterested. Said the judges of King's Bench, it is "a fundamental Rule of Reason and of natural Justice 'That *no* man can be Judge in his *own* Cause.' "[28]

When the Ashford citizens had appealed to Quarter Sessions, one justice had reproved Toke for acting "more like a Party than a Judge."[29] But in making a settlement order about a pauper in his own parish, Toke had not overstepped the bounds of normal judicial conduct. England's local government was based upon justices who made decisions which affected taxation of the parishes in which they held property, and Parliament immediately passed an act which declared these decisions valid, whatever the opinions of the judges may be. 16 George II c. 18 decreed that justices could continue to make decisions

27. Hants. R.O., 18/M51/595, Edward Tenison to Gabriel Walters, Lambeth Palace, May 26, 1709; G. Eland, ed., *Purefoy Letters, 1735–1753* (London, 1931), vol. 1, p. 8, Henry Purefoy to Edward Davis, Mar. 15, 1737 [8]; *Verney Letters,* vol. 2, p. 207, John Millward to Lord Fermanagh, July 2, 1740; pp. 207–208, Lord Fermanagh to Earl Verney, Sept. 15, 1743; J. Wake and D. C. Webster, eds., *The Letters of Daniel Eaton to the Third Earl of Cardigan, 1725–1732,* Northamptonshire Record Society, vol. 24 (Kettering, Northamptonshire, 1971), p. 11, Daniel Eaton to Lord Cardigan [April 10, 1755]; T. Gisborne, *An Enquiry into the Duties of Men in the Higher and Middle Classes of Society* (London, 1795), vol. 1, pp. 436–437.

28. Sir J. Burrow, *Decisions of the Court of King's Bench upon Settlement Cases . . . from March 1732 to June 1776, inclusive,* 2nd ed. (London, 1786), pp. 194–198.

29. Kent A.O., U951/O4, p. 44.

on poor relief, settlement, passing of vagrants, and repair of the highways, and that justices could continue to wield their powers concerning "parochial taxes, levies or rates" in any parish in which they were rateable or chargeable. As Parliament recognized, a justice could be an interested party to almost any administrative decision that he was empowered to make.

Since the office of justice endowed its possessor with power to maintain and extend his interest, it was expected that a justice would make use of his powers in political contests, for politics was the major arena for the combat of interests. Justices wielded their powers so as to influence voters. Contemporaries, well aware of the nature of such influence, did not usually consider it necessary to describe the precise manner of its application. In 1733, a correspondent of the Duke of Dorset simply stated: "Your G[race] will find a furious Opposition to the Government's Interest from some late-made Just[i]ces in E[ast] K[ent]. One (whose Name I forget) will by Blustering and Threatening, make 40 Votes against Lord M[iddlesex] and his Friend; who could not, in Statu quo—have made 10." As usual, Toke's activity merited more detailed description. An innkeeper on the northeastern border of the division informed Toke that he had already pledged his votes to the Whig candidate, and had received an "Emphatical Reply—D——m Ye, do if you dare: I'll take away your Licence." The law vested the power to take away an alehouse licence in the double justice, but both Toke and his audience knew that his was not an empty threat. Confident that the majority of justices in his division would sanction his use of judicial power for the Tory cause, Toke could act as if he alone embodied the power of the double justice. As Dorset's Whig ally commented, "Some of our Friends will either be deterr'd or expos'd to a Sort of Martyrdom for the Cause."[30]

His influence amplified by the support of his judicial colleagues, Toke dominated the electors of his neighbourhood. In the autumn of 1733, the Whig candidate opposing Sir Edward Dering for the east Kent seat came to Ashford to canvas for votes.[31] Knatchbull, in the Whig candidate's entourage, reported on the results of the excursion:

30. Kent A.O., U269/C148/26, Thomas Curteis to the Duke of Dorset, Nov. 2, 1733. Lord Middlesex's "Friend" was Sir George Oxenden, Middlesex's partner in contesting the county's seats in the Whig and government interest. For the denial of alehouse licences as a means of political retaliation, see: J. D. Chambers, *Nottinghamshire in the Eighteenth Century* (London, 1932), p. 48, n.1; R. Robson, *The Oxfordshire Election of 1754* (London, 1949), p. 53; Gisborne, *Duties of Men*, vol. 1, p. 443.

31. Kent was divided for administrative purposes into an east and a west division. It was accepted practice that, when two candidates stood as a team for the county's seats, one stood as representative of the east and the other as representative of the west.

> ... there were no more than three or four Freeholders of the place who wou'd come near us. The Ringers were not suffer'd to give us a peal, and Mr. Toke was immediately sent for, who posted himself at a house just opposite to us, and brought some of the Freeholders with him to drink Sir Edward's health, and, according to his usual generosity, as I am inform'd next day, he made them all pay four shillings a piece for their reckoning.[32]

No Whig candidate would get a hearing in Ashford if Toke could prevent it; and he could. In the 1734 election, 79 percent of the seventy-five Ashford electors who voted supported both Tory candidates.

Likewise in 1734, 78 percent of those who voted in the Ashford division supported both Tory candidates. The only parish in the division where more voters preferred Whig than Tory candidates was Mersham, Knatchbull's parish. A justice could influence those living under his gaze, but the power of the single justice was inadequate for the domination of an extensive area. More compelling were the powers of the double justice, usually exercised within the division. In 1734, the Ashford division was the only division in the county boasting a majority of Tory justices on its bench, and in 1734 the Ashford division produced a greater proportion of Tories among its voters than did any other division in the county.[33] Similarly, in 1734 contemporaries attributed the Tory vote in a Gloucestershire petty sessional division to the preponderance of active Tory justices in that division.[34] The administrative powers bestowed upon the double justice made the division the most appropriate geographical arena and petty sessions the most appropriate institutional arena for the defence of an interest.

3. QUARTER SESSIONS AND ASSIZES

Most impressive among the courts which administered local government were Quarter Sessions and Assizes. The single justice performed before a few inferiors summoned to his justice's parlour; petty sessions was a small local meeting; but Quarter Sessions and Assizes were public occasions. In theory and to some extent in practice, both Quarter Sessions and Assizes assembled the county, there to behold

32. Kent A.O., U269/C148/12, Knatchbull to the Duke of Dorset, Oct. 4, 1733.

33. *The Poll for Knights of the Shire to Represent the County of Kent . . . May 1734* (London, 1734).

34. B.L., Add. MSS 35586, f. 163, J. Dutton to Hardwicke, Apr. 28, 1739; also see unsigned and undated letter in Gloucestershire R.O., Sherborne MSS D 678 Fam Sett D/57.

the actions of their governors. Both courts made decisions on the administration of the county, and so in both courts decisions on seemingly minor matters masked battles for local power. A challenge issued through these courts was a gauntlet thrown in the face of an opponent, daring him to step forth and defend his interest in view of the entire county.

Though Assizes was the more awesome of the two courts, by the eighteenth century it provided less opportunity for attack on a rival justice's use of his power than did Quarter Sessions. In preceding centuries the judges of Assizes had consulted with the justices attending Assizes and then issued orders regulating the justices' conduct of local government. Rarely did an eighteenth-century judge so intervene in the county's government;[35] and decline in Assizes' surveillance of county administration was reflected in decline of the justices' interest in attending Assizes. In the 1670s, between forty and fifty justices (at least half of those active in the commission) were present at any one Kentish Assizes; by the last decade of Anne's reign an Assizes attracted only twenty or so justices, about one-fifth of those governing the county.[36] The law, too, tended to diminish Assizes' administrative importance: some administrative tasks were specifically allocated to Quarter Sessions, but Assizes did not monopolize the power to determine any one administrative matter. The structure of Assizes further diminished the justices' ability to shape this court to their ends. While the justices as a body presided at Quarter Sessions, the sovereign's judges ruled at Assizes.

Nonetheless, by the eighteenth century the justices had invented a means of using Assizes to promote their interests. By the early eighteenth century, many of the members of the grand jury at Assizes were justices of the peace.[37] A grand jury indicted offenders, that is, it decided whether there was sufficient evidence to cause an accused to undergo the expense and inconvenience of a trial. The category of offenders was not restricted to persons. Those groups which the law had made responsible for various governmental duties could also be

35. Compare the Assize orders in J. S. Cockburn, *Western Circuit Assize Orders 1629–1648,* Camden Society, 4th ser., vol. 17 (London, 1976), with those for the western circuit in the 1730s in P.R.O., Ass 24/24. In the reign of Charles I an average of eight orders were issued at each Assizes. In the first ten years of the reign of George II, most Assizes produced only one order, that delegating the responsibility for arranging for the transportation of convicted felons.

36. See the *nomina ministrorum* in P.R.O., Ass 35.

37. For further examination of change in the composition of the grand jury, see chapter II.

indicted for misdemeanour if they failed to perform their duties. So parishes could be indicted for failure to maintain parish stocks, roads, and bridges. When the grand jury delivered an indictment for negligence in the maintenance of such facilities, the indictment was usually transformed into an order that they be repaired, an order usually resented by the inhabitants of the parish which had to pay for these repairs. So, a seemingly innocuous indictment of a parish for failure to maintain its public facilities could in fact signal that a battle between interests had begun.

Consider the quarrel between Sir Edward Filmer, J.P., and Bowyer Hendley, J.P., over a road through Otham. When Filmer sat on the grand jury, he arranged for the indictment of the inhabitants of Otham for failure to maintain the road. Hendley was the leading citizen of Otham, and Hendley was indignant. He averred that it was impossible to build a coach road on clay soil; he accused Filmer of putting Otham's inhabitants to needless expense for repair of roads and legal fees; and he opined, ominously, that a road in Filmer's parish was in equally lamentable condition.[38] As Hendley well knew, the indictment had revealed him before the county assembled at Assizes as incapable of defending his interest and insuring the good government of his parish.

It is possible that indictment for failure to maintain a road was the best weapon afforded by Assizes to warring interests. Certainly William Colepeper thought the road the most usual avenue for attack. In 1726, he published a splenetic pamphlet directed against the justices of the county, and in particular against William Hamilton, his brother-in-law and a justice. Colepeper lived on the one street of the village of Hollingbourne, a short way down the road from Lord Culpeper, his cousin, and like most of his family and acquaintance, his enemy. Colepeper alleged that he had overheard a conversation between Hamilton and Lord Culpeper while they were walking in Culpeper's grove. As Lord Culpeper was deaf, Hamilton had had to shout: "My Lord, indict him [meaning Colepeper]. I'll be on the Grand Jury and find your Bills." According to Colepeper, his noble relative had made a most reasonable reply: "For what shall I indict Him?" For what indeed—rejoined Colepeper. "I could not be indicted for any Thing there, because I had, to the Convenience of all Travellers, and to the

38. Kent A.O., U120/C43, Filmer to Hendley, July 17, 1733; Same to Same, Sept. 27, 1736; Hendley to Filmer, July 17, 1733; Same to Same, Sept. 23, 1736.

Beauty of My Lord's House, taken so much from my own Ground, as to make the Highway so much the broader, the whole Front of my Lord's house that Four or Five Coaches in Breadth, could pass, where but one could pass before. . . ."[39] Private individuals could be indicted for negligence in the maintenance of their property which affected the condition of the roads—for not scouring ditches bordering the highway, allowing their hedges to encroach on the highway, or for obstructing the highway. Since Colepeper had so admirably maintained that part of his property which bordered the highway, he considered himself immune from attack by Assizes' grand jury.

If Colepeper had been a justice at the time of this plot, as he had been several years earlier, it is likely that the conspirators would have contemplated challenging his interest at Quarter Sessions, for the administrative responsibilities of Quarter Sessions meant that this court provided a multitude of weapons for battle between justices. Like Assizes, Quarter Sessions was equipped with a grand jury, and at Quarter Sessions as at Assizes parishes could be indicted for failure to maintain the appurtenances of government. True, justices did not sit on the grand jury at Quarter Sessions; instead they presided on the bench, and their control of the bench allowed them to manipulate the decisions of the grand jury.[40] Even more opportunity for a demonstration of power was afforded by those matters which the justices could determine without reference to the jury. The justices decided these matters by vote, and so the composition of the bench was crucial to Quarter Sessions' adjudication. At Quarter Sessions the justices decided whether to levy a rate on a parish for repair of its roads, on a hundred (a group of parishes) for repair of its bridges, and on both parishes and hundreds for reimbursement of the expenses of high and petty constables.[41] As these decisions affected local taxes and so taxpayers, they revealed who among the elite could maintain his interest.

The justices meeting at Quarter Sessions were also responsible for

39. Extensive excerpts from the pamphlet, entitled *The Case Between the King and Richard Bigs, alias Blue Dick . . .*, are quoted in R. Goodsall, *Stede Hill* (London, 1950), pp. 129–139.

40. Especially did the chairman of Quarter Sessions have power to manipulate the decisions of the grand jury by deciding whether evidence was admissible. See, for instance, B.L., Add. MSS 42590, f. 66, W. Brockman to J. Brockman, Jan. 20, 1736/1737.

41. Under 3 William III c. 12, two justices at the division's highway sessions could order a rate on the parish to reimburse a surveyor for payments for materials used in the repair of a road. The same statute authorized the justices in Quarter Sessions to levy a highway rate on a parish if they decided that its roads could not otherwise be sufficiently repaired.

the county's facilities—most notably for the county's jail and houses of correction. As administration of county facilities involved the distribution of county patronage, this category of decision allowed the justices to proclaim the prevalence of an interest. When in 1693 the Buckinghamshire bench dismissed the master of the county's house of correction, the decision informed the electorate of the dominance of the Wharton interest, a message reinforced a year later by the removal of one of those who had opposed that decision from the county's commission.[42] Yet another category of administrative matters subject to the will of the bench had even more obvious political implications. After the Glorious Revolution the justices were given power to license Dissenting teachers and places of worship. Whigs were sympathetic to Dissent; Tories were not. And so when the justices decided whether to grant these licences, they informed the voters of the relative strength of the Whig and Tory parties on the bench.[43]

Probably most potent among the weapons wielded by the majority of justices in Quarter Sessions was appellate jurisdiction. The law constituted the justices in Quarter Sessions judges on appeals from orders of the single and double justice—the latter including orders on tithes, bastardy, settlement, ratification of the accounts of parish officials, and assessments to the poor and highway rates. So, the majority of justices at Quarter Sessions had the power to uphold or undermine the authority of both individual justices and justices acting as a group out of Quarter Sessions. However dominant his interest might be in a division, no justice could feel entirely secure unless he were assured of the support of the majority at Quarter Sessions. Likewise, a justice unable to obtain the aid of his divisional colleagues could not obtain support from Quarter Sessions if he were not allied to the majority on the bench. As one justice explained to Lord Chancellor Hardwicke:

> . . . we are four Justices of the peace in the Parish of Westbury in the County of Wilts, all Phipps by Name, to Say, my Self of Heywood, Thomas Phipps the Father, Thomas Phipps the Son, both living in the same house and William Phipps the Nephew, all three in the Village of Westbury Leigh. . . . These may, as your Lordship knows, make a Sessions for confirming any parish business to my prejudice if they please, which am by farr the greatest Pay Master, the rest of the parish are alike lyable to Suffer when their business is transacted by a Majority so nearly related, And frequent Appeals my Lord to Quarter Ses-

42. A. Hassel Smith, *County and Court: Government and Politics in Norfolk, 1558–1603* (Oxford, 1974), pp. 93–94.

43. P. J. W. Higson, "A Dissenting Northern Family," *Northern History* 7 (1972): 46.

sions in cases of partiality must prove vexatious, besides not allways likely to meet a Remedy where those on the Bench are ingaged in the Interest complained of. . . .[44]

At Quarter Sessions, as at petty sessions, justices formed alliances to safeguard their interests and attack the influence of their opponents.

When in 1715 magnates pleaded for the removal of members of the opposing party from the bench, they argued that it was necessary to insure that the majority of justices be of the proper party. Some opponents, it was alleged, never "appeare at the Sessions but when sent for . . . to Serve a Turn, having been put into the Commission for that purpose." Similarly, party supporters at mid-century instanced the possibility of "being out-voted at Quarter Sessions" as reason sufficient for the removal of opponents from the commission and the veto of the appointment of others.[45] In 1732, a proposal to make Quarter Sessions the final court of appeal for cases in which it was not the court of first instance was defeated in the House of Commons because, "It was thought that the Judges' determination of appeals would be more equitable than the judgment of Justices of Peace at present that party reigns everywhere so much."[46] The administrative matters with which Quarter Sessions dealt may appear ludicrously trifling, fit subject for satire, but England's governors knew that the justices' administrative decisions affected gentlemen's ability to maintain their interests and to wield political influence.

Justices, observed one Elizabethan, used their powers "to serve the pryvate affeccon of them selves and frends."[47] The office of justice of the peace had always bestowed influence upon its tenants, but evolution of the office altered the justices' assessment of the influence inherent in their armoury of powers. The office had originally been instituted as an aid in the maintenance of the peace, and in earlier eras justices had used powers designed to frustrate disturbers of the peace in the harassment of opponents. By the eighteenth century, the jus-

44. B.L., Add. MSS 35601, ff. 61–62, Mr. William Phipps to Hardwicke, May 27, 1742.

45. Herts. R.O., Panshanger MSS, D/EP/F153, Earl of Suffolk to Cowper, Jan. 6, 1714[5], and D/EP/F154, signed T. Fitzwilliam; B.L., Add. MSS 35604, ff. 187–188, Lord Ducie to Hardwicke, June 22, 1754; see also Add. MSS 35603, ff. 253–254, Sir Francis Fust to Hardwicke, Sept. 17, 1750; Kent A.O., U269/C148/31, Sir Basil Dixwell to Duke of Dorset, Nov. 10, 1733, and U269/C148/42, Same to Same, Dec. 19, 1733.

46. *HMC, Egmont Diary* I, pp. 222–223.

47. Smith, *County and Court,* p. 77.

tices' powers to deal with criminals only rarely and indirectly allowed them to embarrass their enemies. Unlike their Elizabethan predecessors, eighteenth-century gentlemen were not, for example, wont to ambush their rivals.[48] So, eighteenth-century justices engaged in a form of combat which may appear more civilized and therefore less evident, though it was no less serious. In place of contests over might to which the criminal law was applicable, they substituted dispute over matters to which their administrative powers were suited. For by the early eighteenth century, the justices had acquired far more administrative authority than had their Plantagenet and even their Tudor predecessors. Not only had stacks of statutes increased their administrative duties, but the development of institutions of local government had also increased the impact of their administrative decisions upon the communities they governed. By the late seventeenth century, the experiments of the Tudor and early Stuart state had produced a comprehensive, effective, and newly expensive system of local government. For instance, though Tudor statutes had sketched the structure of an administrative system for maintenance of the highways, it was not until the late seventeenth century that justices acquired the power of levying rates to provide for that maintenance.[49] Similarly, it was not until 1662 that Tudor and early Stuart innovations in poor relief achieved their definitive structure, and from the 1660s onwards, English readers were treated to diatribes against the mounting burden of the poor rate.[50] By the late seventeenth century, the development of the justices' administrative powers and the consolidation of their administrative structures had made administrative decision the justices' preferred weapon in their contests for interest.

Since the justices' administrative decisions affected taxpayers, many of whom were voters, the justices' use of administrative decision to maintain their interests inevitably involved them in national politics. Voting was a more regular feature of later Stuart and early Hanoverian political life than it had been in preceding eras. Given the influence wielded by the justices, it is not surprising that later Stuart and early Hanoverian ministries took care to appoint their allies to the

48. *Ibid.*, pp. 197–198; J. S. Cockburn, *A History of English Assizes 1558–1714* (Cambridge, 1972), p. 104.

49. S. and B. Webb, *English Local Government from the Revolution to the Municipal Corporations Act*, vol. 5, *The Story of the King's Highway* (London, 1913), pp. 21–23.

50. D. Marshall, *The English Poor In The Eighteenth Century* (London, 1926), pp. 74–79.

local bench and were wary of bestowing judicial power upon their opponents. The attention with which these ministries inspected and regulated the composition of the bench, inspections and regulations which will be examined in later chapters, indicates that the office of justice was not merely an honour which could be dispensed by the sovereign's ministers without cost to the sovereign's coffers. The justices possessed powers which they employed in political combat. In 1710 the Bishop of London warned Harley, whose Tory ministry had just taken office, that unless the government altered the composition of the commissions many "well disposed people" would not be able "to choose whom they like for fear of ill usage from tyrants." In 1714 the Whig ministry, which had just taken office, was advised that if a large number of the Tories who comprised the majority on the Warwickshire bench were not removed from the commission, so taking "the Freeholders more out of the power of the other Party, It will not signifye any thing to proceed to a Pol[l] in this County for Representatives." The same theme was echoed throughout the reigns of the first two Hanoverians. In 1754, allies of the ministry urged the issue of a new commission for Gloucestershire because "there are people too well dispos'd to exert their power over meek and quiett Whigs."[51]

Because political influence was inherent in the justices' powers, and because the justice exercised his influence through administrative decisions, the office of justice yoked politics to administration. Change in either politics or administration would engender alteration in the commission of the peace, and under the later Stuarts and early Hanoverians the concepts and structure of both administration and politics changed. The following chapters analyze the interaction of politics and administration with the institutions, composition, behaviour, and ideals of England's local governors.

51. B.L., Loan 29/131/7, Henry, Bishop of London to Harley, dated 1710 by G. Holmes, *British Politics in the Age of Anne,* p. 25, n. 2; Herts. R.O., Panshanger MSS, D/EP/F154, George Lucy to [?], Nov. 21, 1714; B.L., Add. MSS 35604, f. 166, Abraham Isaac Elton to Joseph Matthews, May 11, 1754.

CHAPTER TWO

Lex Loquens

Sir Roger de Coverly is Dead. . . . Sir Andrew Freeport has a Letter from one of his Correspondents in those Parts that informs him the Old Man caught a Cold at the County Sessions, as he was very warmly promoting an Address of his own penning, in which he succeeded according to his Wishes. But this Particular comes from a Whig-Justice of Peace, who was always Sir Roger's Enemy and Antagonist.

D. Bond, ed., *The Spectator,* by Joseph Addison (Oxford, 1965), vol. 4, p. 339.

It has long been apparent that in the early seventeenth century the law courts were a major arena for constitutional debate. In the eighteenth century, debate over constitutional issues no longer disturbed legal proceedings. This lack of legal argument about constitutional principles has contributed to the impression that disputes about political ideologies, and hence parties based on political ideology, played little part in early Hanoverian politics. Though early Hanoverian law courts did not make definitive pronouncements on fundamental constitutional issues, they nonetheless did pronounce. Courts have to speak, for their job is to make decisions which define what is right and what is wrong. It has not been realized that in the later Stuart and early Hanoverian eras the rituals of court proceedings were modified so as to allow greater opportunity for speech in court, and that these modifications were instituted to disseminate and validate party propaganda. Charges given by judges at Assizes and by chairmen at Quarter Sessions, addresses of grand juries at Assizes and Quarter Sessions, sermons at Assizes, and even cases heard at Assizes and Quarter Sessions: all were designed to advertise party principles. While the justices' elaboration of structures for legal rhetoric reveals the permeation of party among England's gentry and illustrates the justices' ability to shape their institutions for their own purposes, the very fact that justices used the courts to disseminate party propaganda testifies to their conviction that they could influence the political activity of their compatriots by inculcation of political principles. Under both the later Stuarts and the early Hanoverians, England's rulers acted on twin assumptions: that politics involved debate on political principles, and that the elite could affect the outcome of that debate by their pronouncements in court. Since it would be presumptuous to argue that England's justices were unable to understand the operation of influence in English politics, it is quite likely that the justices were right.

In using the courts to disseminate propaganda, the justices were building upon established precedent. The national government had long been aware that Assizes provided a unique oppotunity for broadcasting a political message. In theory, all the county was present at Assizes. In fact, Assizes and Quarter Sessions were the only institutions which regularly assembled the county's rulers, and at Assizes all had to listen to the sovereign's judge as he charged the grand jurors, informing them of the laws they were sworn to uphold. That the judge's charge had political potential is obvious. Regular use of the charge for political purposes had begun in the late sixteenth century when judges were summoned to Star Chamber to be informed of the message they were to proclaim throughout the land,[1] and the governments of the later Stuarts and early Hanoverians continued to instruct their judges in the charge.[2] In an age when relatively few of the county great would journey annually to London to hear the government present its view of national affairs, and when newspapers were in hyperactive and unreliable infancy, the judge became a messenger of the monarch to his subjects in the hinterlands, and the judge's charge to the grand jury a provincial address from under the throne. In 1688, James II's judges were instructed to rouse due appreciation of the king's religious policies, and to convey the tidings that Parliament would soon be summoned, instructions which some judges sensibly translated into charges advocating the election of those who concurred with the king's programme.[3] In 1715, the judges were told that it was

1. J. S. Cockburn, *A History of English Assizes 1558–1714* (Cambridge 1972), pp. 57–58, 181–186, 228, 230, 235, 237, 239, 247, 249, 252, 255–256, 259–260.

2. For example, P.R.O., PC 2/76, p. 301, Feb. 27, 1695[6]; PC 2/77, p. 425, Feb. 22, 1699[1700]; *CSPD, William III,* vol. 10, pp. 237–238, July 13, 1699; B.L., Add. MSS 35600, f. 2, Feb. 26, 1720[1].

3. *CSPD, James II,* vol. 3, no. 2126; G. A. Ellis, *The Ellis Correspondence,* 2 vols. (London, 1829), vol. 2, p. 61, London, July 21, 1688.

"his M[ajesty']s pleasur—That, to the utmost of your Power, you *Excite* in his *Subjects* a *just* Abhorrence of the intended *Invasion* from Sea; and of that *implacable* and *ungratefull* Faction, by whose *instigation* and incouragement it was undertaken."[4]

As the judges realized, their incorporation of a political message in their instructions to the grand jury endowed their observations on politics with the authority of law. The judges' task was not merely the determination of legal disputes. The judges were pillars of the government. They symbolized the legality of the current regime, and they fully accepted their responsiblities in the maintenance of that regime. Just before Sir Littleton Powys was to give his charge to the Hampshire grand jury in 1715, several justices informed him that reports that the Habeas Corpus Act had been repealed and that the king was establishing a standing army were being circulated in the county. "Whereupon," Littleton proudly reported, "I did in my charge not only Inculcate very fully the several matters directed us in Council at St. James's, but I did Undeceive the People as to those 2 false Reports spread abroad maliciously by seditious persons, who if discovered should be most severely punished. . . ."[5] In less parlous times, judges would excite in his majesty's subjects a due sense of the wisdom and beneficence of his majesty's government. In 1736, Middlesex heard of the king's—read Walpole's—manifest perspicacity in preserving the nation from the horrors of war.[6]

The judges presided at Assizes, but a justice, the chairman of Quarter Sessions, directed the deliberations of his court. Like the judge at Assizes, the chairman of Quarter Sessions delivered a charge to the grand jury. Elizabethan and early Stuart chairmen had, on occasion, included a homily on the wonder and majesty of England's government in their charges, and in the political climate of Charles II's reign these homilies could easily become a partisan exposition of England's constitutional structure. It was only natural that a chairman discourse on the iniquities of republicanism in 1660; by 1677, the same chairman was endorsing the king's right to continue the Pension Parliament.[7] By the early eigh-

4. Herts. R.O., Panshanger MSS D/EP/F150, "Orders to Judges on their Circuits."

5. Herts. R.O., Panshanger MSS D/EP/F150, Sir Littleton Powys to Cowper, Salisbury, Aug. 10, 1715.

6. *The Charge of J——ge P—— to the Grand Jury of M——x, on Saturday, May 22, 1736* (London, 1738), pp. 4ff.

7. E. M.. Halcron, ed., *Charges to the Grand Jury at Quarter Sessions 1660–1677 by Sir Peter Leicester,* Chetham Society, 3rd ser., vol. 5 (Manchester, 1953), pp. 2ff., 80ff.

teenth century, change in the structure of politics and change in the procedure of selecting a chairman were both reinforcing the tendency to use the charge to state party principles. Chairmen of early Stuart Quarter Sessions were appointed by the central government,[8] but chairmen of later Stuart Quarter Sessions were elected by the justices at Quarter Sessions. By the accession of George I, the permeation of party among the local elite had turned the election of chairmen into a party contest. A bench with a majority of Whigs elected a Whig chairman, and a Tory bench chose a Tory chairman. Through the chairman, the majority of justices at Quarter Sessions instructed the populace in the validity of their party's principles and the iniquity of those of their opponents. So, Whig chairmen under George I expounded on the iniquity of Jacobites and their fellow-travellers—of High Churchmen and of those whose minions disseminated "Popery and Slavery" under "the Titles of *Orphans, Scourges, Saturday's Posts,* and the like Traiterous and Seditious Libels."[9] The charge allowed the chairman to demonstrate that his party's principles accorded with the laws of the land, and conveniently, to remind the grand jury that some adherents of the opposing party were committing indictable offences.

So eager were the justices to instruct their audience in party principles that they found the chairman's charge insufficient for their purposes. Spurred by the needs of party, the justices elaborated upon one of the forms for speech in court so as to produce a new vehicle for political propaganda. The form that they developed was the address of the grand jury. From 1680 onwards grand juries issued addresses which were statements of party propaganda, and the justices manipulated the pronouncements of the grand juries. At Quarter Sessions, justices associated themselves with the grand jury in the issue of an

8. T. G. Barnes, *Somerset 1625–1640, A County's Government During the 'Personal Rule'* (Cambridge, Mass., 1961), pp. 70–71. For further examination of the election of chairmen, see chapter IX.

9. W. Cowper, *The Charge of William Cowper, Esq., to the Grand-Jury of the City and Liberty of Westminster, etc., at the General Quarter-Sessions of the Peace, held October the 7th, 1719* (London, 1719), pp. 10ff.; J. Montagu, *The Charge of James Montagu, Esq., to the Grand Jury . . . of the County of Wilts: At the General Quarter-Sessions of the Peace, held at the Devizes, April 26, 1720* (London, 1720), pp. 36ff.; Sir Richard Cocks, Bart., *A Charge given to the Grand-Jury of the County of Gloucester, at the Midsummer-Sessions* (London, 1723), passim; Sir Richard Cocks, *His Charge to the Grand-Jury of the County of Gloucester. At the General Quarter-Sessions Held for that County, April the 30th, 1717* (London, 1717), passim; Sir John Gonson, Knt., *A Charge to the Grand Jury of the City and Liberty of Westminster, etc., At the General Quarter Sessions of the Peace held the third Day of July, 1729 . . .* (London, 1729), pp. 32ff.

address. Indeed, many addresses from the grand jury at Quarter Sessions were written by the justices, and the bench at Quarter Sessions rejected those political statements of the grand jury which the majority of justices opposed.[10] The justices also assumed direction of the grand jury at Assizes: from the early 1680s onwards some of the grand jurors at Assizes were justices.

Since the address was a statement of party principle, it is pleasingly logical that the impetus for its appearance was the same as that for the first appearance of the Whig and Tory parties. Both the address and the parties emerged in 1679, as a response to the Exclusion crisis. In 1679, English politics revolved around the problem posed by the likelihood that James would succeed his brother on the throne. As it was thought that Parliament would pass a bill excluding James from his inheritance, those for Exclusion tried to exert pressure on Charles II to convoke Parliament. Shaftesbury, the Whigs' leader, caused petitions calling for the repudiation of the ministers responsible for the prorogation of Parliament to be carried from house to house throughout the towns and counties of England. Here, the Whigs proclaimed, was the voice of the nation. Charles II responded. Not only did he issue a proclamation against petitioning, but he also thought it expedient to counter Whig national voice with Tory. Bodies that could claim to be representative of the nation—town corporations, deputy lieutenants of the county, and grand juries—were persuaded to address approbatory remarks on the prorogation to the king. According to the Tories, the Whig petitions were misrepresentations of the nation's opinion. They were signed by those who could not claim to represent the opinions of their compatriots by virtue of either their local standing or their office. In January 1680, three Wiltshire Whigs presented a petition to the king "*in the Name of the County*. His Majesty was pleas'd to ask them, *Whether they had their Directions from the Grand Jury?* [They] answer'd, *No*. His Majesty was pleas'd to reply, *Why say you then that you come from the County? You come from a Company of loose disaffected people*."[11]

According to law, and in later Stuart political thought, the grand

10. J. Oldmixon, *The History of Addresses*, 2 vols. (London, 1709–1711), vol. 1, p. 19; R. L'Estrange, *Citt and Bumpkin, in a Dialogue Over a Pot of Ale, Concerning Matters of Religion and Government*, 3rd ed. (London, 1680), pp. 5–6; M. Child, "Prelude to Revolution: Politics in County Durham, 1678–1688," (Ph.D. diss., University of Maryland, 1972), pp. 71–74; *The Case between the King and Richard Biggs alias Blue Dick* . . . quoted in R. Goodsall, *Stede Hill* (London, 1950), pp. 131–132.

11. Oldmixon, *History of Addresses*, vol. 1, p. 20.

jury spoke for the county. It was "the body of the county"[12] and therefore aware of all that affected the community. A recent legal decision emphasized the validity of a jury's pronouncements. Later Stuart legal manuals cited the declaration of Lord Chief Justice Vaughan in 1671 that the petty jury was able to weigh evidence better than the judge:

> . . . 'tis impossible for the Judge to know the Fact as the Jury may; for the Judge knows it no otherwise but by the Evidence given in Court, but the Jury are supposed to know it by other Methods, *viz.*
>
> By being returned of the Vicinage, by their own personal Knowledge, by knowing the Witnesses to be Persons of no Credit.[13]

A pronouncement of the grand jury was accounted as the voice of the county speaking true, and that is why Charles II first obtained and then boasted of addresses from grand juries supporting his policies.

Charles II's use of the grand jury as a forum for political propaganda was not entirely unprecedented. The grand jury had always had the task of presenting those persons and matters dangerous to the county. Presentment was the first stage of legal proceedings leading to condemnation. Until shortly before the Civil War, grand juries had confined their pronouncements to those matters affecting the condition of the county that fell within the jurisdiction of the court. They presented unrepaired roads, recusants, unlicensed alehouses—all matters remediable by legal action. During the Civil War, grand juries elevated the plane of their deliberations. Now they occasionally thought it their duty to consider the state of the nation, to address their remarks to Parliament or to the nation's ruler, and to engage leading representatives of the shire to deliver their sentiments. During Richard Cromwell's Protectorate, addresses had been organized on a large scale, but the address had ceased to be a feature of political life shortly after the Restoration.[14] When Oldmixon wrote his *History of Addresses* in Anne's reign, he found that twelve pages were sufficient

12. *Ibid.*, vol. 1, p. 120.

13. W. Nelson, *Office and Authority of a Justice of Peace . . .*, 6th ed. (London, 1718), p. 385.

14. J. S. Morrill, *The Cheshire Grand Jury 1625–1659*, Occasional Papers of the Department of English Local History, Leicester University, 3rd series, no. 1 (Leicester, 1976), pp. 33–39; J. S. Morrill, *Cheshire 1630–1660; County Government and Society During the English Revolution* (London, 1974), pp. 12, 141, 259; F. W. Jessup, *Sir Roger Twysden, 1597–1672* (London, 1965), pp. 40, 44–45; D. Underdown, *Somerset in the Civil War and Interregnum* (Newton Abbot, 1973), p. 23; J. R. Jones, "James II's Whig Collaborators," *Historical Journal* 3 (1960): 71; J. S. Cockburn, ed., *Somerset Assize Orders 1640–1659*, Somerset Record Society, vol. 71 (Frome, 1971), p. xxiii.

to chronicle all addresses before the Exclusion crisis. The rest of his two volumes was devoted to the addresses of 1679 to 1710. Upon its reintroduction in 1679 the address became a fixture in party politics.

Within a year after Charles II had boasted of grand jury support, the Whigs could also claim that they "had their directions from the county."[15] From 1680 onwards statements of party ideology flowed forth from the grand juries of England. Unlike the grand jury's presentments, its address did not depend on alleged infraction of the law. The address was an editorial on the state of the nation, and in later Stuart England almost any event could furnish sufficient matter for partisan reflection. Grand juries commented on Charles II's prorogation and dissolution of Parliament, on James II's proclamation of toleration, and on plots to assassinate William III. They attested their fidelity to the monarch on James's accession, William and Mary's coronation, Mary's death, and the accession of George I. They congratulated James on the birth of a son. They proclaimed, in measured cadences, the widsom of the Peace of Ryswick and the Treaty of Utrecht. They gravely pronounced on Sacheverell.[16] Even the nation's victories provided occasion for partisan address. When, in the summer of 1704, Rooke triumphed at sea and Marlborough on land, addresses congratulated the monarch on her kingdom's glory. Some addresses mentioned both Rooke and Marlborough. Others omitted mention of Rooke, the Tory hero, while still others coupled praise of Marlborough with approbation of her majesty's ecclesiastical policies—policies which the Tories' High Church allies were condemning.[17] If current affairs did not provide material for patent party statement, the increasing sophistication of the early eighteenth-century address allowed covert partisan propaganda.

Since grand juries now issued political statements, it was only politic to insure that their statements be valid. The list of grand jurors was compiled by the sheriff. So, sheriffs packed grand juries with adherents of their party. A Staffordshire address congratulating James II on the happy prospect of the Queen's pregnancy began with an apology for the county's delay in communicating their sentiments: they had been "de-

15. J. R. Jones, *The First Whigs: The Politics of the Exclusion Crisis* (London, 1961), p. 171.

16. For accounts of addresses, see N. Luttrell, *A Brief Historical Relation of State Affairs from September 1678 to April 1714,* 6 vols. (Oxford, 1857), passim, and Oldmixon, *History of Addresses.*

17. For example, compare Sandwich's address (*London Gazette,* Sept. 18–21, 1704) with those of Dover and Rochester (*London Gazette,* Sept. 21–25, 1704).

tain'd from paying their Duty by an over-ruling Party."[18] In 1711, it was alleged that the Kent and Gloucestershire addresses favouring Sacheverell had been obtained from packed juries. Kent's definitely was. A High Church clergyman resident in Kent reported that the majority of the gentry in west Kent would support the Whig candidates in the 1710 election. "The High Sheriff could find but 40 . . . against them, all these he put in the list for the Grand-jury. . . ."[19] The sheriff knew his men. The grand jury for the summer Assizes of 1710 numbered twenty-seven (the largest grand jury in the history of the later Stuart Kent), and when the county went to the polls in 1713, nineteen of the jury's twenty-three surviving members voted for both Tory candidates; two of the four nonvoters were the Tory candidates. Nor were the Whigs less adept than the Tories in obtaining serviceable juries. The Tory grand juries of the last years of Anne's reign were succeeded by Whig grand juries on the accession of George I. Of the twenty-two members of Kent's grand jury at the first Assizes of the first Hanoverian, twenty had voted for the Whigs in the 1715 election.[20] So prevalent was the packing of juries that in 1711 a Whig historian could argue that those grand jury addresses which supported Sacheverell did not reflect the opinion of the county. The House of Commons which condemned Sacheverell was elected, Oldmixon declared, while grand juries were merely picked by the sheriff.[21]

That Oldmixon felt impelled to refute the notion that addresses might express national opinion and legal truth more accurately than Parliament reveals the power of the address in early eighteenth-century politics. After all, Sacheverell had been impeached. Nonetheless a Whig propagandist felt bound to discredit those addresses which supported the Tory hero. In theory, the address of the grand jury did embody the truth as seen by the county. In fact it proved, at the least, which party had power sufficient to dominate the grand jury. But it was not simply the power to manipulate a grand jury which the address expressed. The address was designed to convince both members

18. Oldmixon, *History of Addresses,* vol. 1, p. 159.

19. Oldmixon, *History of Addresses,* vol. 2, pp. 18, 219; Bodleian Library, Ballard MSS, vol. 15, f. 96, Jo. Johnson to [Dr. Charlett], Sept. 15, 1710; Kent A.O., U820/Z1 is the signed address.

20. Of the remaining two grand jurors of 1715, one voted at neither the 1713 nor 1715 election, and the other voted in 1713 for the Whigs. Lists of Kent's grand juries are in the Assize indictment rolls, P.R.O., Ass 35. Kent A. O., Q/RPe1 is a copy of the poll book for the 1713 election, and Bodleian Library, Rawlinson MSS B338 is a copy of the poll book of the 1715 election.

21. Oldmixon, *History of Addresses,* vol. 2, p. 27.

of the elite and their inferiors of the validity of a party's principles. And the address was persuasive. Addresses were published. Gentlemen even copied paragraphs from addresses they admired into their notebooks.[22] So those with influence carefully drafted addresses which they hoped a grand jury or a town corporation or some other body would endorse,[23] and members of the grand jury argued over the phrases their address would broadcast.[24] Prominent adherents of the party attacked in a grand jury address feared that voters might be conjured into belief in the opposing party's ideology or local prominence. So, in 1710 Whigs promoted addresses to counter those of Tory grand juries which supported Sacheverell.[25] Even the timing of an address was regarded as pertinent to its propaganda. In 1714, it was urged that the Whig address for Glamorganshire be written and signed as soon as possible, for "if the Toryes hear of it to cross us they will address before us."[26] Still more important was the prestige of those signing the address. The more eminent the signators, the more illustrious the members of the grand jury, the more persuasive the address.

Therefore, the introduction of the address necessitated change in the composition of the grand jury at Assizes. Until the 1680s grand jurors were drawn from the freeholders of the county. Occasionally, justices might be added to a grand jury at Assizes, but a grand jury which boasted a substantial number of justices was so unusual that it signalled exceptional turmoil in the county.[27] From the 1680s onwards, a substantial portion of the grand jury at Assizes were justices of the peace—as well they should be. Since grand juries now regularly issued addresses, and since the address was a statement of party principle, the address and the parties had jointly transformed grand juries into county parliaments. Therefore, grand jurors had now to be gentlemen qualified to represent the county.

22. For example, Hants. R.O., 18/M51/595, p. 47 and 18/M51/596, unpaginated. The latter example is a copy of an address on Sacheverell.

23. B.L., Add. MSS 42593, f. 121, draft of an address, July 28, 1712; Eg. 2985, f. 235, Sir Jo. Heath to Mayor [of Milton and Gravesend], June 11, 1681, and f. 236.

24. Lady Margaret Maria Verney, *Verney Letters of the Eighteenth Century from the Manuscripts at Claydon House* (London, 1930), vol. 1, pp. 340–341, Sir Thomas Cave to Lord Fermanagh, Sept. 13, 1715.

25. Oldmixon, *History of Addresses,* vol. 2, pp. 218–219.

26. Herts. R.O., Panshanger MSS D/EP/F155, Richard Jenkins to George Cowell, Dec. 9, 1714.

27. Morrill, *Cheshire Grand Jury,* pp. 15–20, 41–43; A. Everitt, *The Community of Kent and the Great Rebellion 1640–1660* (Leicester, 1966), pp. 95–96 and p. 95, n.2; T. P. S. Woods, *Prelude to Civil War, 1642, Mr. Justice Malet and the Kentish Petitions* (Salisbury, 1980), p. 31.

Consider the history of Kent's grand jury. During the 1670s, justices rarely graced the grand jury at Kent's Assizes. For instance, of the 106 grand jurors at the six Assizes between summer 1678 and Lent 1681, only one was a justice and just three more were gentlemen who would become justices within the next five years. None of these grand juries issued an address. Then, at the summer Assizes of 1681, Kent's grand jury decided to thank the king for "delivering us from an Incroaching Arbitrary power"—that is, for dismissing the Oxford Parliament, and for preserving "the Antient Monarchy in its due and Legall course of Descent." Five of the nineteen grand jurors were justices and another two became justices within four years.[28] From the summer of 1681 every grand jury at Kent's Assizes included some justices, and those whose deliberations produced unusually partisan pronouncements contained an unusually large number of justices.[29] The grand jury at the Lent Assizes of 1683, which presented Dissenters as a danger to the realm, numbered ten justices among its eighteen members.[30] Of the thirteen gentlemen on the Kentish grand jury which congratulated James on the birth of a son, ten were justices.[31] Thirteen justices sat on the grand jury which both pronounced for Sacheverell and announced its support for the Tory candidates for the county seats.[32] When in 1712 the Tory government concluded an armistice with France, an armistice bitterly opposed by the Whigs, the government's actions were praised by a grand jury of fifteen justices and four gentlemen.[33]

Although it is probable that the history of Kent's grand jury was reenacted throughout England, the evidence currently available is insufficient for a categorical assertion that the composition of the grand juries of all counties was altered so as to include justices in the early 1680s. Most studies of the seventeenth-century grand jury deal with the period before the Restoration, and all these studies have restricted

28. B.L., Eg. 2985, f. 243.

29. Lists of grand jurors at Kent's Assizes are in P.R.O., Ass 35. I have not been able to find grand jury lists for the Assizes of Lent and summer 1682, summer 1683, Lent 1685, and summer 1693.

30. *The Presentment of the Grand-Jury for the County of Kent at Maidstone the 12th day of March . . . 1682* (London, 1683).

31. Luttrell, *Brief Historical Relation*, vol. 1, p. 454.

32. Kent A.O., U820/Z1; *The Post Boy*, Aug. 3–5, 1710.

33. *The Post Boy*, Aug. 12–14, 1712. William Brockman had arrived at east Kent's Quarter Sessions with a draft of an address condemning England's abandonment of her allies, but the grand jury and justices at Quarter Sessions issued an address in support of the government (B.L., Add. MSS 42593, f. 121; *London Gazette*, July 31–Aug. 2, 1712).

their focus to a single county. These studies indicate that justices did not usually sit upon the grand jury.[34] The post-Restoration grand juries of only three counties—Norfolk, Northumberland, and Durham—have been examined. "Gentlemen of quality" graced Norfolk's grand jury at Assizes in Charles II's reign, but a grand jury which included "several baronets and justices" was still sufficiently unusual to merit comment in 1677.[35] Before the 1680s, it was "unusual" for a large number of justices to appear among the grand jurors at Assizes in Northumberland and Durham. Yet in 1681 Northumberland's grand jury included justices, as did Durham's in both 1680 and 1681. In Northumberland and Durham, justices even sat on the grand jury at Quarter Sessions—in Durham in 1682 and 1688, and in Northumberland in 1682—and each of these grand juries likewise produced an address.[36] Scattered references to grand juries at Assizes reveal that in Cheshire in 1684, in Warwickshire in the 1690s, and in Devonshire and Buckinghamshire in 1701, grand jurors were justices, members of Parliament, and gentry boasting a status much higher than that of early Stuart grand jurors.[37] So, it is quite probable that in the late seventeenth century there was a nationwide alteration in the composition of the grand jury at Assizes, and entirely possible that the regular appearance of justices as grand jurors was instituted in the 1680s to endow the grand jury's address

34. The evidence of these studies is summarized in Morrill, *Cheshire Grand Jury*, pp. 41–43, which notes the claim of B. C. Redwood, ed., *Quarter Sessions Order Book, 1642–1649*, Sussex Record Society, vol. 54 (Lewes, 1954), p. xxiii, that justices served on the Sussex grand jury and M. S. Gretton's statement, in *Oxfordshire Justices of the Peace in the Seventeenth Century*, Oxfordshire Record Society, vol. 16 (Oxford, 1934), p. lxxxvi, that the grand jury at Assizes was composed of "gentlemen of the best quality, estate and understanding in the County." However, Redwood's assertion is based on documents whose description is suspiciously similar to the *nomina ministrorum*, which lists the names of all justices. It is not clear whether Gretton is describing early or late seventeenth-century grand juries, and her assertion is confusing as she uses as evidence her earlier analysis of the grand jury at Quarter Sessions. In addition, she bases her argument on the title 'Esquire' given in grand jury lists to all grand jurors, both at Assizes and Quarter Sessions. In mid-seventeenth-century Cheshire, the title 'gentleman' was given to all grand jurors, but this has been proved to be a "mere legal fiction" (J. S. Morrill, "The Northern Gentry and the Great Rebellion," *Northern History* 15 [1979]: 72, n. 19). It seems likely that the title 'Esquire' was also a legal fiction. Gretton does note that in a later unspecified century only the justices were permitted to sit on Oxfordshire's grand jury.

35. James Rosenheim, "The Gentry of Restoration Norfolk, 1660–1720" (Ph.D. diss., Princeton University, 1981), pp. 104–105, and p. 130, notes 40, 41.

36. Child, "Prelude to Revolution," pp. 55–64, 72–75, 199. See also Cockburn, *History of English Assizes*, p. 251.

37. Luttrell, *Brief Historical Relation*, vol. 1, p. 305; vol. 5, pp. 79, 88; H. C. Johnson and N. J. Williams, eds., *Warwick County Records*, vol. 9, (Warwick, 1964), p. xlv.

with the justices' prestige. Certainly, descriptions of the grand jury at Assizes indicate that its composition had altered. An early Stuart manual detailing procedure at Assizes stated that, if an unsufficient number of grand jurors appeared when the sheriff called the list of those summoned, the sheriff "must return some Free-holders of the same County, that are present, even the Justices of Peace upon the Bench, if he please." In the mid-eighteenth century, Blackstone declared that grand juries at Assizes usually consisted of "gentlemen of the best figure in the county," and in Blackstone's day, gentlemen of the best figure were justices.[38]

So the practice of placing justices on the grand jury persisted into the reigns of the early Hanoverians. By the second decade of the eighteenth century, at least one-third and sometimes more than half of the grand jurors at Kent's Assizes were justices, and their worships were still dominating the grand jury in the 1750s. Likewise, early Hanoverian grand juries continued to issue political statements. Though the intensity of political debate had declined, Hanoverian politicians could rouse themselves to perform deeds worthy of their forbears when they glimpsed an opportunity to exert pressure on the government or the electorate. As late as 1763 the Grenville administration strove to obtain grand jury addresses applauding the Treaty of Paris, and members of Parliament dependent on the ministry's largesse were expected to promote these addresses when they sat on the grand jury.[39] When those opposing the government had the chance to influence the grand jury, they too insured that the jury's pronouncements validated party rhetoric. So grand juries condemned Walpole's excise bill, protested against the act for the naturalization of Jews, deprecated the mismanagement of the war which resulted in the loss of Minorca, and reiterated Tory demands for free elections, a place bill, and repeal of the Riot and Septennial acts.[40] Perhaps one of the most intensive opposition campaigns occurred in the summer of 1742 when

38. Anon., *The Office of the Clerk of Assize,* 2nd ed. corrected and amended (London, 1682), p. 30 (Morrill, *Cheshire Grand Jury,* p. 52, n. 117, states that this manual was probably written about 1610); Sir W. Blackstone, *Commentaries on the Laws of England* (Philadelphia, 1771–1772), vol. 4, p. 299.

39. Sir L. Namier, *The Structure of Politics at the Accession of George III,* 2nd ed. (London, 1961), p. 416.

40. *Gentleman's Magazine* 3 (1733): 378, 379; 12 (1742): 160, 486, 487; 23 (1753): 467, 468; 26 (1756): 476; Verney, *Verney Letters,* vol. 2, p. 206, John Milward to Lord Fermanagh, July 23, 1740; B.L., Add. MSS 35351, ff. 343–344, Lord Royston to Hardwicke, Aug. 24, 1756; P. Langford, "William Pitt and Public Opinion, 1757," *English Historical Review* 88 (1973): 56, 71.

addresses applauding the resignation of Walpole and urging further opposition initiatives rained upon members of Parliament. Undoubtedly some emanated from juries packed with Tories. When in 1745 an extraordinary series of political negotiations yielded the Tory leaders in Cambridgeshire the right to nominate their adherents to the commission of the peace, the Whig Lord Chancellor noted that their list included the foreman and all but one of the esquires on the county's grand jury for the summer of 1742.[41]

So, though the honours of shrievalty were regarded as so inconsiderable that they could be bestowed on lesser gentry, and the burdens of shrievalty sufficiently irritating that they might be awarded to opponents, canny politicians nonetheless took care to procure amenable sheriffs when they had to issue election propaganda. Shortly after he announced his intention of standing for Gloucestershire in 1741, Robert Tracy was commenting upon nominees to the county's shrievalty for 1740 and observing: "it is of some Importance even this year to have a Sheriff who is so well inclin'd to the Cause as to name a proper Grand Jury and Foreman."[42] In 1753, the actions of Kent's grand jury illustrated the consequences of inadequate attention to the choice of a sheriff in the year before an election. In 1753 Sir Roger Twisden, one of the two Tory incumbents for Kent, declared himself unwilling to stand for reelection, thereby leaving Sir Edward Dering the sole Kentish Tory willing to undertake a contest against the county's resurgent Whigs. Since Dering could not even find a partner, he desperately needed to find some method of persuading the voters of his party's strength in the county. Literature has made his tactics immortal.

> D——g's cause is so bad he no second could find
> So a strange declaration the pack'd jury signed
> And that none of the Pannel might be but true friends
> In his own hand the list to the Sheriff he sends.

The grand jury at Kent's summer Assizes, a grand jury which numbered nine justices among its members, had issued a declaration praising the opposition of both Tories to the Jew bill, thanking both Tories for their "disinterested service," endorsing Dering's candidacy, and lamenting the withdrawal of Sir Roger Twisden—for reasons of bad

41. B.L., Add. MSS 35601, ff. 109–110; Add. MSS 35602, f. 79, Lord Montfort to Hardwicke, June 19, 1745, and ff. 87, 67, 111.

42. Gloucestershire R.O., Sherborne MSS, D678 Fam Sett 57/D, Tracy to [Dutton], Nov. 24, 1739.

health.[43] Even in the political climate of the 1750s, propaganda and the pronouncements of eminent grand jurors had their uses.

As both the address and the eminent grand jury had originated in response to the promptings of the national government in the early 1680s, both testify to the impact of the national government and national parties upon England's local rulers. On the other hand, both also enabled local rulers to increase their power within their localities. Justices soon found that they could adapt their service on the grand jury to suit their own purposes. Most obviously, they could use the new grand jury to strengthen local party. When justices and prospective justices sat on grand juries, and grand juries issued addresses, the grand jury became a recruiting office for party. When a gentleman served on a grand jury determined to deliver itself of an address, he could not escape enunciation and definition of his political principles. The address did not allow for neutrality. It proferred but two choices—to subscribe or not to subscribe—and both denoted partisan sympathies. Willy-nilly, grand jurors were drawn into party politics. Therefore local political leaders used the address and the grand jury to discover potential opponents and supporters, and then communicated their findings to their allies at Westminster. The report that four Kentish justices had at Quarter Sessions endeavoured to secure the grand jury's endorsement of a petition for the convocation of Parliament in January 1680 most probably caused their immediate removal from the bench.[44] At Kent's summer Assizes of 1681, seven justices refused to sign an address applauding the kings's dismissal of Parliament, and another withheld his signature from an anti-Whig address at the Lent Assizes of 1682. Three of these eight justices were forthwith deprived of office, and the report of their recalcitrance probably contributed to the dismissal of four more in 1686.[45] On the other hand, six months after a Kentish grand jury composed of thirteen justices and fourteen gentlemen proclaimed their support of Sacheverell, ten of the gentlemen were made justices by the new Tory government.[46] The transformation of the grand jury

43. The doggerel is quoted in A. N. Newman, "Elections in Kent and its Parliamentary Representation, 1713–1754" (D.Phil. thesis, Oxford University, 1957), p. 126. For the address, see *Gentleman's Magazine* 23 (1753): 469.

44. Longleat House, Wiltshire, Coventry Papers vi, f. 230, Sir Thomas Peyton to Coventry, Jan. 23, 1679/1680. Shortly before Quarter Sessions met, the government had already ordered that the fifth judicial promoter of the petition be removed from the commission (House of Lords R.O., Main Papers, H.L., Nov. 9, 1680).

45. B.L., Eg. 2985, f. 244; P.R.O., Ind. 4215, p. 67; PC 2/71, p. 368.

46. P.R.O., C 234/18, Feb. 20, 1710[11]; Ass 35/150/5.

both abetted the polarization of the counties' elite and further entangled the local elite in the web of local party and its national allies.

Nonetheless, the new grand jury did not serve to subordinate local government to rule from the centre. On the contrary, the eminent grand jury allowed local governors to gain new freedom from central control. The grand jury of yeomen at early Stuart Assizes had paid due deference to the sovereign's judges,[47] but a judge's frowns were less likely to terrify the more eminent early eighteenth-century grand juror. Despite Lord Chief Justice Trevor's harangue against the address of Buckinghamshire's grand jury in 1701, the address was signed by the majority of the jurors and handed to the judge by their foreman—Sir Richard Temple, M.P.[48] In 1763, Buckinghamshire's grand jury again refused to take directions. This time it defied the county's Lord Lieutenant. The Lord Lieutenant had appeared at Assizes to elicit an address praising the ministry's Treaty of Paris. The grand jury chose instead to condemn another of the ministry's measures—"the odious and oppressive extension of the excise upon cyder and perry" which the "county looks upon as a high violation of private property."[49] The early eighteenth-century grand jury, composed of eminent gentry determined to enunciate partisan principle, had entailed a tradition of independence upon its equally eminent though somewhat less fervent successors. Indeed, it may be suggested that the appointment of justices as grand jurors contributed to decline in the judges' supervision of local government. When an eighteenth-century grand jury pronounced on the state of the county, what judge could pretend that he knew better than the county's rulers?

Just as their grand jury service enabled the justices as a group to increase the autonomy of their rule, so grand jury service afforded each individual justice a new opportunity for the exercise of his influence. Gentlemen charged that justices who were grand jurors had used their influence to procure unjust indictments, indictments whose sole purpose was attack upon personal enemies or opposing interests.[50] It was likewise rumoured that justices persuaded their fellow grand jurors to mitigate the punishment of some select offenders. In 1715, Sir

47. Cockburn, *History of English Assizes,* pp. 114–115, 123, 248.

48. G. P. R. James, ed., *Letters Illustrative of the Reign of William III from 1696 to 1708* . . . (London, 1841), vol. 3, pp. 154–155, Mr. Vernon to Duke of Shrewsbury, Aug. 7, 1701.

49. *Gentleman's Magazine* 33 (1763): 361.

50. See chapter I.

Thomas Cave thought it necessary to deny that he had exerted undue influence to secure a lenient sentence for one defendant. True, Cave was foreman of the grand jury. But, he wrote, it was another juror who had urged that the judge be informed of mitigating circumstances. Sir Thomas had merely seconded this sympathetic soul.[51] "What! Evidence, party and judge too!" wrote one satirist of the powers of a single justice.[52] Grand jury service allowed justices a less obvious but equally potent means of guiding justice.

Nonetheless, a description of the justices' use of the grand jury to increase their autonomy which camouflaged their use of their courts to inculcate party ideology would be misleading. Throughout the later Stuart and early Hanoverian eras, local political leaders attempted to insure that even the cases tried in court conveyed a partisan message. Courts were theatres where legal dramas taught what was right and what was wrong. So in the early 1680s Tory grand juries presented Whigs as disloyal and disaffected. In 1696, it was the turn of Whig grand juries to stigmatize those who had not signed the Whig inspired association to protect William III.[53]

However, the presentment of opponents as dangerous to the realm was likely to be persuasive only in the context of specific national emergencies. While the annals of the later Stuarts abound in emergencies—Rye House plot, Monmouth rebellion, assassination plot, Fenwick conspiracy—the number of occasions when partisan grand juries could realistically impugn their opponents as traitors was still too limited for the parties' purposes. Fortunately for enthusiasts of the political fray, the laws of England provided ample opportunity for legal dramatization of their opponents' iniquity. Before 1689, each party could traduce the other through legal proceedings based on the laws regulating religious conduct. Immediately after the Popish plot, grand juries—some packed with Whigs—indicted Catholics for recusancy. Indeed the presentment of the future James II as a recusant was prevented only by the dismissal of a Middlesex grand jury.[54] While

51. Verney, *Verney Letters,* vol. 1, p. 341, Sir Thomas Cave to Lord Fermanagh, Sept. 13, 1715.

52. Quoted in E. Moir, "Local Government in Gloucestershire" (Ph.D. thesis, Cambridge University, 1955), p. 74.

53. Luttrell, *Brief Historical Relation,* vol. 1, pp. 283–284; vol. 4, p. 99; Jones, *First Whigs,* p. 210.

54. Luttrell, *Brief Historical Relation,* vol. 1, p. 49; Child, "Prelude to Revolution," pp. 340–346, 367; J. C. Cox, *Three Centuries of Derbyshire Annals, as Illustrated by the Records of the County of Derby from Queen Elizabeth to Queen Victoria* (London and Derby, 1890), vol. 1, p. 301; J. Miller, *Popery and Politics in England, 1660–1688*

Whigs rejoiced at the opportunity to tie Toryism to Catholicism, Tories favoured libelling Whigs as Dissenters. So, between 1681 and 1686 Tories indicted Dissenters as recusants.[55] As James suspended the laws against those who were not Anglicans, and the Revolution Settlement exempted Dissenters from the penalties for recusancy, political partisans had to seek a new means for vivifying the illegality of their opponents' activities and principles.

They found their instrument in the laws against sedition. As the Whigs were delighted to discover, one of the glories of the Glorious Revolution was the difficulty in which it placed inflexible supporters of the principle of hereditary monarchy. Since the principle of hereditary monarchy was more sacred to Tories than to Whigs, Tory ideology was more apt than Whig to induce seditious sentiments. Likewise, the revolution placed High Churchmen—the Tories' allies—in an anomalous position. As High Churchmen gloried in the mysteries of religion, many found it difficult to reconcile rebellion against a king anointed by the Archbishop of Canterbury with their concept of the sacerdotal role of the Church. Post-Revolution Whigs were doubtless delighted that the political and religious principles of their opponents made them vulnerable to charges of disloyalty. Prosecution of High Church Tories for sedition was so much more relevant to political debate than the indictment of Catholics for recusancy.

During the latter years of Charles II's reign, it had been Whigs who faced charges of sedition and Whig activities and ideology which were aspersed in the courts.[56] After 1689, Tories still discovered occasion to indict Whigs for sedition,[57] but those most likely to face charges of sedition were Tories. If the accused was an Anglican priest, so much the better for Whig propaganda: both Tory and High Church loyalties could be impugned at one trial. So, in 1690 two Whig justices gathered the affidavits which would result in the trial of Willaim

---

(Cambridge, 1973), pp. 164, 265, 267; G. C. F. Forster, *The East Riding Justices of the Peace in the Seventeenth Century,* East Yorkshire Local History Society Publications, no. 30 (1973), p. 43.

55. Child, "Prelude to Revolution," pp. 305–307, 310–312, 314–318; Miller, *Popery and Politics,* pp. 190–194, 205, 208; Luttrell, *Brief Historical Relation,* vol. 1, p. 213; Cox, *Derbyshire Annals,* vol. 1, pp. 346, 350; Jones, *First Whigs,* p. 208; A. H. A. Hamilton, *Quarter Sessions from Queen Elizabeth to Queen Anne* (London, 1878), p. 222.

56. P.R.O. PC 2/69, pp. 404v–405v.

57. J. P. Kenyon, *Revolution Principles, The Politics of Party 1689–1720* (Cambridge, 1977), p. 96.

Cade, cleric. Cade, it was reported, had stated that William had been enthroned by the mob, and that he prayed for William as he did for Turks, Jews, and infidels. Though Cade avowed that he thought a Protestant king an "absolute necessity," and would willingly declare his allegiance to their majesties, the justices had already received the Privy Council's approbation of their proceedings and had no intention of abandoning the prosecution. Cade deemed the justices' activity malicious. Reflect, he demanded of one of the justices, "whether it be not Hatred of my Function that makes you an Enemy to so many Clergymen, indeed, all you know, if Common fame Say right."[58] Malicious or not, the prosecutions which fill the accounts of later Stuart historians testify to the use of the laws against sedition as a means of dramatizing the righteous zeal of the prosecutors and the villainy of their opponents.[59]

By the early eighteenth century the electorate's increasing acquaintance with party ideology enabled the parties to make even more sophisticated use of the laws against sedition. The parties now assumed that their audience would recognize the connection between the issues embodied in relatively abstruse court cases and party programmes. So, in 1719 the conviction of a schoolmaster and a parson for collecting funds for a charity school was readily identifiable as a Whig victory. Collection of the funds had been authorized by Francis Atterbury, Bishop of Rochester. Four years later, Atterbury would be banished upon discovery of his complicity in a Jacobite conspiracy. Without the benefit of this foreknowledge, a grand jury carefully packed with Whigs framed an indictment accusing parson and schoolmaster of sedition, begging, and vagabondage, and the judge directed the jury to find the defendants guilty. The charity schools had become a bastion of the High Church and so fit objects for political attack through the courts. Defendants and charity schools found an able champion in the press. Daniel Defoe's pamphlet on the case ironically lauded the grand jury as "very instrumental in procuring Conquests Abroad, wise Measures at

58. Luttrell, *Brief Historical Relation,* vol. 2, p. 88; B.L., Add. MSS 42586, f. 100, Cade to Julius Deedes, Aug. 1, 1690; f. 103, Deedes to William Brockman, Aug. 25, 1690; f. 104, J. Holt to Brockman, Aug. 26, 1690; f. 106, Cade to Brockman, Aug. 28, 1690; f. 106v, Brockman to [Cade], Sept. 2, 1690; f. 110, Baron Smith to Brockman, Sept. 11, 1960.

59. Luttrell's *Brief Historical Relation* is filled with accounts of prosecution for sedition, only a few of which are cited here: vol. 2, pp. 24, 35, 45–46, 82, 212, 275, 309; vol. 3, p. 155; vol. 4, p. 94.

Home, and impartial Distribution of Justice to all, except those of a contrary Party to themselves in the Kingdom."[60]

While opportunity for using the laws against sedition as a political weapon decreased after the 1720s, as the generation of Tories most prone to Jacobitism died or learned discretion, the practice of disseminating political propaganda through legal proceedings survived into mid-century. In 1733, when Walpole's plan to extend the excise was a major issue of parliamentary debate and extra-parliamentary riot, and when the imminence of a general election made propaganda most valuable, Kent's opposition party carried the debate on excise into the courts. In January 1733, a farmer had preferred an indictment against a supervisor of the excise for entering upon his property without a warrant to search for "uncustomed" goods. When, in July, the case was removed to Assizes, the supporters of the Tory candidate presented the farmer with thirty guineas to finance his legal charges. Tory ideology stigmatized the excise: it had been introduced by Oliver Cromwell in imitation of Dutch Republican financiers to terrorize the countryside by insinuating paid spies into the households of country gentlemen, whose wives could not even brew small beer in peace. Excise officers, spewed forth from the stewpots of London, were symbols of the government's power to appoint to lucrative positions, thus corrupting both nation and Parliament. As Kent's Tories immediately realized, there could hardly be a more appropriate method for impugning Walpole and the county's Whigs than to indict an excise officer for invading the liberties of a subject. That the farmer lost his case against the excise officer in no way impaired its political argument. Opposition rhetoric presented the case as an example of the excessive power of government officials, power which Walpole was attempting to enlarge.[61]

So intent were the elite upon using the courts to dramatize political philosophy that almost every part of court ritual which allowed for speech was used to convey a political message. As the struggle between Whig and Tory encompassed the conflict of High Church and Low Church, even the sermon which opened Assizes became a partisan

60. [D. Defoe], *Charity Still a Christian Virtue or an Impartial Account of the Tryal and Conviction of the Reverend Mr. Hendley* (London, 1719), p. 31; M. G. Jones, *The Charity School Movement* (Cambridge, 1938), pp. 112–123.

61. *The Kentish Post or Canterbury News-Letter,* Jan. 10–13, 1732[3]; July 21–25, 1733; Aug. 18–22, 1733.

harangue. In 1706, Queen Anne castigaged her judges because "Seditious Invectives against Her Royal Majesty and her Government have been published from the pulpit in Sermons preached at Assizes, which have been in no other respect so reflecting upon her royal authority, as in this, that the Justices of assize, before whom the same were delivered have omitted to censure such proceedings. . . ."[62] But when judges did censure such sermons, they could not guarantee that their courts would teach the authorized partisan lesson. England's elite now directed the court's drama. In 1710, one clergyman directed his sermon against the House of Commons' impeachment of Sacheverell. The judge before whom he preached caused the clergyman to be presented to the grand jury. The grand jury refused to indict him.[63]

In 1710, the two Tory candidates for Cheshire's seats informed Harley that "the Gentlemen of the other party here in charges upon the bench preach up Resistance or any thing to poyson the People against an Election, and in their private Acting declare they may expect to be dealt with, as they shall give their vote." It was not only their legal powers which gave justices political influence. As the justices controlled Quarter Sessions and dominated the grand jury at Assizes, the justices determined which party's principles would receive the imprimatur of law. That, from 1679 to the accession of George III, England's elite expended considerable effort in inculcating party principle through legal proceedings indicates that the elite considered party propaganda an essential weapon in electoral battle. So, the justices' use of the courts to disseminate party propaganda was yet another reason for the interest of later Stuart and early Hanoverian ministries in the composition of the commissions of the peace. Harley's two Tory correspondents advocated change in the composition of Cheshire's commission. It is not surprising that Harley's ministry adopted most of their recommendations.[64] When England's justices adapted their institutions so as to advertise party principles, they also advertised their position as the pivot which joined local to national government, and local to national party.

62. Herts. R.O., Panshanger MSS D/EP/F150, Copy of letter to be sent to the judges, Feb. 24, 1705[6].

63. Luttrell, *Brief Historical Relation,* vol. 6, pp. 563–564.

64. B.L., Loan 29/196, f. 134, G. Warburton and C. Cholmondely to [Harley], 1710; f. 135; P.R.O., C234/5, Mar. 10, 1710 [1711].

PART TWO

The Justices and the Parties

CHAPTER THREE

The Making of a Justice, 1679–1725

In 1745, Lord Chancellor Hardwicke perused a succinct assessment of the motives of Sir Miles Stapylton, M.P., in nominating his adherent to the commission of the peace: "He does it, to gain the Credit of having Influence."[1] Like almost every component of the legal process, the justice could be regarded as an object of both practical use and symbolic value. Every justice, bound to preserve the peace and administer the laws of the land, was a representative of the sovereign to his subjects. Any particular justice, sitting on the bench at Quarter Sessions or in his justice's parlour, was a visible and highly effective symbol of those who had exerted pressure on the national government to secure his appointment. From at least the fourteenth century, justices had symbolized the influence of interest and they continued to do so throughout the later Stuart and early Hanoverian eras.[2] At the same time, later Stuart and early Hanoverian justices also represented a new structure of political power. Unlike their predecessors, justices appointed to the bench from 1680 onwards increasingly personified the might of party. Indeed, when Sir Miles Stapylton pressed for the elevation of his nominee to the bench, he was championing both his own interest and the Tory cause in Yorkshire. The rise of the party meant that parties exerted influence on the national government, and so the composition of the local bench in the age of party reflected the local elites' use of this new political structure for obtaining local power. As

1. B.L., Add. MSS 35602, ff. 71–72, Lord Malton to Hardwicke, June 15, 1745.
2. S. Endelman, "Patronage and Power: A Social Study of the Justices of the Peace in Late Mediaeval Essex" (Ph.D. diss., Brown University, 1977).

justices possessed influence over voters, ministries likewise attempted to insure that the composition of the county commissions mirrored the dominance of their party at Westminster. Therefore, the rise of party altered both the composition and the image of the commission of the peace.

As justices were members of local elites appointed to office by the national government, change in the commission reveals change in the structure of both local and national politics. The Lord Chancellor controlled the composition of the commission, both appointing and dismissing justices. Therefore change in the composition of the commission reflects the impact of national politics upon the alignments of England's local elites. At the same time, change in the commission reflects change in the structure of local politics. However determined a Lord Chancellor might be to appoint adherents of his party and dismiss adherents of the opposing party, no Lord Chancellor could make party appear in the provinces. Only if members of the local elite had already been attracted to a party could party allegiance be used as a test for distinguishing friend from foe. Therefore, the pattern made by Lord Chancellors' alterations of the composition of the commission graphs the increasing tendency of local elites to adopt party as a structure determining their alliances.

It is because the justices were members of local elites that examination of change in the composition of the commission affords a unique perspective on English politics. Most analyses of later Stuart and early Hanoverian politics have focused on the activities of parliamentary politicians, and so party can appear a phenomenon both created and most evident at Westminster. This view of party is somewhat paradoxical, for one of party's major contributions to the conduct of English politics was its alteration of the political horizons of its adherents. Before the rise of party, political alliances had been structured by interest. Interest emphasized the local, but party emphasized the national. For concern with local affairs, party substituted involvement with national issues. To alliances based on the locality and the private connections of a magnate, party added allies throughout the nation. During the reigns of the later Stuarts, party allegiance became a major determinant of appointment to and dismissal from the bench. Therefore the pattern of change in the composition of the commission occasioned by the rise of party is also that of the integration of England's local elites into a national political structure.

To some degree, the government had always had to use political allegiance as a criterion for the selection of justices. Since the national government lacked a police force, the justices were its sole bulwark against disorder and rebellion. It was the justices who reported on activity that might indicate potential treason, and who quelled riot before it could inflame the land. Perhaps even more important, it was the justices who exacted due deference to the current regime from the populace. The justices constituted a *tableau vivant* of the legitimacy of the current regime, and they had the authority to demand that those they ruled participate in the spectacle. In the opinion of the Privy Council, the justices' power to administer the oaths of loyalty and supremacy was one of the most useful weapons in the arsenal of local government, and it was employed on all possible occasions. When in 1696 it was reported that cockfights, bull baitings, and wrestling matches in Dorset might be camouflaging meetings of potential conspirators, the Privy Council ordered the justices to tender the oaths to all sportsmen and spectators suspected of disaffection.[3] Administration of the oaths performed two functions. Failure to take the oaths identified those inclined toward treason. Actual repetition of the oaths before the justices committed those of wavering loyalty to unswerving support of the monarch, and did so in full view of their community. Since both the safety of the realm and acknowledgment of the legitimacy of the current regime depended on the justices' activity, it was of the utmost importance that the justices be committed to active support of the government.

It is therefore not surprising that in the late sixteenth and seventeenth centuries radical change in the national government was accompanied by radical alteration in the composition of the local bench. When Elizabeth came to the throne, Catholic sympathizers were removed from the commissions. As regime followed regime during the Civil War, adherents of former regimes were dismissed and those of the current regime elevated to the bench. When Charles II succeeded Richard Cromwell as chief executive of the land, veritable platoons of justices were ousted from the commissions and replaced by those more eager to support a monarchy.

These manipulations of the commissions were impressive, as indeed they were intended to be, for most Tudor and early Stuart attempts to remodel the commissions differed from those noted above. Since the loosely knit, shifting, and temporary alliances characteristic of the

3. P.R.O., PC 2/76, p. 453, Privy Council to Earl of Bristol, June 18, 1696.

politics of interest made it difficult to distinguish friend from foe, banishment from the bench tended to be impermanent. As interest vied with interest, justices were dismissed, reappointed, dismissed, and reappointed again. Since most manipulations were aimed at securing the dominance of an interest in a few counties, change in the commission of one county rarely coincided with change in those of other counties. Before the age of party, a national regulation of the commission signalled a fundamental change in government, and it could be argued that many of those removed in such a regulation symbolized opposition not simply to those in power but to the authority of government itself.[4] Consider the last great remodelling of the commissions before the rise of party—that of 1660 when all commissions were radically revised. Though this remodelling was obviously partisan, it was also a restoration of the countryside's natural leaders which mirrored the restoration of the country's legitimate ruler. Under the Protectorate, justices had been a relatively undistinguished lot, members of social strata not heretofore awarded the power of local rule. Indeed, so unimpressive were the Kentish commissioners of Cromwell's peace that only 18 percent of the families represented on the bench in 1658 were able to gain judicial eminence at any time between the Restoration and the Glorious Revolution.[5] In 1660, the national government could usually distinguish those who had supported the Commonwealth from their less radical neighbours, and the greater gentry from the lesser. Neither distinction demanded a finely tuned test of political allegiance.

Nor did Charles II's government apply such a test during the first nineteen years of his rule. To be sure, the government continued to inspect the composition of the commissions. Books of the peace were inscribed for the king in 1664, for a secretary of state in 1662, for the Privy Council in 1662, 1663, 1666, 1672, and 1675, and for Lord

4. A. Hassell Smith, *County and Court: Government and Politics in Norfolk, 1558–1603* (Oxford, 1974), pp. 75–86, 227–228.

5. P.R.O., C193/13/5 lists the members of the commissions in 1658. See also: A. Fletcher, *A County Community in Peace and War* (London, 1975), pp. 134, 355–357; G. C. F. Forster, "County Government in Yorkshire During the Interregnum," *Northern History* 12 (1976): 103; L. Stone and J. F. C. Stone, "Country Houses and Their Owners in Hertfordshire 1540–1879," in *The Dimensions of Quantitative Research in History,* ed. W. Aydelotte, A. Bogue, and R. Fogel (Princeton, 1972), pp. 84–85, 106; B. G. Blackwood, *The Lancashire Gentry and the Great Rebellion 1640–1660,* Chetham Society, 3rd ser., vol. 25 (Manchester, 1978), pp. 77–80, 101, 167; S. C. Ratcliff and H. C. Johnson, eds. *Warwick County Records,* vol. 4 (Warwick, 1938), pp. xvii ff; D. Underdown, *Pride's Purge* (London, 1971), p. 313; J. S. Morrill, *Cheshire 1630–1660: County Government and Society during the English Revolution* (London, 1974), pp. 223–225, 327.

Treasurer Danby in 1675. In 1675, Danby advocated a wholesale alteration of the commissions.[6] None took place. In 1678, in the last unruly session of the Pension Parliament, the House of Commons demanded that it be presented with a book of the peace and a list of all those who had been removed from the commission during the last seven years.[7] Lord Chancellor Finch's memorandum of all those he removed from the commissions between November 1673 and July 1678 lists only eighty-two justices, thirty of whom seem to have been charged with misdemeanour or malfeasance; two more were Catholics and another two had been removed at the request of the House of Commons.[8] The grievances provoking the Commons' demand appear minimal in comparison with those relating to appointment to and removal from the commission in the next half century. The advent of party would both impel the national government to rid the bench of those who declared themselves allied to the party opposing the ministry, and provide the government with an increasingly sensitive test for distinguishing friend from foe. In both respects, manipulations of the commissions in the age of party differed significantly from those of the Tudor and early Stuart eras.

The Whig party appeared in 1679, in the aftermath of the Popish plot and the storm over Exclusion. By 1680, the first Whigs were being countered by the first Tories. Immediately after its birth each party attempted to implement a wholesale national alteration of the commissions of the peace. By the spring of 1679, the plot had swept Shaftesbury and his newly created band of Whigs into power in the Commons and Privy Council. One of the first demands of the new councillors was that the commissions of the peace be inspected and those justices deemed insufficiently protective of the English constitution and the Protestant religion removed. (Shaftesbury's opponents considered the scheme a blatant attempt to influence elections.) Charles skilfully stymied this Whig regulation, but when he rid himself of his Whig councillors in the autumn of 1679 he was quite prepared

6. P.R.O., Ind. 4214, pp. 186, 189, 214, 219, 283, 415, 503; A. Browning, *Thomas Osborne Earl of Danby* (Glasgow, 1951), vol. 2, p. 66.

7. House of Commons *Journals* 9: 535, 539, 540.

8. *HMC, Finch MSS* II, pp. 43–46. The list may not be complete. Probably those who were removed and subsequently restored are not noted. Edmund Bohun's name does not appear though he was removed from Suffolk's commission in 1677 (S. W. Rix [ed.], *The Diary and Autobiography of Edmund Bohun, Esq.* [Beccles, 1853], pp. 16–17), and only two of the six Monmouthshire justices mentioned in a March 1678 letter from Sir J. Williams to the marquess of Worcester which requests that their dismissal be reconsidered are noted (*CSPD, Charles II,* vol. 20, pp. 25–26).

to execute his own, rather different, fumigation of the commissions. Under his new Privy Council, justices exhibiting undue sympathy for Shaftesbury and his Whigs were replaced by Tory supporters of the court.[9] Between December 1679 and July 1680, 272 of approximately 2,559 names were expunged from the commissions of England and Wales.[10] Though it is possible that the removal of some of these justices can be attributed to local rivalries, most were eliminated because they had been active in promoting the petitions for the convocation of Parliament mentioned in chapter II, or because they were considered zealous partisans of the Whig cause.[11] In its combination of flagrant and solely partisan design with extensive removals, the measure of 1680 had not had its equal. It would soon be surpassed.

By excising justices supporting Exclusion, the government was attempting to make it impossible for the Exclusionists to use either legal forms or powers to promote their policies or increase their following. Contemporaries contended that the petitioning movement had been based on the actions of "hot headed and busy justices"—justices who promoted petitions at Quarter Sessions, or who, like Dr. Hugh Chamberlain, aided the Exclusionists in bringing charges against some who had torn up a petition being circulated in Westminster.[12] The two

9. P.R.O., PC 2/68, pp. 191, 203, 208–209, 465, 641, 643ff. (new numbering 482–484); R. North, *Examen* (London, 1740), pp. 77–78.

10. The calculation both of the number of those in the commissions and those deleted is based on House of Lords R.O., House of Lords MSS no. 275, Main Papers, Nov. 9, 1680, lists of justices of the peace laid before a committee of the House of Lords. The minute books of this committee (House of Lords R.O., House of Lords MSS no. 274, Main Papers, Nov. $\frac{9}{22}$) has notations deleting or adding names to about half of these lists. Since the lists of only half the counties are so corrected, and since some of these notations are difficult to interpret, the calculation does not incorporate the information in this minute book. It should be noted that these figures are not exact. Examination of the Kent commission reveals that the deletion of some names is noted in neither the lists nor the minute book. Neither lists nor minute book contain information on the changes in Nottinghamshire's commission, and the total of that county's justices and of those deleted is taken from S. N. Esquire, *A Catalogue of All His Majesties Justices of the Peace for the Counties of England According to the late Alteration . . .* (London, 1680). This numeration and all succeeding numerations of justices exclude peers, peers's sons, and all others in the honourary portion of the commission—i.e., all names before the list of regular justices beginning with the list of baronets. In this and all succeeding numerations, justices in liberties—such as Ely and Westminster—and in towns whose justices were nominated by the Crown are not included.

11. R. W. Blencowe, ed., *Diary of the Times of Charles the Second by the Honourable Henry Sidney* (London, 1843), vol. 1, p. 253, Mr. Mountstevens to Mr. Sidney, Jan. 23, 1679[80]; L. K. J. Glassey, *Politics and the Appointment of Justices of the Peace 1675–1720* (Oxford, 1979), pp. 48–52.

12. *Memoirs of Thomas Earl of Ailesbury,* printed for the Roxburghe Club (1890), vol. 1, p. 45; N. Luttrell, *A Brief Historical Relation of State Affairs from September 1678 to April 1714* (Oxford, 1857), vol. 1, p. 33.

purges of 1681 again had obvious political motivation. The purge preceding the election for the Oxford Parliament eliminated known or suspected Whigs;[13] that following the Parliament removed those who, in Burnet's phrase, "did not with zeal go into the honour of the court."[14] By June 1681, the scope of the government's supervisory activities had increased; all deputy lieutenants who had, as justices, been removed from the commission were to be deprived of their posts as deputy lieutenants. Scattered mopping-up operations in the following years further cleansed the county benches of Whigs.[15]

To some extent, these measures had the desired effects. In 1682, Secretary Jenkins received the welcome report that Lincolnshire's grand jury had accepted a resolution sent down by the county's Lord Lieutenant abhorring Shaftesbury's Protestant Association. "By this," wrote the Lord Lieutenant, "you may observe what influence Sheriffs and Justices have in this county, since last summer assizes the address I sent up by my son was rejected by the Grand Jury and endeavoured by the Fanatic party to be turned into ridicule. . . . If some justices that favour the factious were removed, this county would be absolutely at the King's command and the royal party might once more hope to carry elections. . . .

"If you order the printing of this address with the names of the Grand Jury, who are men of considerable estates and fortunes, it will give great encouragement.[16]

Those many justices who had managed to retain their judicial seats were well advised to conform to government policy. Prosecution of defaulters may have been encouraged. In 1684, a justice of Cumberland appeared in King's Bench to answer charges of keeping conventicles in his house, not receiving the sacrament in two and a half years, and not baptizing his children; and Mr. Cole, justice of Lancashire, was commanded to enter into a recognizance of £1,000 to answer

13. *CSPD, Charles II,* vol. 22, p. 175, Secretary Jenkins to Lord Chancellor, Feb. 19, 1681; p. 168, Same to Same, Feb. 24, 1681. J. R. Jones, *The First Whigs: The Politics of the Exclusion Crisis* (London, 1961), p. 159.

14. G. Burnet, *History of His Own Time,* 2nd ed., enlarged (Oxford, 1833), vol. 2, p. 285; *CSPD, Charles II,* vol 22, p. 477, Secretary Jenkins to Lord Chancellor, Sept. 29, 1681, and p. 355, June 29, 1681, Same to Same.

15. P.R.O., PC 2/69, p. 295, June 2, 1681; *CSPD, Charles II,* vol. 23, pp. 73–74, Secretary Jenkins to Lord Chancellor, Feb. 11, 1682; p. 77, Same to Same, Feb. 13, 1682; p. 85, Same to Same, Feb. 18, 1682; p. 111, Same to Same, March 6, 1682; p. 218, Same to Same, May 26, 1682; p. 441, Same to Same, Sept. 30, 1682; *CSPD, Charles II,* vol. 25, p. 406, Sunderland to Secretary Jenkins, Sept. 9, 1683.

16. *CSPD, Charles II,* vol. 23, pp. 137–138, Earl of Lindsey to Secretary Jenkins, March 24, 1682.

charges of refraining from suppressing conventicles. The prosecutions reflect the extent and limits of Charles's purges. Cole at least remained on the bench, and in 1685 was reported to have incited the county's grand jury to reject a presentment designed to forestall riots against the parliamentary candidates favoured by the court. The report continued: "whilst he is in the commission of the peace, the rabble will always be factious, for he encourages faction." His removal was most earnestly recommended.[17]

Removals aplenty there would be in James's reign, but justices such as Cole were not the main target of James's campaigns. In October 1686, a select committee of the Privy Council was appointed to review the commissions, and a widespread revision of the commissions soon followed. The Council's order that there be 248 dismissals from the bench was directed against those most likely to oppose the admission of Catholics to positions of power.[18] At the same time, the Council ordered 460 additions to the commission, and the majority of the new appointees were Catholics.[19] It was therefore logical that in April 1687 the government inserted in the commission a clause dispensing justices from the legal penalties for failure to take the oaths of allegiance and supremacy and the Sacraments according to the rites of the Church of England.[20] But in the drama of the commissions of the peace, what had just passed was merely prologue. In August, James looked down upon his Lords Lieutenant and found several politically unsatisfactory. These he replaced. Then, in October and November, the Lords Lieutenant were ordered to repair to their counties, there to submit the justices to an intensive political examination. The Lords Lieutenant were to ask every justice and deputy lieutenant three questions: whether he would approve of the repeal of the Penal and Test acts; whether he would vote for candidates pledged to such repeal; and whether he would live in harmony with his neighbours. The Lords were to note

17. *CSPD, Charles II,* vol. 27, p. 181, Newsletter, Oct. 23, 1684; *CSPD, James II,* vol. 1, pp. 119–120, no. 496, Sir Roger Bradshaugh to Col. Werden, April 3, 1685.

18. Glassey's figure of 245 (*Politics and the Appointment of Justices,* p. 74) includes justices dismissed from the commissions of Westminster and Ely and those in the honourary portion of the commission, and excludes justices dismissed from Lancashire's commission.

19. For the Council's order, see P.R.O., PC 2/71, pp. 363–379, Dec. 17, 1686. The lists of those to be appointed and dismissed are not a totally accurate guide to changes in the commission, for examination of Kent's commission shows that some of those ordered to be added were already justices and some recommended deletions were not executed. See also J. Miller, *Popery and Politics in England, 1660–1688* (Cambridge, 1973), pp. 208–209.

20. *CSPD, James II,* vol. 2, no. 1665.

which justices were Catholics and to list gentlemen who might be added to the commissions, noting those nominees who were Catholics or Dissenters, and to return the answers to St. James's.

While the political intent of the survey was unmistakably evident, the political motivation of the government's subsequent action was shamelessly blatant. Returns for thirty English counties have survived,[21] as have lists of justices to be placed in the new commissions for twenty-four of these counties.[22] Mathematically precise analysis of the political sentiments of the justices and the actions of the government is not possible; the lists do not always specify which deputy lieutenants were not also justices; the returns do not always list the answers of the entire commission, justices on the commission by virtue of other office sometimes being omitted; and duplicate but not identical lists survive for some counties. As the returns and lists are sufficiently complete that arbitrary decisions on the number of justices in the commission and the number of those not questioned are infrequent and minor, the following summation of the lists and returns represents an almost exact account of the sentiments of the justices and the actions of the government.[23]

According to these documents, there were 1,244 names on the commissions of the thirty counties. (As names were counted rather than justices, a justice can be represented more than once in this total. The analysis aims at revealing the percentage change in each commission and therefore the multiple numeration of justices was necessary.) Of the 1,244 names, 216 gave affirmative answers to all three questions, 238 replied in the negative to the first two questions, 383 gave ambiguous answers to the first and/or second questions, 122 were

21. Sir G. Duckett, *Penal Laws and Test Act, 1687–88,* 2 vols. (London, 1882). This excludes the return for Lincolnshire, which was too confusing to use and those for Cambridgeshire, the Isle of Ely, Sussex, Durham, and Northumberland, which gave too little information.

22. This excludes the proposed list of new justices for Derbyshire, which was too confusing to use.

23. These lists have also been used by J. Carswell, *The Descent on England* (London, 1969), pp. 240–243. Carswell did not attempt to distinguish the justices from the deputy lieutenants, nor did he notice that some justices were not questioned. His "doubtful" category did not include all those answers I considered ambiguous. My analysis also differs from his in excluding all peers and their sons. As the proposed new commission for Kent became its commission and the proposed new commissions for Leicestershire, Northamptonshire, and Devon became these counties' commissions (Glassey, *Politics and the Appointment of Justices,* pp. 83–84), I have assumed that the lists of proposed commissions for all counties in Duckett were adopted. J. Miller, *Popery and Politics,* pp. 270–271, shows that these returns seriously underestimate the number of Catholics in these counties' commissions.

Roman Catholics or Dissenters, 248 were not available for questioning, and a further 37 were not questioned. In the twenty-four counties for which lists of the remodelled commissions are available, all but two of those who replied in the negative, 84 percent of those who answered ambiguously, and 82 percent of those who were not available for questioning were removed from the commissions. Sixty-three percent of the justices who had graced the bench in December 1687 no longer sat thereon by August of 1688. In their places were Catholics, Dissenters, and others who would support James's policies.

Obviously, this "regulation" of the commissions, the August 1687 reallocation of Lord Lieutenancies, and the subsequent replacement of the Lords Lieutenant who had refused to put the three questions to the justices removed many of the more powerful men of England from positions in which they could exercise their power within a constitutional framework.[24] This manipulation of the commissions therefore altered the local rulers' concept of local government. Many former justices considered that their standing gave them a legitimate claim to office. In appointing them, the sovereign recognized their eminence; in serving the sovereign they executed the tasks incumbent upon persons of their station. Their judicial activity, therefore, simultaneously emphasized the private prestige which guaranteed their independence and their voluntary decision to uphold the English law, the English constitution, and the English monarch. James's measures made it clear that all government appointees—be they judges or Lords Lieutenant—were agents of the central government. Even those who retained their positions under James found that they were unable freely to wield the powers with which their positions had formerly been associated. The Earl of Ailesbury, who would later join James in exile, indignantly expostulated against commands that he nominate specified justices and deputy lieutenants; the power of appointment of the latter lay in the Lord Lieutenant, and while the Lord Chancellor appointed justices, he "ought to consult . . . with the Lords Lieutenants." Ailesbury decided to resign his Lord Lieutenancies, for, he wrote, he had "become very insignificant in the counties where I was Lord Lieutenant."[25]

When, in September and October of 1688, James attempted to rally

24. Luttrell, *Brief Relation*, vol. 1, pp. 420, 422. F. C. Turner, *James II* (London, 1948), pp. 329–330.

25. *Memoirs*, vol. 1, pp. 166–167, 176. James persuaded him to withdraw his resignation, p. 178.

his unenthusiastic subjects to his support by reappointing deputy lieutenants and justices who had been dismissed in the preceding twelve months, it was found that James's policy had altered the justices' concept of voluntary service. The deputy lieutenants and justices in some counties refused to serve under Catholic Lords Lieutenant, while, in Norfolk, the justices refused to serve at all. In Bedfordshire, the Earl of Ailesbury summoned the reinstated deputy lieutenants to dinner, where they unanimously desired to be excused from the honour lately bestowed upon them. Finally, Ailesbury persuaded them to accept office, but all stated that they served only because of their obligation to Ailesbury and would never serve under another Lord Lieutenant. As a former deputy lieutenant of Essex remarked, "some would think one kick of the breech enough for a gentleman."[26] Service under a sovereign—even if the servant was a mere justice of the peace far removed from the sovereign's presence—now implied support for his clearly defined and highly controversial political program.

In 1689, parliamentary orators declared that the Glorious Revolution had restored England's ancient constitution. The contradictions inherent in their argument soon became as evident in local government as they were at Westminster. The Glorious Revolution did restore England's greater gentry to the county bench, but it did not wholly restore the justices' vaunted independence. During William's reign, both appointment to the bench and activity as a justice increasingly signalled a gentleman's party allegiance. In 1689, the problem posed by the oaths of office made the connection between party and the local bench immediately apparent. As James had restored many of the justices he had previously removed, and as the new monarchs continued all Protestant justices in office, justices who had sworn allegiance to James had now to swear support for his usurpers.[27] Although the oaths declared William and Mary monarchs in fact, while maintaining a diplomatic silence about the legality of the fact, some of the less flexible Tories were not prepared to forswear themselves. Shrewsbury, Secretary of State for the South, directed that the Lords Commissioners of the Great Seal report which justices had refused to take the oaths or declined to act, so that the commissions of the peace could be

26. *HMC, Lothian MSS*, pp. 132, 133; J. P. Kenyon, *The Nobility in the Revolution of 1688* (Hull, 1963), p. 14; Luttrell, *Brief Relation*, vol. 1, p. 465. *The Autobiography of Sir John Bramston, K.B.*, Camden Society, vol. 32 (London, 1845), pp. 325, 326; *CSPD, James II*, vol. 3, no. 1642, Lord Teynham to the Earl of Sunderland, Oct. 3, 1688. *Memoirs*, vol. 1, pp. 181–182.

27. P.R.O., PC 2/73, p. 3, Feb. 14, 1688[9].

altered in accordance with their report. Shrewsbury, a Whig, was ready to interpret failure to act as a mime of the rejection of government explicit in failure to take the oaths.[28]

Despite Shrewsbury's enthusiasm for partisan inspection of the commission, partisan manipulation of the bench had to await party domination of the national government. In the first years of his reign William appointed both moderate Tories and moderate Whigs as his ministers; likewise, neither Whigs nor Tories clearly dominated the local bench.[29] Then, in 1693 Sir John Somers gained custody of the Great Seal. Somers was a Whig, and his appointment and those of the Junto mark the commencement of party domination of the national government. Change in the political structure at Whitehall reverberated throughout the nation. Judges of Assize were instructed to discover which justices refused to act because they were disaffected,[30] and the first attempt to impose a party stamp on every commission of the peace in the country began. In 1693, and then, more markedly, in 1694, justices were removed from the commissions because of their political connections.[31] According to one biased ex-justice: "They strook out the most active men, but left the trimmers and those that would not act at all; and put in whiggs of mean estate and education, or gentlemen of little or no spirit. So that the getting the government into their hands was the apparent end of this alteration."[32] The Whigs were preparing for the general election.

Whatever the extent of this purge—and the absence of complete records makes it impossible to gauge its extent—it is unlikely that it rivalled the measures of Charles II or James II. Greater opportunity for ridding the commissions of political opponents arose from the aftermath of the attempted assassination of William III in 1696. Throughout the country, gentlemen formed associations acknowledging William as "rightful and lawful King" and vowing to assist each other in

28. *CSPD, William and Mary,* vol. 1, p. 148, Earl of Shrewsbury to the Lords Commissioners of the Great Seal, June 13, 1689.

29. Dr. Williams' Library, Morrice MSS Q, pp. 508–510; Glassey, *Politics and the Appointment of Justices,* pp. 104–105; H. C. Johnson, ed., *Proceedings in Quarter Sessions, 1682–1690, Warwick County Records,* vol. 8 (Warwick, 1953), pp. xxiff.

30. Luttrell, *Brief Relation,* vol. 3, pp. 37–38, 42; P.R.O., PC 2/75, p. 97, Feb. 23, 1692[3]; University of Nottingham Library, Pw A 1171, Somers to Portland, June 20, 1693; Pw A 1172, Same to Same, July 25, 1693.

31. D. Rubini, *Court and Country 1688–1702* (London, 1967), pp. 48–49; Luttrell, *Brief Relation,* vol. 3, pp. 131, 237, 274, 304, 393; *Bohun Diary,* pp. 120–121, 124, Aug. 3, 1694; J. P. Kenyon, *Robert Spencer, Earl of Sunderland, 1641–1702* (New York, 1958), p. 263.

32. *Bohun Diary,* p. 122

the defence of His Majesty and his government. Parliament passed an act making the oath mandatory for all office holders; the Junto persuaded William that it was necessary to remove all justices and deputy lieutenants who had not taken the oath before Parliament had passed the act, while Somers suggested that all those "notoriously disaffected"—oath or not oath—be dismissed. Though Somers' proposal did not meet with approval, the 1696 revision of the commissions was again a nationwide political purge that highlighted the political differences of neighbouring gentlemen and turned Quarter Sessions into county parliaments where party battled party for support. Sir John Elwill reported: "A great deal of sourness was shown by some of our neighbours the last sessions week." Those opposed to the measures had solicited support for a letter to the Lord Lieutenant requesting that those dismissed be restored, and averring that the consequences of the purge would be "feuds and animosities amongst us and they would be transmitted to posterity."[33]

By 1700, a renascent Tory party had captured the House of Commons and was besieging the executive. All members of the Junto except Somers had been deprived of office, and, in April 1700, the Tories directed their charges against the Lord Chancellor, alleging that improper use of his office, including his manipulation of the commissions of the peace, rendered him unfit for public trust.[34] Somers was replaced by Lord Keeper Wright, the remaining Whigs dismissed, and a new cycle in the politics of the commissions begun. Again the Privy Council reviewed the commissions of the peace; again they ordered the dismissal of magistrates; again revision of the commissions preceded a general election, and, as in Somers' heyday, the new justices were excused from payment for their *dedimus*—the writ that author-

33. *HMC, Fitzherbert MSS,* p. 40, Sir J. Elwill to Sir George Treby, July 22, 1696. *CSPD, William III,* vol. 7, p. 177, Shrewsbury to deputy lieutenants of Worcester, May 14, 1696; p. 213, Minutes of Proceedings of Lords Justices, June 4, 1696; p. 217, Same, June 5, 1696; J. P. Kenyon, *Sunderland,* p. 278; Luttrell, *Brief Relations,* vol. 4, p. 88; W. Coxe, ed., *Private and Original Correspondence of Charles Talbot, Duke of Shrewsbury* (London, 1821), pp. 122–123, Shrewsbury to the king, June 5–15, 1696; K. Feiling, *A History of the Tory Party, 1640–1714* (Oxford, 1924), p. 320. The Privy Council register reveals that the Council ordered the removal of 145 justices from the commissions of England and Wales between July 2, 1696, and March 25, 1697 (P.R.O., PC 2/76, pp. 458, 463, 470, 483, 504, 522–524, 543, 572, 580, 598). However, examination of the changes in Kent's commission reveals that it is likely that justices were removed from county commissions during this period whose removal was either not ordered by the Privy Council or not noted by the records of Council proceedings.

34. Lord J. Campbell, *Lives of the Lord Chancellors* (London, 1846), vol. 4, pp. 146–147; Burnet, *History,* vol. 4, p. 443.

ized them to take the oaths of office.[35] If the purpose of remodelling the commissions was the appointment of justices favourable to the ministry so that the justices would take action that encouraged voters to favour the ministry, it was advisable that obstacles preventing such activities be removed.

Between midsummer 1700 and March 20, 1704, approximately 656 gentlemen were removed from the commissions of England and Wales, excluding Lancashire. In 1702, the number of names in the commissions, excluding Lancashire and excluding all names in the honourary section of the commission reserved for aristocrats, sons of aristocrats, Privy Councillors, and members of the judiciary, was 3,700. Therefore, approximately one out of every six justices in England and Wales had been removed because of their political affiliation. As the number of appointees exceeded the number of dismissals, an even greater percentage of those sitting on the bench had taken their seats in circumstances unmistakably revealing the connection between local government and national politics.[36] The appointees themselves were symbols of party and ideological rivalry. When the Duke of Devonshire—a Whig—had objected to the appointment of some of the new justices, Lord Keeper Wright had calmly informed him that "those who would never own the government in the last reign are very fit to be employed if they will own it in this." Noted Devonshire: "he

35. Luttrell, *Brief Relation,* vol. 4, pp. 654–655, 659; G. P. R. James, *Letters Illustrative of the Reign of William III from 1696 to 1708 . . .* (London, 1841), vol. 3, pp. 109–110, Vernon to Shrewsbury, July 9, 1700. *CSPD, William III,* vol. 11, p. 63, Petition of Thomas Chute; P.R.O., PC 2/78, pp. 13, 16, 17, 18, 19, 32, 63–69, 71, 74, 83–84, April 25, 1700 through Sept. 26, 1700.

36. B.L., Harleian MSS 7512, a book of the peace. Internal evidence shows the book to be that inscribed in Apr. 1702 (P.R.O., Index 4216, p. 42). House of Lords R.O., House of Lords, MSS no. 2011, Main Papers, "List of all the Justices who have been out of the Commission of the Peace since Mid-summer 1700, Delivered March 20, 1703[4]." The names of all justices left out of the commission are supposedly included in the 1704 list. The notation *mort* has been placed opposite many of the names and these names have not been included in the 656. Comparison of the names for Kent with commissions and *nomina* for Kent shows that some justices were left out whose names were not on the House of Lords list. Several of these justices were no longer on the commission because they had died, but three were still living in 1704. Two of these three justices had been placed on the commission because of their posts under the central government, and when they lost these posts they were removed from the commission. On the other hand, five justices not marked *mort* on the House of Lords list were dead when their names were removed from the commission, and four marked *mort* died after the date of omission. The House of Lords list does not include those removed between 1700 and 1704 who were restored to the commission before March 1704. Glassey, *Politics and the Appointment of Justices,* pp. 150–151, reveals that the Whig ministry appointed shortly before William's death made few alterations in the commissions.

has left out some of the usefullest men, and put in Jacobites, or men of no estates, and that have nothing to recommend them, but that they are violently of a party."[37] A familiar refrain.

The next verse was written in 1705. Marlborough and Godolphin's decision to ally with moderate Whigs rather than moderate Tories eventually led to the replacement by Lord Keeper Cowper of Lord Keeper Wright—on the grounds, it was rumoured, that Wright would not appoint the Whig justices nominated by Lord Wharton.[38] Compared to his predecessor, Cowper made abstemious use of his power to alter the face of justice. There is no comprehensive list of the alterations made by Cowper during his term of office, but there is a list of the changes made in forty counties between October 11, 1705—the date of Cowper's appointment—and early 1707. Cowper dismissed seventy-nine justices in counties where Wright had removed approximately 587.[39] While extensive revisions of the commissions did not follow upon the Whigs' successful attempt to oust all remaining Tories from the ministry in February 1708, less sympathetic examination of the conduct of certain justices led to a few scattered, but symbolic, dismissals. In 1706, John Lade, justice of Surrey, was charged with conniving at the enlistment of a corkcutter because that unlucky artisan had "often voted for Mr. Cox, but never for Mr. Lade." In 1705, it had been reported that Lade supported the pretensions of the Pretender. In April 1708, Lade was removed from the Surrey bench at the order of Lord Sunderland, Secretary of State.[40]

In 1711, Lade was restored to the Surrey bench by a fiat—that is, a document commanding that a commission of the peace be inscribed—signed by Lord Keeper Harcourt, a Tory.[41] Once again, the wheel of

37. G. Holmes and W. A. Speck, *The Divided Society, Party Conflict in England 1694–1710* (London, 1967), p. 47, Duke of Devonshire to the Duke of Somerset, Aug. 3, 1702.

38. Lady Margaret Maria Verney, *Letters of the Eighteenth Century from the Manuscripts at Claydon House* (London, 1930), vol. 1, p. 227, Sir Thomas Cave to Lord Fermanagh, July 10, 1705.

39. Herts. R.O., Panshanger MSS D/EP/F152, list of those put in and out of commission "by my Lord Keeper."

40. Herts. R.O., Panshanger MSS D/EP/F153, affidavit of Walter Carwardine, July 20, 1706; P.R.O., C234/36, Apr. 10, 1708; B.L., Blenheim MSS C1–36, Charles Cox to Sunderland, March 27, 1706; and affidavits of William Pryour, March 27, 1708, and of J. S. Rowles, May 7, 1705; P.R.O., SP 44/106, p. 207, Sunderland to Lord Chancellor, Mar. 31, 1708; Holmes and Speck, *Divided Society*, p. 102, Charles Cox to John Gelibrand, Feb. 24, 1705.

41. P.R.O., C234/36, Feb. 20, 1710[11].

political fortune had revolved. Ministry replaced ministry, Lord Keeper replaced Lord Chancellor, and justice replaced justice. Harcourt's renovation was more thorough then Cowper's and almost as extensive as that of Wright.[42] Like those of all his predecessors, his reformation of the commissions diminished the honour denoted by appointment to the bench.

Even the parchment commission which authorized the justices' activities bears witness to the dilution of judicial prestige. A commission of the peace is divided into two parts: the first lists all justices, and the second, those justices who were of the *quorum*. The presence of at least two justices of the quorum at Quarter Sessions and the signature of at least one justice of the quorum on most judicial orders issued by justices out of sessions were demanded by law. Some justices were more equal than others. In 1680, 14 percent, and in 1702, 12 percent of the justices were not members of the quorum.[43] By 1714, it was a rare commission that did not list all but three or four justices as members of the quorum. Decay in the honour of the quorum, already evident in 1680, had become rampant with the appointment of Cowper. Cowper rarely, and Harcourt never, appointed a new justice who was not also a justice of the quorum. If a man were to be attached to party through gratitude for appointment, it was wisest not to insult the appointee by making invidious distinctions between justices. It was more politic to pursue a policy that extinguished the eminence of the quorum.

Similarly, the eminence of appointees to the bench declined, and this too was a consequence of party. When disgruntled former justices remarked on the relatively low status of their replacements, their rancour was at least partly based on fact. Once again the parchment on which the commission was inscribed testifies to the appointment of justices of lesser status, for during the reigns of the last two Stuarts its list of justices grew ever longer. In 1680, the number of names in the nonhonourary portion of all English and Welsh commissions totalled

42. L. Glassey, *Politics and the Appointment of Justices*, pp. 228–229, states that Harcourt dismissed at least 405 justices and added at least 1,725, while Cowper dismissed at least 195 and added at least 1,044. All Glassey's figures include those in the honourary portion of the commission and so are not precisely comparable to the previous numerations, which excluded these honourary justices. Glassey's calculations are based on the fiats in P.R.O., C234, which are not an entirely exact account of changes in the commissions; see L. Glassey and N. Landau, "The Commission of the Peace in the Eighteenth Century: A New Source," *B.I.H.R.* 45 (1972): 250–253.

43. S. N. Esquire, *A Catalogue of All His Majesties Justices of the Peace*; B.L., Harleian MSS 7512.

2,572.[44] By 1702, the sum of all names in the nonhonourary portions of the commissions, excluding that of Lancashire, was 3,700.[45] Most of the increase had occurred after the Glorious Revolution, when party struggle became a feature of national government. Though there is no source which lists all the justices in all commissions at any one date after 1702, it is clear that during Anne's reign party strife produced an equally rapid expansion of the commissions.[46] The sum of those appointed by Cowper and Harcourt between 1705 and 1714 exceeds the number of justices in all commissions in 1680, and these new appointees were merely additions to an already crowded bench.[47] Inevitably, so great and rapid an expansion of the commissions entailed the appointment of an increasing number of justices of lesser status.

Obviously, expansion of the commissions occurred because more men were placed upon the bench than were removed from it. Party considerations dictated restraint in the dismissal of justices, for omission from the commission might transform a potential ally into an implacable foe. As one gentleman noted: "The honor of being in is not so great as the disgrace of being turned out."[48] So, under the last two Stuarts, Lord Chancellors were wary of insulting any justice who might become amenable. At the same time, the structure of the justices' powers impelled Lord Chancellors to flood the bench with new appointees allied to their party. The justices exercised their most politically effective powers not as individuals but in groups—at petty and Quarter Sessions. The appointment or removal of one or two justices could not affect the outcome of an election for a county seat, nor can estimates of the justices' political influence be based on correlations of the appointment or removal of a few justices with the results of a county election.[49] Because justices acted in groups, it was the party affiliation of the majority in any group of justices that was crucial in calculations of the commissions' powers of political persuasion. Since

44. This calculation is based on the number of justices in the commissions after the purge of 1680 listed in House of Lords R.O., House of Lords MSS no. 275, Main Papers, Nov. 9, 1680. As Nottinghamshire's justices are not included in these lists, information on the number of justices on that county's bench is taken from S. N. Esquire, *A Catalogue of All His Majesties Justices of the Peace.*

45. B.L., Harleian MSS 7512.

46. See appendix A.

47. See n. 42 above.

48. Herts. R.O., Panshanger MSS D/EP/F154, W. Lloyd to [Cowper], July 9, 1709.

49. Cf. Glassey, *Politics and the Apppointment of Justices,* pp. 127–128, 149, 244, 266–268.

the Lord Chancellors who served the last two Stuarts did not dismiss most of the justices who had been appointed under a preceding and opposing ministry, they had to appoint an ever increasing number of new justices in order to secure a majority for their party.

Even as party considerations prompted successive Lord Chancellors so to expand the commissions that they increasingly included men of lesser status, party also brought lesser gentry and gentlemen into the political arena. Party, after all, had an emotional and ideological appeal. It attracted those who could not, in the politics of interest, have hoped to gain the attention of a magnate. As party spread across the counties, joining interest in loose alliance to interest and recruiting new adherents, magnates involved in party found that the number of those whom they might consider members of their connection had increased. A magnate's connection might now include men in relatively inferior social stations, men he might never meet. In 1733, an ally of the Whig Duke of Dorset wrote to urge the appointment of one Mr. Hey to the Kentish bench: "hee seems to be a very good sort of man; I was not acquainted with him before Lord Middlesex and Sir G. Oxenden [the Whig candidates] were Named for the County, but in that hee has been Soe Zealous, I have much good opinion of him, and I hope he is entitled to your Favour." Hey was made a justice shortly after the election.[50] The introduction of party meant that gentlemen were more likely to participate in politics, and that their activity was more likely to attract the attention of those influential enough to secure their appointment to the bench. Expansion of the commissions and the concomitant decline in the status of the justices is indicative of the integration of mere gentry and gentlemen into the framework of national politics.

Indeed, the actions of George I's Lord Chancellors suggest that by 1714 so many mere gentry and gentlemen graced the bench that further expansion of the commission might have endangered its authority. Unlike their predecessors, both Cowper and Macclesfield chose to dismiss justices suspected of alliance with the opposition rather than to swamp their opponents with a host of new appointees. When Cowper wielded the Great Seal under Queen Anne, he had adopted a different policy. Between 1705 and early 1707—the period of his intensive examination of the composition of the bench—he had added

50. Kent A.O., U269/C148/19, Sir Basil Dixwell to Dorset, Oct. 30, 1733; P.R.O., C234/18, Mar. 7, 1734[5].

336 names to the commissions of forty counties and eradicated only 79.[51] Cowper had been succeeded by Harcourt, who appointed more than quadruple the number of justices he dismissed. When in 1714 the Whigs returned to office and Cowper to the woolsack, Cowper evidently decided that such expansion of the commissions could no longer continue. A thorough purge was now the only possible policy. As the new Lord Lieutenant of Essex observed, Harcourt had added above fifty gentlemen "to a very full Commission before, which has so much increas'd that Commission that its impossible to ballance soe great a number, without naming such Persons, as I should be very much ashamed off." Therefore, there was "but one way left, and that is by turning out some of the most obnoctious, and such others as may best be spared."[52] During the reign of George I growth in the commission ceased and the number of justices may even have declined.[53] For the first time since 1689, England's Lord Chancellors preferred the enmity of those they removed to the gratitude of hordes of newly elevated and ever less eminent justices. Possibly, they calculated both the gain to be derived from the appointment of justices sufficient to control the bench and the loss inherent in large-scale dismissals, and concluded that dismissals were more appropriate: the appointment of justices sufficient to control the bench would necessitate reliance upon justices possessed of prestige insufficient to influence the political activity of their compatriots.

Cowper immediately implemented a policy which evoked protests from even those Tories allied to the Whig government.[54] Yet, so accustomed were the English to change in their local judges as an accompaniment to change in the national government that Cowper's far from modest revision of the composition of the county bench seemed treacherously nonpartisan. Cowper soon found himself preparing a memorial informing the king of his reasons for eliminating some justices and not eliminating all those whose dismissal was recommended by their Whiggish neighbours.[55]

51. Herts. R.O., Panshanger MSS D/EP/F152, list of those put in and out by "my Lord Keeper" [n.d.].

52. Herts. R.O., Panshanger MSS D/EP/F153, Earl of Suffolk to Cowper, Jan. 6, 1714[5].

53. For a detailed chart of the growth of the commissions, see appendix A.

54. H. Horwitz, *Revolution Politicks: The Career of Daniel Finch Second Earl of Nottingham, 1647–1730* (Cambridge, 1968), p. 249.

55. Cowper's memorial is printed in J. Campbell's *Lives of the Lord Chancellors,* vol. 4, pp. 373–377. As there are some mistakes in the transcription, references to this document will be based on the original in Herts. R.O., Panshanger MSS D/EP/F152.

According to the Lord Chancellor, justices should be replaced "as fast as they shew any signs of disaffection to your Majesty's Government by so much as a neglect of their Duty: to which the frequent tumults which are either incouraged or neglected by such magistrates will often give a sufficient handle." As for the charge that he had not used his office to rid the bench of unfit justices:

I did . . . turn out according to the best accounts I could get, great numbers of persons disaffected and otherwise not well qualifyed . . . : and as to those who wer of Estate and quality sufficient in their Country, but were represented by your M[ajesty]'s friends as of suspected inclinations; I thought it for your M[ajesty]'s interest not to displace them on bare general suspicion; unless they who sollicited their Removal would give in writing some p[ar]ticular instance or objection to their Conduct, and either prove it or at least subscribe to their knowledge or beleif [sic] of it.

As some, though not all, of Cowper's papers have survived, the extent to which his practice accorded with his theory can be partially measured, and his definition of "persons disaffected and otherwise not well qualifyed" discovered. In 1714, Cowper apparently requested that the custodes rotulorum, to whom supervision of the commissions was entrusted, submit lists of the present commissions of the peace, noting which justices had not been sworn.[56] Willingness to swear fidelity to the Hanoverian would, in some cases, become a touchstone of fitness. For instance, before the issue of the 1715 commission for Kent, Cowper received three lists of justices whose elimination was recommended: one from the clerk of the peace, one from the Earl of Rockingham, the county's Lord Lieutenant and custos rotulorum, and one from the Duke of Dorset, a powerful Whig magnate resident in the county.[57] (Kent's judicial complement was then 240.) The list from the clerk of the peace noted justices dead, justices not sworn, and justices not resident in the county. Of twenty-five not resident in the county, all but six were eliminated; five of these six were members of the commission by virtue of office held under the central government, and the remaining justice, John Lade—the same gentleman who was removed from and restored to the Surrey commission—lived in nearby

56. Herts. R.O., Panshanger MSS D/EP/F153, Holles, Earl of Newcastle to Lord Cowper, Nov. 21, 1715. See also the lists of justices of several counties with the names of those not sworn noted throughout D/EP/F153–155.

57. Herts. R.O., Panshanger MSS D/EP/F153, "Justices to be left out in the Commission of the Peace, From E of Rockinghams hand July 1715"; list of commission of peace for Kent, Oct. 19, 1714; list "received from the E. of Dorset's hand, Monday, 27 July, 1715."

Southwark and probably owed his good fortune to his parliamentary seat and to contemporary assessment of his current political stance as a Whig who would, on occasion, vote Tory.[58] Dorset and Rockingham requested that an additional twenty-six gentlemen be removed from the county's commission. Nineteen were so disgraced. All of the privileged seven were marked as sworn on the clerk of the peace's list; all appeared in the Rockingham list only, and no specific allegations were there noted against any. Only one justice whom the clerk of the peace had noted as sworn and against whom there was no specific allegation was omitted. All those whose elimination was recommended by both Dorset and Rockingham and marked as "not sworn" on the clerk of the peace's list, and all those whose lack of fitness for office was sketched by notes from Dorset and Rockingham were removed from office by the 1715 commission.[59]

In January 1715, it was recommended that at least eighteen justices be dismissed from Leicestershire's commission. (There were eighty-three justices in Leicestershire's commission at the end of Anne's reign.) Notations against ten of the names on the list sketch specific reasons for removal. Six more justices were either noted as "never sworn" on this list or on another list of the commission possibly submitted by the clerk of the peace. The elimination of two more justices was simply requested. None of these justices was in Leicestershire's commission as of January 4, 1716.[60]

A summary of the allegations brought against justices whose removal was requested reveals the government's stereotype of the "man least qualified to be in the commission of the peace." Most frequently, he was a man of "small estate," "no estate in the county," or just "of no estate." Oddly enough, such charges seem almost entirely confined to men appointed by Harcourt and rarely sullied the reputations of those appointed by Cowper during his previous term as Lord Chancellor. Nine justices of Carmarthenshire were so labelled. Six had been

58. R. Sedgwick, ed., *The History of Parliament: the House of Commons 1715–1754* (London, 1970), vol. 2, under "John Lade."

59. Kent A.O., Q/JC/39, July 28, 1715.

60. P.R.O., C234/19, Jan. 4, 1715[6]; Herts. R.O., Panshanger MSS D/EP/F153, lists for the county of Leicester. Other examples of Cowper's thorough supervision can be found by comparing recommendations of dismissals in Cowper's papers (the Panshanger MSS) with the fiats ordering the preparation of a new commission, P.R.O., C234. Specific allegations were brought against all those removed from Glamorgan's commission by fiat of Jan. 10, 1714[5], all those removed from Carmarthen's commission by fiat of Mar. 15, 1714–1715, and all those removed from Cardigan's commission by fiat of Jan. 15, 1714–1715.

appointed by Harcourt and two of these had been previously removed by Cowper. One more had been appointed by Cowper in 1708, who by that act had obliterated the disgrace incurred by that justice when he had been dismissed by Cowper in 1706.[61] Lack of estate befitting a justice was only one of the numerous disabilities enfeebling the administration of justice by six of the seven justices dismissed from Glamorganshire's commission in 1715. All seven had been appointed by Harcourt.[62] Similarly, six of the eight Leicestershire justices reputedly unencumbered by landed property had been appointed by Harcourt.

Ranking second in the list of characteristics of the justice least liable to do justice was partisan political activity—if the party supported were Tory. Justices were charged with making use of their powers to oblige the people to vote their way, of being quarrelsome and "litigious in the late election," of being "troublesome to the county," or to put it plainly, of being "a flaming Tory." Such justices, it was charged, had been "put in by the late Ministry to Serve A turn," or, like Sir William Keyt, of Warwickshire, had been "put into the Commission of the Peace only to be a Check on the Whigg Interest in Barlichway Hundred."[63] Such justices were removed.

Opportunity, too, there was to remove those justices who acted unjustly and otherwise disgraced the bench. Mr. Cole of Oxfordshire, known locally as "Firecoal," who refused to punish those who sold underweight bread and committed the informers to jail, who refused to punish carriers whose wagons were drawn by an illegally large number of horses, and who encouraged the carriers to drag the informers at the tail of their wagons was no longer to persecute his neighbours. He had been previously dismissed by Cowper and reappointed by Harcourt.[64] John Goodere alias Dineley was likewise removed from the bench. He was accused of fabricating an accusation so that he could jail a woman who had been evidence against him in his suit against his cousin, of violating laws against Sunday work, and

61. Herts. R.O., Panshanger MSS D/EP/F155, list from Marquis of Winchester; P.R.O., C234/85.

62. Herts. R.O., Panshanger MSS D/EP/F155; P.R.O., C234/81.

63. Herts. R.O., Panshanger MSS D/EP/F154, "These Objections to the Names, Received the 9 January 1714[5] of my Lord Uxbridge, Custos Rotulorum," Staffordshire; D/EP/F155, list of the Marquis of Winchester, Carmarthenshire; D/EP/F153, "My Lord Clare's List for Nottinghamshire given in the 13 January 1714[5]"; Bedfordshire, "From the Duke of Kent;" D/EP/F154, Warwickshire, George Lucy to [?], Charlott, Nov. 21, 1714; D/EP/F155, Cardiganshire.

64. Herts. R.O., Panshanger MSS D/EP/F154, "From E[ar]l G[odolphin];" P.R.O., C234/30, Jan. 30, 1708[9], Feb. 14, 1710[11], Jan. 13, 1714[5].

of inappropriate conduct at a test for witchcraft. The alleged witch had been thrown into a sluice to see if she would float. After she was pulled out, Dineley stripped, jumped into the sluice, and "swam about it on his Back, exposing his nakedness to the Men and Women that were present." On emerging from the sluice, he pulled on his breeches "before several Women that were present and asked which of them would be kn——kt." Dineley had been appointed by Harcourt. William Lloyd, D.D., the justice who took the depositions against him, had been appointed by Cowper in 1705, removed by Harcourt, and reappointed by Cowper in 1714.[65] It was remarkable how nearly the dictates of politics and demands of morality coincided. What if Dineley had been a Whig?

Of course, accusations against justices might have been motivated by personal, family, and local party feuds, and it would hardly further the government of the realm if such biased allegations were given credence. For instance, it was alleged that several justices of the counties of Caernarvon and Anglesey had rioted in the main street of Beaumaris, had led a mob marching to the beat of a drum and, bravely shouldering muskets from the castle through the town, had broken windows, had beaten some of the inhabitants with whips and others with the blade of a naked sword, had run a sword through the town constable's thigh, had drunk damnation and confusion to "the pitiful one-eyed Lord Bulkeley," Constable of the Castle, and had fired at a fellow on horseback whom they believed to be one of Bulkeley's retainers. Several of the justices were further charged with bending the rules of judicial procedure to the disadvantage of their personal enemies. Of the maligned nine gentlemen whom the records of the central government identify as justices, all but one had been appointed by Cowper early in his second term of office. Two of the nine had originally been honoured by appointment to the bench during Cowper's first term of office and had been subsequently dismissed by Harcourt. None of the nine was removed.[66]

65. Herts. R.O., Panshanger MSS D/EP/F154, deposition of Edward Cromer of Fladbury parish, Worcestershire, Oct. 5, 1716; information of Samuel Jackson of Fladbury parish, Worcestershire, Oct. 26, 1716; Dineley's warrant for the commitment of Elizabeth Eden, May 2, 1716; P.R.O., C234/41, Dec. 13, 1705, Feb. 15, 1710[11], Mar. 3, 1711[2], Dec. 1, 1714, Dec. 12, 1716.

66. P.R.O., C234/82, Oct. 12, 1714, June 8, 1715, July 25, 1729; C234/79, July 26, 1704, Feb. 7, 1706[7], Aug. 2, 1707, Sept. 24, 1715, Aug. 30, 1720, Jan. 2, 1727[8]. Herts. R.O., Panshanger MSS D/EP/F155, "Beaumares Borough: Information given upon oath by the Persons following before the Mayor, Recorder and Bayliffes of the said Borough touching a Riot committed there on the First and Second of August last by several Justices of the Peace for the said County of Anglesey and Caernarvonshire."

While Cowper was reluctant to act upon charges brought against Whig justices, it is possible that the restraint which characterized his evaluation of requests to dismiss Tories became less noticeable toward the end of his term of office. For example, two of the seven Kentish justices whom he had not removed, though their dismissal had been recommended, were removed in 1716.[67] On the other hand, Cowper may already have been labouring under the strains and ideological commitments that later caused him to turn Tory, and conducted himself accordingly. When, in May 1718, Thomas Parker, later first Earl of Macclesfield, succeeded Cowper on the woolsack, any protective barrier placed between the triumphant Whigs and Tory justices, or justices simply allied to interests opposing that local Whig faction supported by the government, disappeared. The justices of the peace were exposed to the full force of the prevailing political winds.

The growth of the use of the commission as an instrument of party politics can be gathered from table 1, a table of the number of justices removed from the commission in seven counties for reasons other than death between 1700 and 1725.[68] As the records of the central government noting the removal of justices sometimes obscure the difference between a dead justice and a live one, it has not been possible to ascertain the number of justices dismissed after 1714. Where two figures are shown in the last two columns, the top figure is the number

67. P.R.O., C234/18, June 22, 1716; Herts. R.O., Panshanger MSS D/EP/F153, list from the Earl of Rockingham.

68. Justices eliminated and then restored within the period covered by a column are not noted in the table. Those in the honourary portion of the commission, including peers and their sons, are not noted in the table. The figures in the column for 1700–1704 are taken from House of Lords R.O., House of Lords MSS No. 2011, Main Papers, March 20, 1703[4] for which see n. 36 above. The column for 1705–1710 is based on Herts. R.O., Panshanger MSS D/EP/F152, "List of those put in and out by my Lord Keeper," and on the fiats in P.R.O., C234. The justice eliminated from Kent's commission—in 1706—is not noted in either of these two sources. Again, the records of the national government may not be entirely accurate. The remaining columns are based on the fiats in P.R.O., C234 and on lists in Herts. R.O., Panshanger MSS D/EP/F153. As the fiat for Herefordshire's first commission under George I is missing, the number of those eliminated in 1714 has been calculated from B.L., Loan 29/27/19, "The Names of such Justices . . . who have been left out. . . ." This list was drawn up after the omissions of March 6, 1719[20]. Since this list may note only those former justices who were still alive in or after 1720, the number of those eliminated may be greater than shown here. The Cambridgeshire fiats for Nov. 10, 1714, and Feb. 20, 1721[2], the Hampshire fiats for Oct. 5, 1714, and Aug. 5, 1715, and the Bedfordshire fiat for June 27, 1718, are all lists of the entire commission. As the number of removals made by these fiats was calculated by comparing these lists to Harcourt's fiats appointing justices, the number of removals may be greater than shown here. As two of Macclesfield's fiats for Oxfordshire are missing and a third is a list of the commission, I have not attempted to numerate his removals in Oxfordshire.

of all justices the records show were alive at the time of dismissal, and the bottom figure is the number of all whose state of health at the time of dismissal is not indicated in the records of the central government or in county histories. It is very probable that many, and possibly most, of these justices were alive when removed from the commission; yet it is also very probable that several were dead when the order for erasure of their names was given.

As table 1 suggests, party warfare had stimulated increased ferocity in the political manipulation of local government. Party now permeated all institutions whose officers were appointed at Westminster. Even the land tax commission was not exempt. In William's reign, only a few of the justices removed from Kent's bench lost their place on the land tax commission. By George I's accession almost every Kentish justice who was dismissed from the commission of the peace was also removed from the land tax commission.[69] Since the justices comprised the overwhelming majority of those land tax commissioners who actually acted as land tax commissioners, it is possible that the elevation of a land tax commissioner to the bench may have increased the probability that he would be marked as a suitable candidate for removal from the land tax commission whenever a change in the balance of party power at Westminster enabled his opponents to alter the balance of power in local institutions.

Party warfare was now so intense that when Lord Chancellor Macclesfield succeeded a Lord Chancellor of his own party (the only Lord Chancellor in table 1 to do so), he thought it appropriate to dismiss many justices who had survived Cowper's earlier campaigns against their Tory allies. Indeed, both the extent and manner of the early Hanoverian purge might profitably be compared to that conducted under James II. James had had to canvas his justices in order to determine their political sympathies, but even though the expansion of the commissions insured that most of the justices removed in the reign of George I were less prominent than those dismissed in James's reign, George I's Lord Chancellors did not have to resort to

69. For lists of the land tax commissioners between the Glorious Revolution and the death of Queen Anne, see the land tax acts in *The Statutes of The Realm printed by Command of His Majesty King George The Third,* 11 vols. (London, 1820–1828, reprinted 1963). The composition of the land tax commissions in the reign of George I can be traced through the land tax acts in the British Library's collection of statutes. I want to thank Richard Grover for giving me lists of the land tax commissioners who acted on their commission in Kent. See also R. J. Grover, "The Land Tax in East Kent" (M. Phil. thesis, University of Kent, 1980), p. 145.

TABLE 1 JUSTICES REMOVED 1700–1725

Number of Justices Removed by:

County	*Wright* Midsummer 1700– March 1704	*Cowper* Oct. 1705– Sept. 1710	*Harcourt* Sept. 1710– Aug. 1714	*Cowper* Aug. 1714– May 1718	*Macclesfield* May 1718– Dec. 1725
Bedfordshire	1	2	3	22	6
				5	1
Cambridgeshire	3	5	6	14	2
				3	2
Gloucestershire	28	21	6[a]	39	6
				16[b]	
Hampshire	6	0	6	14	7
				9	
Herefordshire	1	0	2	11	7
Kent	38	1	36[c]	53[b]	31
Oxfordshire	20	1	16[d]	26	incomplete information

a. One of those removed had been appointed by Harcourt.
b. Three of those removed had been appointed in 1714 by Cowper.
c. Three of those removed had been appointed by Harcourt. An additional two were removed, reappointed, and again removed.
d. Two of those removed had been appointed by Harcourt.

such an extraordinary device. Because party had integrated lesser gentry and gentlemen into a national political framework, Cowper and Macclesfield could rely on local magnates' knowledge of the justices' political affiliations. So, though they did not canvas the justices, George I's Lord Chancellors made few errors in their assessment of the justices' political allegiance. For instance, of the eighty-four justices whom Cowper and Macclesfield removed from Kent's commission, fifty-four had voted for the Tory candidates at either or both of the county elections of 1713 and 1715, three had split their vote, and only three had voted for the Whigs.[70] Cowper and Macclesfield's manipulation of the commissions based forty years of 'Whig Supremacy' upon the firm rock of local government. So, too, their policy of party manipulation of the commissions, a policy which elaborated upon that of their predecessors and extended its effects over the next half-century of local government, spattered the contemporary image of the justice with the mud of partisan politics.

Between 1680 and 1725, party conflict had given rise to a partisan policy of manipulation of the commission, a policy which reflected and reinforced the permeation of party among England's local rulers. So, the tale of the justices is the local counterpart of the stories of the birth of parliamentary parties long told by historians of national politics. During the reigns of the first two Hanoverians, the triumphant chorus resounding at the birth of Whig and Tory orchestrated by Macaulay, and the martial blare of party strife trumpeted in Trevelyan no longer obliterated all other anthems in the nation's political life. Yet, though the score was rewritten for different players, the melody would linger on.

70. Kent A.O., Q/RPe1/1713; Bodleian Library, Rawlinson MSS B338. All three Whigs, it was noted, no longer resided in the county (Herts. R.O., Panshanger MSS D/EP/F153, list of Kent's commission as of Oct. 19, 1714).

CHAPTER FOUR

The Making of a Justice, 1725–1760

Preceded by the age of Civil War and Glorious Revolution, succeeded by that of the Industrial Revolution, the early Hanoverian era seems a brief moment of stability amidst centuries of turmoil. Even interpretations of the era's politics—the sphere in which conflict is made articulate—have reinforced the impression of Augustan tranquillity. Most interpretations of early Hanoverian politics have declared that during the reign of George I party struggle ceased to disturb England's political landscape.[1] Whig hegemony at Westminister transformed politics into a contest for place and pension. Politics became a mere tournament, a mock battle among oligarchs. To the victor went the prize, but the identity of the victor affected neither the rules of the tournament nor the structure of the social and political arena.

Interpretations of early Hanoverian politics have focused upon Parliament, but it is possible that concentration on Parliament has obscured the importance of party struggle. So complete was Whig dominance of the national government that some historians have claimed that the Tories ceased to function as a parliamentary party.[2] Yet, historians have also noted that conflict between Whig and Tory persisted in the localities even when party seemed to have vanished at

1. W. Speck, "Whigs and Tories dim their glories: English political parties under the first two Georges"; G. Holmes, "Colloquy on chapter 3"; and J. Cannon, "Final discussion," in *The Whig Ascendancy,* ed. J. Cannon (London, 1981).

2. However, see L. Colley, *In Defiance of Oligarchy: The Tory Party 1714–1760* (Cambridge, 1982).

Westminster.[3] Indeed, since the king's ministers used their power to secure a parliamentary majority, it is likely that both party struggle and Tory power were more evident and important in the localities than at Westminster. Analysis of the political structure of early Hanoverian England must therefore penetrate behind parliamentary stratagems and examine the alliances of England's local elites. If Tory groups in the localities threatened Whig hegemony, then Whig hegemony and perhaps even oligarchy were less secure than their triumph has made them appear.

Since Lord Chancellors determined the composition of the commissions of the peace and since justices wielded political power, Lord Chancellors had to assess the extent to which party struggle permeated local elites. Therefore the Lord Chancellors' manipulations of the county commissions delineate their definitions of the structure of politics. Loss of some or all of the personal papers of Lord Chancellors, and the absence of records of the central government detailing changes in the commissions before 1705, render close analysis of the policy and process of appointment and dismissal in the reigns of the last Stuarts and first Hanoverian impossible. In 1737 Hardwicke became Lord Chancellor and remained so for twenty years. His papers survive in bulk, and a comparison of the Lord Chancellor's policies, as recorded in his correspondence, with his activities, as revealed in the records of appointments and dismissals, becomes a series of sketches of the interaction of mid-century politics and local government. Since, in mid-century, party was slowly though never completely disintegrating and since the structure of politics was therefore constantly subject to readjustments simultaneously minor and fundamental, it might seem that a series of line drawings would resemble one of those books of cartoons in which the figures seem to perform consecutive actions as the pages are flipped. Instead, the sketches in Hardwicke's papers bear more resemblance to a series of transparencies placed one on top of another until a composite picture is formed. Since the presentation of these sketches in a sequence roughly chronological creates a partially deceptive impression of development, it should be remembered that many of the sketches could be hung in a room furnished in the style pervading squirearchic residences during the reigns of the first two Hanoverians—a style now known as "Queen Anne."

3. Sir L. Namier, "Monarchy and the Party System," *Personalities and Powers* (London, 1955), p. 33, quoted in Speck, n. 1 above.

1. PARTY AND APPOINTMENT TO THE COMMISSION, 1737–1745

In every sketch, one figure is always present, always active, always decisive. Lord Chancellor Hardwicke determined the composition of the commissions. Especially is his surveillance evident in the process of appointment to the local bench. A presentation of the scrutiny of the nominees to the Westminster and Middlesex commissions in 1743 may seem atypical, but, like most caricatures, it firmly establishes the outstanding features of participants and activity.

At some date prior to May 11, 1743, Gabriel Mallett, the secretary for commissions, compiled two lists of nominees to the Westminster and Middlesex commissions. The secretary of commissions was a Crown Office position in the patronage of the Lord Chancellor. As names of nominees sometimes seem to have been left "at the office" in the custody of the secretary, it appears that the secretary worked at the Crown Office performing some of the more menial and tiresome chores necessary if the Lord Chancellor were to receive information about prospective justices. Mallett's lists of seventy-one nominees and their sponsors were presented to Hardwicke, who examined them, added five names, crossed out five, and queried thirty. Some time later a list of twenty-three "additional names left in the office since the former list was left in the office"[4] was presented: two were crossed out and fourteen queried. At this point, inquiries were made of the suitability of the forty-four questionable names, the results recorded, and five new names added. Further investigations were made of the characters of ten of the forty-four and one of the new names, and the results again recorded. It was now September. As Hardwicke's secretary of commissions had secured information about the 104 nominees whose names had either been left in the office or forwarded by the Lord Lieutenant and custos rotulorum of the county of Middlesex, it was time to meet with that grandee. In 1743, the Lord Lieutenant and custos rotulorum of Middlesex was the Duke of Newcastle—Hardwicke's friend, constant consultee, and political ally. Newcastle, Hardwicke, Hardwicke's secretary of commissions Gabriel Mallett, and Newcastle's "man of business," Peter Forbes—or some combination of the four—met to consider yet another list. This one, totaling forty-one new names, was entitled "a list of Gentlemen appearing in the Duke of Newcastle's list but not on my lord's"—i.e., Hard-

4. B.L., Add. MSS 35601, ff. 281–284, 294.

wicke's.[5] Newcastle's secretary made a copy of the list, added the name of a former justice who had requested reinstatement on October 4, and either at or after the meeting eliminated seventeen names, including that of the former justice. On October 17, one more list of seven names was compiled in Hardwicke's office and a final investigation of the suspect nominees in this list, Newcastle's lists, Hardwicke's previous lists, and five new nominees was launched. Sometime in November another four names were recommended, and then, finally, two grand alphabetical lists—the lists penultimate to the issue of the commissions—were engrossed. Three new names appear on these lists. Of a total of 165 nominees, 98 had secured the approval of the Lord Chancellor.[6] The information on the lists, information which is frequently an incomplete summary of the details communicated to Hardwicke by numerous correspondents, reveals that Hardwicke knew who had sponsored almost every nominee and had discovered the occupation, profession, social position, and/or income of at least one hundred applicants. As the lists detail the occupation, etc., of forty-eight of the sixty-seven nominees judged unacceptable, and of only fifty-two of the ninety-eight accepted, it can perhaps be assumed that Hardwicke or Newcastle knew or knew of several of the successful applicants or their sponsors and had considered further investigation of these applicants to be unnecessary.

Westminister and Middlesex may seem too atypical to provide a basis for generalization. In no other area were there seventy-seven different persons, of sufficient wealth, estate, position, and connection to nominate justices of the peace. No other areas were within walking distance of the Crown Office. Few, if any, Lords Lieutenant and custodes rotulorum were as closely connected with the Lord Chancellor as the Duke of Newcastle—and, indeed, it may be that Newcastle relied on Hardwicke to conduct investigations that he would have conducted himself if Hardwicke had not been Lord Chancellor. Yet, it can also be argued that the issue of the Westminster and Middlesex commissions reveals merely the essential and regular procedure behind the issue of each commission. While few other areas could boast of seventy-seven nominators, several could put forward over one hundred nominees, and many of these nominees were of sufficient status

5. B.L., Add. MSS 35601, ff. 289–290, 292–293, 296–297.

6. B.L., Add. MSS 35601, ff. 287–288, 273–274, 291, 285, 270, 254–259, and f. 236, Clifford William Philips to Hardwicke, Goodmans Fields, Oct. 4, 1743; P.R.O., C 234/25, Dec. 12, 1743.

to stand as their own sponsors. Time, distance, and less amenable or trustworthy Lords Lieutenant and custodes rotulorum introduced problems, but then, Lord Chancellor Hardwicke was not noted for inability to discover solutions.

According to nineteenth-century expositors, control of appointment to his county's commission rested with the Lord Lieutenant. In law, the custos rotulorum was head of the commission.[7] But, in fact, the Lord Chancellor determined the composition of eighteenth-century commissions of the peace. The Lord Chancellor's secretary received recommendations from persons other than the Lord Lieutenant and custos, and such applications for appointment to the commission could be successful. When Lord Chancellor Hardwicke's correspondence provides a complete record of his activity, it appears to reveal that recommendations were always eventually passed to the Lord Lieutenant and custos rotulorum. Yet, in 1737, shortly after Hardwicke had assumed office, one Lord Lieutenant considered it necessary to enclose with his list of nominees an instruction that the Lord Chancellor "direct your Clerk, not to let any others Slip in, for by that means some Persons altogether unfit for the Station have formerly been nominated," and apparently appointed. By 1751, Halifax, Lord Lieutenant and custos rotulorum of Northamptonshire, was meekly requesting that Hardwicke send him the names of those recommended so that Halifax could put them on his list.[8] Lord Brooke, Lord Lieutenant and custos rotulorum of Warwickshire, reacted to Hardwicke's referral of two nominees in a somewhat different manner: if the nomi-

7. The position of custos rotulorum seems to have been slighted by historians of local government—possibly because these historians have relied upon sixteenth- and nineteenth-century evidence. As the office of Lord Lieutenant, with its powers of supervision of the militia and appointment of deputy lieutenants was instituted in the sixteenth century, the figure of the sixteenth-century Lord Lieutenant has attracted attention not given to the older post of custos rotulorum. Yet, the militia was nearly moribund in the first half of the eighteenth century, and so the office of lieutenancy bestowed less immediate power upon its early eighteenth-century possessors than it had upon its earlier tenants. The Militia Act of 1757 and the reorganization of the militia during the French Revolution revived the militia and so once again increased the powers of the Lord Lieutenant. Since the nineteenth-century Lords Lieutenant were almost always also custodes rotulorum, nineteenth-century commentators and their historians have invariably labelled the possessor of both offices the 'Lord Lieutenant' and attributed the sum total of his powers to this one office. In the late seventeenth and early eighteenth centuries, the offices were not always united. As the custos, not the Lord Lieutenant, was legally the official charged with responsibility for the commission of the peace, the custos influenced the appointment of justices in equal or even greater degree than the Lord Lieutenant.

8. B.L., Add. MSS 35600, f. 85, Lord Malton to Hardwicke, Oct. 17, 1737; Add. MSS 35603, f. 333, Dec. 17, 1751.

nees were suitable, he stated, they would have been on his list; "I have always endeavoured to Serve the King to the utmost of my power in the station I am in, and whatever further I can do, His Majesty may depend upon my utmost endeavours and zeal to promote his Interest and that of the Common Cause, in those parts where I am settled, and where give me Leave to say proper attention and due care should be given to what passes by whoever is the Person his Majesty shall think Proper to constitute his Lord Lieutenant and Custos Rotulorum." Nonetheless, one of the nominees was appointed.[9]

Despite Brooke's pretensions, the power of appointment was the Lord Chancellor's. The Lord Chancellor could, if he wished, receive nominations from any quarter. In some instances, he may have judged such activity to be essential. Consider the negotiations over Huntingdonshire's commission in 1746, negotiations which featured the Duke of Manchester, who was the county's Lord Lieutenant and custos, and the Earl of Sandwich, a magnate with an interest in the county who had recently been attached to the Pelhamite ministry by the Broad-Bottom alliance. In 1746, Sandwich was in Breda conducting England's diplomacy, and he had forwarded both his list of nominees and his objections to one of Manchester's nominees to Hardwicke. Hardwicke informed Sandwich that it was usual for lists of nominees to be forwarded through the custos. Sandwich's reply was succinct: ". . . in the situation I am in that county I can certainly never make any application thro' his Graces Chanel. . . ." As the grandees disagreed over the appointment of one of Manchester's nominees, Hardwicke postponed issue of the new commission. The new commission finally appeared in 1749, after Sandwich had again been consulted about the list submitted by Manchester and had again objected to the same nominee, and Hardwicke had decided that the objectionable nominee should not be made a justice.[10] In arbitrating disputes between the powers of a county, in assuaging Lords Lieutenant and custodes rotulorum with whom he was not closely allied, in circumventing the barriers placed by such grandees to his supervision of their exercise of the right to nominate, Hardwicke elaborated his own policy of appointment.

9. B.L., Add. MSS 35603, f. 170, July 15, 1749; P.R.O., C234/38, July 21, 1749.

10. B.L., Add. MSS 35602, f. 210, draft from Hardwicke to Earl of Sandwich, Oct. 1, 1746; ff. 224–225, Sandwich to Hardwicke, Oct. 20, 1746, N.S.; Add. MSS 35603, f. 166, Sandwich to Hardwicke, June 28, 1749; f. 168, Manchester to Hardwicke, July 7, 1749; P.R.O., C234/17, July 8, 1749.

Almost every recommendation of a nominee to the commission in the Hardwicke correspondence contains a vague and indefinite reference to the nominee's status and a more direct and unambiguous reference to politics. As in the reign of the last Stuart, political allegiance was a major determinant of appointment. The points at issue are whether political allegiance in the later Stuart period is comparable to political allegiance from 1737 to 1756, and whether the influence of political allegiance as a determinant of appointment was diminished by other considerations. To appreciate Hardwicke's policy of appointment, it is therefore first necessary to outline the effect of his predecessors' policies on the political composition of the commission.

Cowper and Macclesfield had aimed at Whig dominance of the county benches, but they had nonetheless allowed some Tories to remain on the commissions. Indeed, in some petty sessional divisions and perhaps even in some counties, Tories were so predominant that they still formed the majority.[11] Since the removal of a justice was an insult greater than refusal to appoint a gentleman to the commission, some Tories remained justices in the 1720s whom neither Lord Chancellor would have elevated to the bench. By 1725, when Macclesfield was ousted from office, a very large number of Tories no longer graced the commissions and Whigs were in the majority on most commissions. Since Cowper and Macclesfield had wielded the weapon of removal to the fullest extent practicable, in the future, manipulation of the political composition of the bench would depend on Lord Chancellors' decisions about appointment.

Macclesfield was succeeded by Lord Chancellor King, whom George II instructed to "put into the commission of the peace all gentlemen of rank and quality in the several counties, unless they were in direct opposition to his Government; but still keep a majority of those who were known to be most firmly in his interest." George directed the Lord Chancellor to "declare the former part as his sentiment."[12] Though the correspondence of neither King nor his successor Talbot survives, central government records reveal that neither Lord Chancellor continued the practice of national purgation of the commission. Though, on occasion, King eliminated some justices from the commissions, he also reinstated a few of those dismissed by his predecessors, while Talbot refrained both from removing justices and from

11. See, for instance, the case of Herefordshire in chapter IV, part 2 below.

12. Peter, seventh Baron King, *The Life and Letters of John Locke* (London, 1858), "Notes on Domestic and Foreign Affairs," pp. 454–455.

loading the bench with Tories. So, when Hardwicke received the Great Seal, most commissions were dominated by a Whig majority, but Tory applications for a seat on the bench were no longer always automatically vetoed. Nonetheless, greater consideration of Tory wishes was not necessarily indicative of the disintegration of Toryism as a political force. Lord Chancellor Hardwicke's assessment of the structure of English politics, as revealed in his policy of appointment to the commission, was that Tories and Toryism constituted a threat to Whig hegemony.

In May 1738, Hardwicke had received a list of four nominees to the commission of Flint, all dwelling in the same hundred, from Sir Thomas Hanmer, leader of the parliamentary Tories. Hardwicke was evidently contemplating renewal of the commission, and, within the next few weeks, initiated correspondence with Lord Cholmondeley, Flintshire's Lord Lieutenant. Despite intensive canvassing Cholmondeley could find only two suitable nominees with influence in the area, and, as one was a member of Parliament resident in Sussex, and the other unwilling to act, he concluded that he must "intreat your Lordship to take only two of the four Persons recommended by Sir Thomas Hanmer . . . or we Entirely loose the Burrough of Flint" which controlled one parliamentary seat. Only two of Hanmer's nominees were appointed.[13] In 1739, Hardwicke had received three lists of nominees to Norfolk's commission from Lord Townshend, the county's former Lord Lieutenant and custos rotulorum. In 1738, he had been relieved of these offices, and nine years later, a rival grandee of the county attributed his loss of office to "his desire to bring in Tory Justices." Of the one bishop, one dean, four baronets, twenty-eight gentlemen, and two clerics recommended by Townshend, Hardwicke appointed one bishop, one dean, one baronet, and nine gentlemen. The same commission elevated one peer's son, one baronet, and fourteen gentlemen not distinguished by the earl to the bench.[14] In Hardwicke's opinion, there were political interests tightly allied to political parties, and it was the duty of the Lord Chancellor to insure that the commissions were controlled by the political interest in alliance with his party.

Yet, in Hardwicke's opinion there were, unfortunately, gentlemen

13. B.L., Add. MSS 35600, f. 124; ff. 128–129, Lord Cholmondeley to Hardwicke, June 19, 1738; P.R.O., C234/83, July 8, 1738.

14. B.L., Add. MSS 35602, f. 314, Earl of Leicester to Hardwicke, Sept. 5, 1747; Add. MSS 35600, f. 214; f. 213; f. 211, Townshend to Hardwicke, Aug. 1, 1739; P.R.O., C234/26, June 23, 1740.

so prominent that they had to be appointed. Total exclusion of all in opposition to the government was no longer acceptable. In 1738, Lord Hertford, custos rotulorum of Wiltshire, had objected to three nominees on the following grounds: one was "the hottest party man in the County"; so was the second; and the third was "a Scotch Parson." The last two nominees lived just by Lord Bruce—a Tory magnate—and "would be tools of his to do anything"; all lived near enough to Hertford's neighbourhood "that they know I could not but have heard of them, which was the reason they did not apply to me." Four days later, Hertford was brought to agree to the inclusion of one of the three, but only for Hardwicke's ease, and "upon no other account." And so, the "Scotch Parson," the Honourable and Reverend Thomas Bruce, was added to Wiltshire's commission.[15]

A somewhat analogous pattern appeared in the West Riding of Yorkshire where, some time after the issue of a commission in 1734, the justices had made complaint at Quarter Sessions "of the Partiall and Unjustifyable way of making Justices of the Peace." As the justices noted, they had represented the lack of magistrates in the wapentake of Staincross and submitted a list of appropriate candidates. None of their nominees had been appointed. In particular, Mr. Wentworth of Wooley, "A Gentleman of above £5000 a year," had been eliminated from the list of nominees "Because he was against Sir Rowland Wynn [a Whig candidate] in the last Election, though otherwise, A Gentleman of the Fairest Character of any in the County." Instead, "one Zouch Vicar of Sundale, was put in a Justice of Peace, Who was but th'other day School Master in the Neighbourhood, To the Great Scandal and Dissatisfaction of Most of the Justices of the Peace in the County of York." (As the justices did not note, the Rev. Mr. Zouch was a political agent of the Riding's Lord Lieutenant and had laboured valiantly for the Whig candidates in the 1734 election.) The justices' indignation was communicated to Hardwicke, who consulted the Earl of Malton, the Riding's Lord Lieutenant and custos rotulorum. Wentworth, it appeared, was the earl's neighbour and personal friend; it was "very fitting" that he be in the commission. As of November 15, 1737, he was.[16]

15. B.L., Add. MSS 35600, f. 181, Hartford to Hardwicke, Nov. 15, 1738; f. 183, Same to Same, Nov. 19, 1738; P.R.O., C234/40, Nov. 24, 1738.

16. B.L., Add. MSS 35600, f. 89; f. 92, Malton to Hardwicke, Oct. 29, 1737; P.R.O., C234/44; C. Collyer, "The Yorkshire Election of 1734," *Proceedings of the Leeds Philosophical and Literary Society, Literary and Historical Section* 7:1 (1952):59–60.

Even as Whig hegemony was being undermined by Whig reluctance to appear unreasonably partisan, fissures within Whig ranks posed problems in the identification of Whig adherents. Consider Hardwicke's difficulties in the renewal of the Denbighshire commission in 1742. Denbighshire's commission had last been renewed in 1740, but, by June 1742, Sir Robert Cotton, the county's custos rotulorum and Lord Lieutenant, seemed to think it necessary that substantial additions be made to the commission. In June 1742, he submitted a list numbering two baronets, twenty-six esquires, and one doctor of laws. As the commission of 1740 had contained a total of sixty-three baronets, esquires, and clerics, the Cotton list might conceivably alter the balance of power within the commission.[17] The gentlemen of Denbighshire were sure it would. In July, Hardwicke received letters from the Bishop of St. Asaph and the Bishop of Bangor requesting that the issue of the new commission be postponed, and reporting that Mr. Wynn, member of Parliament for Denbigh, shared their sentiments. To some extent, their objections had been forestalled. Hardwicke must have instituted inquiries into the Cotton list, for a memorandum noting salient facts about twelve of the Cotton nominees appears among his papers. One of the twelve had either £1,000 or £1,000 per annum. Of the rest, five had little or no estate, one had a father living and therefore probably had no estate, one was not of age, one lived out of the county, one was "weak," one "bad," and one reputedly lunatic. By mid-July, the Cotton list of twenty-nine had been pared to eight. According to the Bishop of Bangor, the justices of Denbighshire considered that the request to add eight "is only an artful way of undermining His Majesty's and their Interest, because these eight would give a Majority of two against them. They apprehend too, that there is no occasion for any alteration at all, That the present Number is rather too large, and no other wise defective, but upon Party Considerations." Upon receipt of this advice, Hardwicke suspended the issue of the commission for three weeks and urged the gentlemen of the county to consult with Sir Robert. Consultation did not produce amity. The subsequent report stated, ominously, that the gentlemen would indeed have approached Sir Robert even sooner, "had they not found, that, by appointment, he was engaged with Sir Watkin Williams Wynne," the Tory and Jacobite King of the West. By August, the Bishop of St. Asaph was urging: "to be sure your Lordship will not lay it down as

17. B.L., Add. MSS 35601, f. 73; Add. MSS 35600, ff. 237–238.

an invariable Rule," that the representations of a custos "are to be final. There is a recent Instance where a List was not only rejected, but the Custos himself tho' of Great Quality removed upon giving in an improper one." The commission was now suspended indefinitely. In October, Hardwicke was apprised of the myrmidons of active justices in Denbighshire—nineteen, in fact—and suspension continued. In June 1743, Hardwicke urged Cotton to come to an "equitable compromise" with the gentlemen of Denbighshire. No compromise was reached. In 1745, Cotton was again pressing the need of a commission, but the next commission for Denbighshire was issued on George III's accession, in 1761.[18]

Yet, at first glance, there seems little political reason for Hardwicke's refusal to accept Cotton's nominees. Cotton was an "old Whig," heir of a Whig family, and possessor of a parliamentary seat bestowed upon him by the Treasury. However, in 1734, he had lost his seat as member of Parliament for Cheshire to a Tory candidate, and in 1741 he was on the point of entering into an agreement with Sir Watkin Williams Wynn: according to the proposed treaty, he would support Wynn's candidacy for Denbighshire's seat if Wynn would support his campaign to represent Denbigh borough. The ministry must have considered the bargain particularly obnoxious. It was decided that Cotton should represent a Treasury borough, and that his brother would be given a government position, but it was understood that Cotton would continue to support Wynn's candidacy.[19] By 1742, it could not be assumed that the Whig Lord Lieutenant and custos rotulorum of Denbighshire would sponsor an unimpeachably Whig list of nominees.

Whiggish members' of Parliament flirtations with Toryism were by no means the only threats to Whig rule. In January 1742, Walpole had had to resign, bested by a combination of Tories and dissident Whigs. By March, the ministry was composed of the Pelhamites—Walpole's political heirs, leaders of one faction of Whig malcontents, and even two Tory aristocrats. So intimate was the connection between national

18. B.L., Add. MSS 35601, f. 90, Bishop of St. Asaph to Hardwicke, July 16, 1742; ff. 97–98, Thomas, Bishop of Bangor to Hardwicke, July 19, 1742; f. 74; f. 98v; ff. 116–117, Isa., Bishop of St. Asaph to Hardwicke, received Aug. 9, 1742; ff. 125–126, draft of letter from Hardwicke to Sir Robert Cotton, Aug. 14, 1742; ff. 143–144, Jo. Myddleton to Hardwicke, Oct. 12, 1742; ff. 211–212, draft of letter from Hardwicke to Sir Robert Cotton, June 30, 1743; Add. MSS 35602, f. 48, Sir Robert Cotton to Hardwicke, April 4, 1745.

19. R. Sedgwick, *The History of Parliament: the House of Commons 1715–1754* (London, 1970), vol. 1, p. 586.

politics and the commissions of the peace that the reconstruction of the ministry immediately reverberated in negotiations over the appointment of justices.

The tale of the Wiltshire commission reflects in miniature changes in the greater and distant political world of Westminster. In 1743, the Earl of Ailesbury, a magnate resident in the county, sent Hardwicke his lists of nominees to the county's commission. Ailesbury thought it appropriate to compliment the Pelhamites on their "national ways of thinking," and had continued: "now . . . that we are engaged very seriously in a War with Spain, and pretty like it with France, its my poor opinion that keeping up a ferment here at home, is not for the good of any one that means well, and the keeping out of many Gentlemen of figure, purely for their being of one certain complexion, and on the other hand putting in some no ways fit for it, as is the practice of most of the Custos's without England, is surely a great national hurt, and to one in your Lordship's post a most troublesome thing." The list forwarded by Ailesbury in 1743 was a shortened version of a list he had tendered a year earlier. The Earl of Hertford, Wiltshire's custos rotulorum, had considered that all but one of the twenty-six on the first list were "violent Tories" and had observed: "most live in the Chippenham Division, so that the design is to get a majority of their Party there. . . ." According to Hertford, the new list of eight old nominees and two new ones was hardly less objectionable—all but one were "violent" Tories—and Hertford concluded: "I leave it to You to put in who You think proper among them." The disgusted earl had not heard the last of the Tory renaissance. A few days later he received another list containing five old and four new nominees "every one of them Tories," and again consigned the responsibility for decision to Hardwicke. Of the twenty-six new justices on Wiltshire's commission of July 29, 1743, nineteen had either been recommended by Ailesbury or dubbed Tory by Hertford. Even so, fourteen of Ailesbury's nominees had been rejected.[20] Changes in the distribution of power at Westminster might have yielded more power to those opposed to the Walpoleian Whigs, but the Lord Chancellor still thought it possible to distinguish between Whigs and Tories.

Nor did the commissions of the peace merely reflect national poli-

20. B.L., Add. MSS 35601, f. 201, Earl of Ailesbury to Hardwicke, June 3, 1743; f. 253; f. 43, Lord Hartford to Hardwicke, Apr. 12, 1742; f. 203; f. 209, Earl of Hartford to Hardwicke, June 23, 1743; ff. 205–206; f. 219, Earl of Hartford to Hardwicke, July 10, 1743; P.R.O., C234/40, July 29, 1743.

tics. Changes in the configuration of party alliances at Westminster made the composition and quality of the county bench a major issue of national politics. By November of 1744, the Pelhamites had entered into an uneasy alliance with yet another segment of the opposition, a segment including the Tories, some of whom were rewarded with government office. By the winter of 1745, their new allies had made support of the Pelhamites contingent upon two concessions. The first was an act that would enforce earlier legislation raising the qualifications for appointment to the commissions. The act was duly passed, but not before one member of Parliament noted that "it was by no means agreeable to the Whigs, not only as it seemed to cast a general reproach on those of that party, with whom most of the commissions were filled up, but as they apprehended it would be followed by a further concession, in admitting the Tories into a larger share of that power, which would increase their influence in elections."[21] Such forebodings were not unwarranted. The second opposition demand was the admission of Tories to the commissions of the peace.

So important and complex was this issue that it caused a schism in the alliance. Denied an unequivocal commitment to an unlimited remodelling of all county benches, the Pelhamites' new allies voted against the government, imperilling its stability.[22] Negotiations ensued. Finally, on April 7, 1745, it was agreed that,

> In all Commissions of the peace, hereafter to be issued, all proper Regard shall be had to Gentlemen of Figure and Fortune, well-affected to His Majesty's Government, without Distinction of Parties.
>
> Application having been made That Six new Commissions, to be agreed upon, should be Forthwith made out, The Same shall be issued, as soon as possible, as a Specimen of the Manner of carrying this into Execution: And, whenever any further Application shall be made for the Renewal of other Commissions, Such Resolution shall be had thereupon, as shall be liable to no just Objection, and shall be agreeable to what is mention'd in the Beginning of the Paper.[23]

21. [T. Cobbett, ed.] *The Parliamentary History of England from the Earliest Period to the Year 1803,* vol. 13 (London, 1812), p. 1243.

22. *A Letter to the Author of the Case Fairly Stated* (London, 1745), pp. 29–30; B.L., Add. MSS 35602, f. 46, Mar. 20, 1744[5]; f. 56; Add. MSS 32804, ff. 286–287, Newcastle to Chesterfield, Mar. 26, 1745.

23. B.L., Add. MSS 32993, f. 308. The wording of the treaty as proposed by the opposition leaders on April 3 is to be found in Add. MSS 35602, f. 52, and Add. MSS 32993, f. 304. Newcastle's draft of April 4 amending the wording is Add. MSS 32993, f. 306, and an intermediate form, shown to the king on April 5, is in Add. MSS 35602, f. 50, and Add. MSS 32993, f. 289. The opposition's amended version, delivered to Pelham on April 6, is in Add. MSS 32993, f. 291, and Hardwicke's copy of the defini-

Passage of the act and conclusion of the treaty on the appointment of justices temporarily reinforced the uneasy alliance between Pelhamites, opposition leaders, and Tories. The ministry based on this alliance, known as the "Broad-Bottomed," was the first since 1716 to employ unregenerate Tories in the service of the crown. The Broad-Bottomed ministry was therefore both an anomaly in English politics and a symbol of English political life. In accepting the Tories as partners in local and national administration, the Pelhamites acknowledged that Toryism was no longer synonymous with Jacobitism, and that the Tories were loyal and legitimate possessors of political power, entitled to a share in the government of the nation. The alliance, adumbrating the nonparty government basic to "Broad-Bottom" principles, points to the disintegration of national party fundamental to the Namierian political world of 1761. Nonetheless, Tory behaviour attests to the reality of party in 1745. That the more inveterate Tories resigned their offices within a few months, finding the demand that they support the ministry while they held office inconsistent with their habits and concept of responsible behaviour, illustrates the effect of Tory party and ideology on Tory actions. Similarly, the necessity of parliamentary negotiations to gain Tory representation on the county bench evidences the reality of mid-eighteenth-century party and the close ties between national politics, political party, electoral power, and the composition of the commissions of the peace. It was neither backward provincialism nor ignorance of the structure of politics which made stipulations about justices "the Darling"[24] of the opposition's leaders.

2. LOCAL PARTY IN 1745

Of necessity, examination of Hardwicke's policy in the appointment of justices before 1745 has to be based on a selection from the tales told by the lists, letters, and notes remaining in his papers. In most cases, these stories are fragmentary and incomplete, frequently lacking setting, motivation, and even plot. In contrast, the setting of the six new commissions guaranteed the opposition leaders in 1745 is

---

tive wording of the treaty in Add. MSS 35602, f. 57. The political negotiations over both the bill and the treaty are thoroughly analysed in J. B. Owen, *The Rise of the Pelhams* (London, 1957), pp. 258–264.

24. *A Letter to the Author of the Case Fairly Stated*, p. 27.

clearly and decisively established by the negotiations between the Pelhamites and their new allies. Their motivation was explicitly political: the admission to the magistracy of "Gentlemen of Figure and Fortune, well-affected to His Majesty's Government," hitherto excluded by "Distinction of Parties." Presentation of the dramas outlined by the fragmentary papers on the issue of these six commissions therefore sketches both the structure and contemporary assessments of local party in 1745.

Examination of the health and nature of mid-century local party is peculiarly difficult. The least ambiguous evidence of a gentleman's party affiliation is his vote at an election which pits adherents of one party against those of another. But, as the balance of power in most counties was so well known at the mid-century, few counties proceeded to the expensive formality of a contested election to determine their representation, and those contests which did occur did not always involve a choice between candidates of different parties campaigning on party issues. The most famous mid-century party contest was the Oxfordshire election of 1754, when Tory candidates battled Whig over the Jew bill. Fortunately, Oxfordshire was one of the six counties chosen to receive a commission on the new model in 1745. It is indicative of the strength of party ties that an election held almost ten years after the renewal of Oxfordshire's commission should illuminate the role of party in its politics of appointment.

The reason for the choice of Oxfordshire as one of the six counties must remain a mystery. Since 1710, the county's knights had been Tory, and in 1745 its Lord Lieutenant and custos was the Duke of Marlborough, an opposition Whig who had made his peace with the Court in 1740 while retaining ties with both the opposition and the Prince of Wales.[25] Perhaps the duke's political alliances persuaded both Pelhamites and Tories that Oxfordshire would be a suitable county for judicial experiment.

The chief piece of evidence for the appointment of Oxfordshire's new justices in 1745 is a piece of paper listing names in two columns.[26] As one column is in the same hand as that which wrote the copy of Oxfordshire's commission of 1739, forwarded to the Lord Chancellor,[27] it can be assumed that this column of twenty-five names was

25. A.S. Foord, *His Majesty's Opposition 1714–1830* (Oxford, 1964), p. 275; R. Robson, *The Oxfordshire Election of 1754* (London, 1949), p. 1, n. 6.
26. B.L., Add. MSS 35602, f. 131.
27. B.L., Add. MSS 35602, ff. 132–133.

written by an associate of the Duke of Marlborough.[28] The other column is in a different hand: let us suppose that it is the list of twenty-four Tory nominees. There is ample evidence for this assumption. Only one of these gentlemen can be suspected of Whiggery. The Hon. John Spencer was brother to the Duke of Marlborough. Yet, as a member of Parliament, he voted consistently against the administration, as well he should. He owed his seat to his grandmother, the first Duchess of Marlborough, an inveterate opponent of Walpole. The overwhelming majority of the other nominees on the putatively Tory list displayed even more marked signs of opposition both to the ministry and to Whiggery. One of the nominees was a Tory member of Parliament. Another two were Jacobites;[29] one was crossed off the list, and the gentleman substituted in his place on the fiat ordering the renewal of Oxfordshire's commission was among those prominent county residents who had refused to sign the county's association against the Pretender. Two of the list's three peers and three more of its gentlemen also appeared in Whig propaganda for the 1754 election as non-associators.[30] Indeed only one of the putatively Tory nominees associated in 1745, and in 1754 that gentleman split his vote between Whig and Tory candidates. In 1754, thirteen of the twenty non-aristocrats on the putatively Tory list would vote for both Tory candidates and only one would vote for both Whigs.[31] However, that renegade had been a Tory in the 1740s.[32] In all, nineteen of the twenty-five putatively Tory nominees were undoubtedly Tory; the one gentleman who signed the county's association and split his vote in 1754 surely nourished Tory sympathies; and the Hon. John Spencer had only a fraternal tie to Whiggery. None of the remaining four putatively Tory nominees can be identified as Whig. That the Oxfordshire Tories could produce such an overwhelmingly partisan list of nominees reveals the strength and cohesion of their party.

Evidence of a similarly cohesive Whig party is somewhat less impressive. The list of Marlborough's nominees, headed by the duke

28. One name was added to the bottom of the Marlborough list in a different hand. This nominee is considered as sponsored by Marlborough.

29. Robson, *Oxfordshire Election*, pp. 6, 9.

30. *An Authentick Copy of the Association entered into by Part of the Nobility, Gentlemen and Clergy of the County of Oxford at the Time of the late Unnatural Rebellion in the Year 1745 together with the Names of all the Persons who Subscribed thereto; An Authentick Copy of another Part of the Nobility, Gentlemen and Clergy . . . who did NOT enter into the Association.*

31. *A copy of the poll . . .* (Oxford, at the Theatre, 1754).

32. Dr. Theophilus Leigh (Robson, *Oxfordshire Election*, p. 74).

himself, included four of the prominent Oxfordshire residents whom Whig propaganda for the 1754 election stigmatized as non-associators. Nonetheless, there may have been reason for the county's Lord Lieutenant to think himself bound to nominate at least three of these men: two, the Earls of Abingdon and Lichfield, were resident peers; and the third, Norreys Bertie, was member of Parliament for the county. Despite the inclusion of these men on his list, Marlborough might still claim that the list revealed the presence of a Whig party in Oxfordshire, of a party whose principles inspired its adherents to action which differentiated them from the Tories. While only one gentleman on the Tory list joined the association against the Pretender in 1745, two of the five aristocrats and twelve of the twenty non-aristocrats on the Marlborough list had subscribed to the county's association. Unfortunately for the Whigs, subscription was not so clearly a mark of total commitment to Whiggery as nonsubscription was a symptom of Tory sympathies. In 1754, two of the subscribers and another two nonsubscribers voted for the Tories, while only five of the subscribers and one of the nonsubscribers voted for the Whigs. It may be that Oxfordshire's bench was already graced by so many of the county's Whigs that the duke had difficulty discovering staunch party adherents who were not already justices. Hardwicke evidently felt the need for both further advice and more Whig justices. The lists were sent to Lord Harcourt, a rabidly Whig peer resident in Oxfordshire, but the response was not particularly promising: "I wish I could assist his Grace in making out a list that might not be liable to any exceptions. But I fear that would be a medlor undertaking, and that we should not have active Justices sufficient to dispatch the common busyness of the County." Harcourt recommended five more gentlemen, all of whom Marlborough found "proper persons."[33] Yet, Harcourt had good reason to entertain doubts: in 1754, one of his nominees would support the Whigs and two the Tories. Analyses of the politics of the reigns of the first two Hanoverians have usually ascribed the disappearance of party to attrition in the Tory ranks. In the Oxfordshire of 1745, even Whig actions attest to Tory strength, and when in 1754 Marlborough carried the Whig standard into electoral battle, the county reverberated with party contest.

33. B.L., Add. MSS 35602, f. 128, Harcourt to [Hardwicke], Sept. 15, 1745; f. 130; f. 134, Marlborough to Hardwicke, Sept. 19, 1745. Besides the Harcourt nominees and those on the Whig and Tory lists, the fiat (P.R.O., C234/30, Sept. 21, 1745) lists three gentlemen of unknown sponsorship plus the non-associating gentleman inserted in the Jacobite's place.

In Hampshire, the appointment of the justices of 1745 again reveals the presence of two distinct party groupings. Most probably, Hampshire's inclusion in the list of six counties can be attributed to the local and parliamentary influence of its Lord Lieutenant and custos rotulorum—Charles, Duke of Bolton. As an opposition Whig, Bolton had been stripped of his offices in 1733 and reinstated upon the alliance of opposition Whigs and Pelhamites in 1742. Even before the 1745 treaty was negotiated, Bolton had been urging the renewal of Hampshire's commission, and when the list of new justices appeared, it included all eight of Bolton's nominees.[34] Three of Bolton's candidates can be identified as adherents of the Walpoleian or opposition Whigs.[35] Also inscribed upon the new commission were the names of one aristocrat and six gentlemen which had been culled from a list of seventeen that had not been written by Bolton.[36] The list of seventeen may, therefore, be that submitted by Hampshire's Tories. Six of the seventeen were Tory members of Parliament; Hardwicke doubted whether a seventh was "a proper Person," and an eighth would in 1749 be labelled "formerly a Tory tho' no Jacobite" and then appointed to the commission.[37] Yet, the list is neither an unadulterated honour roll of Hampshire's Tories nor a martyrology of judicial exclusion. Two of the Tory members of Parliament were already justices; so were three other gentlemen, two of whom were Whigs.[38] After carefully inspecting the list, Hardwicke selected the aristocrat, the four remaining members of Parliament, and two gentlemen against whom no objections were recorded, added the heir of a dead justice and two aristocratic grandees, and issued the new commission. In balancing eight Whigs against seven Tories, the new commission reflected the presence of party in Hampshire. In submitting a list which revealed lack of complete knowledge of their nominees' political predilections and local office, the Tories exposed the weakness which made Hampshire a Whig county.

Like Hampshire, each of the remaining four counties was a stronghold of a prominent member of the opposition. Since Hampshire's opposition leader had not joined forces with his county's Tories, the

34. B.L., Add. MSS 35602, f. 36, Bolton to Hardwicke, Feb. 14, 1744[5]; f. 136, Sept. 19, 1745.

35. George Anson, Thomas Knollys, Hon. Robert Fairfax.

36. B.L., Add. MSS 35602, f. 124; P.R.O., C234/14, Sept. 16, 1745.

37. John Popham. B.L., Add. MSS 35603, f. 143, Earl of Portsmouth to Hardwicke, Feb. 20, 1748[9]; P.R.O., C234/14, June 12, 1749.

38. Francis Whithead, Richard Mill.

nomination of justices in 1745 provides evidence both of a Tory party independent of a county potentate and of a past policy of exclusion of prominent Tories from the bench. Since opposition leaders were more intimately connected with local Toryism in the remaining counties, it is more difficult to determine whether a list of nominees represents local interest or local party. Nonetheless, the negotiations over these commissions reflect Tory opinion that the bench had been unjustifiably barred to gentlemen whose only offence was political affiliation. Herefordshire and Bedfordshire are cases in point.

There is no difficulty in determining why Herefordshire was one of the chosen six. In April 1745, the Earl of Chesterfield had advised the Pelhams that "little things, and . . . prudent things . . . would . . . strip this new opposition of Watkin Williams [Wynn], and Lord Oxford, the only people to be regarded in it." Lord Oxford reigned in Herefordshire. In July, Hardwicke received lists of nominees from Oxford and from Mr. Westphaling, a Whig, and only at this juncture did he contact Sir Charles Hanbury Williams, the county's Lord Lieutenant and custos rotulorum. Oxford had informed Hardwicke that his nominees were either the heirs of dead justices or "Gentlemen of Estates in their Several Hundreds who are very proper to be in Commission," and Hardwicke, knowing that Oxford's list would rouse objection, yet wishing to avoid battle, echoed Oxford's assurance. Sir Charles was not mollified: "You do me a great deal of honour, My Lord, in communicating the two Lists that have been offer'd to your Lordship. I have the honour to be Custos Rotulorum of that County but as yet I protest to you no application has ever been made to me for a new commission and however insignificant I may in myself be yet the dignity of the Kings Commission shall never suffer in my hands and therefore I must say that I know of no occasion at all for a new Commission." Westphaling's list was irreproachable, but: "There are some on the other that have with me (who think this constitution and the Hanover family so blended that the ruin of the one involves the other in the same destruction) great exception to their being trusted with any Authority under King George. Tis disagreeable to mention Names, but I will say that The Reverend Dr. Coningsby notwithstanding the Gown he wears, and the oaths he has taken deserves no trust from his Majesty, he having formerly preached Sermons full of Sedition and Treason instead of Morality and divinity." Sir Charles named no more names, but contented himself with damning the list entire.

Hardwicke had now to perform his usual role as arbitrator between two outraged dignitaries. Sir Charles's sentiments were communicated to Oxford, who asked for the details of the charge against Coningsby, and then with one fell blow preserved the rest of his list: "Your Lordship will be pleased to remember that a Lieutenant's Negative without reasons from him to support it, was one of the Grievances which the Country Gentlemen complained of." Oxford also thought it timely to recommend another gentleman, the secretary to the Dean of Lichfield. Coningsby was not appointed; the rest of the Oxford list—five aristocrats, one cleric, and twenty-two gentlemen—became justices of Herefordshire. Westphaling's ten nominees, the Lord Lieutenant himself and his one nominee, one gentleman recommended by a Mr. Price—a guaranteed Whig—and two more of unknown sponsorship brought the total of new justices to forty-three.[39]

It cannot be automatically assumed that all of Oxford's nominees were strict Tories: one gentleman had been recommended by the Whig Mr. Price and two of the aristocrats, both administration supporters, by Sir Charles. As Oxford assumed the duties of Lord Lieutenant and custos rotulorum in these negotiations—to the extent of performing the custos' function of forwarding lists of dead justices to the Crown Office—it may be that he had also played the role of Lieutenant and custos and submitted a list not totally partisan. Yet, it would appear that at least one participant in the Herefordshire negotiations had been able to distinguish Whig from Tory.

Similarly, at least one magnate would have had little doubt that the majority of Bedfordshire's new justices were Tories joined in an unholy alliance to the Duke of Bedford. The Duke of Bedford, appointed Lord Lieutenant and custos of the county of Bedford in April 1745,[40] was an opposition Whig and one of the leaders of the opposition group that had concluded the treaty of April 1745 with the Pelhamites.[41] When the county's commission had last been renewed in 1738, Bedford had attempted to elevate nine gentlemen to the bench. His stratagem had been effectively countered. The Duke of Kent, then the county's Lord Lieutenant and custos, had stormed into the office

39. B.L., Add. MSS 32804, f. 291, Chesterfield to Newcastle, Apr. 13, 1745, N.S.; Add. MSS 35602, f. 116, Westphaling's list and f. 101, Oxford's list; f. 97, Oxford to Hardwicke, July 9, 1745; ff. 99–100, Herefordshire commission of 1736, with dead noted; f. 102, draft of letter from Hardwicke to Sir Charles Hanbury Williams, July 13, 1745; ff. 108–109, Sir Charles Hanbury Williams to Hardwicke, July 19, 1745; ff. 114–115, Earl of Oxford to Hardwicke, Aug. 13, 1745; f. 118, Price's list; P.R.O., C234/15, Aug. 9, 1745.

40. B.L., Add. MSS 35602, f. 59.

41. B.L., Add. MSS 32993, f. 304.

of Hardwicke's secretary, charging that "most of all these Gentlemen were Tories and Jacobites. . . . That if those Gentlemen (Chernock and Napier) were put in it would loose the Elections and putt all the County in a Flame," and that if they were put in he would not act as Lord Lieutenant. Direct evidence of appointment in 1738 is missing. Yet, examination of later lists of the commission reveals that it is entirely probable that only the two Bedford nominees who were already in Kent's list and the one baronet whom Kent found acceptable were appointed to the commission.[42] In 1745, Bedford again nominated four of the six rejects of 1738, including Sir Boteler Chernock, Bart., and Sir John Napier, Bart. Both of the baronets appeared on the commission of 1745; the remaining two gentlemen did not, and neither did eight other gentlemen whom Hardwicke eliminated from the duke's 1745 list. Nonetheless, the duke's twenty-four successful candidates included four Tory members of Parliament, and the father of another Tory member of Parliament. Evidence of affiliation with the Pelhamite Whigs tainted just one of the duke's nominees: in 1746 the Hon. John Trevor would be returned to Parliament on the Duke of Marlborough's interest and would support the government. Only one of Bedford's thirty-four nominees was the heir of a justice who had died after the issue of the last commission; so were two of the six gentlemen not on Bedford's list who became justices in 1745.[43] In Bedfordshire, gentlemen of "Figure and Fortune" adhering to the Duke of Bedford and/or to the Tories had been excluded from the commission, and the 1745 treaty had been necessary to secure their appointment.

The 1745 nominations for Cambridgeshire again reveal a past policy of the omission of Tories from the group of gentlemen considered eligible for judicial office and also introduce evidence of the status of those excluded. Sir John Hynde Cotton, Cambridgeshire's knight of the shire from 1722 to 1727 and a Tory leader who had joined the government in 1744, had been removed from the county's commission in 1726 and never reinstated. On March 24, 1745, Cotton submitted a list of fifteen candidates for Cambridgeshire's commission, including himself and his son. Hardwicke apparently vetoed the appointment of the two clerics on the list; as Hardwicke noted, appointment of the attorney on the Cotton list would violate the provisions of the 1745

42. B.L., Add. MSS 35604, ff. 338, 339, 343, 346, 348.
43. B.L., Add. MSS 35602, ff. 104–105; P.R.O., C234/1, July 12, 1745.

act for the further qualification of justices of the peace, while appointment of the one gentleman on the list who was already a justice would clearly have been superfluous.[44] All of the eleven remaining nominees became justices of the peace of Cambridgeshire.

All of these nominees were regarded as Tories in Cotton's interest. As one of Hardwicke's informants remarked, most of Cotton's candidates had served on Cambridgeshire's grand jury at the Summer Assizes of 1742, a grand jury headed by Sir John himself. Only ten of those summoned to that jury were accorded the rank of esquire, and nine of the ten esquires appeared on the Cotton list. Tory solidarity was matched by Whig. The leaders of Cambridgeshire's Whig interest had agreed "not to add any of our Friends to the Commission and to Use that as an Argument for not putting in more of Sir John Cotton's list than the Number . . . fixt upon."[45]

As Lord Chancellor and as a newly established member of Cambridgeshire's Whigs, Hardwicke had also thought it necessary to investigate thoroughly the status of the Cotton nominees. The status of two—Sir John and his son of the same name—he knew only too well. A Mr. "St. L." reported on five of the remaining nine. Two had estates of £1,000 per annum; one an estate of £500 per annum, one of £600 per annum, and one an estate near Hagginton of "about £300 per annum but is reputed to have other estates elsewhere."[46] In 1745, gentlemen of "Fortune and Estate, well affected to His Majesty's Government" and members of a Tory group excluded from the commission became justices of Cambridgeshire.

Somewhat paradoxically, the available information on the effect of the negotiations of 1745 on Gloucestershire's commission is both more complete and more fragmentary than that for the other counties. Though Hardwicke's papers do not yield information on the party allegiance of all the nominees, the tale of the Gloucestershire appointments both illustrates Hardwicke's use of his office and furnishes clues to a riddle so far unexamined—the relation between the Tories of 1745 and those of 1714.

The story told in the Hardwicke papers begins in 1739 with the issue of a new commission for the county. Augustus, Earl of Berkeley,

44. B.L., Add. MSS 35602, ff. 47, 89.

45. B.L., Add. MSS 35601, ff. 109–110; Add. MSS 35602, f. 87; f. 79, Montford to Hardwicke, June 19, 1745; f. 85, Same to Same, June 21, 1745. Nevertheless, the recorder of Cambridge, a Whig, managed to insinuate himself into the new commission, as did one baronet whose sponsor is unknown (P.R.O., C234/4, Oct. 8, 1745).

46. B.L., Add. MSS 35602, f. 87.

Lord Lieutenant and custos rotulorum of Gloucestershire, was head of the county's Whig interest. Yet, when a new commission was requested Hardwicke consulted Sir John Dutton, former Whig member of Parliament for Gloucestershire. According to Dutton, justices were wanted in Berkeley hundred—the earl's territory. Issue of a new commission adding Whig justices who would act in that region only—for only there was there a shortage—"would be of great consequence in the next Election for this county." Dutton thereupon persuaded Berkeley to apply for a new commission, never disclosing that he had previously been in communication with Hardwicke or that he had requested that Hardwicke send him Berkeley's list so he could inspect it. After examination of Berkeley's nominees, Gloucestershire's Whigs concluded that several were "improper Persons" who would "give a bad turn to our affairs," especially in the forthcoming election. In the event, it was Dutton who forwarded the list of nominees on which the new commission was based.[47]

The first threat to this eminently satisfactory working alliance appeared when Lord Bathurst stepped on stage in 1742. A member of the Whig opposition grouped round Pulteney, Bathurst had accepted office when Pulteney had joined the ministry, and, as Hardwicke informed Dutton, "as my Lord is now come to Court . . . he will expect some Regard to be shown him in the County." It would be advisable, Hardwicke counseled, to confer with Lord Bathurst and to reach an agreement that would prevent future difficulties. As Hardwicke had predicted, Bathurst galloped over one day in October to consult Dutton about a new commission, sat down for breakfast, and pulled a list of nominees from his pocket. "In that list," wrote Dutton, "there was not one Person who would not . . . apply to the Prejudice of the King, as farr as he was able, the Powers with which that Commission would have invested him; . . . Many of them also are Persons who are not entitled to such a Trust for their Rank, Fortune, or Capacities, so that this List can be calculated only for impropper Purposes." Dutton's action had been decisive: "I have prepared my Lord Berkeley to put a negative upon a New Commission."[48] No commission was issued.

47. B.L., Add. MSS 35586, f. 163, Dutton to Hardwicke, Apr. 28, 1739; f. 165, Same to Same, May 12, 1739; Gloucestershire R.O., Sherborne MSS, D678, Fam Sett 57/D, Robert Tracy to [Dutton], Nov. 24, 1739; Lord Ducie to Sir John Dutton, Sept. 1, 1739; W. Young to Dutton, Jan. 19, 1739 [1740]; B.L., Add. MSS 35600, f. 244; f. 220; ff. 235–236, Dutton to Hardwicke, Jan. 16, 1739[40]; f. 242, Same to Same, Jan. 25, 1739[40]; P.R.O., C234/13, Jan. 16, 1739[40].

48. B.L., Add. MSS 35601, f. 128, draft letter by Hardwicke, Aug. 26, 1742; ff. 145–146, Sir John Dutton to Hardwicke, Oct. 18, 1742.

Yet, rumours of impending renewal continued to circulate. In April 1744, one agitated gentleman reported that the Tories of the county were confident of installation, and continued: "I must beg leave to declare for one, that the general Notion, which prevail'd upon Lord Orford going out, of uniting all Parties under the cant Term of broad bottom is to me absurd and ridiculous." By December, the Earl of Berkeley had been persuaded to apply for the renewal of the commission.[49] Negotiations for a new commission were almost certainly in progress in early 1745, and since the Earl of Beaufort had at one point been entrusted with the negotiations for the justices' treaty by the opposition, it may have been his desire to increase his influence in his county that caused Gloucestershire to be included in the list of six.[50]

Once the county had been chosen, seemingly everyone recommended candidates. Surviving lists, fragments of lists, and extracts from lists evidence that the Earl of Berkeley submitted a list, Norborne Berkeley—Tory knight of the shire—submitted a list, and Thomas Chester—Gloucestershire's second and Tory knight—submitted at least two lists. Hardwicke investigated lists, correlated lists, produced lists of names "on Mr. Berkeley's list and Not Mr. Chester's," of "further names from Mr. Chester's list" and of "persons named in both lists"—leaving it unclear as to which lists the "both" referred.[51] Dutton had died in 1743, but Hardwicke evidently found someone else willing to comment—though briefly and ineffectually—on the nominees.[52] Of the sixty-four added to Gloucestershire's commission, it is possible to identify the sponsors of forty. At least thirty-four had been nominated by Thomas Chester and Norborne Berkeley. Fourteen of this group of thirty-four had also been sponsored by the Earl of Berkeley, who had at the same time nominated another six of the new justices. Further analysis of these lists in terms of party allegiance is, at present, impossible.

Further investigation of the lists in terms of the relation between the nominees of 1745 and those ejected by Cowper and Macclesfield is

49. B.L., Add. MSS 35601, f. 317, Mr. Robert Tracy to Hardwicke, Apr. 25, 1744; f. 332, Earl of Berkeley to Hardwicke, Dec. 5, 1744.

50. B.L., Add. MSS 35602, f. 46, March 20, 1744[5], and f. 56 which may be the paper of the names of six counties delivered by Beaufort on March 20. The only county in this list which appears in the list of counties finally chosen is Gloucestershire. Add. MSS 32804, ff. 286–287, Duke of Newcastle to Earl of Chesterfield, March 26, 1745; W. S. Lewis, ed., *Horace Walpole Correspondence,* vol. 19 (New Haven, 1954), p. 26, Horace Walpole to Sir Horace Mann, Mar. 29, 1745.

51. B.L., Add. MSS 35601, ff. 321, 334–335, 341, 338, 339.

52. B.L., Add. MSS 35601, f. 337.

more illuminating. Forty-eight families lost their place on the bench at some time during the reign of George I due to the excision from the commission of a justice alive at the time of his removal.[53] Another fourteen families probably suffered the indignity of the dismissal of a justice, but neither the order for removal nor Gloucestershire's county histories disclose whether these fourteen justices were dead or alive when their names were omitted from the commission. Of the fourteen families represented by those who may or may not have been ousted from the commission, four had been restored to judicial rank before 1745. Of the forty-eight families represented by those known to have been alive when removed, eight obtained a place on the bench before 1745. In 1745, these forty-eight families were again represented; four of the new justices were direct heirs of three families who had lost judicial seats in the reign of George I and had never been reinstated, and one more justice headed a family whose representative had been omitted and subsequently restored. There was, therefore, a tenuous connection, but nevertheless a connection, between Gloucestershire's sixty-four new justices and those removed from the bench by Cowper and Macclesfield.

But, what had happened to the families whose representatives were omitted in George I's reign and were not restored to the bench before 1745 or in 1745? Thanks to Thomas Chester, Gloucestershire's Tory knight of the shire, surmise is possible for the county of Gloucester. Chester had initiated his campaign for capture of the Gloucestershire bench by submitting a lengthy list entitled "Names of Gentlemen not in the Commission of Peace for Gloucester with their Places of Aboad." Of the fifty-one non-aristocrats on this list, twenty-one appear on Gloucestershire's commission for 1745.[54] Three of the successful twenty-one are descendants of those removed by Cowper and Macclesfield; so are eleven of the unsuccessful thirty.[55] At least some of the families ejected in the days of Whig triumph and not since restored could still put forward claims to local eminence. That the claims of a majority of these families could be ignored in 1745 and that only 24

53. This and all further calculations of the number of families which lost their representatives on the bench in the reign of George I do not include those justices who were removed but had a father, son, or brother still in the commission at the date of their removal.

54. B.L., Add. MSS 35601, ff. 334–335. This enumeration omits the gentleman already on the commission.

55. One of the successful three represents a family restored to the bench before 1745, as do two of the unsuccessful eleven.

percent of the families omitted in George I's reign recovered seats upon the bench by 1745 may be substantiation of the Whig claim that Harcourt had found his justices among the lesser gentry. That the nominees of Tory lineage were considered unsuitable by Hardwicke is indicative of the tenacity of the Tory faith in the provinces.

The existence of a link, however tenuous, between the appointees of 1745 and the ejections of 1714 to 1727 is evidenced in Oxfordshire, Bedfordshire, Cambridgeshire, and Hampshire. (See table 2.)

In the examination of the 1745 appointments to the Oxfordshire, Gloucestershire, Cambridgeshire, and Hampshire commissions, it was possible to identify some lists as Tory. All those noted in table 2 as representing families omitted during the reign of George I and restored in 1745 appear on the Tory lists for Oxfordshire, Cambridgeshire, and Hampshire. Three of the five justices representing Gloucestershire families omitted during George I's reign appear on the Tory list, and the sponsor of the two other justices cannot be identified. Perhaps the political location of Bedford as a county magnate enlisting Tories among his followers is reinforced by the information that every one of the five Bedfordshire justices representing families restored in 1745 was nominated by the Duke of Bedford.

Analysis of Herefordshire's 1745 appointees in terms of the justices eliminated in George I's reign presents a very different problem. Perhaps the difference can be attributed to the Tory faith of almost every leading family in the county. Or, perhaps it should be attributed to the quixotic Thomas, Lord Coningsby, Lord Lieutenant and custos rotulorum of the counties of Radnor and Hereford. It appears that my Lord Coningsby was enthusiastic in recommending the removal of justices from the Herefordshire and Radnorshire commissions, and that, by 1720, both the Lord Chancellor and the Lords Justices of England had begun to question the perspicacity of his political judgment. In 1720, he was informed that several of those removed from Radnorshire's commission on his recommendation would be restored: they had had "a very good character . . . given of them by a very impartiall person."[56] In 1721, Lord Coningsby was replaced as Lord Lieutenant and custos of the counties of Herefordshire and Radnorshire; in 1724, he was removed from Herefordshire's commission by

56. Public Record Office of Northern Ireland, D638/85/1, Lord Chancellor Parker to Coningsby, July 28, 1720. See also T1135/18, Lord Coningsby to Lord Chancellor Parker, Jan. 7, 1720–1721.

TABLE 2 APPOINTMENT OF JUSTICES REPRESENTING FAMILIES REMOVED FROM THE BENCH DURING THE REIGN OF GEORGE I, 1714–1727[a]

County	*Removed, known alive*	*Restored pre-1745*	*Restored 1745*	*Removed, not known if alive*	*Restored pre-1745*	*Restored 1745*
Bedfordshire	27	6	5	6	1	0
Cambridgeshire	16	3	2	5	0	0
Gloucestershire	48	8	3 (1)	14	4	0
Hampshire	22	3	0	9	1	1
Oxfordshire[b]	23	5	1 (1)			

a. Unlike table 1, this table notes all justices removed, whether restored by the Lord Chancellor who removed them or not. Again, unlike table 1, this table does not note a justice whose father, son, or brother remained on the commission when the justice was removed. Similarly, if more than one representative of a single family was placed on the bench in 1745, the table records the reinstatement of one family, and not the multiple reinstatement of justices. The figures in parentheses represent justices whose families had been omitted and then restored before 1745 and who had another representative put on the bench in 1745.

b. As in table 1, the total of Oxfordshire removals is restricted to those removed by Cowper.

order of the Privy Council, and by 1727 there was some reason to doubt his sanity.[57]

Coningsby's actions were, at the least, politically inept. Among those he ousted was the Earl of Oxford, and in 1721 the earl was opining that, since those removed "had been unjustly marked out by what They called a brand of infamy," they "should so far reverence themselves as not to be restored again but together." This unity would best be demonstrated at "Elections . . . and wil [sic] render them so considerable that it wil be a Stated united Interest upon all other occasions for the Good of the County. . . ." Herefordshire's new Lord Lieutenant and custos, the Duke of Chandos, promptly moved the Lord Chancellor to restore almost all of those his predecessor had removed from the commission, "taking it for granted that they were wrongfully displaced."[58] Their brief vacation from the burdens of judicial office may have actually strengthened the cohesion of Here-

57. B.L., Add. MSS 35585, f. 68, Clerk of Peace of Herefordshire to Duke of Chandos, July 3, 1727; f. 70; P.R.O., C234/15.

58. University of Nottingham Lib., Pw 2 Hy929, Oxford to [Foley], Dec. 21, 1721; Huntington Lib., ST. 57, vol. 19, pp. 142–143, Chandos to Henning, July 27, 1721; vol. 18, pp. 311–312, Same to Same, Oct. 2, 1721; vol. 26, pp. 345–346, Chandos to Davis, Sept. 26, 1725; P.R.O., C234/15, Jan. 12, 1721[2].

fordshire's Tories. Even those few who were excised after Chandos gained office were soon reinstated.

Since the families of all but one of the twenty-three gentlemen removed from Herefordshire's commission at some time during George I's reign regained their judicial status,[59] it is not to be expected that the Herefordshire nominees of 1745 would bear the same relation to justices removed during the reign of George I as the nominees of the other five counties. Fourteen of the twenty-three families omitted from Herefordshire's commision in the reign of George I would have had representatives on the bench even if the commission had not been renewed in 1745. In the other five counties, only one-third or less of the families purged from the commission had managed to return to the bench, and not all of these families were represented on the 1745 commission. Of Herefordshire's nominees in 1745, three were of families removed during George I's reign and subsequently restored. All three had been sponsored by the Earl of Oxford.

Since the parliamentary Tories who negotiated the agreement of 1745 thought that it would allow leaders of county groups allied to the Tories to place their adherents on the bench, it would seem logical to categorize some of the 1745 nominees as Tories. Since there seems to be a connection between those appointees whom other evidence indicates are Tories, and the justices excluded by Cowper and Macclesfield, it would seem logical to posit the survival of Tory party groups at the county level for at least thirty years after the accession of the first Hanoverian. Indeed, the historical casuist can convert the rather slender thread of group continuity revealed by the evidence of justices' appointments into a double-edged logician's sword: since by far the greater portion of the Tory nominees were not descendants of those excluded in George I's reign, it can be argued that Toryism continued to thrive in the counties; since the purges of 1714 to 1727 did not wipe all Tories from the bench, and since some of the 1745 nominees were heirs of justices whose families had simply ceased to be represented on the bench when the justice died,[60] it can be argued that

59. For the method of calculating the number of those removed from Herefordshire's commission, see chapter III, n. 68. Table 1 in chapter III enumerates only those justices who were removed from the commission and not restored by the Lord Chancellor who had removed them. This numeration of the justices removed from Herefordshire's commission includes all justices who were removed, whether they were restored by the Lord Chancellor who first removed them or not.

60. Detailed comparison of the 1745 nominees to lists of those left out of the commission because of death and not replaced by successors nine or more years prior to 1745 has proven impossible, as fiats are missing and as some fiats simply list the new commission and do not list the names of those omitted as dead. At least one Bedford-

the connection between the Tories of 1714 and 1745 is less apparent than real; since the case of Herefordshire proves that gentlemen who were suspected of harbouring fervent Tory views could remain on the bench in the days of George I and continue to wield influence in the days of George II, it can be argued that, in 1745, the Tory parties in the counties still posed a real threat to the maintenance of Whig hegemony. The very label 'Whig hegemony' may cover a political situation less stable than the term implies. When Hardwicke sat in his study and examined lists of nominees to the commissions, when he entered into lengthy correspondence simply to ascertain the politics of the nominees, when he conducted tedious negotiations about the appointment of a few justices of uncertain or inimical political allegiance, he did not consider that he was fighting a chimera. The evidence of the justices' negotiations of 1745 would at least suggest that—to rework Butterfield's phrase—the thing he thought he was fighting was what he was fighting: the Tory groups—parties or party if you will—in the counties.[61]

3. LORD CHANCELLOR HARDWICKE AND THE ATTENUATION OF TIES BETWEEN PARTY AND THE LOCAL BENCH

In 1745, as a result of a treaty specifying that "distinction of parties" ought not to affect the appointment of justices, justices were placed upon the bench because of their affiliation to party: Tories were appointed because they were Tories and Whigs because they were Whigs. In 1745, the justice was a symbol of party. Nonetheless, during Hardwicke's tenure of office the tie between party and the bench gradually became attenuated. As the appointment of justices in the decade after 1745 reveals, attenuation was in part a consequence of the etiolation of the Tory party and the partial disintegration of the Whigs. In part, attenuation can also be credited to Lord Chancellor Hardwicke. In elaborating a set of criteria and procedures for the

---

shire, two Gloucestershire, four Herefordshire, two Cambridgeshire, and three Oxfordshire appointees were apparently successors of justices left out as "dead" nine or more years prior to 1745. All of these Bedfordshire, Cambridgeshire, and Herefordshire appointees appear on the Tory lists. Two of the three Oxfordshire appointees appear on the Tory list. Both the Gloucestershire appointees were nominated by Mr. Chester, Tory member of Parliament for the county.

61. H. Butterfield, *George III and the Historians,* rev. ed. (New York, 1959), p. 228.

dismissal of justices, Hardwicke removed much of the tarnish of political jobbery from the justices' image. According to the Tories, justices should not represent party; instead they should, like the judges, symbolize the impartiality of the law. Somewhat paradoxically, the policies of the Whig Lord Chancellor heightened the resemblance between justice and judge.

Above all, the glorious revolutionaries had declared, judges should be disinterested. The value of an apparently disinterested judiciary became increasingly evident in the course of the eighteenth century. When neither the majesty of the Crown nor the mystery of the church roused sufficient awe to legitimize the structure of England's government, eighteenth-century Englishmen perceived that their rulers derived their ultimate sanction from English law, and forthwith the sovereign's judges became the vestal virgins of law's sacred temple. Judges were to be above politics, free from the control of the sovereign or the sovereign's ministers. Under James II judges had been removable at the pleasure of the monarch, and it had been James's pleasure to remove those judges who disagreed with his interpretation of English law. William III thought it politic to appoint his judges on terms which guaranteed that they could be removed for misconduct only and, in 1701, Parliament ordained that judges appointed after Anne's death could be dismissed only for misconduct proven in a trial before Parliament. Once lions under the throne, judges were now servants of the law.

Unlike the judges, the justices were still removable at the pleasure of the sovereign, and as the Lord Chancellor exercised control of the commission for the sovereign, Lord Chancellors had interpreted the sovereign's pleasure. It was Hardwicke's interpretation of the sovereign's pleasure that justices, like judges, should be dismissed only for opprobrious conduct. Through the implementation of his policy on the dismissal of justices, Hardwicke separated the office of justice from politics.

When Hardwicke became Lord Chancellor it was not commonly assumed that the era of partisan purges of the bench had passed. King, Lord Chancellor from 1726 to 1733, had excised a few opponents of the ministry from the commissions, and when Talbot became Lord Chancellor in 1733, some hoped that his appointment signalled a remodelling of the commissions.[62] When Hardwicke gained the seals in

62. Kent A.O., U269/C148/42, Sir Basil Dixwell to the Duke of Dorset, Dec. 19, 1733.

1737, he was presented with a request for the elimination of justices. The Archbishop of York submitted a list of justices for the liberty of Ripon which omitted several then on the bench. Hardwicke must have requested an explanation, for Mr. Hayter, writing for the archbishop replied: "As to the Justices omitted tho' Stil living, the Reason of omitting them was either that they have never acted, or live at too great a distance, or have distinguish'd themselves in Support of an Interest which his Grace hath ever thought it his Duty to oppose in Every Shape. But he is Sensible this Political Consideration cannot be properly alleged as an objection in Form." There is no evidence that any justices were erased from Ripon's commission.[63] Hardwicke's policy would make removal from the bench an apolitical censure.

The usual method of removing a justice was simply the omission of the justice's name from the commission on its renewal. Commissions were inscribed by the clerks of the Crown Office, and the Lord Chancellor informed the clerks of the alterations that the new commission would make to the preceding commission by a fiat—an instruction—signed by the Lord Chancellor listing either all members of the new commission or those to be added to and eliminated from the preceding commission. Before 1733, the fiats did not always distinguish justices to be omitted because of their death from living justices ousted from the bench. After 1733, fiats which listed the names of those eliminated almost always specified whether these former justices were now dead or alive. Since those fiats which list the entire commission did not specify omissions, the fiats provide a guide to removals rather than a record of all removals; since the vast majority of fiats are instructions to change the commission rather than a list of the commission, the fiats constitute a reasonably accurate index of the frequency of removal.

According to the fiats, which survive for all counties but Middlesex, in his twenty years in office Hardwicke ordered that a total of twenty-two justices be deprived of their place on the bench of thirteen counties when their commissions were renewed.[64] Little evidence of the reasons for the dismissal of these justices survives in Hardwicke's papers, but what record there is suggests that removal by omission followed upon the Lord Chancellor's cognizance of gross misconduct or abuse of office. When in 1738 Hardwicke removed seventy-five

63. B.L., Add. MSS 35586, f. 23, T. Hayter to [Hardwicke's secretary or secretary of commissions], June 11, 1737; P.R.O., C234/96, June 13, 1737.

64. P.R.O., C234/1–22, 26–44, 78–90. These fiats exclude Lancashire, for the Chancellor of the Duchy of Lancaster appointed that county's justices.

justices from the Middlesex bench, the *Gentleman's Magazine* celebrated the action with a suitable tribute.

Full 75 turn'd out—a handsome Drench
Tho' much too late. Sure this will purge the Bench.
Informers now may find th' Employment bad
And Justice may from Justices be had.
So surely did the trading Harpies roast us,
We suffer'd less by Spanish Guarda Costa's.
O Liberty! defend these harras'd Nations
From Foreign and Domestic Depradations.[65]

The vices of the seventy-five are not chronicled in the Hardwicke papers, but those of justices whose removal was recommended to Hardwicke in the 1740s included: setting up "shop" as a justice, debt, imprisoning for pleasure and at will, irregular licensing of alehouses, taking bribes from gaming and bawdy houses, extorting money under the cover of office, and smuggling. The justices so accused were almost certainly removed.[66]

Of course, it is quite possible that motives other than the pursuit of justice prompted Englishmen to complain of the actions of certain justices to the Lord Chancellor; nonetheless, there is no evidence in Hardwicke's papers that he ever removed a justice simply because that justice favoured a party hostile to the ministry. There is evidence that he did not dismiss justices against whom no objection was alleged but that of their political affiliations. When, in 1740, five justices of Cardiganshire learned of "publick and repeated Declarations" by some gentlemen that they would be removed from the commission, they protested to the Lord Chancellor: the application for their removal could not be grounded upon "the least pretense of Misbehaviour unless the right and Independency we now Claim of Choosing our Representatives to Parliament may be Deem'd Criminal." The justices remained on Cardiganshire's bench.[67] When Hardwicke refused to use renewal of the commission to rid the bench of political opponents, he

65. *Gentleman's Magazine* 8 (August 31, 1738):435.

66. B.L., Add. MSS 35604, f. 366; Add. MSS 35601, ff. 260–262, "A True Account of some Justices of the Peace" (reprinted with the more salacious passages expurgated in C. Harris, *The Life of Lord Chancellor Hardwicke* [London, 1847], vol. 1, pp. 390–391); P.R.O., C234/25, Dec. 12, 1743; B.L., Add. MSS 35603, ff. 300–301, "Petition of Henry Broadhead"; A. Babington, *A House in Bow Street: Crime and the Magistracy* (London, 1969), p. 60.

67. B.L., Add. MSS 35600, f. 265, Thomas Powell, Thomas Lloyd, James Lewes, Richard Stedman, John Lloyd to Hardwicke, Nov. 25, 1740; P.R.O., C234/80, Feb. 5, 1740[1].

contributed to change in the justices' image. Like the judges, justices now held office for life. By 1745 one magnate was observing: "when a Justice of Peace is once in the Commission there is no getting him out again."[68]

Hardwicke indeed devised a new procedure to get a few select justices out, but this procedure served to emphasize the justices' role as servants of the law. The new procedure distinguished those justices whose conduct was merely reprehensible from those whose conduct was vile. The former Hardwicke omitted from the commissions on their renewal. The latter had to be removed from the bench immediately, and renewal of the commission no longer afforded the opportunity for immediate removal. During Anne's reign, the average English and Welsh county had received a new commission about once every fifteen months. When Hardwicke became Lord Chancellor, the interval between renewals of a commission had increased to about three years.[69] To censure promptly and publicly those justices totally unfit for public trust, Hardwicke invented a new procedure for the dismissal of justices.

Hardwicke based his new procedure on the writ of *supersedeas*. In his capacity as premier judge of the court of Chancery, the Lord Chancellor could issue a writ of *supersedeas,* ordering the justice to cease executing his office. The *supersedeas* could be superseded by a writ of *procedendo,* again at the order of the Lord Chancellor, and issued, like the *supersedeas,* through the court of Chancery. Lambard, writing in the sixteenth century, cited the *supersedeas* as the only method of suspending a justice other than removal from the commission,[70] and the device was still in use in the eighteenth century. In 1732, Lord Chancellor King suspended Justice Midford after the constables of St. Giles, Middlesex, had presented a petition against his "illegal practices," and after a formal hearing of the case. (Midford, restored to active duty within ten months of his suspension, continued in his office until removed from the commission by Hardwicke, when he turned to management of a gaming house.[71])

68. B.L., Add. MSS 35602, ff. 71–72, Lord Malton to Hardwicke, June 15, 1745.

69. This calculation is based on P.R.O., Index 4216, 4217. Durham has been omitted from the calculation as a new commission for that county was issued annually and conjointly with that for gaol delivery.

70. W. Lambarde, *Eirenarcha: or of the Office of the Justices of Peace* (London, 1594), pp. 74–75.

71. *Grub Street Journal,* April 6, 1732, no. 118; B.L., Add. MSS 35604, f. 382; P.R.O., SP 44/85, f. 18, Thomas Burdus to Secretary of State, Bow St., Covent Garden, Nov. 3, 1747.

Records of the writs of *supersedeas* issued by Hardwicke's predecessors would be kept by the six clerks in Chancery. In 1737, records of the issue of writs of *supersedeas* begin to form a portion of the records of the Crown Office.[72] It is evident that these writs are of a different order from those issued by the court. Writs issued from the Crown Office removed a justice from the commission permanently; the only means of again attaining office would be reappointment, but no justice so superseded by Hardwicke was ever reinstated. Hardwicke's use of *supersedeas* was an elaboration of earlier unusual procedure. In 1685, the Crown Office had issued a writ of *supersedeas* to the entire commission of St. Albans, and in 1711 it issued the writ to the commission of Macclesfield.[73] The only *supersedeas* directed against a single justice, prior to those issued under Hardwicke, had been inscribed at the order of Lord Chancellor Macclesfield. It is probable that he was seeking a prompt and public means of disgracing its recipient: the superseded justice had imprisoned one of the servants of the Russian ambassador.[74] No further issue of the Crown Office writ is recorded until Hardwicke's possession of the Great Seal, when fourteen justices were superseded in twenty years. An additional twenty-two justices would be the dismayed recipients of the writ during the remainder of the century.

Evidence of Hardwicke's procedure in issuing this writ of *supersedeas* is rather ambiguous. In 1736, he stated, in his capacity as head of the court of Chancery, that the court could not sit as court of first instance in an action brought to punish a justice. A complainant could move the court of King's Bench for an information against a justice and then apply to Chancery to remove the justice from the commission. Yet, few of the justices permanently erased from the commission by Hardwicke's writ of *supersedeas* were the target of informations issued by or requested in King's Bench. In 1756, when a gentleman complained of a justice's biased decisions and requested his removal, Hardwicke replied: "The Great Seal is always open to receive such a Complaint by proof, and after That for me to direct Notice to be given to the Justice complained of, and appoint a Time for him to give in his answer by affidavits also, after which the Chancellor considers the

72. These writs are indexed under "supersedeas" in P.R.O., Index 4217–4220, and notes recording the use of the writs are in C234.

73. P.R.O., Index 4215, p. 120; Index 4216, p. 230.

74. L.K.J. Glassey, *Politics and the Appointment of Justices of the Peace 1675–1720* (Oxford, 1979), pp. 19–20.

weight of the Evidence, and the merits of the Case, and if he finds just grounds for it orders a Supersedeas." What Hardwicke considered "proof of the complaint" is unclear, especially since this complainant proceeded to apply for an information in King's Bench,[75] but it is likely that other methods of establishing judicial malfeasance were permitted. Other evidence does support Hardwicke's assertion that the issue of a *supersedeas* was preceded by a formal hearing, a procedure well suited to present removal by *supersedeas* as legal retribution for illegal activity.[76]

It may be that the documents related to these hearings were placed in a special file, which would explain why they cannot be found among Hardwicke's papers. What evidence is available in other sources indicates that the writ followed upon representation to the Lord Chancellor of proceedings sufficiently injudicious to constitute grounds for removal. Thomas Robe, the first justice superseded by Hardwicke, had as clerk of the market within the verge attempted to collect the fees of his office throughout the county of Middlesex. When his campaign was frustrated by Middlesex Quarter Sessions, he had levied a seven-years war against the Sessions, interfering with the collection of taxes and accusing the justices of embezzlement.[77] A series of charges provide the background to the supersession of Simon Michell, the second justice awarded this signal dishonour. Fourteen years before he was superseded he had been reprimanded by the Middlesex bench for improper bailing. Six months prior to supersession, an information was brought against him in King's Bench for directing that an "aged poor lame and impotent" widow be evicted from the parish workhouse and subsequently refusing to order the parish officials to give her relief, for refusing to order the relief of a poor man, and for so assaulting a pregnant woman who came to plead for this man's relief that she subsequently miscarried. A few days before his removal from the bench he had been confined in Fleet Prison for a contempt of the court of Chancery entailed in his complicity in a scheme to marry an heiress and ward of the court to a

75. *Ex parte Rooke,* 2 Atk. 2; B.L., Add. MSS 35604, f. 331, draft of letter from Hardwicke to Sir J. Astley, Aug. 14, 1756; *Rex* v. *Young and Pitts, Esquires,* 1 Burr. 557–564.

76. B.L., Add. MSS 35602, f. 271, Sir Nathaniel Mead to Hardwicke, Feb. 6, 1746[7].

77. S. and B. Webb, *English Local Government from the Revolution to the Municipal Corporations Act,* vol. 1, *The Parish and the County* (London, 1906), p. 560 and n. 3; E. G. Dowdell, *A Hundred Years of Quarter Sessions: the Government of Middlesex from 1660 to 1760* (Cambridge, 1932), pp. 77, 162–163.

watchmaker.[78] Similarly, the writ of *supersedeas* which removed Herbert Lloyd and George Jones from Cardiganshire's commission was issued shortly after these two justices led a mob which seized one of the Crown's mines and clapped the king's superintendent in jail.[79]

Hardwicke's use of the *supersedeas* was copied by his successors, and perhaps a review of the activities likely to lead to supersession ends on a woodnote suitably wild with a summary of the charges against Thomas Johnes Senior and Thomas Johnes Junior, justices of Cardiganshire, relieved of the burdens of maintaining the peace in 1773. Issue of their *supersedeas* was prompted by the record of a case in the court of Chancery. Both Johnes were defendants in the case, and the plaintiff had found it rather difficult to bring them into court. When his solicitor had requested the sheriff's office to serve a writ on the defendants, the officer "refused to do [so] declaring He was afraid of his Life." Another individual was finally prevailed upon to serve the writ. Gaining entry to the Johnes' household by pretending to seek a warrant from the justices, he served the writs, which the Johnes' retainers then made him eat. Having dined, he was struck with an oak stick by Johnes Junior and chased through the grounds by Junior and retinue, caught and beaten until, feigning death, he was thrown in the river. When another warrant was served on the Johnes, the server managed to maintain the peace by drawing a pistol and declaring that he would shoot the first person who attempted to bar his retreat.[80]

Hardwicke's invention of the *supersedeas* to brand such justices as unfit for office reinforced the tendency to view dismissal from the commission as an impartial judgment upon the justices' conduct. In Anne's reign, the inadvertent omission of Harley's name from Herefordshire's commission had evoked a political statement: "I have learnt not to be surprised with affairs of this nature, because my father was turned out by the regulators in King James' time." By 1747, the response to elimination was rather different. Sir Nathaniel Mead pleaded with Hardwicke to rescind his supersession: "My Lord; My Life Cannot Be Very Long; And I Should Be Very Sorry To Go Down To My Grave; Stigmatized With Such A Marque Of Infamy (As A

78. Webb and Webb, *The Parish and the County,* p. 559, n. 7; P.R.O., Index 6658, Mich. 15 George II; KB 10/25, Mich. 1740, information 59; KB 28/159, Mich. 15 George II; [Anonymous] 2 Atk. 173–174.

79. O. Brynon, "Lead Mining at Esgair y Mwyn in the time of Lewis Morris," *Cardiganshire Antiquarian Society Transactions* 16 (1936): 39–40; D. L. Thomas, "Lewis Morris in Cardiganshire," *Cymmrodor* 15 (1902):15–17.

80. P.R.O., C234/80, Mar. 19, 1773.

Supersedeas Manifestly Imparteth) By A Lord Chancellor Of Your Lordship's Character."[81] Under Hardwicke, removal from the commission became a legal and apolitical censure.

Hardwicke was less inclined to make appointment to the bench an apolitical honour. As a politician, he was well aware that the justices of the peace wielded political influence. As a leading member of the Pelhamite ministry, he wanted to insure that this influence was wielded by the ministry's allies. Though the treaty of 1745 unfortunately guaranteed Tories greater access to the bench than they had hitherto enjoyed, Lord Chancellor Hardwicke still thought it necessary to distinguish Whigs from Tories. His treatment of the Suffolk commission is a case in point. In August 1745, just after the conclusion of the treaty, Suffolk's gentlemen had met at the summer Assizes, drawn up a list of those they wished to nominate to the commission, and requested that the county's two Tory representatives submit their list to the Lord Chancellor. The Tories accordingly forwarded the list, together with a note referring to the "Hopes that were given in the Spring." Hardwicke countered with a suggestion that they direct their application to the county's Lord Lieutenant and custos rotulorum, and he had considered adding: "As to what is alluded to in your letter relating to what passed in the Spring on the Subject of Commissions of the peace, I never heard that any particular mention was made of the County of Suffolk on that occasion, but when a new Commission shall be issued, it will certainly be considered and settled according to the general Rule then laid down." When a new commission was issued in 1747, the Suffolk gentry would probably note that only nine of the seventy-five lords, baronets, and gentlemen recommended in 1745 were put on the commission. They might also have remarked that the nine were almost half of the twenty-two elevated to the bench by this commission.[82]

A similar tension between attempt to abide by the letter of the 1745 agreement and desire to retain appointment to the commission as a political weapon permeates negotiations over five Welsh commissions. In 1745, Robert Williams, Tory member of Parliament for Montgomeryshire, applied for a new commission for his county. The com-

81. *HMC, Portland IV*, p. 554, Harley to Cowper, Aug. 2, 1710; B.L., Add. MSS 35589, f. 331, Nathaniel Mead to Hardwicke, Nov. 2, 1747.

82. B.L., Add. MSS 35602, ff. 110–111, Sir Cordel Firebrace and Mr. Affleck to [Hardwicke], Aug. 5, 1745; ff. 112–113; f. 120, draft to Sir C. Firebrace and Mr. Affleck, Aug. 15, 1745; P.R.O., C234/35, Mar. 25, 1747.

mission, issued in 1749, listed five of the twenty-six gentlemen nominated by Williams; the five comprised almost one-third of the new justices of 1749.[83] Sir John Philipps, a Tory seated at the Board of Trade by Broad-Bottom, submitted lists of nominees for three Welsh counties and one borough. Five of the sixteen appointees on Carmarthenshire's commission of 1747 had appeared on his list of twenty-one. Thirteen of the thirty-eight new rulers given Cardiganshire in 1748 had first achieved national notice in the list of thirty-nine nominees concocted by Philipps three years earlier.[84] Hardwicke chose to postpone renewal of the commissions for the county of Pembroke and the borough of Haverford West. The first finally received a new commission in 1757, and the second in 1761.

So Hardwicke manoeuvered to maintain Whig predominance without repudiating the treaty with the Tories, but by the late 1740s he was encountering yet another obstacle to his political manipulations. Even the Lord Chancellor could not produce a county bench which embodied the might of the Whig party if party were not the dominant structure determining alliances in the county. By the late 1740s changes in attitude were undermining Hardwicke's policy. In 1746, the Lord Lieutenant of Essex thought he ought to nominate two Tory baronets "by way of experiment, being both very young men, and may at least take away any pretense of disgust at being neglected." Both were put in the commission.[85] In the West Riding of Yorkshire, the Lord Lieutenant thought it proper to appoint a Tory against whom he had raised serious objections just one year earlier. In the intervening months, the gentleman had supported the measures taken against the Pretender at York.[86] In 1750, two Gloucestershire Whigs reported that the county's Lord Lieutenant now thought it mandatory that "Gentlemen of the Opposite Party" be included in any list of nominees for the county's new commission, though he would "take care to have a Majority on the Right Side."[87]

The Lord Chancellor might endeavour to maintain his party's inter-

83. P.R.O., C234/88, June 23, 1749; B.L., Add. MSS 35602, f. 95.

84. P.R.O., C234/81, July 20, 1747; C234/80, Feb. 26, 1747[8]; B.L., Add. MSS 35602, ff. 38, 40, 42, 44.

85. B.L., Add. MSS 35589, f. 67, Earl Fitzwalter to Hardwicke, Oct. 3, 1746; P.R.O., C234/12, Oct. 27, 1746.

86. B.L., Add. MSS 35602, ff. 69–70, Lord Malton to Hardwicke, June 8, 1745; f. 192, Earl of Rockingham [to Hardwicke], May 4, 1746; P.R.O., C234/44, June 18, 1746.

87. B.L., Add. MSS 35603, ff. 253–254, Sir Francis Fust to Hardwicke, Sept. 17, 1750; ff. 251–252, Mr. Tracy to Hardwicke, Sept. 10, 1750.

est in the counties by making affiliation with the right interest a virtual guarantee of appointment, but party in the localities was no longer what it had been. Bristol's Union Club—the Whig political organization—had only to request that its nominees be put on the Gloucestershire and Somersetshire commissions, there to give "countenance and protection to many of our friends against the partial views of enrag'd and disappointed people" (who had just lost the Bristol election)—and the thing was done, or almost done. For one of the Union Club's nominees was considered a raging Tory by Hardwicke's principal consultant in Gloucestershire and one other a Tory supporter. When Lord Ducie, enlisted by Hardwicke in 1754 to act as the Chancellor's lieutenant in the county, examined the list submitted by one of the Whigs who in 1750 had been astounded at the Lord Lieutenant's desire to include Tories, he found that of the twenty-eight nominees, four were violent Tories, three Tory sympathizers, and one "improper." All those whom Ducie considered wildly Tory or improper were struck from the lists of nominees, as were three of the five he considered "exceptionable."[88] Hardwicke's employment of Ducie parallels his earlier use of Sir John Dutton, and Ducie's care in inspecting the nominees and his adjurations of the need to maintain a Whig supremacy in the commission are reminiscent of Dutton's similar conduct. Nonetheless, the confusion among genuine Whigs about the party allegiance of their fellows is indicative of the partial disintegration of local party so striking in an examination of the structure of politics at the accession of George III.

The negotiations terminating in the Devonshire commission of 1754 seem a more perfect reproduction of the cartoons of Hardwicke's first decade in office. In 1754, the county's Lord Lieutenant and custos rotulorum was the Duke of Bedford. As Bedford admitted to Hardwicke, he had little acquaintance with the gentlemen of the county. Bedford soon found himself supplied with an adviser, Sir Francis Drake, who both recommended nominees to the duke, and, at Hardwicke's invitation, inspected the list of all those nominated by Bedford. So did Sir John Wynn, a Whig member of Parliament. Be-

88. B.L., Add. MSS 35604, f. 164, Abraham Isaac Elton to Joseph Mathews, May 7, 1754; f. 166, Same to Same, May 11, 1754; f. 181, Lord Ducie to Hardwicke, June 3, 1754; f. 200, Same to Same, July 13, 1754; f. 187, Same to Same, June 22, 1754; ff. 189, 241; Add. MSS 35603, ff. 255, 256; Add. MSS 35604, f. 199, Union Committee, Bristol, to Robert Nugent, Esq., July 13, 1754; f. 206, John Berrowe to the Honourable Robert Nugent, July 15, 1754; f. 208, N. Tooker to John Berrowe, July 14, 1754; f. 224, Robert Nugent to [Hardwicke?], July 19, 1754; P.R.O., C234/33, July 21, 1757; C234/13, July 20, 1754.

tween them, Drake, Wynn, and Hardwicke eliminated nine gentlemen from lists totalling 133 nominees, all nine of whom, so Hardwicke assured the duke, were members of a Devonshire political club hostile to the government's interest and perhaps Jacobite. Drake also vetted the four nominees of Sir William Yonge, Bart., Whig member of Parliament for Honiton. One, the Rev. William Palmer, Drake thought a Tory and a "wrangling litigious Parson" to boot. Palmer was added to the unsuitable nine, and the remaining 127 nominees were placed in the first commission Devon had received since 1744. Palmer's patron protested: "I have daily Accounts . . . of the Malice and Oppression exercised by Attorney Gill, since his Exaltation as a Justice: and my poor Friends have no place to fly for Relief in the Neighbourhood. . . . Mr. Palmer has both Abilities and Resolution sufficient to save my poor helpless Friends from Destruction, when it shall be legally in his Power." An almost perfect mid-century parallel to the Bishop of London's observation in 1710 that, unless the justices in the commission were changed, it would not be in the power of voters "to choose whom they liked for fear of ill usage from Tyrants." But not quite. A year later, Palmer was finally placed on the commission.

Nor was the Lord Lieutenant's attitude precisely that which one would expect of the noblemen Queen Anne's ministers would have placed at the head of a county. Improper persons he would not nominate. Otherwise, his list was "as general as possible with regard to all Persons of fortune and character without regard to Party denominations," though he thought it best to wait until the elections were over before he initiated the procedure for issue of a new commission. As Bedford had himself been allied to the Tories of Bedfordshire, it is not surprising that he did not wish to make distinctions among judicial nominees. Accordingly, he adopted a new form for his list of justices, a form which guaranteed that none of the new justices could consider himself slighted. Both Bedford's list and the list of new justices added to the commission ranked the justices alphabetically.[89]

89. B.L., Add. MSS 35604, f. 168, Duke of Bedford to Hardwicke, May 22, 1754; ff. 177–178, Bedford's list in alphabetical order; ff. 191–193, Bedford to Hardwicke, July 6, 1754; f. 194, Sir William Yonge to Hardwicke, July 6, 1754; f. 196, Yonge's list; f. 202, Sir Francis Drake to Hardwicke, July 13, 1754; f. 204, Duke of Bedford to Hardwicke, July 14, 1754; ff. 216, 355, lists of objectionable nominees; f. 210, Sir Francis Drake to Hardwicke, July 15, 1754; ff. 212–213, Drake's comments on Bedford's list; ff. 214–215, 217, Drake's lists; ff. 219–220, draft from Hardwicke to Bedford, July 16, 1754; f. 234, Sir F. Drake to Hardwicke, received July 26, 1754; f. 236, Sir John Wynne to Mr. Jephson, July 27, 1754; f. 268, Sir William Yonge to Hardwicke, Feb. 15, 1755; P.R.O., C234/9, July 23, 1754; B.L., Loan 29/131/7, f. 64, Henry, Bishop of London to Harley, Aug.

The new ranking symbolized a new order. In the late seventeenth century, justices had contended for precedence in the commission, complaining if they were omitted from the quorum or if their names followed those they considered their inferiors.[90] The seventeenth-century commission was regarded as a list of individuals, each possessing considerable power as a private person. Both justices and Lord Chancellors thought the prestige of each justice so nicely distinguished that it could be graded and ranked. By the early eighteenth century, Lord Chancellors were no longer attempting to distinguish among the entire group of justices. Instead, the justices added to a commission were listed at the end of the commission, the most eminent among the new justices heading the list of new appointees. Bedford's alphabetical list therefore represents the logical culmination of a gradual change in attitude: justices were now regarded as a fairly homogeneous group of gentlemen. Distinctions among gentlemen were invidious, and among justices pernicious. The private prestige and alliances of any individual justice were now less important than the prestige and cohesion of the justices as a group. Similarly, Hardwicke's abstention from dismissal of political opponents served to minimize the importance of the justices' political affiliations, while his invention of a procedure to disgrace egregiously errant justices enhanced the prestige of all justices as representatives of the law. In 1753, just one year before Bedford submitted his alphabetical list, Parliament all but abolished the commission's legal distinctions among justices. 26 George II c.27 ordained that, even if an act specified that a document had to be signed by two or more justices of the quorum, the document was legally valid though none of the signator justices were of the quorum. Henceforth no justice would be any more judicial than his brother justices.

4. ADMINISTRATION, SOCIAL STATUS, AND APPOINTMENT TO THE BENCH, 1745–1756

Change in the structure of politics may indicate why it was possible for the national government to subordinate emphasis on the justices as eminent individuals to their eminence as a group. But it does not explain why the national government or the justices might consider it logical or desirable to do so. While the disintegration of party was making distinctions among the justices impolitic, change in both the

90. For example, B.L., Eg. MSS 2985, vol. 8, f. 350.

government's perception of the justices and the social composition of the bench were contributing to alteration of the justices' image. By the mid-eighteenth century the national government was evincing a new interest in the justices' more purely judicial and administrative functions. At the same time, the Lord Chancellor was elevating an increasing number of the less eminent gentry and gentlemen to the bench. Therefore, change in the commission's diplomatic hinted at change both in emphasis on the justices' functions and in their status. As the commission's alphabetical ranking of justices subordinated the individual to the group, it could also imply a new emphasis on the group's work: the identity of any one justice may now be regarded as less significant than the work the justices performed, work any gentleman could perform no matter what his ranking within or alliances among England's upper orders.

Of course, the national government had always been concerned about the justices' work. For example, in 1721 Lord Chancellor Macclesfield had requested that the judges "Use their Endeavours with well Affected Gentlemen to Act in the Commission of the Peace."[91] Well affected gentlemen were the bulwarks of the Hanoverian regime and the Whig ministry. In contrast, in 1754 Hardwicke urged the judges to persuade those appointed to the commission to assume the burdens of office because crime "of the deepest dye, and most flagitous nature" was infecting the realm.[92] By mid-century the Lord Chancellor was emphasizing the justices' role as a bulwark of social order.

Likewise, by mid-century Parliament was also becoming interested in the more routine problems of local government. In 1751, the House of Commons ordered clerks of the peace to return accounts of monies raised and expended on poor relief in the past four years.[93] Between 1745 and 1747, the Privy Council proclaimed and Parliament then enacted regulations designed to halt spread of the cattle plague, regulations which the justices were to enforce. The justices proved essential but insufficient. By 1747 it was found necessary to associate commissioners of the land tax with the justices in the supervision of the movement of cattle.[94] In 1757, when Parliament remodelled the militia, the House of Commons added a clause to the Militia Act em-

91. B.L., Add. MSS 35600, f. 2, Feb. 26, 1720[1].
92. B.L., Add. MSS 35870, ff. 241–243.
93. House of Commons *Journals* 26:140, Mar. 20, 1750[1].
94. PC 2/99, pp. 254, 261–262, 388–394; PC 2/100, pp. 60–65, 99–101, 175–180, 300–313, 416, 420–424; 19 George II c. 5.

powering land tax commissioners to associate themselves with the deputy lieutenants in enlisting, for there were too few justices and the commissioners were more often resident.[95] Just when the Lord Chancellor was expressing a new interest in the justices' role as judges and Parliament was beginning to attend to local administration, both noted that there was a shortage of active local governors. As Hardwicke told the judges, "Gentlemen are apt to be very pressing to get into the Commission of the Peace, and when they are appointed, to be very backward in Acting."

Reports of a lack of active justices flowed in from county after county. In Hertfordshire, the Lord Lieutenant declared, "we have so few who do act that the common necessary business of the County can scarce be carried on without great hardship and Expence to the People in general." Only one magistrate dispensed justice to a division of Hampshire. In Devonshire, a justice reported that there were only two justices acting in a "District of 51 parishes, 5 of them large and populous towns." In Warwickshire, a justice of one division found that there was no second justice with whom he could hold a petty sessions. In Somerset, one entire division had no resident justice; few justices resided in the northern portion of the county, and one justice was forced to ride 28 miles before he could get an order signed. The clergy and inhabitants of the Isle of Wight informed their Lord Lieutenant that the presence of only one active justice on the island had rendered "the Execution of several laws of this Realm . . . impracticable."[96]

In part, Hardwicke himself was responsible for the inadequate supply of justices. Once change in the alliance of parties at Westminster afforded rivals to the Pelhams claims to nominate justices, Hardwicke found that the renewal of commissions was impolitic. For example, in 1742 the Pelhams had allied with members of the opposition, including Lord Bathurst, and Bathurst had forthwith attempted to place his adherents on the Gloucestershire bench. "It may be easier," reasoned Hardwicke's Gloucestershire adviser, "to avoid renewing that Com-

95. The clause was rejected by the House of Lords (J. R. Western, *The English Militia in the Eighteenth Century* [London, 1965], pp. 138–140).

96. For Hertfordshire, see B.L., Add. MSS 35604, f. 117, Earl Cowper to Hardwicke, July 15, 1753; for Hampshire, see f. 12, Earl of Portsmouth to Hardwicke, May 19, 1752; for Devonshire, see Add. MSS 35601, Thomas, Bishop of Oxford to Hardwicke, Nov. 8, 1744; for Warwickshire, see Add. MSS 35600, ff. 168–169, T. Archer to Duke of Montagu, July 19, 1738; for Somerset, see Add. MSS 35603, f. 132, Jo. Wood to [?], Jan. 25, 1748/1749; for the Isle of Wight, see Add. MSS 35602, ff. 283–284.

mission, then to put a negative on any of the Persons his Lordship may think proper to recommend; and if improper Persons are once admitted, it is I think always deigned invidious to put them out without having a Publick and a legal Cause assigned to such a procedure."[97] Gloucestershire's commission was not renewed.

When the Gloucestershire commission was renewed, as part of the 1745 treaty with the Tories, Hardwicke immediately received evidence that the treaty had increased the number of those who could be offended upon issue of a new commission. Before 1745, gentlemen disappointed in their hopes of judicial office might derive consolation from the knowledge that those suspected of Tory affiliation were likely to be denied a place on the bench. After 1745, omission from the commission was a personal affront. So perturbed was one barrister denied a place on Gloucestershire's bench in 1745 that he sought an explanation from the Lord Chancellor:

> My Lord I know I have no merit in any respect, so as to particularly expect such honour, but when I consider the general and impartial nomination your Lordship hath made in the present Commission, My profession, My share of property in the County, my recommendation to your Lordship without any previous application or knowledge of my own, My Father being above thirty years in the Commission, and as many Years a Representative in Parliament for the City and a Burrough in this County, when I consider every Clothier round about me of Substance, is in Commission and Scarce any one Gentlemen of Fortune excepted but my self, and not one of the profession except one, whose Brother is in, I must confess to your Lordship, it gives me and my Friends a real uneasiness, to be so mark'd and distinguish'd by the insinuations, which the Malice or unwarrantable views of two or three of my Neighbours may have suggested to Your Lordship.[98]

Hardwicke could only assure the plaintiff that omission had proceeded neither from malicious reports nor "from any prejudice or disrespect in me towards You."[99] When every gentleman considered himself entitled to be a justice, and renewal of the commission was more apt to insult those excluded than compliment those appointed, all the more reason to postpone renewal of the commission. During Hardwicke's tenure as Lord Chancellor, the interval between receipt of a new com-

97. B.L., Add. MSS 35601, f. 131, Dutton to Hardwicke, Sept. 4, 1742; Gloucestershire R.O., Sherborne MSS, D678, Fam Sett 57/D, Dutton to Young, Apr. 18, 1742.

98. B.L., Add. MSS 35588, f. 87, J. Coxe to Hardwicke, July 20, 1745. Coxe had been nominated in the list of "Names of Gentlemen not in the Commission . . . ", Add. MSS 35601, f. 334.

99. B.L., Add. MSS 35602, f. 125, draft of letter by Hardwicke, Aug. 31, 1745.

mission by the average English and Welsh county increased from three years to six or seven years.[100]

Hardwicke's postponement of the day of reckoning decreased the number of justices. As the interval between the issue of commissions increased, the proportion of justices named in the commissions who remained alive dwindled. In Kent, which received a new commission about once every eight years between 1735 and 1758, approximately one-third of the justices listed in a commission were dead when that commission was renewed.

Nonetheless, scarcity of active justices cannot be attributed solely to Hardwicke's politic solution to the problem posed by reconciliation with the Tories. The justices had also made themselves scarce. For example, on average only a quarter of those appointed to the commissions of Kent, Hampshire, Bedfordshire, Oxfordshire, Herefordshire, Cambridgeshire, and Gloucestershire between 1738 and 1760 took out a dedimus—the document which authorized the justice to take the oaths of office—within five years of appointment. In contrast, half of the justices appointed to the commissions of the same seven counties between 1706 and 1713 had taken out a dedimus within five years of appointment.[101] Not only had Hardwicke's manipulation of renewal diminished the supply of justices, but the proportion of justices willing to act had also declined.

Administrative expediency therefore impelled the Lord Chancellor to search for those who would serve their sovereign, and if acknowledged gentlemen spurned the duties of their station, then there was little choice but to lower the standards for assessment of gentility. In 1738 the Duke of Chandos, resident in a rural area of Middlesex, found himself seriously inconvenienced by the death or retirement of an active justice. He canvassed the neighbouring gentlemen, all of whom declined to act, until he discovered one Mr. Stanmour: "He is indeed a Distiller, but one of a setled Reputation, and void of all manner of Reproach; if the Profession he follows is no Objection to Him, I am sure the County will be extreamly well pleased with Him,

100. This calculation is based on P.R.O., Ind. 4217–4218. Durham has been omitted from the calculation, as a new commission was issued annually and conjointly with that for gaol delivery.

101. P.R.O., C234, C193/43–45. It is possible that P.R.O., C193/43, on which the numeration of those obtaining a dedimus in Anne's reign is based, does not list all those who obtained a dedimus. This calculation excludes both the appointment of and the obtaining of a dedimus by those justices listed in the honourary clause. For a graph of the number of dedimuses obtained from 1728 to 1833 see appendix E, figure 1.

and very well serv'd by Him. . . ."[102] Similarly, political expediency forced adjustment of social principle to pressing realities. If those hostile to the administration were to be admitted to the commission, then the appointment of more judicial allies and of all those whom the insult of omission might antagonize was essential to the maintenance of Pelhamite dominance. When one of Hardwicke's allies agreed to search for "Proper persons" for Gloucestershire's commission at mid-century, he felt obliged to caution: "To Say the Truth, I believe we have descended as Low already, in filling up the Commission as is right."[103]

By all indications they would descend lower yet. By 1761, there were over 8,402 justices in the commissions of England and Wales, more than double the number of justices in 1702, and under George III the commission continued to expand.[104] Inevitably, expansion entailed the admission of gentlemen of lower status.[105] Prominent among the new appointees were the clergy, a hitherto unused source of potential magistrates.

Early in his career as Lord Chancellor, Hardwicke had occasionally found it politically necessary to appoint a cleric to the bench. Consider his difficulties in the renewal of the Warwickshire commission in late 1742. The county's Tory members of Parliament had submitted a list of seventeen nominees, almost all of whom were labelled fervent Tories by the county's Lord Lieutenant. Nonetheless the Lord Lieutenant had also concluded that "as severall of them are men of Quality and of Considerable Estates in the County, I recon it will be proper that they should be in the Commission." As the list submitted by a Whig member of Parliament resident in the county was not nearly so impressive, Hardwicke had urged him to find more judicial candidates. The Whig could find only two more, neither of whom would act. Since it was believed that most of the Tories would act, he informed Hardwicke that "our Friends are apprehensive of great incon-

102. B.L., Add. MSS 35600, f. 164, Chandos to Hardwicke, July 4, 1738.

103. B.L., Add. MSS 35602, f. 75, Col. Selwyn to Hardwicke [n.d.].

104. The figure 8,402 is the sum of all names, excluding those in the honourary clause, in the commissions of all counties except Lancashire, Cornwall, and Durham in the lists of commissions for 1761 in P.R.O., C234 and of those listed in the Middlesex commission in 1761, Greater London R.O., MJP/L11a. The comparable figure in 1702 is 3,535, B.L., Harleian MSS 7512. For the growth of the commissions see appendix A.

105. L. Stone and J. F. C. Stone, "Country Houses and Their Owners in Hertfordshire 1540–1879," in *The Dimensions of Quantitative Research in History*, W. Aydelotte, A. Bogue, and R. Fogel, ed. (Princeton, 1972), p. 85, notes the decline in status of those attending Hertfordshire's Quarter Sessions.

veniences, and therefore are in hopes, and desire your Lordship will be so good as to shorten their lists, as much as conveniently may be. . . ." Hardwicke found it convenient to appoint nine of the seventeen Tories and thirteen of the fourteen Whigs (so obscure was the one Whig whom he did not appoint that the Lord Lieutenant could not even identify him). Among those elevated to the bench on the Whig's recommendation was a cleric who was chaplain of a regiment, possessed of a living of £100 per annum, and "a little touched in the head."[106]

Even when psychologically sound, the country cleric could not boast a status equal to that of the gentry. Though possessed of a university education, of influence over the inhabitants of his parish, and of claims to deference based on his moral authority, the country cleric was nonetheless an appendage of the gentleman who had endowed him with a benefice. Therefore, sponsors of clerical nominees would stress, when they could, that their nomination was based on "the temporal Estates they have among us."[107] By the 1750s emphasis on the private landholdings of many a clerical justice would have been misplaced. In Devon, for instance, a cleric whose sole sustenance was a living of £113 per annum became a justice of the peace.[108]

True, the clerical justice performed a variety of useful services. According to the Earl of Ailesbury, the appointment of one cleric would be "a particular convenience to my self, he being situated in the middle of my Estates, where we are very thin of Justices, and besides the trouble of it, it would be improper in me, who does act sometimes, to be trying my own causes. . . ." Timothy Neve, D.D., could represent his usefulness to the Earl of Sandwich in an equally acceptable manner: "I fear his Lordship will have no one Friend in the Commission in this part of the County, except my self; and that, added to the Station I am in (as the first Clergyman in the County, next after the Bishop) will enable me upon occasion to serve his Lordship's Interest in the country more effectually." The Earl of Sandwich saw fit to promote his cause. In a larger context, the appointment of suitably

106. B.L., Add. MSS 35601, f. 83, Lord Montagu to Hardwicke, July 15, 1742; f. 152, Same to Same, Nov. 11, 1742; ff. 171–172, T. Archer to Hardwicke, Dec. 22, 1742; Add. MSS 35604, ff. 374–376, lists and comments thereon; P.R.O., C234/38, Jan. 22, 1742[3].

107. B.L., Add. MSS 35602, f. 97, Earl of Oxford to Hardwicke, July 9, 1745; Add. MSS 35603, ff. 307–308, Duke of Dorset to Hardwicke, July 12, 1751.

108. B.L., Add. MSS 35604, f. 234, Sir Francis Drake to Hardwicke, received July 26, 1754.

Whig clergymen would contribute to the maintenance of a proper imbalance between Whig and Tory.[109] But probably most important in the advancement of clerics to judicial honours was a characteristic noted even by their detractors: clerics were constantly resident in their parishes.[110] They were also more likely to act.[111]

The consequences were inescapable. Given the reluctance of the gentry to act, a Lord Chancellor intent on providing an adequate number of local governors had little option but to appoint members of social groups whose status bordered on gentility, including the clergy. Even though Hardwicke used his veto against clerics more frequently than against other nominees, the number of clerics in the commission swelled. In 1702, there had been fifty-one clerics in the commissions of England and Wales. In 1761, there were over 932, and almost all of the increase had occurred after 1740.[112] Indeed, so common had the appointment of clerics become that the omission of any clerical dignitary, including a prebend, could be deemed a slight.[113] When in 1761 all commissions were renewed at the accession of George III, almost every commission ended with a special section devoted to judicial brethren of the cloth, two of whom would be the only justices in the commission not of the quorum.

The mid-century remodelling of the commission's diplomatic—the adoption both of alphabetical listing of laymen and of a section reserved for clerics—reflects alteration in the government's and the elite's perception of the justices. Concern both for his party and for local administration had inspired the Lord Chancellor to appoint clerics and gentlemen of relatively low status. Accordingly, the commission's new diplomatic replaced emphasis on the prestige of the individ-

109. B.L., Add. MSS 35601, f. 201, Earl of Ailesbury to Hardwicke, June 3, 1743; Add. MSS 35603, f. 160, Neve to the Hon. Edward Wortley, June 20, 1749; f. 159, Sandwich to Hardwicke, June 24 [1749]; Add. MSS 35604, f. 27, Lord Fitzwalter to Hardwicke, June 16, 1752; Kent A.O., U269/C147/14, Abraham Tilghman to Duke of Dorset, Sept. 20, 1756.

110. B. L., Add. MSS 35604, ff. 70–71, Sir Thomas Prendergast to Hardwicke, Jan. 4, 1753; f. 319, Henry Hoare to Perkins, May 24, 1756; Add. MSS 35602, f. 198, Dr. George Rooke to [Hardwicke], Sept. 8, 1746.

111. See appendix E, table E-2.

112. All clerical ranks except bishops and vice-chancellors of universities have been included in this numeration, and all doctors of law are deemed clerics. The numeration for 1702 is based on B.L., Harleian MSS 7512, which includes every county except Lancashire. That for 1761 is based on the lists in P.R.O., C234 and on Greater London R.O., MJP/L11a, and includes all counties except Lancashire, Durham, and Cornwall.

113. B.L., Add. MSS 35603, f. 264 [Edward Leeds to Hardwicke, ca. 1754]; Add. MSS 35602, f. 216, Manchester to Hardwicke, Oct. 28, 1746; Add. MSS 35604, f. 40, Bolton to Hardwicke, Oct. 1, 1752.

ual justice with emphasis on the justices as a group. As Hardwicke's motives for appointing these new justices indicate, the commission remained a political institution, but increasing attention was focused upon the justices' administrative and judicial functions. And, at the same time as Hardwicke's policy of removal was distancing the justices from politics and the central government's concerns were emphasizing the justices' administrative functions, local elites were also contributing to alteration of the justices' image. Partial disintegration of local party and increasing disinclination of local elites to act had affected the Lord Chancellor's policy of appointment. Likewise, Hardwicke found that he had to respond to a new interest in administration evinced by those local governors who cared to act. The tale of the Caernarvonshire commission may symbolize the paradoxes of the commission at mid-century.

In 1748, Sir Thomas Prendergast applied for the issue of a new commission for the county of Caernarvon. In 1747, Sir Thomas, a Whig, had entered the contest for the county seat under the sponsorship of Sir Watkins Williams Wynn, the inveterate and unrepentant Tory "King of the West," and had lost to William Bodvell, another Whig. Prendergast's request was repeated on at least five occasions in the next six years—once at the end of 1748, and four times between 1752 and 1754, when, it was noted, the election was drawing near. According to the Earl of Powis, "the new Commission, under the Circumstances it will appear will be a means of giving Weight Credit and Power to the Tories . . . ; and of effecting or at least trying, the Schemes They have been forming to the Prejudice of the Whig Interest." Sir Thomas submitted a list of twenty-two nominees, and Hardwicke was informed that two were disaffected, one the Watkin of Caernarvonshire, one a "Bullocking Teague," one low and unfit, and one, a cleric, not qualified. Sir Thomas replied that one of the so-called Jacobites was his cousin and Irish "where a Protestant-Jacobite is a thing unknown," and stressed the need for immediate renewal of the commission. The county suffered from an "unparallel'd scarcity of Justices." Hardwicke's other informants declared that there were ten active justices in the county, "[I]f true . . . a small number for a length of above fifty miles," Sir Thomas replied and submitted a list of the six justices then active in the county—of whom one was too infirm to ride to Quarter Sessions, one nearly seventy years old, and one lived on the borders of Caernarvonshire and Denbighshire and frequently attended Quarter Sessions for the county of Denbigh.

Sir William Yonge, the county's custos, Mr. Bodvell, member of Parliament for the county from 1747 to 1754, and Sir John Wynn, who would represent the county from 1754 to 1761, had conferred and drawn up their own list, in case Hardwicke decided to be persuaded by Prendergast. Instead, on July 4, 1753, he declared to Sir Thomas, "that for reasons (which I gave him in general) I did not think fit to issue a new Commission for the County till after the next general Election should be over; . . ." The new Parliament convened on May 31, 1754. Of the forty-eight new justices on the Caernarvonshire commission of August 8, 1754, seventeen—including Prendergast's Irish cousin and the reputedly unqualified cleric—were Prendergast nominees. The sponsors of the candidacy of most of the other new justices are not known, but at least ten had been nominated by Sir John Wynn, the successful Whig candidate for the county in the 1754 election who would become a government placeman in 1755. All but one—a cleric—nominated by Wynn were appointed. The addition of forty-eight justices must have altered the face of justice in Caernarvonshire. Only seventeen of the sixty-five justices listed in the commission of 1754 had also been named in the previous commission, issued in 1739.[114]

When Sir Thomas had been stressing the necessity of a new commission he had thought it plausible to note that there was "a Spirit of repairing roads (never before known in these parts) which grows very strong in this County . . . ; as well as in neighbouring countys; and I am sure that your Lordship will judge it fit to be encouraged." Lack of justices was impeding the advancement of the county. When the Oxfordshire Whigs of 1754 wished to present a favourable view of their candidates to the voters, they advertised "the faithful and diligent discharge of the important office of Justice of the Peace" of one candidate, and "pledged a similarly 'laudable zeal' " from the other.[115] Another layer of meaning was accruing to the symbol of the justice.

114. P.R.O., C234/82, July 2, 1739 and Aug. 8, 1754; Sedgwick, *House of Commons*, vol. 1, p. 372, and vol. 2, p. 469; B.L., Add. MSS 35603, f. 19, Sir Thomas Prendergast to Hardwicke, Jan. 27, 1747/1748; f. 72, Same to Same, Dec. 9, 1748; Add. MSS 35604, f. 16, Earl of Powis to Hardwicke, May 31, 1752; f. 20, Sir William Yonge to Hardwicke, June 3, 1752; ff. 23, 25; ff. 29–30, Earl of Powis to Hardwicke, June 19, 1752; ff. 31–32, Sir Thomas Prendergast to Hardwicke, July 30, 1752; f. 70, Same to Same, Jan. 4, 1753; f. 71v, Hardwicke's decision on request, July 4, 1753; f. 87, Earl of Powis to Hardwicke, Feb. 16, 1753; ff. 112–113, Sir Thomas Prendergast to Hardwicke, May 30, 1753; f. 233, Sir John Wynn's list, July 25, 1754.

115. R. Robson, *Oxfordshire Election*, p. 43. It was noted that the commission for Oxfordshire issued in 1755 was markedly Whig, p. 157.

CHAPTER FIVE

Political Ideologies and Partisan Portraits

> The King himself is called *Summus Justiciarus*, the Supreme *Justice* of the Realm, and to shew the *Craftsman*, that the People are not desperate Losers on this Head, *the very Supream Justice has been chosen by the People;* if they chuse the First, and he the rest, they chuse all.[1]

Party warfare for control of the local bench involved the elaboration of party ideologies. Partisan manipulation of the commission evoked partisan protest; protest was answered by justification; and both protest and justification articulated the structure of partisan political ideologies. Ever since Namier's revelation that the actions and rhetoric of eighteenth-century politicians tended to be self-serving, there has been considerable debate as to whether the political ideologies seemingly espoused by those active in eighteenth-century politics affected their actions, and indeed, as to whether political rhetoric during the reigns of the first two Hanoverians reflected a combat of political ideologies. Just as examination of the policy of appointment to the bench revealed the rise of later Stuart party and its persistence under the early Hanoverians, so analysis of the debate over the appointment of justices reveals the development of Whig and Tory ideologies. In vindicating or condemning the government's policy on appointment to the bench, Whigs and Tories broadcast partisan definitions of the function of the justice, definitions which illuminate the nature of both political ideology and judicial office.

1. *The Hyp-Doctor*, No. 88, August 8, 1732.

1. 1678–1720

As one would expect, party, partisan manipulation of the commission, and partisan protest against partisan manipulation were simultaneous and related developments. Party may be said to have been born—though not yet baptized—in 1678, when the last session of the Pension Parliament erupted over the issue of the Popish Plot, and at the same sitting requested lists of all justices and of all who had been removed from the commission during the last seven years. By 1680 both parties had been christened; the first in the series of purges had been completed; and the House of Lords had appointed a committee to inspect Charles's reconstruction of the commissions, while the House of Commons had sent an address to the monarch, urging him to place the commissions of the peace and deputy lieutenancy in good hands.[2]

The composition and structure of both parties changed considerably in the period following the Glorious Revolution, as adherents of the Court decided whether there was sufficient reason to join the Whigs and those of the Country considered whether there was sufficient reason to desert them. The reappearance of the tactics of inspection and address, like the renewal of the government's use of its powers over the commission for party purposes, is indicative of the emergence of the parties whose struggle would dominate the political history of Anne's reign. It was the second session of the Parliament of 1698 when the Commons again considered it necessary to inspect the commissions and the alterations to the commissions, and then to frame their conclusions in an address advising the monarch that the state of the commissions was unsatisfactory. William replied that he would "do what is good for the Publick," and, in the following year, the Commons again appointed a committee to determine if the royal definition of public welfare coincided with that of the majority of the members of the House of Commons. Three years later, it was the turn of the House of Lords, first to inspect, then to address, and finally to review governmental action.[3]

2. *HMC, House of Lords MSS,* 11th report, appendix II, p. 172, no. 274; House of Commons *Journals* 9:535, Nov. 8, 1678; R. W. Blencowe, ed., *Diary of the Times of Charles the Second by the Honourable Henry Sidney* (London, 1843), vol. 2, p. 152, Lady Sunderland to Mr. Evelyn, Sunday night.

3. House of Commons *Journals* 13:8, Nov. 28, 1699; pp. 300–302, Mar. 26, 1700; p. 378, Mar. 5, 1700[01]; p. 314, Apr. 5, 1700; House of Lords *Journals* 17:482a, Mar. 15, 1703[4]; p. 557a, Mar. 31, 1704; p. 659a, Feb. 12, 1704[5].

Even though the latter years of William's reign mark a period of unusual flux in the composition and nature of party, the inspection and address of his reign, as well as those of Anne's reign are distinguished by an obvious party bias. The period subjected to the examination of the committee of Commons was roughly that of Somers' tenure of office, and the period surveyed by the Lords was roughly that of Wright's. While the Commons had thought it would "conduce to the service of his Majesty" to advise that "Gentlemen of Quality and Good Estates" be "restored and put into the Commissions" and "Men of small Estates" be "neither continued, nor put into the Commissions," it had declined to accept an amendment specifying that His Majesty's servants should be "well affected to his Majesty, and his Government." On the other hand, the address emanating from the Lords had stated that "it is our Opinion, That no Person that refused to take the Oaths to the late King is fit to be in the Commission of the Peace under your Majesty," and requested that gentlemen "of Quality and Estates, and of known Affection to your Majesty's Title and Government, and the Protestant Succession and the Church of *England,* as they are both established by Law," be restored. In both instances, governmental measures blatantly favouring one party had evoked an equally partisan protest.

As both Whig and Tory addresses reveal, partisans of both parties considered it proper that only "men of quality and estates" be appointed justices of the peace. While the Whigs could drape their demands in an ideology positing loyalty to the monarch as the *sine qua non* of office, the Tories were unable to relate their claims to such a plausible and immediate political issue, and so were forced to develop a more philosophical framework for their proposals. The Tories elaborated their concept of the justice at a time when a shift of alliances within national politics presaged the identification of the Tory party with the Country interest.[4] Consequently, the form of protest originally adopted by Tory and Country groups in Parliament against the threat to their position gradually became a basic tenet of a renovated Tory ideology.

That the maintenance of stability in the political structure of the realm depended on the continued existence of a substantial number of independent gentlemen, able to fight for themselves and bound to fight

4. J. H. Plumb, *The Growth of Political Stability in England, 1675–1725* (London, 1967), pp. 143–153.

for no other; that the martial independence of these guardians of the realm was based on their ownership of property; that their proper role in the state was to act as an uncorruptible check upon the government; that their assemblage in county meeting was, therefore, comparable to an assemblage of Roman *cives* were fundamental principles of neo-Harringtonian doctrine adapted, during the last quarter of the seventeenth century, by the spokesmen of the Country interest as a philosophical platform for the criticism of changes within the government of England.[5] To wage war against Louis XIV, England's government had found it necessary to create a new and massive financial structure, based on the Bank of England, and to enroll in its expanding bureaucracy armies of administrators and tax collectors. The new grandees of finance and government, deriving their wealth from war and office in mysterious and therefore reprehensible ways, were portrayed as the agents of corruption within the state. Using their ill-gotten gains to insinuate themselves into parliamentary and county seats, they seemed to threaten the dominance of the way of life personified by the independent country gentleman. Since their power was not rooted in the land, it was inherently unstable. Since they derived wealth from the favour of government and the chimeras of finance, they were dependents of the executive. Since wealth which was not based on land did not instill virtue in its possessors, these men could be corrupted by the executive.[6] England was threatened with arbitrary government. To the country gentleman, it was evident that the preservation of the English constitution depended upon the maintenance of the just and necessary prerogatives of the landed interest.

To combat the corruption of the age, members of Parliament sponsored bills to increase the frequency of elections and the landed qualifications of members of Parliament, to preserve honesty in electoral practices, to limit the expense of election, and to decrease the number of placemen in Parliament.[7] While some of these bills were forwarded by the Whigs—notably that which became the Triennial Act of 1694—the limitation of government's ability to corrupt gradually became a doctrine associated with reconstituted Toryism. When, in 1711, a moderately Tory government pushed by a rabidly Tory pres-

5. J. G. A. Pocock, "Machiavelli, Harrington, and English Political Ideologies in the Eighteenth Century," *William and Mary Quarterly*, 3rd ser. 22 (1965):549–583.

6. J. G. A. Pocock, *The Machiavellian Moment, Florentine Political Thought and the Altantic Republican Tradition* (Princeton, 1975), pp. 431, 450–452.

7. D. Rubini, *Court and Country 1688–1702* (London, 1967), pp. 100–117.

sure group enacted a measure to increase the landed qualifications of members of Parliament, the news led one country gentleman to exult: "Tha[t] for qualifying Justices of the Peace will I hope meet with th[e] same succe[ss] for when Landed Gent[lemen] represent us in Parliament and do our business at hom[e] in the Country, we may justly look for better times and that our tottering Constitution may be once more fix't to the confusion and amazement of all its adversaries."[8]

The bill of 1711 was the sixth measure for altering the qualification requisite for a seat on the county bench introduced in the Parliaments of William and Anne. While the first two bills—those of 1699 and 1700—were sponsored by relatively obscure members of Parliament arguably representative of Country rather than Tory interests, the cry for insurance that justices possess landed estates gradually became part of the Tory programme. In 1708, the Tories made agreement to promote a bill on judicial qualifications one of the conditions for their rapprochement with Harley, but it remained for the sponsors of the bill of 1711 to symbolize the complete absorption of Country protest by Tory measure. That bill was prepared by Sir Gilbert Dolben, a prominent High-Church Tory, and Sir George Parker and Henry Campion, both members of the October Club.[9] The October Club was an organization of Country Tory members of Parliament—the soubriquet commemorated the bumpers of October ale downed by country gentlemen at the time of annual harvest and brewing—formed in the autumn of 1710 for the purpose of forcing Tory measures on a government it considered only moderately Tory. The club wielded most influence and most harassed the ministry in the three months succeeding February 1711—precisely when the bill for qualifying justices was introduced into the Commons.[10] As the October Club initiated the 1711 campaign for a qualification act for members of Parliament, it is not improbable that it was also the instigator of this very similar measure. It would be difficult to find a more unimpeachably Tory

8. Lincs. A. O., Massingberd MSS 20/93, William Masssingberd to Burrell Massingberd, Apr. 1, 1711.

9. For the introduction and sponsors of the six bills see: House of Commons *Journals* 12:527, Feb. 25, 1698[9]; 12:605, Mar. 21, 1698[9]; 13:72, Dec. 18, 1699; 13:95, Jan. 4, 1699[1700]; 13:516, May 7, 1701; 13:611, June 10, 1701; 13:730, Feb. 6, 1701[2]; 13:752, Feb. 21, 1701[2]; 14:465, Dec. 19, 1704; 14:475, Jan. 10, 1704[5]; 16:536, Mar. 6, 1710[11]; 16:554, Mar. 16, 1710[11]. G. Holmes and W. A. Speck, "The Fall of Harley in 1708 Reconsidered," *English Historical Review* 80 (1965):683–684.

10. G. Holmes, *British Politics in the Age of Anne* (London, 1967), p. 342.

imprimata for the justices' bill than the joint sponsorship of the October Club and Sir Gilbert Dolben.

Obviously, the Lords thought so too. They never managed to give the bill a third reading even after being reminded of their legislative responsibilities in a message from the Commons carried to the upper House by Mr. Cholmondeley, another member of the October Club.[11] Before their lordships allowed the bill to perish unread at the end of the parliamentary session, they thought it necessary to instruct the judges to draft a clause excluding from the commission all those who neglected to take the oaths of office—including the oaths of allegiance and supremacy. By 1711, party position on the justices' qualification bill, like party stance on the appointment of justices, was clearly defined. The bill represented a revivified and persuasive Tory philosophy.

According to the last act regulating the qualifications of justices, passed in 1439, all justices except those "learned in the law" had to possess a landed estate yielding £20 per annum.[12] Each of the six bills introduced in the later Stuart Parliaments sought to increase the landed qualification demanded of the justice. In the justifications offered for these bills and the increasing sophistication of their provisions lie clues to the manner in which Country bias became annexed to Tory doctrine.[13]

Since the bills of 1699, 1700, and 1702 never reached the Lords, there to be preserved in the archives of the upper House, examination of their contents is not possible. Yet, it is probable that the bill of 1701 is representative of their tenor.[14] Its preamble argued: "by several statutes heretofore made, the justices of the peace in the counties and shires of England ought to be assigned of the most sufficient knights, esquires and gentlemen of the law in the said counties and of the best reputation, notwithstanding which statutes, of late divers persons of small estates and mean education have been deputed and assigned to be justices of peace in the said counties, whereof great inconveniences may arise. . . ." The 1701 bill sought to restore conformity between the spirit of English law and the administration of

11. House of Commons *Journals* 16:691, June 9, 1711.

12. 18 Henry VI c. 11.

13. The surviving bills are transcribed in *HMC, House of Lords MSS.* The bill of 1701 is in New Series IV, pp. 391–392, that of 1705 in VI, pp. 260–261, and that of 1711 in IX, pp. 154–155.

14. Like the bill of 1701, that of 1700 required an income of £200 per annum from land for justices of Westmorland. (Cumbria County R.O., Lonsdale MSS, no. 76, James Lowther to Sir John Lowther of Whitehaven, 9 Jan. [1700]. I wish to thank Professor H. Horwitz for this reference.)

government by increasing the landed income requisite for appointment to the bench, but its argument was not entirely persuasive. As the bill's preamble revealed, its argument was an appeal to tradition. Like the last statute regulating the qualifications of justices, that of 1439, the bill rested its case for landed qualification on the inconvenience nonlanded justices were likely to cause the governed. According to the 1439 statute, nonlanded justices "for their necessity do great extortion and oppression among the people." In 1701, the formula that equated lack of a sizeable landed estate with a slender purse was no longer valid. By the late seventeenth century and increasingly throughout the eighteenth century, those aspiring to gentry status solaced their vanity with a country seat and small adjoining estate while investing the rest of their capital in more profitable ventures.[15] If the Tories wished to justify the exclusion of those whose income did not spring from landed estates, they would have to reformulate the natural law binding justice to land.

By 1705, they had. The bill for qualification of justices introduced in that year began: "Whereas justices of the peace are, by the laws and statutes of this Realm, invested with many large powers and authorities, and the public welfare does in some measure depend upon the discreet and impartial execution of the same, and whereas experience has manifested that when persons of low condition and mean estates have been entrusted with the said office they have acted therein with more regard to their own private interest than the public welfare, to the great detriment of the good people of this kingdom. . . ." The school of Court and Exchange taught a man to further his immediate private gain. In contrast, land inspired its possessor to think of the long-term interest of the nation, for a landed gentleman's fortune and the future of his family were indissolubly bound to the fate of his country. Land likewise endowed its possessors with the autonomy prerequisite for virtuous action. Therefore, it was obvious that, for England's own good, the power of government ought to inhere in the gentry.

Such would be the reasoning assumed by the bill of 1711. Its preamble stated simply: "it has been found by experience that the Constituting persons of mean estates to be Justices of the Peace is highly prejudicial to the public welfare." By 1711, a Country protest articu-

15. H. J. Habbakuk, "English Landownership 1680–1740," *Economic History Review* 10 (Feb. 1940):2–17.

lated in inapposite rhetoric had been transformed into a confident assertion based on an emerging Tory philosophy.

Similarly, by 1711 refinement of the bill's provisions had altered its message. The bill of 1701 suggested a desperate attempt to monopolize power by a gentry fearful of extinction. Its major provision was a demand that justices possess lands and tenements yielding an annual income of £400. To insure that the justices' qualification be based on rural estates the bill excluded hereditaments from the definition of the estate requisite for qualification. Gregory King had recently estimated that there were only 4,400 baronets, knights, and esquires in receipt of incomes upwards of £400.[16] Even though King had probably undervalued the incomes of the landed gentry,[17] the new qualification would severely constrain the Lord Chancellor in his choice of justices, for by 1702 over 3,700 justices were listed in the commissions.[18] If the bill had become law, the governmental privileges of the gentry would have been transformed into rights protected from change in the structure of politics and society alike. In contrast, the 1705 bill eschewed the gratuitous and probably ineffective insult to urban property holders,[19] and also reduced the qualification from £400 to £300, thereby allowing a considerable proportion of the 12,000 gentlemen whose annual incomes averaged £280 to aspire to the bench. As the 1705 bill implicitly acknowledged, the gentry were not as landed as they found it psychologically necessary to claim. The 1701 bill had reconciled the conflict between the gentry's vision of themselves and the reality of their circumstances by a series of clauses which endowed some lesser gentry with the requisite qualification, at the expense of complicating its regulations. For instance, the bill's insistence on the possession of landed income free of encumbrances was mitigated by a clause exempting gentlemen who would have possessed the requisite estate, if only they had not settled some part of it upon their sons. By 1711, this

16. The figure usually given is £450, but Mathias points out that it should be £400 if King's calculations are to make mathematical sense (P. Mathias, "The Social Structure in the Eighteenth Century: A Calculation by Joseph Massie," *Economic History Review*, 2nd ser. 10 [1957]:32, n. 1).

17. G. Holmes, "Gregory King and the Social Structure of Pre-Industrial England," *Transactions of the Royal Historical Society*, 5th ser. vol. 27 (1977), pp. 53–58.

18. B.L., Harleian MSS 7512, excluding all those in the commissions' honourary clause, and sons of peers. This figure does not include the justices of Lancashire, who are not listed in this book of the peace.

19. It is likely that the property denoted by "hereditaments" would also be denoted by "tenements," a variety of property recognized by the 1701 bill as suitable for a judicial qualification. (See Giles Jacob, *A New Law-Dictionary*, 7th ed. [London, 1756], *sub* hereditaments, tenements, inheritance).

clause no longer marred the bill's clear statement of principle. Likewise, the 1701 bill had exempted the justices of Rutland and Cardigan from all its provisions and declared that a landed estate of £200 per annum was sufficient for justices of Wales, Monmouthshire, Westmorland, Cumberland, and Northumberland. By 1711, the attempt to rank counties in a hierarchy of judicial wealth was almost, though not entirely, abandoned. Instead, the exemptions of the 1711 bill recognized the legitimate needs of government: those officers of the central government who were routinely placed upon county commissions need not possess a landed qualification.[20] In fact, the 1711 bill was so well constructed that little change in its regulatory provisions was deemed necessary when an act to increase the qualification of justices of the peace was passed by Walpole's Parliament in 1732.

Though the Tories of Anne's reign were unable to enact a justices' qualification bill, their manufacture of the bill reveals the creation of both a philosophy and a measure which would sustain the Tory party through half a century of political exile. When, in the winter of 1720, the combined opposition of Walpole, his opposition Whigs, Tories, and Jacobites had defeated the government's peerage bill, and the government was being challenged by the most successful opposition to appear between 1714 and 1733, leave was requested to bring in a bill for the further qualification of justices of the peace. The motion was defeated by a vote of 107 to 103.[21] Proponents of the hypothesis of the disappearance of the Tory party might present this near victory as the last grin of the Cheshire cat. But the history of the justices' qualification bill suggests a different interpretation.

2. 1720–1750

On April 9, 1742, the House of Commons directed that lists of all the justices in England and Wales be laid before the House. The lists were produced on May 10, and the Commons then ordered that the records of the proceedings of March 26, 1700, upon the report of the committee to inspect the commissions of the peace and deputy lieutenants be recited to the House. Thereupon, the Commons granted leave to bring in a bill for the further qualification of justices of the peace.[22]

20. The officers of the Board of Green Cloth, and the commissioners and principal officers of the Navy.

21. House of Commons *Journals* 19:273, Feb. 20, 1719[20].

22. House of Commons *Journals* 24:170, 220.

As the members of the Parliament of 1742 reflected upon the proceedings of the Parliament of 1700, as they heard that Parliament's address to King William beseeching the monarch to remove from the commission men of small estates and reinstate therein gentlemen of quality and good estates, as they identified the rhetoric of the address with the proceedings of a Parliament that had attacked the Whig Junto and brought charges against Lord Somers, the members of the Parliament of 1742 would have entertained little doubt about the continuity of party and party ideology from 1700 to May 1742. That the justices' qualification bill symbolized the continuity of Toryism indicates the modifications in Tory ideology which enabled the Tories to survive as a party in early Hanoverian England.

Indeed, if the Tories had not modified their ideology, it is possible that they would not have survived as a party, for the accession of the first Hanoverian terminated many of the debates which had structured political discussion under the later Stuarts—and terminated them in favour of the Whigs. A Hanoverian on the throne was empirical validation of Whig arguments about the nature of kingship, the power of Parliament, and the meaning of the Glorious Revolution. Henceforth Tory arguments about these issues, which had been central to the politics of Anne's reign, could be dubbed Jacobite, and Jacobitism was not a platform on which many candidates could win elections. Because Jacobitism entailed the threat of absolutism, Catholicism, and civil disruption, Walpole insisted that Tories were Jacobites and thereby extended the Whigs' appeal. So powerful was the argument against Jacobitism that even some Tory members of Parliament voted for Walpole's government when a vote against it might aid the Pretender.[23] Walpole would have been delighted if the Tories had been content simply to reiterate the arguments which they had emphasized in Anne's reign. But the Tory party was neither moribund nor stagnant. As the Tories realized, a politician who allows his opponent to decide which issues will be debated has lost the debate before it has begun. The Tories did not make that mistake. Instead of merely rebutting Whig charges of Jacobitism, the Tories proclaimed their own definition of the issues which should preoccupy the political nation, and their definition was in large part based upon the Country ideology which had been incorporated into Toryism in Anne's reign.

23. L. Colley, *In Defiance of Oligarchy: The Tory Party 1714–1760* (Cambridge, 1982), p. 82.

The Tories' choice of issues was shrewd. Country ideology had developed out of several centuries of discussion about the relation between virtue and the state. "It was endowed with all the riches of the complex and articulate vocabulary of civic humanism. . . . Its paradigms therefore tended to dominate discourse."[24] In identifying their argument with a Country programme, the Tories had defined a debate that they might win. Moreover, an argument whose paradigms dominated discourse possessed an appeal beyond mere Toryism. In the late seventeenth century, the Whigs had associated their party with Country measures. Their own political history therefore led some Whigs to support both Whiggery and Country measures, while many more Whigs respected the Country analysis of the relation between political structure and political action. If Walpole could transform potential Tories into supporters of his ministry by labelling Tories as Jacobites, Tories could enlist potential Whigs in their cause by insisting upon the importance of Country issues.[25] In depicting Walpole as the epitome of corruption, the Tories associated Walpole, and by extension Whig government, with the decay which the era's dominant mode of discourse posited as the major threat to private virtue and public good. So, while early Hanoverian Tories retained a distinctive respect for the sovereign's prerogative and maintained their support of High Church principles[26] (thereby proclaiming their inheritance of the attitudes most emphasized in later Stuart Toryism), they also gave increasing prominence to Country issues which had played a more subordinate role in later Stuart Toryism. As a result, much of the political debate in early Hanoverian England focused on the dispute between Court and Country. That Country issues so preoccupied the political nation testifies to the persistence and resilience of the Tory party.[27]

Because early Hanoverian Tories prided themselves on promoting Country measures—measures to reduce the number of placemen in Parliament, to decrease the size of the army, and to shorten the duration of Parliaments[28]—their efforts to insure that justices possess sub-

24. Pocock, *Machiavellian Moment,* p. 486.

25. Colley, *In Defiance of Oligarchy,* p. 233.

26. *Ibid.,* pp. 102–112.

27. For a summary of the contention that the importance of Country issues indicates the decline of party, see W. A. Speck, "Whigs and Tories dim their glories," and J. Cannon, "Final Discussion," in *The Whig Ascendancy,* ed. J. Cannon (London, 1981), pp. 60–70, 190–192.

28. Colley, *In Defiance of Oligarchy,* pp. 93–97; H. T. Dickinson, *Liberty and Property, Political Ideology in Eighteenth-Century England* (London, 1977), pp. 184–186.

stantial landed estates acquired a special significance. The rural justice was the symbol of the 'Country,' as even the Whigs acknowledged. When, in 1732, a ministerial newspaper printed a fictitious debate between an adherent of the Court and a Country sympathizer, the figure the Whig writer chose to represent the Country was a justice of the peace.[29] The rural justice, living on his lands which in turn inspired his altruistic public service, personified Country virtue. In presenting bills for the qualification of the justice, the Tories identified themselves with a hero of Country ideology and extended their appeal to all who thought themselves independent country gentlemen.

As the Parliament of 1742 was well aware, the sponsors of that year's qualification bill symbolized both the Tory party and the wider appeal of its Country measures. Three of the bill's four sponsors—Carew, Fazackerley, and Winford—were acknowledged as Tories by contemporaries and posterity alike. The political alignment of the bill's fourth sponsor was somewhat more problematic. William Pulteney's sponsorship of the qualification bill of 1742 is emblematic of the changes in political structure that had occurred since 1714.

Pulteney was the Whig leader of the parliamentary opposition groups—a heterodox combination of Whigs opposed to Walpole's monopoly of the disposition of power and profit, of Whigs opposed to Walpole's conduct of the war, and of Tories opposed to Walpole and Whiggery—which had forced Sir Robert to resign the office of First Lord of the Treasury on January 31, 1742. By May 1742, when the justices' qualification bill was presented, Pulteney and some of his Whig followers were members of the ministry. Alliance with the Tories had enabled Walpole's Whig opponents to win places of power and profit, but in 1742 only two of Pulteney's Tory allies were similarly rewarded. Pulteney had used the Tories to gain office, for the Tories were vulnerable to Whig exploitation.

The Tories formed a large, but still limited, bloc in the House of Commons. In early 1742, they numbered 136.[30] Their electoral strongholds were in the counties and in boroughs with large electorates, but they possessed insufficient influence to expand or even maintain their base in the far more numerous smaller boroughs.[31] The Tories could inconvenience a ministry, but they could not muster sufficient numbers to threaten it. Nor could they persuade aspiring politi-

29. *London Journal,* Feb. 19, 1731–1732.
30. J. B. Owen, *The Rise of the Pelhams* (London, 1975), p. 66.
31. Colley, *In Defiance of Oligarchy,* p. 296.

cians to convert to the Tory creed. Aspiring politicians aspired to office, and the first two Hanoverian monarchs did not like awarding office to Tories. So, by the 1740s the Tories boasted relatively few leading speakers—a deficiency which Country ideology proclaimed a virtue. In Country thought, the ideal parliamentary representative was the independent member who could not be corrupted by hope of place or pension. As a member of the grand jury of the nation, the independent parliamentarian listened to the evidence presented by the sovereign's ministers and declared his verdict on their activities by his vote. But since the independent member did not take action in any matters which were likely to be adjudged by the House, he had no need to persuade others of the righteousness of his own actions. Indeed, those endowed with the gift of tongues were suspect. Sustained demonstration of oratorical skill was likely to appear as an attempt to gain office and so as notice of willingness to be corrupted. Since the Tories constituted a large bloc opposed to the ministry, since many of the Tories' Country measures were not inherently antithetical to Whiggery, and since the Tories lacked leading speakers, dissident Whigs presented Country measures to gain Tory support and embarrass the ministry. But contemporaries could distinguish between men and measures. That Pulteney endorsed the qualification bill did not make him any less a Whig. That the qualification bill was presented under Pulteney's aegis did not make it any less a Tory measure.

This, at any rate, was the interpretation of the House of Commons. Pulteney's promotion of the qualification bill, like his nearly simultaneous endorsement of a place bill,[32] was an obvious attempt to retain Tory support and so maintain effective leverage within the ministry. In June 1742, the House voted to postpone consideration of the qualification bill for two months, thus blocking further consideration of the measure during the remainder of the session. The tellers for the negative were Carew and Winford—Tories. Those for the affirmative were Osbaldeston and Glanville—adherents of the Walpoleian faction in the ministry.[33]

Three years later, a bill for the further qualification of justices of the peace received the approbation of Lords and Commons and the assent of the monarch. The bill passed through the Lords without amendment; indeed, that House did not even divide to vote on it.

32. W.S. Lewis, ed., *Horace Walpole Correspondence,* vol. 17 (New Haven, 1954), p. 431, Walpole to Mann, May 20, 1742.

33. House of Commons *Journals* 24:278, June 16, 1742.

Agreement both to the bill and to appointment of justices without distinction of party was the basis of the treaty between the Pelhamites and the Tories. In 1745, a measure to insure that justices were gentlemen of substance was a Tory symbol of the continuity and development of their own distinctive political ideology.

The 1745 bill was a modification of that sponsored by Pulteney and his Tory allies in 1742, which in turn was a refinement of an act sponsored by Pulteney's followers and the Tories[34] in 1732 which, in its turn, was almost identical to the bill for the further qualification of justices of the peace presented to Parliament by members of the October Club in 1711. The only major difference between the 1711 bill and that of 1732 was that the 1711 bill's requirement that a justice be in possession of an annual income from estates, tenements, and hereditaments of at least £300 per annum was reduced by the 1732 bill to £200. Since the projected bill of 1720 would have required an income of £200, the 1732 bill may be that which would have been introduced in 1720.[35]

That Walpole allowed the 1732 measure to pass the House of Commons and eventually become an act of Parliament is surprising. It may be that the act was an attempt to pacify Tories and gentry, as was the contemporaneous attempt to reduce the land tax by imposition of a salt tax and excise. The government did expunge the less seemly provisions of the bill in the House of Lords. Tory propaganda was not permissible in an act of Parliament, and so, the bill's preamble charging that "experience" had revealed "that the constituting Persons of mean Estates to be Justices of the Peace is highly prejudicial to the Public Welfare" became, in the hands of the Lords, a calm and disinterested statement of a philosophical problem that had not yet affected the lives of Englishmen: "the constituting Persons of mean Estates to be Justices of the Peace may be highly prejudicial to the publick Welfare." The remote possibility that the act would disqualify any justices

34. House of Commons *Journals* 21:803, Feb. 17, 1731[2].

35. *Political State of Great Britain*, vol. 19 (1720), p. 236. The 1732 bill is 357.b.12 (35) in the British Library Collection. There are only two other variations from the 1711 bill. The 1711 bill set the qualification for J.P.s of Wales, Monmouth, Westmorland, Durham, Lancaster, Rutland, and Cumberland at £150 per annum. The 1732 bill set the qualification for J.P.s of eight Welsh counties, Westmorland, Lancaster, Cumberland, Rutland, and the Isle of Wight at £100 per annum. The 1711 bill exempted sergeants at law from its provisions; the 1732 bill did not. This alteration is probably a reflection of the decline in the importance of the sergeants. While seventeenth-century and early eighteenth-century commissions usually listed one of the sergeants who rode the circuit, mid-eighteenth-century commissions did not.

in the provincial commissions became an impossibility after the Lords had changed the qualification from £200 per annum to £100 per annum and altered the definition of leasehold land admissible as a qualification from land held for a term of at least sixty years or two lives to land held for a term of at least twenty-one years or one life. In 1732, the Tory qualification bill of 1711, suitably shorn of almost every effective or affective provision, became the law of the land.[36]

That the act was both ineffectual and unenforceable is suggested by the attempt of Pulteney and the Tories to introduce a further bill for the further qualification of justices of the peace in 1742.[37] As the bill left blank the qualification to be demanded of justices, it is quite probable that the Tories were hoping to increase the qualification and thereby disqualify some of Hardwicke's appointees. In 1742, a Tory writer was suggesting that only those in possession of estates yielding annual incomes of £500 or £1,000 enjoyed estates equivalent to those required of justices in 1439, while in 1745 some thought the minimum qualification should be £300 or £500.[38] In the event, the act of 1745 settled for the £100 qualification of 1732 while sanctioning a new candidate for judicial honours: the heir of a person who possessed an estate of £300 per annum. Nor did the act unduly constrain the justice in his definition of his estate. The estate could include messuage, land, rent, tithe, office, benefice or, as the act stated, "what else."[39] The act's principles enshrined the concept of a landed magistracy, while its specifics defined "land" so broadly that the term almost lost its meaning. Pragmatists might scorn such an act. But the Tories were idealists, committed to a political ideology and its symbols.

Perhaps the Tories considered the act an achievement because it contained a provision which made the requirement of a qualification enforceable. Every justice had to take an oath swearing that he had the requisite estate and specifying that estate. The 1745 act decreed that any justice acting without proper qualification was liable to a fine of £100, half of which would become the property of the plaintiff once lack of qualification had been proved in any of the king's courts at

36. 5 George II c. 18.

37. B. L., Abbot B1—erroneously catalogued in S. Lambert, *List of House of Commons Sessional Papers 1701–1750*, List and Index Society, Special Series, vol. 1, (London, 1968), as the bill of 1732.

38. [Thomas Carte], *A Full Answer to the Letter from a By-Stander, Etc., . . . By R—H—Esq.* (London, 1742), p. 192; *London Magazine* 15 (Feb., 1745):82.

39. 18 George II c. 20. Contrary to Owen, *Rise of the Pelhams*, p. 260, the act does not require that the estate lie in the county for which the justice was commissioned.

Westminster. In the trial of the suit, the only estates admissible as proof of qualification would be those specified when the justice took the oath plus those listed by the justice when he received notice that his qualification was being contested. The burden of proof of qualification therefore rested upon the justice. English common law generally placed at least some of the burden of proof upon the plaintiff. It would have been very difficult to prove that a justice did not have an estate of proper proportions. By limiting the estate upon which a justice could base his claim to qualification to that specified in a sworn document open to public inspection, the act would allow a complainant to estimate whether the justice actually had the proper qualification. By placing the burden of proof of the income from the estate upon the justice, the act allowed the complainant to circumvent the obvious difficulties of proving that the estate did not yield the required income. By offering a reward to those who successfully prosecuted an unqualified justice, the act encouraged private citizens to cleanse the bench of unqualified and therefore corrupt magistrates. It remains to be seen whether Tory remedy was applicable to Whig evil.

It would be surprising if it were. Despite Tory rhetoric on the necessary connection between landed estate, independence, and judicial virtue, the ultimate Tory valuation of the landed estate requisite to a justice was hardly rigorous. Surviving debates on the acts of 1732 and 1745 do not make reference to the definition of the estate of a gentleman. But, in 1732, Parliament was also discussing the effect of a salt tax on the English taxpayer, and in the course of that debate, Pulteney, who sponsored the 1732 act, and Walpole, who allowed it to pass, presented their own definitions of the estate essential to gentility. Pulteney referred to a farmer of £100 a year and to landed gentlemen of £400 a year. Walpole's assessment of the structure of English society differs somewhat from that of Pulteney, but his definition of a gentleman is remarkably suitable for an evaluation of his opinion of the justices' act. "I believe," he said, "there are few landed Gentlemen in *England,* whose Estates do not amount to £100 per Annum; . . ."[40] The acts of 1732 and 1745 would not hinder any Englishman who thought himself a country gentleman from becoming a justice of the peace.

Nor would either act force the Lord Chancellors to modify their

40. *Political State of Great Britain,* vol. 44 (1732), p. 393; *Historical Register for 1732,* vol. 17, p. 320.

policies of appointment. When Hardwicke's informants noted the income of judicial nominees, they almost invariably recorded a figure much higher than £100 per annum. Indeed, it was rare for a figure so low to be mentioned.[41] Even the dubious gentility of the justices of Middlesex would have survived the test. As the Tory *Craftsman* acknowledged, estates could be bought in or near London at prices which were only four or five times their annual rental value.[42] Perhaps the acts may have eliminated some Welsh contenders for a place on the bench. The acts may very probably have barred trading justices from the county bench. Trading justices lived by their judicial trade. They had to reside in areas where there was sufficient judicial business to enable them to make a living from the fees of their office and the bribes of those who wished the justice to neglect the suppression of alehouses and bawdy houses. Therefore, trading justices lived in towns and cities, but both acts stated that their provisions did not extend "to any City or Town, being a County of itself, or to any other City, Town, Cinque-Port, or Liberty, having Justices of the Peace within their respective Limits and precincts, by Charter, Commission, or otherwise." The acts might affect a few of the trading justices of Surrey and Middlesex; they would not touch the justices of Westminster, and they were almost irrelevant to the local government of England.

It is not, therefore, surprising that there is little evidence that the 1745 act had to be enforced. Burn's *Justice* usually mentions legal decisions relevant to the execution of the office of justice. There could be few acts more relevant to the office than those of 1732 and 1745; yet, no mention of any case connected with the act appears in the edition of 1756, and there is still no whisper of decision on the act in the edition of 1780. It had been the opinion of the Duke of Newcastle that the 1745 bill was an "innocent" measure; according to the Earl of Chesterfield, it was a mere "trifle," one of those "little objects Tory Boobys had set their hearts upon."[43] They appear to have been entirely correct.

That the Tories insisted on an act for the further qualification of justices must be considered a triumph of ideology over *realpolitik*. Similarly, only Tories firmly committed to a developing political ideol-

41. A. M. Mimardiere, "The Warwickshire Gentry, 1660–1730" (M.A. thesis, University of Birmingham, 1963), pp. 104ff. and 160 states that the income of Warwickshire's justices ranged between £600 and £1,000 per annum.

42. *The Craftsman* 318 (Aug. 5, 1732):201.

43. B.L., Add. MSS 32804, f. 257, Newcastle to Chesterfield, Mar. 12, 1744–1745; ff. 291–292, Chesterfield to Newcastle, Apr. 13, 1745, N.S.

ogy would have been convinced that the aim of the acts of 1732 and 1745 was that which had directed the rhetoric of the Tories of Anne's reign. In fact, discussion of the acts revealed that Whig as well as Tory views of the justice were closely tied to distinct political ideologies.

In Anne's reign, protest against the threat to free government posed by the growth of bureaucracy and the permeation of politics by money had constituted the core of an emerging political ideology. Under Bolingbroke's guidance, Toryism in the reign of George II became a continuous call to the defence of vanishing freedoms. Government, it was declared, was becoming increasingly corrupt and increasingly arbitrary. So Tory publications reminded Britons of their rights under the more free and perfect constitution of pre-Conquest and Tudor England, when their members of Parliament had been freely elected and subjected to constant reminders of their dependence upon the electorate.[44] In elaborating a criticism of Walpole's regime, Tory ideology became more comprehensive and its charges more specific. Tory publications condemned the Riot Act, for it increased the arbitrary powers of government. They denounced the laws of customs and excise, because those charged with evasion of duties might be tried before a board of customs commissioners rather than by a jury of their peers. And so, too, they deplored all those laws of the past half-century which had increased the justices' summary jurisdiction, so that justices were now "vested with a Power by far too discretionary for a free nation."

> [L]et any thinking man reflect seriously on the prodigious Number of Penal Laws, made for the Security of the Government, and on other Accounts and Pretences, since the *Revolution;* and the Multitude of Taxes that have been laid since that Time, upon Windows and all excisable and other Commodities; and an enormous Accession of Power and Influence over all Ranks and Orders of Men, by putting the Laws of all these into their Hands, hath occurred to *Justices of Peace,* the Jack-calls of bad Ministers.

Since, it was charged, justices collaborated with excise officers in unfair administration of the excise laws, since justices possessed new powers under the Riot Act, and since justices delivered judicial verdicts without benefit of jury, Tory emphasis on the dangers of arbitrary rule resulted in new scrutiny of the powers and composition of the commission.

44. I. Kramnick, *Bolingbroke and His Circle; The Politics of Nostalgia in the Age of Walpole* (Cambridge, Mass., 1968), pp. 78, 178ff; Pocock, *The Machiavellian Moment,* p. 480.

No man, stated the Tory *Craftsman,* ought to be entrusted with arbitrary authority, but Walpole's justices were particularly suspect. If justices were incorrupt and impartial, if they served the law rather than party, Englishmen would have less cause to fear for their freedoms. But bad ministers had the power to appoint bad justices. The government had removed those "who are actuated by higher Motives, and scorn to prostitute their Office, or sacrifice the Interest of their Country, to the Views of the Court." Instead, commissions were filled with Walpole's minions, necessitous creatures who derived their sustenance from office. "When *Men in Office* are thus suffer'd to make a *Trade* of their Duty, They will be obliged, in Return, to become the Tools of a *Minister* . . . by making Use of their Authority to influence *Elections,* or carry on any other *dirty Job,* which his Service requires." For the Tories, both the justices' powers and their use of their powers proved the charge that Walpole's government was a venal tyranny.

Similarly, Tory depiction of the plight of local government mirrored their analysis of the decay of Parliament. In days of yore, Englishmen had freely elected their parliamentary representatives; now English liberties were threatened by the corruption of Parliament. Under the ancient constitution justices were elected. It were better so. When Englishmen lost the right to choose their magistrates and the appointment of justices devolved upon the Crown, both justices and government used the augmented powers of local government to pervert the execution of law and prevent the free election of members of Parliament.[45] That Tory analysis of judicial administration accorded so well with their analysis of the deterioration of England's constitution reveals the extent to which party ideology permeated the political debate of Walpole's England.

Yet, though Tory discussion of the justice disclosed the presence of a pervasive Tory ideology, it also betrayed internal inconsistencies within Toryism, inconsistencies which by the 1740s were making Tory doctrine an increasingly nebulous idealization of gentry rule. Advocating both representative government and government under a strong and moral sovereign, dreaming of the days of benevolent paternalism under

45. The following provided the quotations in the preceding paragraphs and the basis for their assertions: *The Craftsman* 318 (Aug. 5, 1732):197–198, 200–203; 471 (July 12, 1735):40–41, and Appendix to 355 (April 21, 1733):225–226, 247–248; *The Measures of the Late Administration Examin'd* (London, 1745), p. 32; [Thomas Carte] *A Full Answer to the Letter from a By-Stander,* pp. 188, 191–194, 206–207; *Opposition not Faction or the Rectitude of the Present Parliamentary Opposition . . . In Answer to a late Book, Intitled, Faction Detected Etc.* (London, 1743), pp. 50–57.

elected justices, Toryism might be used as a doctrine of radicalism or revisionism—neither acceptable to the Tories of George II's England. So, though Tory argument might imply and even recommend that justices ought to be elected, Tories were not slaves to the logic of their rhetoric. Tories might like to believe that, if justices were elected, Tories would be elected. Yet, Tories also believed that good government was government by the independent country gentlemen, the natural leaders of the people. Since the gentry were independent and incorruptible, they wielded their powers in the true interests of the governed. Even as Toryism subjected the powers of the justice to critical examination, it refrained from wholesale condemnation of appointive magistracy. If only party affiliation did not affect appointment and the venal were not endowed with office, England's gentry would be restored to their rightful place upon the bench and local government to its pristine purity. Having raised the problem of arbitrary rule inherent in an appointed and powerful magistracy, Toryism refused to acknowledge that there was a problem. Similarly, Bolingbroke's Tories criticized the management of Parliament by ministers whom the king had chosen, but refused to acknowledge that maintenance of the powers of both king and Parliament required parliamentary management.

Consequently both Tory debate and parliamentary programme reflect the dissipation of Tory ideology before the conflicting tenets of its argument. In the case of the justices, the problem of reconciling the claims of liberty and authority was partially solved by a facile but useful identification of trading justices, and usually trading justices only, as instruments of arbitrary power. Gentry justices were obeyed because they were respected; only the trading justice had to call upon the army to enforce an authority not respected because of its abuse by both justices and government.[46] So, while the Tories of Anne's reign had regarded a justices' qualification act as a means of restoring the rightful leaders of England to the county benches, the Tories ruled by George II acknowledged that their acts were directed solely against trading justices, and that trading justices were confined to the county of Middlesex and the liberty of Westminster.[47] Tory ideology as well as Whig power had deflected the aim of Tory measure. Yet, that the

46. *Gentleman's Magazine* 8 (1738):513.

47. *The Kentish Post or Canterbury News-Letter,* Mar. 1–4, 1731/1732, Feb. 3–6, 1730/1731; *The Craftsman* 313 (July 1, 1732):158; *HMC, Egmont Diary,* vol. 1, p. 223, Feb. 17, 1731–1732; Charles Grey, *Considerations on Several Proposals, lately made for the Better Maintenance of the Poor* (London, 1751), pp. 24–25.

Tories of 1745 imagined there was a direct connection between the act for the further qualification of justices and an agreement to restore Tories to the commissions reveals the commitment of mid-century Tories to a party ideology formed in the reign of Queen Anne.[48]

Caught in a trap of their own making, the Tories had sold their votes for a politically ineffectual act. Nonetheless, they were neither politically inept nor politically defunct. It remained for the Tories of 1747 to foreshadow the demise of their party in their new programme for the commission of the peace. Having realized that the treaty of 1745 would not secure the bench for their party, the Tories of 1747 proposed that all gentlemen paying land tax for estates assessed at £300 per annum be appointed justices.[49] By mid-century, Tory circumvention of the problem of the nature of arbitrary rule and insistence on the virtues of the gentry had culminated in a self-interested advocacy of untrammelled gentry government. Even the Tories of Anne's reign had not claimed that an estate automatically and invariably instilled in its possessor the qualities and capacities necessary for good governance. Though in succeeding decades most gentlemen of fortune and estate would gain a seat on the bench, whatever their politics, this realization of Tory dreams signalled the demise of their party and its vision. When the Tory party became so weak that the government could appoint justices without fear of the effect of their political affiliation, and Tory doctrine so vague and generalized that Whig and Tory alike could accept a modified version of the doctrine of gentry rule, Toryism was a sentiment and not a party ideology.

Yet, though Toryism was moribund at the accession of George III, Tory ideology informed the debate of the Walpoliean era, and an attempt to describe political debate in the 1730s and 1740s that omitted the influence of ideology would distort the character of early Hanoverian politics. Under Walpole, as in the reigns of the last Stuarts, Tory ideology was countered by Whig ideology. But, unlike their later Stuart predecessors, Walpoleian Whigs found it necessary to present a distinctive analysis of the justices. Later Stuart Whigs had responded to Tory charges about the composition of the commission by impugning Tory loyalty to the constitution as defined by the Revolution of 1688. Unlike the later Stuart Tories, their successors discovered

48. *The Case Fairly Stated In a Letter from a Member of Parliament in the Country Interest* (London, 1745), pp. 29–31.

49. B.L., Add. MSS 35870, ff. 129–130; see also C. Grey, *Considerations on Several Proposals*, p. 24.

an appropriate reply. In refocusing their ideology so as to emphasize and refashion their depiction of corruption, early Hanoverian Tories elaborated a framework for continual complaint that Whig government and Whig justices were violating the liberties of Englishmen, including those guaranteed by the Revolution of 1688. So, Walpole's pamphleteers riposted with an alternative explanation of English government and English history, an explanation which incorporated an alternative analysis of the office of the justice of the peace.

If, wrote the Whigs, present English rights were neither identical to rights of Englishmen in the distant past nor shadows of ancient liberties; if present rights were superior to those of the past; then the legal assertions of royal power which altered the shape of government—preeminently the establishment of Parliament—were contributions to the improvement of English government.[50] So it was with the justices. "The Election of Justices," one Whig paper stated, "was not a Privilege inherent in the People, they had no original right to it in our Law, it was a grant from the Crown, and Seditions, Insurrections, Riots, Tumults, Disorders, Fogpates, and Calebites made it necessary for the King to reinvest it in the more immediate Appointment of the Crown." If justices were elected, wrote another Whig, they would favour their supporters. "Therefore, . . . the Power of chusing their *Magistrates* was never wrested from the People by the violence of the Crown, but [was] freely given up by the People to avoid those Inconveniences and Confusions, which long Experience had found to be the Consequence of that Privilege [the *Craftsman*] complains we have lost." Besides, the Glorious Revolution had allowed the people to choose their sovereign and "if they chuse the First, and he the rest, they chuse all."[51] Whiggish explanations of the Glorious Revolution served to justify Court power, Walpole's government, and the policy adopted by Whig Lord Chancellors in their choice of Whig justices.

Similarly, Walpole's propagandists posited an interpretation of his methods of government designed to counter Tory argument, and again a Whig interpretation structured to answer criticisms of national government was applied in a consistent manner to rebut Tory analysis of

50. Kramnick, *Bolingbroke*, pp. 130f; Dickinson, *Liberty and Property*, pp. 140–141.

51. Fogpates refers to the writers of *Fog's*, a Tory journal, and Calebites to those of the *Craftsman*. *The Hyp-Doctor*, No. 88 (Aug. 8, 1732); *Applebee's Original Weekly-Journal*, Aug. 19, 1732.

local government. Tories insisted that good government demanded virtuous and therefore disinterested governors; Whigs replied that the governor's virtue was less important than the results of his activity. If a gentleman's actions produced good government, then his motives need not be examined. Indeed man's baser passions should be channelled so as to serve the public interest. What the Tories termed corruption in national government was actually a system that made parliamentary government work. In Mandeville's terms, private evil was public good.[52] And so while the *Craftsman* might argue that a qualification of £100 per annum was an insufficient estate for a justice, especially in those parts of Middlesex near London where estates might be bought for four or five years' purchase, the Whig would reply that it was necessary that gentlemen of lesser estates be appointed to the Middlesex bench. "In places inhabited by the *Scum* and *Dregs* of the People, and the most profligate Class of Life, *Gentlemen* of any great *Figure* or *Fortune,* will not take such a Drudgery upon them; . . ." Gentlemen had better taste than to reside amongst the lower orders, were disgusted by their brutish and inhumane treatment of one another, and would decline to listen to "their lothesome and ridiculous relations."[53] Government which functioned, albeit by appealing to the vanity or greed of minor gentlemen, was superior to a governmental structure which would prevent government from functioning at all. Indeed, a society whose government refused to recognize the public benefit which could flow from private vice was a society doomed to decay.[54]

In the interstices of their ideological debate, Whig and Tory sketched portraits of the justice at once complementary and contradictory but always lighted by their political beliefs. Distrusting arbitrary government and the growth of the power of the Crown—especially when that power was wielded by Whig ministers—the Tories emphasized the more purely judicial powers of the justice and their abuse. In Tory ideology the justice was a "Sort of *inferior Judge,* on whose Determination the Liberty and Property of his Fellow Subjects in a great Measure, depend."[55] Since justices were judges they should be disinterested, above party, subject neither to fear nor favour. Like the

52. Kramnick, *Bolingbroke,* pp. 120f; Pocock, *The Machiavellian Moment,* p. 487.
53. *Applebee's Original Weekly-Journal,* Aug. 19, 1732.
54. T. Horne, "Politics in a Corrupt Society: William Arnall's Defence of Robert Walpole," *Journal of the History of Ideas* 41 (1980):612.
55. *The Craftsman* 318 (Aug. 5, 1732):197.

judges, justices should be independent. Unfortunately, they were not. Naturally, the Whigs considered the Tory analogy of justice to judge unrealistic. Whig writers preferred to approach the question of judicial function empirically, asking not what powers the law allowed the justice to wield, but what justices most frequently did. Since they wished to justify the appointment of minor gentlemen to the Middlesex bench, the Whigs were delighted to discover that the justice's most usual role was that of proto-social worker. "A *Justice* of *Peace,*" proclaimed a Whig paper, "is not a Magistrate of so extraordinary a Power. Whoever knows any thing of the Laws of the Land and of Proceedings of *Justices of the Peace* cannot be insensible that by far the Greater Part of those Strifes and Dissensions which come before them, are such as are determinable, no otherwise by them than as *Moderators* and *Reconcilers* of Differences, and not as *Magistrates,* in which they can Act by any Authority of Law. . . . A judicious and compassionate *Justice of the Peace,* heals innumerable trifling Discords and Animosities, which for want of such a Prudent Interposition might terminate in the utter Ruin of the Contenders."[56]

Political debate structured by the framework of ideological conflict need not be divorced from reality. Englishmen of the Walpoleian era were engaged in a debate about the role and function of the justice, and while the debate was based upon philosophical definitions of the proper conduct of government, it was given point and emphasis by the use of concrete observations from contemporary life. Tories decried the political uses of the justice and, as has been shown, their estimate of local government was not completely unfounded. Whigs depicted the justice as both more and less than a judicial officer. Only by examination of the work usually performed by a justice can the accuracy of their portraiture be evaluated. In Kent change in the political and social composition of the bench, in the administrative structure of local government, in the work demanded of local governors, as well as in assumptions about rule implicit in gentry culture, altered the roles which justices chose to assume.

56. *Applebee's Original Weekly-Journal,* Aug. 19, 1732.

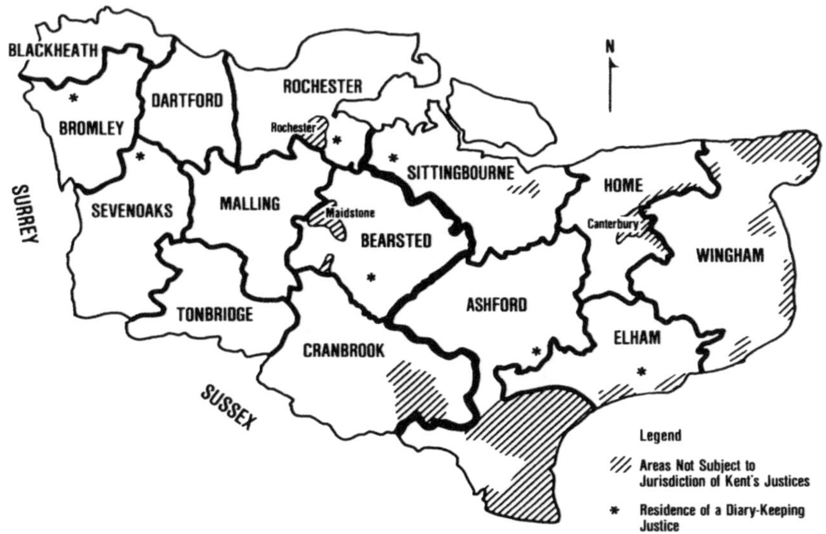

KENT'S PETTY SESSIONAL DIVISIONS, 1753

PART THREE

The Work of Kent's Justices

CHAPTER SIX

The Single Justice: Varieties of Paternalism

Elizabeth soon perceived, that though this great lady was not in the commission of the peace for the county, she was a most active magistrate in her own parish, the minutest concerns of which were carried to her by Mr. Collins; and whenever any of the cottagers were disposed to be quarrelsome, discontented, or too poor, she sallied forth into the village to settle their differences, silence their complaints, and scold them into harmony and plenty.

Jane Austen, *Pride and Prejudice*
(New York, 1962), p. 176

Whether depicted as petty tyrant or benevolent overlord, the justice has always been credited with guiding the conduct of those fortunate enough to live in his neighbourhood. The justice, it is assumed, knew of the most intimate details of the lives of those he governed; he stood *in statu parentis,* eager to give advice, ready to heal quarrels, and willing to interfere in the lives of his inferiors when necessary. Though some critics have deplored such judicial surveillance, the justices' activities as fatherly arbiters of their communities have more usually been presented as the most important and praiseworthy of their functions. In 1837 Sir J. Eardley-Wilmot, M.P., summarized this somewhat Arcadian concept of judicial paternalism in straightforward Victorian prose: "the most important part of their duties was their residence in the various places in the county where they lived and where they were enabled to act as friends of the poor and heal disputes as arbitrators and referees. In cases of assault, differences between masters and servants, and cases of trespass, their interposition was most constant and useful."[1] By counselling his inferiors, the justice enabled them to live in harmony without rancorous recourse to the expense and severity of the law.

Frequent reliance upon a governor's informal guidance and extra-legal aid is a hallmark of paternalist rule. When the justice used his legal powers, the law defined and so limited his authority. Resort to the law implied the failure of the justice's persuasive power as both social superior and magistrate. On the other hand, dependence of the governed upon the extra-legal intervention of a justice implied that the governed accepted the justice as the natural leader of his community. A fatherly ruler preserving the peace of England's green fields by beneficent guidance: the image is most pleasing.

That the image also reflected fact, that the justice did indeed act as arbiter and arbitrator of his community, is suggested by a venerable tradition of contemporary observation and historians' commentary. In the late sixteenth century, William Lambard observed that though his classic manual for justices dealt with the purely legal functions of the magistracy, he assumed that the justice would "occupie himself also in pacifying the suits and controversies that do arise among his neighbors etc. Yea, rather I wish him to be as wel . . . a Compounder as a Commissioner of the Peace. . . ."[2] According to Blackstone, the justice's most vital function was "healing petty disputes and preventing vexatious prosecutions"; in the 1790s, Thomas Gisborne deemed the conciliation of disputants and prevention of lawsuits the "most useful" of the justice's duties, and the frequent citation of Wilmot's encomium of magisterial arbitration indicates the acceptance by both historians and the justice's peers of the importance of this role.[3] Amongst such a chorus, the opinion of mid-eighteenth-century Whigs that justices were "Reconcilers," who healed "innumerable trifling Discords and Animosities, which for want of such a Prudent Interposition might

1. R. Quinault, "The Warwickshire County Magistracy and Public Order, c. 1830–70," in *Popular Protest and Public Order,* ed. J. Stevenson and R. Quinault (London, 1974), p. 191.

2. W. Lambarde, *Eirenarcha: or of the Office of the Justices of Peace* (London, 1594), p. 10.

3. Sir W. Blackstone, *Commentaries on the Laws of England* (Philadelphia, 1771–1772), vol. 1, p. 8; T. Gisborne, *An Enquiry into the Duties of Men in the Higher and Middle Classes of Society* (London, 1795), vol. 1, p. 423; C. H. E. Zangerl, "The Social Composition of the County Magistracy in England and Wales, 1831–1837," *Journal of British Studies* 11 (1971–1972): 181; D. McClatchey, *Oxfordshire Clergy, 1777–1869* (Oxford, 1960), p. 181. See also P. Clarke, *English Provincial Society from the Reformation to the Revolution: Religion, Politics and Society in Kent 1550–1640* (Hassocks, Sussex, 1977), pp. 119–120.

terminate in the utter Ruin of the Contenders,"[4] seems little more than a truism—until it is remembered that this description of judicial duties was part of an argument designed to justify the appointment of men of lesser status to the bench in urban areas. It is, of course, possible that the Whig argument was a completely accurate description of the normal work of both rural and urban justices. Yet, the congruity of a partisan description of urban justices with the venerated image of rural paternalism raises doubts about the activity of urban justices and/or rural paternalism. Only by analysing the work of single justices out of sessions can the reality of justices' normal business be reconstructed. As the Whig argument would suggest, examination of the work of urban and rural justices illuminates a rather peculiar relation between the image and reality of rural paternalism.

The most direct and obvious route to a view of a justice's activities is the record of those activities kept by the justice himself. Justices' manuals advised the local governor to keep a record of his activity so that he could remember what he did and why he did it.[5] At least ten Kentish justices heeded this advice.[6] At Beachborough, an Elizabethan mansion about two and a half miles inland from the small port of Hythe, three generations of Brockmans surveyed their considerable acres and ruled the southern corner of Kent's Elham division. Their impressive and conscientious magisterial service is attested by a continuous series of justice's notebooks stretching from William Brockman's record of his activity from 1689 to 1701, and from 1713 to 1724, through the notes of his son James from 1725 to 1767, to those of James's heir, Ralph Drake Brockman, an active justice from 1770 to 1781.[7] Though the Brockmans were landowners sufficiently wealthy and powerful to exhibit political pretensions, their lineage and landed power was overshadowed by that of two more eminent note-taking justices. Sir Edward Filmer, fifth Bart., premier representative of a family that had guided Kent's activities during the Civil War and would in the late eighteenth century send a baronet to Parliament, resided at his family seat in East Sutton, about six miles from Maid-

4. *Applebee's Original Weekly-Journal,* Aug. 19, 1732.

5. W. Nelson, *The Office and Authority of a Justice of Peace,* 6th ed. (London, 1718), p. 489; E. Bohun, *The Justice of Peace, His Calling and Qualifications* (London, 1693), p. 153.

6. Ralph Buffkin also kept a diary, Kent A.O., U23/O1, but comparison of the diary with Quarter Sessions records reveals that it is a very incomplete account of his activity.

7. B.L., Add. MSS 42598, 42599, 42600; notes on William Brockman's activities in the 1690s are also to be found in B.L., Add. MSS 42596, 42597.

stone, where he stored documents taken in the course of his judicial duties and kept a notebook of his activity from 1750 to 1754.[8] Sir Wyndham Knatchbull, fifth Bart., justice from 1729 until his death in 1749, recorded judicial decisions made during his summer retirements to his seat a few miles from Ashford.[9] Like these five representatives of the greater gentry, Paul D'Aranda was also a rural justice. Unlike them, he possessed but a moderate landed estate—Preston, situated in the parish of Shoreham in the Sevenoaks division, where he compiled a diary of his activities for the year 1708.[10] Thomas Osborne was probably slightly more prosperous and eminent. His estate at Hartlip, an inland parish about five miles from Sittingbourne, encompassed over 600 acres and was in 1720 worth more than £1,200 per annum. Like his father before him, Osborne was a justice in the Sittingbourne division, and his papers include a notebook of his activities as a single justice from June 1692 to July 1693.[11] In contrast, George Norman was a gentleman lessee of the rectory in Bromley, a market town ten miles from London. Between 1792 and 1796 he continued the justice's diary begun eighty-one years earlier by William Emmett, whose family properties the Normans had inherited. Emmett, like Norman a lessee of the Bromley rectory, had gained dignity from his appointment to Kent's commission in 1711, an honour he lost in the purge of 1714 and regained in 1729.[12] His colleague, Gabriel Walters, was even less burdened by landed estate and prestige. Were it not for mention of his activities in the records of Quarter Sessions and his justice's diary, it could not now be discovered that Walters lived in the Rochester division, in or near Chatham, where he acted from 1708 to 1718.[13] Fortunately, the ten justices run almost the gamut of judicial stereotypes—from greater gentry rejoicing in lordly acres, to country gentlemen enjoying pastoral peace, petty notables of a market town, and the obscure gentleman residing near a bustling ship-building centre. As the map of Kent reveals, only the justice of an urban area is missing. In Kent, most of the urban justices lived in the Blackheath division, that portion of Kent which bordered London and would in the nineteenth century be swallowed by the metropolitan colossus.

8. Kent A.O., U120/O11, U120/O22.
9. Kent A.O., U951/O3.
10. Kent A.O., U442/O45.
11. D. A. Baker, "Agriculture in Kent, 1660–1760: A Regional and Comparative Study" (Ph.D. thesis, Kent University, 1976), pp. 16, 268; Kent A.O., U771/A14.
12. Kent A.O., U310/O14.
13. Hants. R.O., 18/M51/595, 18/M51/596.

As the justices fit the stereotypes suggested by their places of residence, so do their judicial duties. Table 3 reveals that Gabriel Walters, living near Chatham, was by far the busiest of the later Stuart justices. His diary records his activity in 304 cases in twenty-four months between July 1708 and December 1710.[14] A large portion of these cases required merely *pro forma* activity. Walters signed 123 certificates that decedents had been buried in wool, and gave his legal imprimatur to 67 attestations. Most of the latter involved naval affairs: a ship's officer would make oath that victuals delivered to his ship were defective or underweight; a sailor would swear that one of his mates was dead, or that he himself merited a certificate so that he could be granted money from the Chatham Chest. Walters also issued or acted on twenty-seven passes for vagrants, issued warrants or orders in sixteen cases involving the administration of the poor laws, took examinations and sometimes other action in seven cases of bastardy, and issued warrants or took note of five disputes between masters and servants. Of the 304 cases aired in his parlour, 54 involved quarrels or charges of criminal activity.

Only the activity of William Emmett, the justice in the market town of Bromley, can even be compared to that of Walters. Unfortunately, Emmett's diary is peculiarly cryptic: he noted warrants for unspecified misdemeanours and used the term *misdemeanour* to encompass both complaints of assault and the demand of parish officers that a poor person be examined as to his settlement. It is clear that in 1712 through 1713 Emmett heard at least 42 complaints of crime and quarrel and at least 136 such complaints in the seven years between 1730 and 1736. Although Emmett's activity in criminal cases may appear quite similar to Walter's, their decisions indicate that the two justices were confronted by different varieties of miscreant. In the nine years of 1712 to 1713 and 1730 to 1737, Emmett took recognizances forwarding just four cases to Quarter Sessions and three to Assizes. In two years, Walters took recognizances which sent two cases to Quarter Sessions and five to Assizes.[15] Unlike Emmett, Walters routinely recorded cases of burglary, highway robbery, and forgery of certificates to the Chatham Chest. Nonetheless, both justices could claim that their sovereign had constant need of their services. Emmett

14. No notes are recorded in his diary from January through June 1710.
15. Numerations of cases forwarded to Quarter Sessions and Assizes ignore recognizances taken in bastardy cases.

TABLE 3 FREQUENCY OF ACTIVITY OF SINGLE JUSTICE

Justice	*Period*	*Annual average number of cases*
Urban or Market Town		
Gabriel Walters	July 1708–Dec. 1710	152
William Emmett	1712–1713	71
William Emmett	1730–1736	56
George Norman	Two years within period 1792–1796	26
Rural		
Thomas Osborne	June 1692–June 1693	43
William Brockman	1696–1699	41
Paul D'Aranda	1708	34
William Brockman	1715–1718	31
James Brockman	1726–1729, 1736–1739	13
Sir Wyndham Knatchbull	40 months within period 1734–1744	9
Sir Edward Filmer	1750–1754	17
James Brockman	1746–1749, 1756–1759	11
Ralph Drake Brockman	Aug. 1770–July 1777	9

acted as a single justice about once or twice a week, Walters about three times a week.

In the last decade of the seventeenth century, rural justices could also boast of continuous activity. Thomas Osborne and William Brockman both acted more than three times each month, and both encountered a similar variety of judicial duties distributed in similar proportions. Twenty-one percent of Brockman's cases revolved about complaints of crime, 11 percent assaults and personal quarrels, 19 percent disputes between masters and servants, and 26 percent administration of the poor laws and laws concerning bastardy. For neither Brockman nor Osborne was rural residence a guarantee of pastoral peace. In the eight years from 1696 to 1699 and 1715 to 1718, Brockman took recognizances which forwarded ten cases of crime and quarrel to Kent's Quarter Sessions and one to the Quarter Sessions of Hythe. Likewise, in the one year recorded in his diary, Osborne sent one dispute to Quarter Sessions. Perhaps Paul D'Aranda's judicial business best fits the slightly comic stereotype of rural placidity. In 1708, D'Aranda heard thirty-four cases. Four involved crime. In two instances, suspected thieves were brought before him and dismissed. The premises of a third culprit, a miller suspected of cheating his customers, were searched and no evidence found. The fourth miscreant confessed that he did indeed grub up young trees, and promised not to do it again. In the same year, D'Aranda settled a family quarrel over some linens, signed four certificates that decedents were buried in wool, took twenty-two settlement examinations, summoned two more persons to petty sessions to be examined about settlements, ordered that the relief allotted two goodwives be reduced because they did not wear the "P" signifying that they were the recipients of parish charity, and then upon appeal from the women, rescinded the order. (Both promised to wear the badge, but next day D'Aranda saw them both unlabelled.)

Only in the frequency of his activity is D'Aranda distinguished from his mid-century successors. When James Brockman was appointed to the commission in 1724, he assumed the magisterial duties formerly borne by his father. As table 3 reveals, they were not unduly onerous. He acted as a single justice about once a month. His successor, Ralph Drake Brockman, acted even less frequently. It is unlikely that the decline of magisterial activity among the Brockmans is evidence of progressive familial debility. In the 1730s and 1740s Sir Wyndham Knatchbull acted, when in rural residence, slightly less frequently than did James Brockman, and in the early 1750s Sir Edward Filmer acted slightly more frequently.[16] By the end of the century, even justices in market towns might successfully avoid undue magisterial strain. George Norman, resident in Bromley in the 1790s, acted about once every two weeks.[17] Well might rural justices of the mid-eighteenth century boast of their service to their country. Their activity as single justices was sufficiently infrequent to require advertisement of their assiduity.

As Walter's, Emmett's, and even Norman's diaries suggest, justices living in country towns or in or near urban areas had to devote more time to judicial business than their rural counterparts, and justices living in urban areas were confronted with a disproportionate number of serious criminal cases. The most densely populated areas in the

16. Knatchbull's warrant book covers the years 1734 through 1744. No activity is recorded for 1735. As almost all of the notations in this book were made in the months from June through September, it seems most logical to regard the book as a record of a justice's activites for three and one-third years—i.e., the forty months he was at residence in Mersham.

17. As there are substantial periods in which no activity is recorded in Norman's diary, and as the diary proves that Norman was residing in Bromley for at least twenty-four months between March 1792 and December 1795, the diary is regarded as evidence of typical judicial activity in a two-year period.

administrative county of Kent were in the Blackheath division. By the late seventeenth century, the combination of London's expansion into Lewisham and Deptford and the growth of naval dockyards at Woolwich and Deptford had imparted a distinctive urban character to large portions of the division. At Chatham, in the Rochester division, the development of naval dockyards had a similar effect.[18] As the older established towns in Kent boasted governments exempt from the jurisdiction of the county's justices, the diaries would lead one to expect that the justices of the Blackheath division—and, to a lesser extent, those of the Rochester division—would be called upon to assume magisterial duties more onerous than those of their rural colleagues. This hypothesis is confirmed by the jail calendars of mid-eighteenth century Assizes and by the recognizances returned to Quarter Sessions.

Table 4 displays the number of cases in each petty sessional division requiring commitment to jail before trial at Assizes in 1748 and 1749, and 1758 and 1759.[19] As can be seen, one-quarter of the cases involving prisoners awaiting the verdict of Assizes were initiated before the justices of the Blackheath division.[20] Their activity is rivalled only by that of the justices of the Rochester division.

Table 5 lists, by petty sessional division, the number of cases leading to the issue of recognizances[21] returned to Kent Quarter Sessions in 1708 and 1709, 1716 and 1717, Michaelmas 1721 through Easter

18. D. C. Coleman, "The Economy of Kent Under the Later Stuarts, 1660–1714" (Ph.D. thesis, University of London, 1951), pp. 15–16, 269, 310–311.

19. This table numerates cases, not number of prisoners. In the late 1740s, two justices named Charles Brown were active in Kent. One was in the Tonbridge division and the other in the Rochester division. It was not possible to determine which of these two justices had committed prisoners in five cases in 1748 to 1749, and these cases are omitted from the table. Also omitted are cases involving prisoners committed by the mayors of Kent's towns, the county's coroners, and justices in commission for other counties.

20. Evidence for commitment to jail before trial at Kent's Quarter Sessions and commitments to the county's houses of correction also support the hypothesis of greater activity of urban justices and the more serious nature of the infractions of the law committed in their vicinity. However, the rather cryptic nature of these Quarter Sessions returns make this evidence difficult to summarize. For more information, see N. Landau, "Gentry and Gentlemen: The Justices of the Peace, 1680–1760" (Ph.D. diss., University of California, Berkeley, 1974), pp. 519–523.

21. Table 5 enumerates all cases which produced a recognizance. So, it enumerates cases in which defendants were bound by recognizance to appear at Quarter Sessions, cases in which both defendant and prosecutor were bound by recognizance to appear at Quarter Sessions, and cases in which only the prosecutor was bound in recognizance to appear at Quarter Sessions. It is very probable that all defendants in the last variety of case were incarcerated until Quarter Sessions met.

TABLE 4 CASES INVOLVING COMMITMENT TO JAIL BEFORE TRIAL AT ASSIZES, BY PETTY SESSIONAL DIVISION

Division	*Cases 1748–1749*	*Cases 1758–1759*
West Kent		
Blackheath	21	17
Bromley	1	3
Dartford	1	2
Sevenoaks	5	1
Rochester	7	10
Malling	7	6
Bearsted	12	2
Tonbridge	1	2
Cranbrook	6	6
East Kent		
Wingham	0	3
Home	0	5
Sittingbourne	0	9
Ashford	3	6
Elham	2	0
Total	66	72

1723, 1748 and 1749, and 1758 and 1759.[22] (Table 5 divides the recognizances of the first quarter of the eighteenth century into ordinary recognizances and recognizances concordantur. The nature of recognizances concordantur will be examined below.)

The Blackheath justices are once again in a commanding lead in the race for divisional honours. In the reign of George II, these justices were responsible for initial supervision of over one-quarter of the cases requiring recognizances returned to Quarter Sessions. In the reign of George I, one-third of the cases resulting in ordinary recognizances and two-thirds of those producing recognizances concordantur had begun before their worships of Blackheath. Only in Anne's reign was the frequency of their activity matched by those of justices elsewhere

22. As the recognizance roll for the Easter meeting of east Kent Quarter Sessions in 1708 is missing, the figures for east Kent note recognizances returned from Michaelmas 1708 through Midsummer 1710. As the recognizance roll for the Epiphany meeting of east Kent Quarter Sessions in 1723 is missing, the figures for east Kent include recognizances returned from Midsummer 1721 through Midsummer 1723. In the 1720s, west Kent Quarter Sessions did not have a Midsummer meeting.

TABLE 5 CASES RESULTING IN RECOGNIZANCES RETURNED TO QUARTER SESSIONS, BY PETTY SESSIONAL DIVISION

	1708–1709		*1716–1717*		*Mich. 1721–Eas. 1723*			
Division	*Ordinary*	*Concordantur*	*Ordinary*	*Concordantur*	*Ordinary*	*Concordantur*	*1748–1749*	*1758–1759*
West Kent								
Blackheath	25	6	38	51	59	38	9	16
Bromley	2	0	4	3	8	0	1	0
Dartford	10	1	1	1	5	0	2	1
Sevenoaks	6	0	3	4	4	3	1	7
Rochester	23	14	12	3	8	0	1	12
Malling	1	0	6	1	3	2	1	3
Bearsted	33	0	10	1	18	2	4	6
Tonbridge	5	0	5	2	6	2	0	1
Cranbrook	2	0	14	4	6	5	1	4
East Kent								
Wingham	12	2	10	0	3	0	1	2
Home	21	1	32	0	15	0	6	4
Sittingbourne	7	2	8	4	13	3	1	5
Ashford	19	4	13	4	0	1	2	2
Elham	7	0	8	0	4	0	0	0
Total	173	30	164	78	152	56	30	63

in the county. Lack of consecutive series of complete recognizance rolls makes it difficult to extend comparison of judicial activity back into the seventeenth century.[23] Nonetheless, surviving records indicate that, in the 1680s, the justices of the Blackheath division were just slightly more active than their rural colleagues. The late seventeenth-century transformation of Blackheath into an urban area had entailed a radical alteration in the nature of its justices' service.

Yet, even these tables are an inadequate reflection of the burden of urban magistracy. They reveal only that portion of a justice's activity which produced returns to the most complete records among the papers of Quarter Sessions and Assizes. Jail calendars, recognizances, and all the other papers returned to Quarter Sessions resulting from the decisions of a single justice are an extremely imprecise guide to judicial activity. For instance, since William Brockman returned no recognizances in 1716 and 1717, and his son neither returned a recognizance nor committed a prisoner to jail for trial at Assizes in 1758 and 1759, these records suggest that neither justice was acting on his commission to keep the peace in these years. Even the continuous activity of Gabriel Walters in 1708 and 1709 is represented only by recognizances for three bastardy cases, two cases of theft, and one case of failure to make tax assessments.

Therefore, the activity of some Blackheath justices must have been enormous. Consider just the evidence left in Quarter Sessions papers of the action of Sir Snelling Thomas as a single justice in 1716 and 1717. In these two years, Thomas took recognizances for sixty-four cases, and placed a minimum of fifteen persons in the Dartford house of correction. Incomplete records of fines on those uttering profanity reveal that he fined a minimum of fifteen persons for swearing in 1716 through 1717 and set three of these offenders in the stocks.[24] Miscellaneous Quarter Sessions papers attest that between mid-January and October 8, 1717, he fined twenty-two bakers and chandlers in the parishes of Deptford, Woolwich, and East Greenwich a total of £1.19.0 for selling bread weighing less than the statutory amount. Sir Snelling was a conscientious servant of the government. Three of the seven cases of seditious words reaching presentation of a bill of indict-

23. Unlike the recognizance rolls of Anne's reign, those of the late seventeenth century frequently consist of loose recognizances, and so the researcher cannot be assured that they are complete.

24. Kent A.O., Q/RSj1/2, is the file of convictions for swearing for this decade. A paper in Kent A.O., Q/SB 1717 reveals that Thomas fined a person for swearing whose fine is not noted in Q/RSj1/2.

ment at west Kent's Quarter Sessions between 1716 and 1717 had begun their legal process under his supervision. The one indictment against a person publishing seditious words was brought by his clerk, James Ruddock.[25] Since Quarter Sessions papers would reveal only a small percentage of his activity, it is quite likely that Sir Snelling acted daily upon his commission. In 1716 and 1717, he was by far the most active justice in the county.

Throughout the first six decades of the eighteenth century, it was quite likely that one justice, usually resident in the Blackheath division, would be responsible for a disproportionately large number of the documents returned to Quarter Sessions. In the 1720s, Sir Snelling was succeeded as the premier justice of the Blackheath division by William Wright, and in the 1740s and 1750s, the palm for most frequent activity was held by Joseph Bell, again of the Blackheath division. Yet, in the first decade of the century, the service of Isaac Loader, Blackheath's most active magistrate, was overshadowed by that of a fellow justice in the Rochester division. In 1708 and 1709, Loader, as a single justice, returned recognizances for twelve cases to Quarter Sessions. John Crompe of Rochester took recognizances for twenty-four cases—a bulky contribution to the recognizance rolls, but one less impressive than those he had made earlier in the decade. At mid-century, a couple of justices in the Rochester division continued to act more frequently than their rural colleagues, but no justice of the Rochester division chose to assume Crompe's mantle as the most active justice in the county. Crompe's career therefore reveals an obvious determinant of judicial activity: not only did the most active justices serve a population which requested their service more frequently than those in rural areas, but the most active justices also wanted to act frequently. Those they governed knew that these justices would hear their complaints and take legal action upon them, and so they conducted an inordinately large amount of judicial business.

It is therefore possible that these outstandingly active Kentish justices were trading justices. The term 'trading justice' is a label—and perhaps a libel—applied to those justices who lived by their judicial trade. Lacking an estate sufficient to support a gentleman and safeguard integrity, these justices converted judicial service into profitable employment. The more frequently they were employed, the greater their profits. As opportunities for judicial service were relatively scarce

25. Kent A.O., Q/SI 1716, west Kent, Mich., f. 7.

in the countryside, and the fees of judicial office a trifling addition to the income of any substantial gentleman, trading justices tended to be men of marginal gentility appointed to govern urban areas. The species' favourite haunts were Westminster and London's annexes in Middlesex and Surrey.

Two charges were regularly levelled against the trading justices. The first has received the most attention. It was alleged that these justices took bribes to license alehouses and to ignore the presence of bawdy and gaming houses in their neighbourhoods. As there is no evidence that Kentish justices entered into such transactions, this charge will not be explored here. The second accusation is more relevant. Trading justices, it was averred, stirred up quarrels amongst their neighbours so that they could bind defendants in recognizances to keep the peace, and then released the disputants from their bonds.[26] In both binding and loosing, the justice exacted a fee. Consequently, justices who returned a large number of recognizances to Quarter Sessions were accused of being trading justices.[27] And, conversely, many of those justices who returned a disproportionately large number of recognizances can be identified, through other evidence, as trading justices. For instance, of the seven justices who returned the most recognizances to Middlesex's Quarter Sessions in 1737, four were definitely trading justices.[28]

Like the trading justices of London, Middlesex, and Westminster, the most active magistrates of Kent inhabited urban areas. Again, like these trading justices, they returned an inordinate number of recognizances to Quarter Sessions. And, like the trading justices, they bound disputants in recognizances to keep the peace and appear at Quarter Sessions, and then at the disputants' plea released those bound from their obligations. This is the procedure represented by the recogni-

26. *CSPD, Anne,* vol. 2, p. 373, petition of Simon Fanshaw, Dec. 4, 1703; B.L., Add. MSS 35601, f. 266, A. Wroth to Hardwicke, Jan. 1743[4]; *Gentleman's Magazine* 39 (1769): 539–540. See also H. Fielding, *The Coffee House Politician or the Justice caught in his own trap* (London, 1730) and Dr. Fitzpatrick, *Directions to Mankind in General* (London [1745]), pp. 62–64.

27. Herts. R.O., Panshanger MSS D/EP/F157, Wm. Ashurst to [Lord Cowper], Oct. 23, 1717.

28. P. Linebaugh, "Crime in London, 1700–1750" (Ph.D. thesis, Warwick University, 1975), pp. 73–74, identifies the seven justices who returned the largest number of recognizances to Quarter Sessions. For a description of Wroth's activities as a trading justice, see B.L., Add. MSS 35601, ff. 265–266; for those of Midford, see Add. MSS 35604, f. 382 and P.R.O., SP44/85, f. 18; for those of Poulson, see B.L., Add. MSS 35603, f. 102 and Add. MSS 35601, f. 269; for DeVeil, see G. Rudé, *Hanoverian London: 1714–1808* (Berkeley and Los Angeles, 1971), p. 129.

zances concordantur. As these recognizances concordantur reveal, a complainant would appear before a justice and accuse another of assault, slander, mistreatment, or other opprobrious behaviour. The accused would be bound in a recognizance to keep the peace. Then, at a later date, sometimes marked on the recognizance, the complainant would inform the justice that the dispute had been settled and the justice would subscribe the recognizance *concordantur*—i.e., "they are agreed." And, since the disputants were reconciled, and there was no reason to prefer charges at Quarter Sessions, the disputants could be released from their bonds. They need not appear at Quarter Sessions.

Obviously, the ability to discharge someone from the obligation of a long, expensive, and time-consuming journey to Quarter Sessions endowed the justice with considerable arbitrary power, and the use of this power was regarded with suspicion. In the 1630s, the judges had prohibited justices from discharging recognizances out of Quarter Sessions. If those bound in recognizances did not fulfill the obligations of their bonds, the king's treasury would be swelled by the amount of the recognizance; release out of Sessions therefore threatened national finances.[29] According to seventeenth-century justices' manuals, a justice could release a recognizance only if the plaintiff agreed to the release, and this instruction was both repeated and qualified in some early eighteenth-century manuals; recognizances issued in cases of petty quarrel, minor trespass, or on a plaintiff's demand that his opponent enter into a recognizance of the peace could be released; but recognizances which might lead to fines delivered to the king's treasury could not.[30] Yet, as even these manuals hinted, release of a recognizance had to be handled with caution. It might be assumed that the justice had been bribed to release his majesty's subjects from their legal obligations, and so manuals reminded the justice that one magistrate had been fined and imprisoned for compounding recognizances and not returning them to Quarter Sessions.[31] Most probably, it was

29. E. H. Bates Harbin, ed., *Quarter Sessions Records for the County of Somerset*, vol. 2, *1625–1639*, Somerset Record Society, vol. 24 (1908), pp. xxiii–xxiv; S. C. Newton, "Staffordshire Quarter Sessions: Archives and Procedure in the Earlier 17th Century," *Collections for a History of Staffordshire*, 4th ser., vol. 6 (Staffordshire Record Society, 1970), p. 73.

30. M. Dalton, *The Countrey Justice* (London, 1643), pp. 213, 215–217; J. Bond, *A Compleat Guide for Justices of Peace*, 2nd ed. (London, 1696), p. 207; S. Blackerby, *The Second Part of the Justice of Peace His Companion, or Cases in Law*, rev. ed. (London, 1729), p. 176; J. Shaw, *The Practical Justice of the Peace*, 4th ed. (London, 1744), vol. 1, p. 15.

31. Shaw, *ibid.*, vol. 1, p. 20; Blackerby, *The Second Part*, p. 181.

his desire to avoid imputations of the dishonourable sale of justice that induced Sir Thomas DeVeil, the premier trading justice of Westminster, to include a solemn prohibition of the release of recognizances in his pamphlet of advice to the justices of the metropolis.[32]

Nonetheless justices—and not just Kentish justices—did release recognizances,[33] but the unclear and contradictory advice on release in justices' manuals suggests that release was not a frequent procedure in the eighteenth century. For instance, some manuals stated that those bound in recognizances which had been released need not appear at Quarter Sessions; others insisted that all those bound—whether released or not—had to journey to Sessions.[34] Nor did the most complete and authoritative manual of the century avoid confusion. Burn's *Justice of the Peace and Parish Officer,* first published in 1755, included a model for the release but also stated, simply, that recognizances should not be released. That Burn based his opinion on ancient authority rather than recent legal decision suggests that the recognizance concordantur was a device not tested in eighteenth-century courts. That his prohibition was a short, terse statement, unembellished by advice, reasons, or cautions reveals that frequent recourse to the release was unknown to the reverend justice of rural Westmorland.[35]

Similarly, the release was unfamiliar to the justices of rural Kent. Their lack of acquaintance with the device is demonstrated by Sir Wyndham Knatchbull, who in 1739 informed the justices of his division that all recognizances had to be certified to Quarter Sessions, and that all those bound in recognizances, released or not, had to attend Quarter Sessions. Knatchbull cited his justices' manual in support of his contention.[36] Yet, in 1724, Kent's clerk of the peace had noted in

32. Sir T. DeVeil, *Observations on the Practice of a Justice of the Peace: Intended for such Gentlemen as design to act for Middlesex or Westminster* (London, 1747), pp. 9–10.

33. D. L. Powell, ed., *Surrey Quarter Sessions Records, 1659–1666,* Surrey Record Society, vol. 35 (London, 1931), p. 173; H. C. Johnson, ed., *Warwick County Records,* vol. 8, *Proceedings in Quarter Sessions, 1682–1690* (Warwick, 1953), p. 8; S. A. Peyton, ed., *Minutes of Proceedings in Quarter Sessions held for the Parts of Kesteven in the County of Lincoln, 1674–1695,* vol. 1, Lincoln Record Society, vol. 25 (Lincoln, 1931), p. 95.

34. W. Nelson, *The Office and Authority of a Justice of Peace,* 7th ed. (London, 1721), p. 498; Shaw, *Practical Justice,* vol. 1, p. 129; see also Sir W. Hawkins, *A Treatise of the Pleas of the Crown,* 3rd ed. (London, 1739), book 1, p. 129.

35. R. Burn, *The Justice of the Peace and Parish Officer,* 3rd ed. (London, 1756), pp. 678 *sub* "Surety for the peace," 689–690 *sub* "Surety," form for release.

36. Kent A.O., U951/O4, pp. 53–54.

his minute book: "Circular Letters are to be sent by the Clerk of the peace to every Division of Justices to desire them NOT to return any Recogn[izances] Concordantur."[37] And the Sessions rolls for the reign of George II prove that the clerk's instruction was heeded. Since recognizances concordantur were not certified to Quarter Sessions, there was no method for determining whether those bound in such recognizances appeared at Sessions. In Kent, those bound in recognizances which had been released definitely did not need to attend Quarter Sessions. If Knatchbull had resided in the urbanizing Blackheath rather than the pastoral Ashford division, it is improbable that he could have been five years an active justice and still unacquainted with his county's customary procedure in the release of recognizances.

Table 5 reveals that it was the justices of the Blackheath division who returned two-thirds of the county's recognizances concordantur in the reign of George I; table 5 also indicates that their reliance upon this device was innovative. More recognizances concordantur were granted in George I's reign than in that of Anne, and more in Anne's reign than in the late seventeenth century. Only some four or five a year, almost invariably issued by justices of the Blackheath and Rochester divisions, appear among the Sessions rolls of the 1680s. The proportion of their recognizances which the Blackheath justices released also differentiates their use of the recognizance from that of their rural colleagues. Of the recognizances issued by these justices in 1716 through 1717 and Michaelmas 1721 through Easter 1723, almost half were discharged before Quarter Sessions met. In contrast, less than one-fifth of the recognizances issued by justices of other divisions in these years were released. Further indicative of difference between the practices of rural and urban justices are the cases in which the Blackheath justices granted release. Almost all of their recognizances concordantur relate to cases in which a plaintiff had accused the defendant of assault, mistreatment, or slander, or had alleged that the defendant had threatened his life. In contrast, more than one-third of the relatively few recognizances concordantur issued by justices of divisions other than Blackheath record agreement on administrative matters—bastardy cases or the conduct of constables and tax collectors. Evidently, the Blackheath justices were issuing recognizances in cases of minor quarrel and then, for a fee, releasing these bonds and at the same time probably settling the disputes which had led to recognizances.

37. Kent A.O., Q/SMa W4, Oct. 6, 1724.

Foremost among these paid arbitrators of disputes were the outstandingly active justices. Eleven of the cases producing recognizances concordantur in 1708 through 1709 were initiated before John Crompe, five before Isaac Loader, and one before Snelling Thomas. Thomas was responsible for thirty-three of the cases leading to recognizances concordantur in 1716 through 1717 and William Wright for eight, while between Michaelmas 1721 and Easter 1723, Wright returned recognizances concordantur for twenty-nine cases to Kent's Quarter Sessions. Between them these four justices accounted for more than half of the recognizances concordantur numerated in table 5. It is possible, but impossible to prove, that the assiduous service of some of these gentlemen in reconciling disputants was the product of their careers as trading justices. Of the four, Loader is the most implausible candidate for notoriety. Isaac Loader of Deptford was a prominent manufacturer of iron, a supplier to the navy, and the possessor of a noteworthy residence in Greenwich.[38] John Crompe of Rochester was less prominent. All that is known of his life is marmorealized in a plaque in Rochester Cathedral: Crompe was the eldest son of one of Rochester's prebendaries.[39] Sir Snelling Thomas was a brewer resident in Deptford, and it is therefore possible that he increased the profits of his brewery by his use of his judicial powers to license alehouses. Thomas earned his knighthood by bearing company to Kent's Lord Lieutenant on the delivery of the county's address to the king in 1715.[40] William Wright, likewise resident in Deptford, also enjoyed landed connections in the gentry dominated regions of east Kent. Nonetheless, his respectability might have been impugned when, in 1710, he was dismissed from his post as commissioner of the navy for irregularities and improper conduct.[41] Possibly, the purses of three of these four magistrates might have been so straitened that judicial emoluments were necessary to sustain their pretensions to gentility. Certainly, the activity of both Wright and Thomas was both sufficiently

38. M. W. Flinn, *Men of Iron, The Crowleys in the Early Iron Industry* (Edinburgh, 1962), pp. 149, 173–174; H. H. Drake, ed., *Hasted's History of Kent, Corrected, Enlarged and Continued to the Present Time, Part I, The Hundred of Blackheath* (London, 1886), p. 31, n. 6; N. Dewes, *The History of Deptford* (London, 1884), p. 154.

39. E. Hasted, *The History and Topographical Survey of the County of Kent,* 2nd ed. (Canterbury, 1797–1801), vol. 4, p. 107.

40. *Ibid.,* vol. 1, p. 209; W. A. Shaw, *The Knights of England* (Baltimore, 1970 [reprint of 1906 ed.]), vol. 2, p. 279.

41. Sir G. F. Duckett, *Naval Commissioners from 12 Charles II to 1 George III* (Lewes, 1889), pp. 12–13, 131; Hasted, *History of Kent,* 2nd edn., vol. 10, p. 46; Wright attended petty sessions in east Kent in 1716 (Kent A.O., PS/W1).

constant and sufficiently congruent to that of the trading justices to warrant suspicion of their motives for judicial service.

Yet the activity of all four justices—indeed, of many of the Blackheath justices—raises a more important question: that of the nature of judicial paternalism. For the recognizances concordantur reveal that the urban population was using their justices as institutions conveniently provided by the state for the settlement of their quarrels. As Gabriel Walters' diary demonstrates, a plaintiff's request that his opponent be brought before a justice was in many instances a prelude to the reconciliation of the disputants. For instance, in 1710 a woman asked Walters to issue a warrant against another woman, whom she accused of slander. The defendant had evidently been declaring that the plaintiff was a drunkard and frequented ill company. The warrant was issued, the putative slanderer brought before Walters, and Walters finally noted "they agreed."[42] Similarly, the issue of a recognizance was a method for compelling reconciliation. That the accused, and frequently the accuser, were bound to attend Sessions must have induced one and sometimes both of the disputants to seek discharge of the bond, and so the settlement of the grievance. Both in issuing so many recognizances and in granting so many releases, these urban justices were arbitrating the quarrels of their communities. True, the exaction of a fee for both recognizance and release was not a hallmark of benevolent paternalism. But the recognizances concordantur do indicate that urban justices—and perhaps particularly trading justices—were knowledgeable about and involved in the lives of those they governed. Therefore, since rural justices issued so few recognizances concordantur, the activity of the Blackheath justices questions the nature and even the existence of rural judicial arbitration. Urban justices certainly heard disputes and participated in the reconciliation of disputants; but did rural justices indulge in similar activity?

It could be argued that the rural justice served his neighbours as assiduously as his rural colleague, but that his altruism has left his service unrecorded. If urban justices composed disputes by demanding recognizances and so garnering fees, rural justices may have settled quarrels without recourse to either recognizances or fees. Examination of records other than recognizances is therefore essential to the investigation of rural paternalism. Two sources—justices' diaries and convictions for profane swearing returned to Quarter Sessions— suggest that

42. Hants. R.O., 18/M51/596, Aug. 30, 1710.

the notion of eighteenth-century rural paternalism has served to camouflage a subtle change in the paternal intervention of rural justices. Eighteenth-century rural justices did mediate disputes; indeed, the single eighteenth-century rural justice was more likely to settle disputes without recourse to other legal tribunals than his pre-Restoration predecessor. Nonetheless, the frequency with which rural justices acted as mediators declined throughout the first three-quarters of the eighteenth century.

All of the ten Kentish justices recorded the issue of warrants in their justice's diaries. By issuing a warrant, a justice could cause any specified person to be brought before him or before another justice. Warrants are therefore the major and most persuasive evidence of a justice's activity in cases of crime and quarrel, for if a plaintiff wanted to secure a remedy in cases of crime and quarrel he had to get his persecutor before a justice. Unless both disputants agreed to appear before a justice, or on report of a quarrel the justice sallied forth to busy himself inquiring into the affairs of his inferiors, the only way that a defendant would be brought under the justice's eye was by warrant. It is unlikely that many disputants jointly agreed to lay their quarrel before a justice or that justices sought out their quarrelsome inferiors. Sir Samuel Whitbread, a very active early nineteenth-century justice, conscientiously recorded every one of his actions which could be deemed judicial in his justice's diary, even noting letters he wrote relating to cases before him. As his diary reveals, Whitbread did not go to disputants; disputants came to him, and only very infrequently did both parties to a dispute ask for his arbitration. In almost every case, a plaintiff appeared in his justice's room requesting a warrant against an alleged oppressor.[43] It is therefore unlikely that these Kentish justices acted in cases of crime and quarrel for which warrants had not at some time been issued. These justices did, very occasionally, settle quarrels on warrants issued by other justices; they also very occasionally issued warrants in cases that other justices mediated. A justice's record of warrants issued on complaint of crime or quarrel is evidence of the frequency with which inferiors appealed for judicial aid in the settlement of their disputes.

All the diaries reveal that the justices issued a great many more warrants on complaint of crime, quarrel, or disagreement between

43. A. F. Cirket, ed., *Samuel Whitbread's Notebooks, 1810–1811, 1813–1814*, Bedfordshire Historical Record Society, vol. 50 (1971).

master and servant than is indicated by the number of recognizances returned to Quarter Sessions. Evidence of their activity after they issued a warrant is slightly more elusive. Seven of the ten justices usually did not note their subsequent action in cases for which they had issued warrants unless that action involved exaction of a fine, an order for punishment, or the demand that the defendant enter into a recognizance. The diaries of D'Aranda, Knatchbull, and Ralph Drake Brockman are more informative. These diaries indicate, as does an even more detailed diary of a mid-century Wiltshire justice,[44] that justices almost always took further action in cases for which they had issued warrants. Their activity rarely produced a document which would be returned to Quarter Sessions. Instead, these justices settled the disputes of their neighbours—sometimes by the exaction of a fine, but most frequently by reconciling the disputants. Indeed, the diary of the Wiltshire justice reveals that the issue of a warrant was sometimes in itself sufficient to produce concord among disputants. In some instances he noted that he had taken no further action because when the warrant was returned he had been informed that the disputants were now agreed. The diaries therefore indicate that rural justices undoubtedly acted in a paternalist fashion.

And the diaries further indicate that late seventeenth- and eighteenth-century justices could claim to be exercising their authority in a more paternalist manner than their pre-Restoration predecessors. They could base this claim on the difference between their practices in demanding recognizances and that of their predecessors. As their diaries reveal, eighteenth-century justices were not apt to demand that those who appeared before them enter into recognizances. While the rather cryptic notes of some of these justices make it impossible to calculate precisely the ratio of recognizances to warrants, it is clear that these justices demanded recognizances in only 10 percent or less of the cases of crime and quarrel for which they had issued warrants. In contrast, when Bostock Fuller served James I as a justice of Surrey he demanded a recognizance in over a quarter of the cases of crime and quarrel for which he had issued a warrant; and Sir Edward Dering, justice of Kent under Charles I, exacted recognizances in over half such cases for which he had issued warrants. Dering's Elizabethan predecessor, William Lambard, did not note the issue of warrants in his justice's diary.

44. Wilts. R.O., Diary of William Hunt, now being edited for the Wiltshire Record Society by Elizabeth Crittall. I wish to thank Miss Crittall for allowing me to see this diary when she was working on it in London.

He did record the exaction of recognizances, and as Lambard made note of an average of eleven recognizances a year between May 1583 and September 1588, it is likely that he too demanded that a considerable proportion of those brought before him by warrant enter into a recognizance. Like Lambard, Captain John Pickering eschewed notation of warrants and enthusiastically wielded the recognizance. The diary he kept when he served Cromwell as a justice of the West Riding records his exaction of about four recognizances every month. Undoubtedly, Pickering settled some disputes by fining defendants for drunkenness or swearing. He levied two or three such fines a month.[45] Nonetheless, it is unlikely that Pickering reconciled the disputants in a majority of the cases brought to his attention. If we postulate that he demanded recognizances in only half of the cases of crime and quarrel for which he issued warrants, then we must conclude that he was confronted by well over one hundred such cases each year. Even Gabriel Walters, living near the expanding dockyard town of Chatham, heard only twenty-seven cases of crime and quarrel a year. In all probability, Pickering demanded that the majority of defendants in cases of crime and quarrel enter into a recognizance.

Unlike their rural successors, and like the eighteenth-century urban justice, pre-Restoration justices relied on the recognizance. Again, like the urban justice, the pre-Restoration justices released recognizances. Neither Dering nor Pickering noted the release, but Lambard and Fuller released those bound in about a quarter of the recognizances they had exacted. Again, like the recognizances concordantur issued by the urban justices, those recognizances which Lambard and Fuller released usually involved cases of quarrel and threats of violence. In exacting and releasing recognizances, urban justices were merely elaborating on the practices of their eminent rural predecessors. By substituting mediation for reliance upon the recognizance, eighteenth-century rural justices were increasing the extra-legal component of their authority emphasized in the label 'paternal ruler.' They had replaced a legal instrument which forwarded disputants to the court of Quarter Sessions with the practice of mediation, and mediation neither sent disputants to another tribunal nor produced a legal document

45. G. Leveson-Gower, "Note-Book of a Surrey Justice", *Surrey Archaelogical Collections,* vol. 9 (1888), pp. 180–277; Kent A.O., U570/O1; C. Read, ed., *William Lambarde and Local Government* (Ithaca, N.Y., 1962), pp. 28–52; G. D. Lumb, "Justice's Note-Book of Captain John Pickering," *Publications of The Thoresby Society,* vol. 11 (1903), pp. 69–100, and vol. 15 (1905, 1906, 1909), pp. 71–80.

which subjected disputants to the rules of law. By substituting mediation for reliance upon the recognizance, the justices enhanced the ability of each individual justice to become the arbiter of his community.

Indeed, throughout the eighteenth century both the procedures adopted by justices and the laws enacted by Parliament enhanced the individual justice's authority as judge and arbitrater of his locality. Increasingly throughout the eighteenth century, Parliament enacted statutes which allocated to the single and double justice power to convict those accused of specified minor offences.[46] In 1778, Parliament granted the justices the right to ascertain and award costs to parties involved in any case which they determined after issue of a warrant or summons, and this, too, increased their power as arbitrators.[47] The justices' diaries reveal that in many instances their mediation of disputes had involved exaction of an agreement that one of the parties pay the other. But unless the statute governing jurisdiction of the offence specifically allocated power to award costs to the justice, this agreement had no force in law. Now, under the guise of awarding costs, the single justice, the double justice, and the justices in Quarter Sessions could exact immediate and direct retribution for an injured party from his opponent. Indeed, if the justice decided both to fine the defendant and award more than £5 in costs to the plaintiff, a portion of the costs was to be deducted from the fine. In so giving precedence to costs paid to parties over fines paid to the parish, Parliament advertised its desire to enhance the attractions of the justices as arbitrators. In both law and practice, eighteenth-century justices were better suited for the role of paternal ruler than their predecessors.

Nonetheless, in a very important respect the mid-eighteenth-century rural justice exercised less paternal authority than his predecessors: he acted as arbitrator and mediator less frequently. The decline in the number of recognizances returned to Quarter Sessions during the reigns of the first two Hanoverians is not simply a reflection of change in the justices' procedure. After all, by the 1690s justices had already ceased to demand recognizances regularly. The procedure of William Brockman and Thomas Osborne was more akin to that of their mid-eighteenth-century successors than to that of their pre-Restoration predecessors. On the whole, fewer recognizances were returned to mid-eighteenth-century Quarter Sessions than to early eighteenth-century

46. See chapter 11.

47. 18 George III c. 19; W. Paley, *The Law and Practice of Summary Convictions on Penal Statutes by Justices of the Peace,* 1st ed. (London, 1814), pp. 173–174.

Quarter Sessions because the rural populace became increasingly disinclined to request judicial aid in the resolution of their disputes. The most impressive evidence of decline is that provided by the diaries of the Brockman clan, who dispensed justice from the mansion of Beachborough for over a century. As table 6 indicates, the diaries of the other rural justices suggest that the Brockmans' activity was representative. However much mid-eighteenth-century justices may have prized their independence as paternal mediators, they did not exercise their paternal authority frequently.

It may be that mid-eighteenth-century rural justices acted less frequently in cases of crime and quarrel because change in the behaviour of some of their neighbours diminished the number of minor crimes and quarrels. Early seventeenth-century justices had been confronted by complaints from members of relatively substantial families against members of equally substantial families. By the late seventeenth century, justices were rarely acting in such cases,[48] and it may be that the less frequent activity of mid-eighteenth-century justices is merely evidence of continuation of that trend. Either the more substantial inhabitants of village society had become less quarrelsome and less litigious, or they thought it inappropriate to request that a justice settle their disputes. It may be that, by the eighteenth century, the more substantial inhabitants of rural society had become accustomed to view the justice as an institution provided to settle cases involving members of the lower orders. Certainly, increase in the single and double justices' powers of summary jurisdiction allowed more substantial inhabitants to demand that the justice punish the less substantial for petty crime. In Wiltshire, for example, William Hunt frequently levied fines on women and labourers for cutting wood on land in the possession of yeomen. Though Kent's petty sessions levied few fines, the records of Sevenoaks petty sessions regularly note the exaction of fines for stealing wood. Change in the nature of the single justice's business would also alter popular perception of the justice. Because complaints of crime and quarrel diminished, an increasing proportion of the rural justices' activity as single justice involved the mediation of disputes between master and servant. During the 1770s, the settlement of cases which pitted master against servant composed one-third of Ralph Drake Brockman's business. Since justices deter-

48. K. Wrightson and D. Levine, *Poverty and Piety in an English Village, Terling 1525–1700* (New York, 1979), pp. 122–125.

TABLE 6 ANNUAL AVERAGE OF THE NUMBER OF CASES OF CRIME AND QUARREL FOR WHICH THE JUSTICE ISSUED A WARRANT OR ANOTHER LEGAL DOCUMENT

Justice	*Year*	*Annual average number of cases*
Thomas Osborne	June 1692–June 1693	17
William Brockman	1696–1699	12
Paul D'Aranda	1708	5
William Brockman	1715–1718	10
James Brockman	1726–1729, 1736–1739	4
Sir Wyndham Knatchbull	1734–1744 (40 months)	4
Sir Edward Filmer	1750–1754	5
James Brockman	1746–1749, 1756–1759	3
Ralph Drake Brockman	1770–1777	2

mined cases of petty crime, which usually involved the less substantial members of rural society, and since settlement of disputes involving servants comprised a large portion of their business, the more substantial inhabitants of rural society may have thought it beneath their dignity to appeal to a justice to settle disputes with their equals.

Instead, they may have appealed to other mediators. In the seventeenth century, gentlemen, clergymen, and even substantial yeomen had settled the disputes of their neighbours,[49] and it is not unreasonable to suppose that they continued to do so in the eighteenth century. The village community had also invented a ceremony for imposing extra-legal sanctions upon their neighbours. In the eighteenth century, those who continually violated accepted standards of behaviour might be the objects of a skimmington—a communal parade or riot which derided the erring villager. The skimmington embodied and symbolized the close-knit community of the village, and the existence of such a close-knit community precluded much of the judicial activity that is commonly associated with paternal mediation.

Comparison of the cases with which urban justices dealt to those confronting the rural justice reveals the limits of rural judicial mediation. Rural justices mediated a more restricted variety of disputes than

49. M. J. Ingram, "Community and the Courts: Law and Disorder in Early Seventeenth-Century Wiltshire," in *Crime in England 1550–1800*, ed. J. S. Cockburn (London, 1977), pp. 126–127.

did urban justices. Most notably, urban justices mediated quarrels between women, and rural justices did not. Approximately 30 percent of the recognizances concordantur and 20 percent of the ordinary recognizances issued by Blackheath's justices revolved about disputes which pitted a female plaintiff against a female defendant. In contrast, only 3 to 5 percent of the recognizances issued by rural justices involved charges brought by a woman against another woman. As the diaries of the rural justices reveal, only 10 percent or less of the cases of minor crime and quarrel for which they issued warrants involved disputes between women. Therefore, even if it is assumed that the recognizances of Blackheath's justices are as accurate a record of activity as the diaries of rural justices, then it must be concluded either that urban women were more disputatious than rural women, or that urban women were very much more inclined to request judicial aid in the settlement of their disputes than were rural women. In part, the greater representation of quarrels between women in urban recognizances may reflect the greater independence of urban women and the greater opportunity for contact with their neighbours afforded by an urban environment. Nonetheless, it is at least arguable that the greater representation of disputes between women in the records emanating from urban justices indicates that rural women settled their own disputes and urban women did not.

Little is known about the ways in which the eighteenth-century rural community, and especially rural women, regulated the conduct of their neighbours. However, it is clear that a considerable proportion of eighteenth-century skimmingtons were directed against women—women who were scolds, who disturbed the peace of the community, or whose behaviour offended their neighbours.[50] No rural disturbances that can be classified indubitably as skimmingtons appear in Kent's Quarter Sessions records of 1708 to 1709, 1716 to 1717, 1748 to 1749, or 1758 to 1759. These records do allow a glimpse of what was undoubtedly an urban skimmington. In the summer of 1708, several women resident in Deptford rioted against one Susannah Messingham, and were bound to keep the peace and answer charges of riot at Quarter Sessions. The women were indicted but not convicted. But, at that same Quarter Sessions, Susannah Messingham was both indicted and convicted of being a common

50. E. P. Thompson, " 'Rough Music': Le Charivari Anglais," *Annales, Économies, Sociétés, Civilisations* 27 (1972):288, 294.

scold and keeping a bawdy house.[51] As Henry Fielding, himself a justice of Middlesex and Westminster, noted, his judicial colleagues were inclined "to construe a little harmless scolding into a riot."[52] Fielding thought it appropriate to append this observation to an account of a dispute between women. In all probability, urban magistrates considered the skimmington a tactic inappropriate to a densely populated urban setting and treated participants in skimmingtons as rioters. Urban women and the urban community were less able to impose their own discipline upon their neighbours than were their country cousins. Similarly, it is probable that urban residents were less able to rely upon nonjudicial mediators than were village residents. Because rural communities were communities, their residents knew persons who were respected by village society. Disputants could therefore agree that certain persons, not necessarily justices, would be suitable mediators. Urban residents were less likely to know persons whom both parties respected and considered appropriate mediators. Since urban communities were neither sufficiently cohesive nor permitted to use extra-legal forms of control, urban residents demanded that their justices regulate the conduct of their neighbours, and urban justices acted in types of dispute that were not brought to the attention of rural justices.

Another set of documents, certificates of convictions for profane swearing returned to Quarter Sessions, also indicates that urban justices arbitrated disputes more frequently than their rural colleagues. As the justices' diaries indicate, returns of fines for swearing are evidence of judicial arbitration. Five of the justices—the Brockmans, Osborne, Emmett—record the imposition of these fines in their diaries. Though the justices resorted to these fines very, very infrequently, their diaries reveal that the majority of these fines were intimately related to disputes brought before them. For example, on April 6, 1733, Mary Granger accused William Wood of an unspecified misdemeanour and obtained from Emmett a warrant ordering that Wood be carried before a justice. On the same day, Emmett fined Wood four shillings for swearing profane oaths the day before. The person on whose information the judgment was granted was Mary Granger, the

51. Kent A.O., Q/SI, west Kent, Mich. 1708, ff. 9, 12; Q/SRc, west Kent, Mich. 1708, ff. 11, 15, 19, 20; Q/SB, 1709, f. 36, Tho. Wellings to Mr. Fuller, Deptford, May 2, 1709.

52. In *Amelia: The Complete Works of Henry Fielding, Esq.*, vol. 6 (New York, 1967 reprint), p. 19. See also J. M. Beattie, "The Pattern of Crime in England, 1660–1800," *Past and Present* 62 (1974):65.

woman who had obtained a warrant against Wood for misdemeanour.[53] In fining Wood, Emmett settled the dispute and exacted vengeance for the plaintiff, and the fine allowed Emmett to administer justice without resort to further legal proceedings. Similarly, in 1728 James Brockman levied two fines for swearing which represented the final arbitration of a dispute. At first, he had determined to fine Robert Beck £1 on the information of Thomas Taylor, but when both men appeared before him Brockman adjudged that "in a quarrel they had both been guilty," and accordingly fined Beck ten shillings and Taylor five shillings.[54] Both Emmett and Brockman were using the fine for swearing as a crude but satisfactory instrument to persuade plaintiffs that justice had been done. In the early nineteenth century, one justice recommended the fine for swearing as a panacea for complainants aggrieved by injuries for which the law allowed no appropriate remedy:

> Complaints are made to magistrates, with respect to a thousand immoral and wicked actions over which they have no jurisdiction whatsoever. In such cases, it will be prudence to conceal the infirmity of their authority: but they will frequently find [the statute against swearing] has been violated by one or both parties. I should then recommend, that they should exert their full authority in the punishment of *this* offence; and to dismiss the parties, with an admonition or a reprimand, when the law has given them no power to act.[55]

The certificates returned to Quarter Sessions recording fines for swearing are the detritus of disputes adjudicated by justices out of Quarter Sessions, and usually by a justice acting alone.

Unfortunately, the files of fines for swearing preserved in the records of Kent's Quarter Sessions are incomplete, and the earlier files are more incomplete than the later ones.[56] Only one certificate from the justices in east Kent survives for the decade 1706 to 1715. Even so, the files reveal a preponderance of urban arbitration. According to the files, in the decade 1706–1715 the Blackheath justices fined 118 persons for profane swearing and the justices of all other divisions fined a total of thirty-three persons. Between 1746 and 1755, Blackheath's justices fined twenty-four persons, and justices in the rest of Kent sixteen. In Blackheath, women were prominent among

53. Kent A.O., U310/O14, p. 65.
54. B.L., Add. MSS 42599, ff. 39–40.
55. Quoted in D. Hay, "Property, Authority and the Criminal Law," in *Albion's Fatal Tree*, ed. D. Hay et al. (New York, 1975), pp. 51–52.
56. The files of fines for swearing are Kent A.O., Q/RSj1.

the swearers. Blackheath's justices fined twenty-six women between 1706 and 1715, and nine women between 1746 and 1755. Rural justices fined three women in the first decade and none in the second. Like recognizances and justices' diaries, fines for swearing indicate that the pattern of urban arbitration differed markedly from that of the countryside.

Likewise, that Blackheath's justices imposed many more fines for swearing than justices in the remainder of the county indicates that Blackheath's justices arbitrated disputes more frequently than their rural colleagues. The disproportionate representation of Blackheath in the fines for swearing is not simply a reflection of the likelihood that societies for reformation of manners were more likely to be active in urban than in rural areas. In the early eighteenth century, these societies were bringing profane swearers to the attention of the justices, but they had ceased securing fines for swearing by the 1730s.[57] Nonetheless, between 1746 and 1755 Blackheath's swearers outnumbered those in the rest of Kent by three to two. Of course, some might argue that comparison of the amount of arbitration performed by urban and rural justices ought not to be based on the number of persons fined: trading justices might be more likely to impose fines than their paternal rural colleagues, just as they were more likely to demand recognizances. The recognizance rolls permitted no reply to this argument, but the files of fines for swearing do. The files include returns of fines imposed by the mayors of Gravesend and Milton, Maidstone, and Rochester. These notables were not trading justices. As they usually held office for just one year, they could not depend on the judicial powers of their office for their livelihood. Their fines therefore illuminate the pattern of urban arbitration without introducing the possibility of distortions associated with the practices of trading justices.

Returns of convictions for swearing in Gravesend and Milton survive for six years of the decade 1706–1715, when thirty-five persons were fined. In seven years of the decade 1746–1755, the mayor of Gravesend and Milton fined fifteen persons; in three years of the latter decade the mayor of Maidstone fined ten persons, and in nine years of that same decade the mayor and justices of the corporation of Ro-

57. Tina Isaacs, "Moral Crime, Moral Reform and the State in Early Eighteenth Century England: A Study of Piety and Politics" (Ph.D. diss., University of Rochester, 1979), pp. 242–244, 257–259.

chester fined forty-six persons.[58] In all three towns, women were proficient in profane swearing. Since the population of Gravesend and Milton was less than half that of Deptford, the most populous parish in Blackheath, it does not appear that the Blackheath justices imposed an undue number of fines. Perhaps Sir Snelling Thomas did have an excessive aversion to swearing. He was a justice of Kent for six years of the decade 1706–1715, and in those six years he fined forty-six persons. Between 1716 and 1719, his activity was matched by that of William Wright. Both Thomas and Wright might have been trading justices, but Quarter Sessions records indicate that it was unlikely that Joseph Bell was likewise a candidate for notoriety, and Bell was the most active justice in mid-century Blackheath.[59] In the decade 1746–1755, Bell fined twenty persons. Convictions for swearing in mid-century Kent therefore suggest that Blackheath's justices were arbitrating a much greater proportion of the disputes arising in their vicinity than were the rural justices. Between 1746 and 1755, Blackheath's justices imposed 60 percent of the fines exacted by the justices in the administrative county of Kent while governing about 15 percent of the population residing in the administrative county.[60] As contemporaries noted, urban residents applied to justices "upon every trivial occasion, to gratify their own spleen and malice against their neighbours."[61] Because urban residents requested judicial aid in "trivial" disputes and rural residents did not, urban justices more frequently regulated the conduct of those resident in their locality than did rural paternalists.

As the urban justices discovered, constant regulation of a neighbourhood can be a trying occupation. Since they were continually requested to mediate petty disputes, urban justices were constantly confronted by the more quarrelsome, troublesome, and unpleasant inhabitants of their

58. The mayor and justices of the corporation of Rochester exercised exclusive jurisdiction over all offences committed within the town. The mayor and justices of the corporation of Maidstone exercised exclusive jurisdiction over all trespasses and misdemeanours committed within the town. The mayor and justices of Gravesend and Milton exercised jurisdiction over the town, but the county justices also exercised concurrent jurisdiction.

59. Bell was a director of the Royal Hospital at Greenwich (E. and J. Chamberlayne, *Angliae Notitia,* 33rd, 35th, and 37th eds. [London, 1737, 1743, 1748]).

60. The Hearth Tax returns of 1663 indicate that 11 percent of those inhabiting the administrative county dwelt in the Blackheath division (Coleman, "The Economy of Kent," pp. 7–9, 398–402). According to the 1801 census, the division contained 20 percent of those resident in the administrative county (House of Commons, Sessional Papers, 1831 [348] XVIII, pp. 121–129).

61. *Memoirs of the Life and Times of Sir Thomas DeVeil, Knight* (London, 1748), p. 18.

neighbourhoods. For instance, on October 26, 1715, Sir Snelling Thomas bound Mary, wife of James Steward, mariner, to keep the peace especially to Anne, the wife of Richard Beach, victualler. Eight months later Thomas again bound Mary Steward to keep the peace, especially toward two victuallers of Deptford, including Richard Beach.[62] On February 7, 1716, Richard Vokins, brewer, was bound by three justices of the Blackheath division to answer charges of contempt against William Wright, J.P. On May 2, 1716, Sir Snelling Thomas bound Benjamin Finch, maltster, to keep the peace to Vokins. This dispute was agreed before Quarter Sessions met. On May 8, Vokins was bound by four justices of Blackheath to keep the peace toward a sailor's wife. On July 28, Vokins was bound by Thomas to keep the peace toward Sir Snelling Thomas and two women. This dispute was reconciled and, either as a result of this dispute or of yet another, Thomas fined Vokins for profane swearing on August 2. Later in August, the honours were taken by Vokins' wife, whom Thomas bound to keep the peace toward another woman. Again, the disputants were brought to agreement before Quarter Sessions met.[63] In 1717, Vokins was again in a recognizance—this time to keep the peace toward the wife of John Rawlings. But on this occasion, Vokins may have met his match. In 1716, Sir Snelling Thomas had bound John Rawlings to keep the peace toward one Mary Hoskins, and in 1717 Thomas bound Rawlings and his wife to keep the peace to the wife of Samuel Smith.[64] The latter recognizance is marked *concordantur.*

Small wonder, then, that justices of status resident in urban areas were reluctant to perform the duties of their office. As early as 1666, John Evelyn, residing in an area of Surrey adjacent to London, was recording that he would not act in the commission because of "the perpetual trouble thereof in these numerous [i.e. populous] parishes."[65] By the mid-eighteenth century, even a prosperous gentlemen resident in Spittlefields would request that his name be removed from the commission for "the multitude of poor persons residing in that part of the Town" meant that he was "continually engaged" in judicial business.[66]

62. Kent A.O., Q/SRc, west Kent, Epiphany, 1715[6], f. 2; Mich., 1716, f. 9.

63. Kent A.O., Q/SRc, west Kent, Easter, 1716, not foliated; Mich., 1716, ff. 27, 38, 21, 19; Q/RSj1/2.

64. Kent A.O., Q/SRc, west Kent, Mich., 1717, ff. 13, 20; Mich., 1716, f. 13.

65. Quoted in S. and B. Webb, *English Local Government from the Revolution to the Municipal Corporations Act,* vol. 1, *The Parish and the County* (London, 1906), p. 321, n.2.

66. B.L., Add. MSS 35601, f. 275, petition of John Peck to Hardwicke.

So, in 1732, those urging the appointment of justices of small estate to the commissions in urban areas were arguing that "Gentlemen of any great Figure or Fortune will not take such a Drudgery upon them." Not only were gentlemen unwilling constantly to devote their time to mediation, but gentlemen were also repelled by the "brutish and inhumane" treatment the urban poor inflicted upon each other, and had little patience to hear the poor's "lothesome and ridiculous relations."[67]

To some extent, the demands of the urban poor therefore created the trading justice. Since gentlemen would not assume the burdens of governing the urban poor, men not endowed with fortune and estate had to be appointed to the commission, and these justices would require payment for their services. In the Blackheath division, as in London, eminent gentlemen would not act, and so the burdens of office were assumed by the least landed and eminent of those appointed to the commission.[68] While it is not possible to determine whether Blackheath's most active magistrates were trading justices, it seems most probable that they were more than willing to hear the causes of their neighbours.

Certainly, those resident in the Blackheath division believed their justices eager to adjudicate their complaints. And, since justices who depended on the poor for their income would adopt a manner which encouraged the poor to bring them their business, the behaviour considered typical of Blackheath's justices suggests that some of these justices may have traded on their office. One Kentish case nicely illustrates the judicial behaviour which Blackheath's poor regarded as normal. The case arose in 1722, when the parish constable of Woolwich—a parish in the Blackheath division—received a warrant directing him to bring a labourer before a justice to answer a woman's complaint. The constable was also an alehousekeeper, and he conspired to use his office to increase his alehouse's profits. Instead of taking the labourer before a justice, the constable procured a "gentleman" to impersonate a justice. The fake justice met with the labourer in the constable's alehouse, where over several pots of ale he questioned the labourer and agreed to settle the dispute. The labourer, in turn, agreed to pay both the charges at the alehouse and those accumulated by the constable at another alehouse.[69] Apparently, the labourer eventually discovered the plot. But it is clear that the labourer

67. *Applebee's Original Weekly-Journal,* Aug. 19, 1732.
68. See chapter X.
69. Kent A.O., Q/SRc, west Kent, Mich. 1722, ff. 38, 40, 45, 49, 50.

thought there was nothing unusual in a justice sitting in a common alehouse to discuss a quarrel with one of the poor, and then expecting the disputant to pay the bill. The urban poor assumed that intimate and relatively easy contact with their rulers was normal.

In contrast, Kent's rural magistrates took care to emphasize the inequality between ruler and ruled. At mid-century, a country clergyman resident near Ashford described a scene which provides a neat comparison to the behaviour of urban justices at business in alehouses. The clergyman was present at a dinner given for the respectable gentlemen of the neighbourhood; so were the area's justices. The clergyman recorded: "Sir E. Knatchbull [a justice] always shakes hands with everybody that comes to dine with him. Toke [a justice], receiving Doctors Rutton, Andrew, Gorse and Whitfield, would shake hands with the two first and stopping short of the other two, would make a ceremonious bow. Brockman [a justice], receiving our club, shook hands only with Honywood. . . . A great awkwardness."[70] And the rural justices used manners, ceremony, and formality to create awkwardness, to emphasize the social distance between the sovereign's commissioners and those they were commissioned to govern. These servants of the king would endanger neither their status nor that of their office by encouraging undue familiarity by their inferiors.

Emphasis on the chasm separating ruler from ruled involved disengagement of the rulers from the lives of those they governed. It is quite possible that, in the first half of the eighteenth century, rural justices strove and strove successfully to increase both the respect due their position and their distance from the populace. Comparison of rural and trading justices' views of fees contrasts two very different concepts of the appropriate relation of governors to the governed. To the trading justices, judicial fees were the product of judicial business, and judicial business was to be encouraged. As the Woolwich incident indicates, fees both formal and informal constituted the nexus of the relationship between the trading justice and those he governed. In return for paying the alehouse bill, the Woolwich labourer expected to obtain a judicial service. The Woolwich labourer was the fake justice's client; both the alehouse honorarium and the fake justice's informal behaviour at the alehouse symbolized a relation of near equality between the magistrate and those he governed. Therefore, rural justices both insisted on ceremony and disdained fees. "My Clerk is not here[;]

70. Sir H. Knatchbull-Hugessen, *A Kentish Family* (London, 1960), p. 82.

I take no fees," declared one justice on bailing a prisoner.[71] Rural magistrates shunned any practice which might imply that either their status or their office might be subject to the regulation of the marketplace. Neither office nor status were commodities to be used in bargaining with the governed. The awesome and mystical attributes of hierarchy had to be protected.

Yet, the rural justice had also to be protected—protected, that is, from the importunities of those he governed. While the urban justice cultivated business in order to garner fees, the rural justice took fees to discourage business. In 1697, William Brockman resolved to take fees to prevent "a Multiplicity of Buseness [sic] or the Scandall of Affecting it too much." His honour and reputation he would protect by donating his fees to the poor. A century later, Brockman's practice was proclaimed a model of beneficent rule. According to Thomas Gisborne, a justice should take fees. If he did not, "the immediate consequence would be an immoderate increase of business to the Magistrate himself; and, what would be still worse, an increase no less immoderate of squabble and contentions among the poor, who would carry every frivolous dispute, every angry word to the nearest tribunal. . . ." Justices who did not wish to keep their fees were advised to put them "to a charitable and useful purpose." In 1788, the *Gloucester Journal* reported that "Some few Justices in different parts of this county have made a practice of officiating as their own clerks," and as they declined to take fees their practice had encouraged applications "on matters extremely frivolous."[72] Kent's justices had solved that problem in the reign of George II. Sir Wyndham Knatchbull recorded that in his division the justices merely forwarded memoranda of the recognizances they had issued to the division's clerk, leaving it to the clerk to both fill up the recognizance and take the two shilling fee, "the Justice with us never taking any fee."[73] To reject judicial income was a mark of status, an evidence that the justice served the Crown but was not the servant of the populace. To insist on judicial fees was also, for the rural justice, to express a desire that his paternal mediation not be demanded too frequently.

That the wish was father to the deed, that the frequency with which

71. B.L., Add. MSS 35601, f. 17, information of Thomas Griffith, Jan. 28, 1741[2].

72. B.L., Add. MSS 42598, f. 40; Gisborne, *Duties of Men*, vol. 1, pp. 433–434; E. Moir, *Local Government in Gloucestershire, 1775–1800*, Bristol and Gloucestershire Archaelogical Society, Records Section, vol. 8 (1969), p. 125.

73. Kent A.O., U951/O2, p. 8. The clerk filled in the recognizance, and then returned it to the justice to be signed (Kent A.O., U951/O3, July 14, 1738).

rural magistrates mediated disputes did indeed decline, is indicated by the justices' diaries, by the decline in the number of recognizances returned to Quarter Sessions, and even by the decline in the number of fines for swearing imposed by rural justices. It may be that increasing civility among the rural populace reduced the demand for judicial aid. It is also possible that decline in the rural demand for judicial intervention was abetted by the rural magistracy. Change in the structure of local government could both enhance the justice's image as paternal mediator and relieve the single justice of his paternal responsibilities.

Undoubtedly, the most important development in the structure of local government in the seventeenth and eighteenth centuries was the establishment, growth, and consolidation of petty sessions. By the last decade of the seventeenth century, Kent's justices were referring complaints arising from quarrels and minor crimes to this new local tribunal. In the 1690s, William Brockman was ordering that some miscreants be taken to petty sessions at Elham; Thomas Osborne was sending some of his supplicants to Sittingbourne petty sessions; and in his incomplete justice's diary Ralph Buffkin was recording warrants mandating that some persons who appeared before him take their grievances to Bearsted petty sessions.[74] Likewise, all the eighteenth-century judicial diarists recorded the issue of warrants ordering that defendants appear at petty sessions.

It is difficult to estimate the extent to which the business of the single rural justice was being redirected to petty sessions. The less than complete information recorded in the justices' diaries makes it impossible to determine whether a greater proportion of cases was directed to petty sessions at mid-century than in the late seventeenth century. Petty sessions minute books are also inadequate as records of mediation in petty sessions. Petty sessions minute books do not note the appearance of disputants unless at least one of the disputants was fined or bound in a recognizance. Nonetheless, the diaries of James and Ralph Drake Brockman reveal that at least one-quarter of their warrants for cases of crime and quarrel demanded that the defendant appear at petty sessions. Sir Wyndham Knatchbull's informal and incomplete account of thirty-three meetings of Ashford's petty sessions between 1734 and 1745 notes judicial consideration of nine quarrels. Three of the quarrels resulted in recognizances to Quarter Sessions; the disputants in two other quarrels were advised to settle their differences.[75]

74. Kent A.O., U23/O1.
75. Kent A.O., U951/O4.

Eighteenth-century justices did mediate disputes at petty sessions, and the growth of petty sessions, inspiring the referral of complainants to this tribunal, may well have affected the justice's role as paternal mediator. Since the ratio of recognizances demanded to warrants issued by rural justices decreased markedly after the Restoration, the justices had to some extent substituted warrants to appear at petty sessions for recognizances demanding appearance at Quarter Sessions. In substituting petty sessions for Quarter Sessions, the justices had increased their authority as a group of governors within their own divisions. In substituting mediation at petty sessions for the discharge of a recognizance—a legal bond—at Quarter Sessions, the justices had emphasized their extra-legal role as paternal arbiters of the community. If single justices sent to petty sessions those cases which they deemed difficult or potentially controversial, they could at one and the same time exercise their paternal authority and avoid the opprobrium of unsatisfied disputants. A decision which one or more of the disputants found unsatisfactory could be declared the judgment of the justices as a group, not that of the single justice. Eighteenth-century justices had reason to be sanguine about adoption of the practice of referring cases to petty sessions.

Plaintiffs may have been less pleased. Indeed, the adoption of the warrant to petty sessions may have discouraged plaintiffs from requesting judicial aid. Before the late seventeenth century, a plaintiff's plaint had frequently resulted in a recognizance binding his persecutor to appear at Quarter Sessions, and so the plaintiff could feel satisfied that he had wreaked vengeance upon his persecutor. The recognizance was in itself a punishment: the defendant had to pay a fee for the recognizance, and undertake a troublesome and expensive journey to Quarter Sessions where he would probably be reprimanded. Plaintiffs did not have to appear at Quarter Sessions unless they intended to prosecute their persecutors or had entered into a recognizance to prosecute or give evidence against their persecutors. On the other hand, if a justice issued a warrant demanding that the plaintiff's persecutor appear at petty sessions, the plaintiff would also have to appear at petty sessions if he wished his plaint to be considered. In rural areas, petty sessions were convened at inns several miles from the residences of most justices. Referral to petty sessions therefore obligated a plaintiff to undertake a moderately inconvenient journey just so that he could air his grievances. A hearing before the justice who granted the warrant would have been more convenient. And, once he arrived at petty sessions, the plaintiff was confronted not by the paternal ruler of his parish, but by the rulers of the division sitting formally as a body of governors. At petty sessions, the formal behaviour adopted by rural justices in their individual dealings with their inferiors was elaborated and emphasized in new ceremonies introduced to eighteenth-century local government.

During the eighteenth century, individual rural justices withdrew from involvement in the lives of those they governed, just as landowners erected walls round their parks to protect their privacy from the gaze of the village and in the first half of the century retreated "from involvement in the working life on their properties."[76] Yet, individual retreat did not imply abdication of either status or rule. In the eighteenth century, landlords would sally forth as a group to balls and hunts, to Assizes and militia drills, to awe their inferiors.[77] And at petty sessions, eighteenth-century justices would construct a theatre of rule to impress their own view of rule upon those they governed. Somewhat paradoxically, examination of the paternalist image of the individual justice leads to inspection of petty sessions, the institution which justices molded to embody their joint authority.

76. P. Roebuck, *Yorkshire Baronets 1640–1760* (Oxford, 1980), pp. 340–341.
77. E. P. Thompson, "Patrician Society, Plebeian Culture," *Journal of Social History* 7 (1974):389.

CHAPTER SEVEN

Petty Sessions

According to its historian, all Kent was divided into two sections, formed out of five lathes, between them comprising fourteen bailiwicks and sixty-three hundreds, which were in turn fragmented into 413 parishes, subdivided into villas, boroughs, and hamlets, plus fourteen areas exempt from the jurisdiction of the county's justices.[1] But when Kent's Lord Lieutenant wished to survey the balance of political power in the county's commission in 1714, and when the county's Lord Lieutenant wished to examine the administration of the county in 1775, they had placed before them lists of justices arranged according to petty sessional division.[2] In the eighteenth century, petty sessions was the prime focus of judicial power.

This central institution of local government has never been examined, in part because it is difficult to find sources which document its activities. Since eighteenth-century petty sessions were not required to explain themselves to any higher authority, official archives contain few accounts of petty sessions' operation. This lack of obvious guides

1. E. Hasted, *The History and Topographical Survey of the County of Kent,* 2nd ed. (Canterbury, 1797–1801) vol. 1, pp. 253–258. Hasted lists Rochester, Canterbury, Romney Marsh, New Romney, Sandwich, Dover, Hythe, Deal, Fordwich, Folkestone, and Tenterden. In his later description of Lydd (2nd ed., vol. 8, p. 421), Hasted states that this town was also exempt from the justices' jurisdiction. The parish of Beaksborne was subject to the jurisdiction of Hastings. Faversham was formally under the supervision of Folkestone, but had its own Quarter Sessions (London School of Economics, Webb Collection on Local Government, vol. 138).

2. Kent A.O., Q/JL1, "Justices Named and Alterations since 1708 to 1713"; U269/O96, "The County of Kent divided into Five Laths and several Divisions of Justices."

to petty sessions is evidence of petty sessions' nature: petty sessions was an institution developed by and for the justices themselves. Its structure reflects the justices' notions of the framework most convenient for themselves in government. Its work reveals what powers the justices thought most important in government. Even change in the justices' concepts of appropriate judicial conduct can be attributed to their association in petty sessions. Examination of Kent's petty sessions therefore demands analysis of the relation of judicial aspirations and behaviour to the institution which the justices built.

Perhaps nowhere is the absence of nonjudicial direction more evident than in the search for the petty sessional division. As petty sessions were not required to define themselves to any higher authority, there is no official list detailing the boundaries of eighteenth-century petty sessional divisions in Kent. Fortunately, documents arising from the operation of county government furnish the requisite evidence. Quarter Sessions' clerk, the clerk of the peace, was entitled to one shilling for each licence to sell ale and spirits.[3] Returns of the licences issued at the licensing meetings in the western half of the county have survived in the county records in the custody of the clerk of peace. These returns reveal that by 1707 the nine petty sessions in west Kent had assumed the geographical shape they would retain for the rest of the century. The last alteration in the geographical limits of these divisions occurred between 1706 and 1707, when the justices in the lower portion of the eastern division of the Lathe of Aylesford formed the Tonbridge division, meeting in Woodgate near Tonbridge, leaving the justices in the remaining portion to form the Wateringbury or Malling division, which would first meet in the parish of Wateringbury at the Kingshead and later in Town Malling at the Swan.[4]

The only surviving returns for the eastern portion of the county prior to mid-century centre upon the item of major concern to the clerk of the peace: the number of licences granted and his portion of the money therefrom.[5] Lists of justices made by the clerk of the peace and an occasional reference in the records of Quarter Sessions indicate

3. Kent A.O., Q/SO W6, Oct. 2, 1705.

4. Kent A.O., Q/RLv1/44–45. For purposes of easier identification, this book christens a petty sessional division with the name of the parish in which the justices of the division held their sessions. The division encompassing the western portion of the Lathe of St. Augustine was and still is known as the Home division. The justices of the division nearest London, encompassing the hundred of Blackheath and that of Little and Lesnes, met at both Greenwich and Lewisham. The division is here labelled 'Blackheath'.

5. Kent A.O., Q/RLv3/3: these returns relate to two divisions only—Wingham and Home.

that there was some change in the geographical limits of the divisions of east Kent during the first half of the eighteenth century. Lists of 1704 and 1708 state that there was one division in the Lathe of St. Augustine, meeting at Wingham.[6] Other records prove this to be an oversimplification. There were two petty sessional divisions in the Lathe, but they shared the same clerk. The minute book of Wingham petty sessions—in the eastern portion of the Lathe—reveals that by the first decade of the eighteenth century the division had acquired the geographical limits that would define its existence throughout the century. The other division in the Lathe seems to have led a more varied life. The list of justices recently removed and appointed prepared in the late summer of 1714 refers to the Ospringe division of the Lathe of St. Augustine,[7] as does an order of Quarter Sessions for 1719.[8] Yet Ospringe was in the Lathe of Scray, not in the Lathe of St. Augustine, and the minute book of the upper division of Scray (Sittingbourne division) records routine action of its justices over Ospringe and surrounding parishes in the early 1720s. After 1726, such entries cease. Ospringe and its vicinity had escaped into the clutches of the justices of the Home division.[9] By 1753, when the shape of all divisions can at last be traced, Ospringe had been ceded to the government of the Sittingbourne division, and the Home division comprised that portion of the Lathe of St. Augustine not in the Wingham division.

The occasion for this complete record of petty sessional divisions was an edict of Parliament. According to 26 George II c. 31, the clerk of the peace was required to keep a register of all alehouse licences issued in the county, and Kent's clerk of the peace arranged his register according to petty sessional division.[10] The map made by the licensing register is that of the fourteen divisions that structured the government of Kent throughout the remainder of the century.[11] As the register illustrates, Parliament was becoming increasingly interested in

6. Kent A.O., Q/JL1, list based on commission of Mar. 1703 [4]; list of justices in divisions Apr. 1708.

7. Kent A.O., Q/JL1.

8. Kent A.O., Q/SMa E2, July 12, 1719.

9. Kent A.O., PS/US1; Q/SO E6, July 14, 1730; Q/SB 1748, untitled list of justices in divisions based on the commission of 1735.

10. Kent A.O., Q/RLv4/1.

11. The map, which is presented at the beginning of Part Two, agrees with that constructed from the land tax returns of 1798. (The map of land tax returns is based on the calendar to these returns in the Kent Archives Office, i.e., the calendar to Q/RP 437–450.)

the work of the justices in petty sessions. As the remainder of the clues to the geography of Kent's petty sessions indicate, in the first decade of the eighteenth century groups of justices were meeting at a fixed time and place to license all the alehouses in the division; such meetings were arranged by no agency other than the justices concerned; and the formal supervision of these meetings was so loose that the principal method of discovering their existence is through the measures taken by the clerk of the peace to obtain his fees. In searching for fees, and in so communicating with the divisions, the clerk left behind him the spoor of petty sessions, and in tracing the institutional evolution of the sessions, recourse will once again be had to the peculiar nature of his trail.

As both the changing map and the difficulties of tracing the map of Kent's petty sessional divisions reveal, Kent's justices at their local meetings altered the boundaries of areas over which groups of justices exercised jurisdiction. As in the early seventeenth century, the extent of the division was left to the determination of the justices themselves. In Kent, petty sessional divisions had existed in the late sixteenth century, and those ancient divisions still survived to shape the county's deputy lieutenancy in the eighteenth century.[12] Such survival indicates the moribund state of the county's military machine and the comparative irrelevance of the deputy lieutenancy to county government. The petty sessional divisions, and with and identical to them the land tax divisions, had subdivided in response to the justices' assessments of the most convenient organization of local government. So, too, the justices in their petty sessions would structure the administrative framework of their institution of local government.

According to law, very few of those powers bestowed upon two or more justices acting out of Quarter Sessions had to be exercised within the confines of a meeting of petty sessions. The justices of Kent found such freedom inconvenient. As early as 1704, the justices of the Wingham division were ordering that all alehousekeepers who had not applied for licences on the division's licensing day be refused licences. By 1716, the Wingham justices were commanding that licences be granted only at the "publick Monthly Meeting" of the division, and only "by generall and open Consent of the Justices present in such said

12. W. Lambarde, *A Perambulation of Kent . . . Written in the Yeere 1570 First published in the Year 1576 And now increased and altered . . .* (London, 1826), pp. 22–26; Kent A.O., U269/O96, "A list of the Principal Gentlemen" [1746].

publick monthly meeting and not otherwise."[13] Yet it was not until 1729 that Parliament endowed the monopoly of licensing upon the justices present at the licensing session of the division. In 1717, the justices of Wingham decreed that poor rates be allowed only at the monthly meeting of the division's justices. Yet statute declared that poor rates could be authorized by any two justices living in or near the division.[14] A similar desire to aggrandize their divisional meeting inspired the justices of the Sevenoaks division to command in 1707 that no accounts of overseers of the poor be passed, no poor rates signed, and no parish or public officer sworn at any time or place other than a meeting of petty sessions.[15] Of the extant minute books of Kent's petty sessions, only those for the Wingham and Sevenoaks divisions cover the first two decades of the eighteenth century. It is clear that the justices of these divisions—and probably of other divisions—were determined to grant petty sessions a monopoly of administrative power.[16] No longer could a single justice rule his parish or combine with a friend to administer the parishes in his neighbourhood. The new restrictions bestowed greater power upon petty sessions, and more particularly upon the justices in the majority at petty sessions. The power in which the majority was interested was administrative power, and analysis of the development of petty sessions reveals that the growth of its administrative activities transformed petty sessions into the major institution of local government.

A marked judicial propensity for local innovation, sometimes effected without the guidance of any central authority whatsoever, prohibits generalization about the activity of seventeenth-century petty sessions. At some time between the late sixteenth century and 1630 divisional meetings of justices had been established in most counties. These meetings gained authority during the Civil War, and though the power of Cheshire's petty sessions declined after the Restoration, historians of other counties suggest that, in the later seventeenth century, petty sessions was a permanent and increasingly important institution of local

13. Wingham minute book at the Red Lion Hotel in Wingham, Kent (hereafter referred to as "Wingham, Lion minute book"), Apr. 25, 1704; Kent A.O., PS/W1, Apr. 4, 1716; for similar regulation in the North Riding of Yorkshire, see J. S. Cockburn, "The Work of the North Riding Quarter Sessions in the Early Eighteenth Century" (LL.M. thesis, Leeds University, 1961), p. 53.

14. Kent A.O., PS/W1, Sept. 3, 1717.

15. Kent A.O., U442/O45, June 14, 1707.

16. By 1721, Westminster's petty sessions were establishing a similar monopoly (S. and B. Webb, *English Local Government from the Revolution to the Municipal Corporations Act,* vol. 1, *The Parish and the County* [London, 1906], p. 406n.).

government.[17] Yet, it is quite probable that the administrative powers of even late seventeenth-century petty sessions were insignificant compared with those wielded in the eighteenth century. Certainly, those of the Sevenoaks division in Kent exhibit a remarkable development.

Among the papers of Sir John Heath are what appear to be formal minutes of seven meetings of Sevenoaks petty sessions from April 1681 to March 1683.[18] As these notes indicate that Sevenoaks petty sessions did not meet every month, Heath's muniments are probably a nearly complete account of the sessions' proceedings over these two years. In the 1680s, the procedure and business of Sevenoaks petty sessions was structured by the presentments of the division's borsholders (petty constables) and high constables, and the attention of borsholders, constables, and justices was focused on those who did not attend the services of the Church of England. Sixty-four recusants were presented and ten borsholders were bound by the justices to prosecute these religious defaulters at Quarter Sessions. In addition, nine persons were presented for selling ale without a licence, and one man who refused to support his family and one bastardy case were brought to the notice of the justices. Their worships learned that one migrant would soon return to his parish of settlement, apprenticed

17. J. S. Morrill, *Cheshire 1630–1660: County Government and Society during the English Revolution* (London, 1974), pp. 8, 233–237; for Sussex, see A. Fletcher, *A County Community in Peace and War* (London, 1975), pp. 137–139, 155; for Herefordshire, see B.L., Loan 29/50, no. 79, Nich. Phillpott to Sir Edward Harley, Hereford, Apr. 22, 1665; for Warwickshire see S. C. Ratcliff and H. C. Johnson, ed., *Warwick County Records,* vol. 4 (Warwick, 1938), p. xxviii, and vol. 7 (Warwick, 1946), p. xxxviii; for the North Riding of Yorkshire, see E. Trotter, *Seventeenth Century Life in the Country Parish with Special Reference to Local Government* (Cambridge, 1919), p. 78; for Hampshire, see J. S. Furley, *Quarter Sessions Government in Hampshire in the Seventeenth Century* (Winchester [n.d.]), pp. 13–14; for Norfolk, see C. H. Dittbrenner, "The Poor Law and the Problem of Poverty in Norwich and Norfolk 1660–1700," (Ph.D. diss., University of Wisconsin, 1973), ch. 4, p. 1; for Nottinghamshire, see J. D. Chambers, *Nottinghamshire in the Eighteenth Century* (London, 1932), p. 53; for Gloucestershire, see I. E. Gray and A. T. Graydon, *Gloucestershire Quarter Sessions Archives, 1660–1889, and Other Official Records* (Gloucester, 1958), pp. 70–71, and S. Rudder, *A New History of Gloucestershire* (Cirencester, 1779), p. 38, and E. Moir, *Local Government in Gloucestershire, 1775–1800,* Bristol and Gloucestershire Archaeological Society, Records Section, vol. 8 (1969), pp. 116–119; for Oxfordshire, see M. S. Gretton, *Oxfordshire Justices of the Peace in the Seventeenth Century,* Oxfordshire Record Society, vol. 16 (1934), p. lxxxiv; for Bedfordshire, see J. Godber, *A History of Bedfordshire 1066–1888* (Luton, Bedfordshire, 1969), p. 375; for Cambridgeshire, see E. M. Hampson, *The Treatment of Poverty in Cambridgeshire 1597–1834* (Cambridge, 1935), pp. 225–229. For early seventeenth-century petty sessions, see T. G. Barnes, *Somerset 1625–1640: A County's Government during the 'Personal Rule'* (Cambridge, Mass., 1961), pp. 81–89, 172–201.

18. B.L., Eg. MSS 2985, ff. 232–233, 246–254, 256, 258, 260–261, 263, 269, 286, 289–292, 299.

two children, tendered the oaths to one borsholder, agreed to write to the justices of another division to secure the pay owed a labourer, and ordered that two vagrants be whipped, four idlers go into service, one migrant bring a certificate from his parish of settlement, and one high constable attend petty sessions to answer for his failure to send his warrants to the borsholders on time. A busy two years, but the business of these justices pales before that of their successors.

Compare the administrative business of the Sevenoaks division in the early 1680s with that of Sevenoaks and other divisions in the first half of the eighteenth century. Table 7 charts the administrative business of those Kentish petty sessions for which minute books of the first six decades of the eighteenth century survive.[19]

Like most attempts to categorize documents which were not compiled in a uniform manner, table 7 conveys a delusive impression of certainty and precision. In this case, the table considerably understates the amount of business conducted by petty sessions. Quite possibly the most deceptive numeration is that of the settlement examinations taken and removal orders issued by the justices of the Blackheath division. So numerous were settlement examinations and subsequent orders that persons be removed to their parish of settlement or that they secure a certificate exempting the parish in which they resided from responsibility for their welfare that Blackheath's clerk kept a separate notebook for settlement business, a notebook which has not survived.[20] Undoubtedly, the orders for removal and the settlement examinations recorded in the division's minute book represent but a small fraction of the settlement cases determined by Blackheath's justices. Similarly illusory are the numerations of settlement certificates signed by the justices of the Blackheath, Malling, Bearsted, Bromley, and Rochester divisions. It is probable that the clerks of these divisions just did not consider it necessary to record the signature of certificates

19. Wingham minute book at the Dog Inn in Wingham, Kent (hereafter referred to as "Wingham, Dog minute book"); Sevenoaks, Kent, Sevenoaks Public Library, Sevenoaks minute book; Kent A.O., PS/US1; PS/W3; PS/Ma1; PS/NA1; Greenwich Local History Library, Blackheath minute book; Maidstone, Maidstone Museum, Bearsted minute book; Bromley, Bromley Central Library, Bromley minute book. The Sevenoaks minute book occasionally notes some documents issued by justices out of petty sessions—the discharge of a servant from his master, recognizances, settlement examinations, removal orders, warrants, bastardy examinations, and mittimuses. As these documents were not issued in petty sessions, they are not enumerated in either table 7 or table 8.

20. Greenwich Local History Library, Blackheath minute book, May 13, Oct. 13, 1747.

TABLE 7 ADMINISTRATIVE BUSINESS OF KENT'S PETTY SESSIONS

	Wingham 1706–1709	*Sevenoaks* 1716–1719	*Sittingbourne* 1723–1726	*Wingham* 1739–1742	*Blackheath* 1745–1748	*Malling* 1749–1752	*Bearsted* 1749–1752	*Bromley* 1749–1752	*Rochester* 1754–1757
Removal order	40	21	80	33	35	27	110	2	54
Settlement examinations and/or orders[a]	1	66	122	0	15	50	21	78	107
Settlement certificates[b]	38	39	81	207	2	6	0	0	0
Poor relief	31	9	22	31	0	3	10	1	1
Poor rates	0	124	70	0	24	8	1	10	105
Overseers' accounts	0	57	58	0	15	0	0	0	54
Poor book	0	0	103	0	0	0	102	0	0
Bastardy cases[c]	7	8	9	5	5	0	0	0	0
Apprentice indentures	0	31	19	0	40	0	0	0	2
Distrain for taxes or highway rates[d]	11	16	37	11	32	6	0	3	8
Borsholder or constable sworn	16	60	9	37	1	0	2	1	16
Borsholder or constable appointed	7	0	1	13	0	0	0	0	0

Reduce land, window, or poor tax assessment[e]	1	7	10	15	0	0	1	0	0
Highway orders	3	0	0	8	2	0	2	0	0
Surveyors' accounts	0	4	7	0	0	0	0	0	18
Pay tithes or church rate[f]	9	0	2	0	0	0	0	0	0
Order to get service	10	4	1	0	0	15	0	0	0
Pass or other vagrant order	0	0	0	0	31	0	0	0	0
Recruits	31	0	0	0	0	0	0	0	0
Cattle plague certificate	0	0	0	0	15	0	0	0	0

[a]Does not include examinations of those removed.
[b]Includes some persons also numerated in the category "settlement examinations and/or orders."
[c]Includes warrants issued for the apprehension of putative fathers.
[d]Numerates warrants granted to parish officers, not persons against whom warrants of distraint were issued.
[e]Orders, but not complaints which did not produce orders, are noted.
[f]Notes only orders, not summonses or warrants to appear.

in their minute books. Though the Bromley minute book contains no indication that justices signed certificates at petty sessions, it is filled with orders that those brought before the justices obtain certificates from their parish of settlement—and parishes in the division did grant certificates.[21] Likewise, the great variation in the number of indentures of apprenticeship signed is most probably explained by the idiosyncratic recording practices of the clerks. Certainly, the absence of notation of signature of overseers' accounts and poor rates in Wingham's minute book reflects clerical practice and not lack of petty sessions' supervision: the Wingham division had ordered that all poor rates be signed at petty sessions only, and its minute books occasionally order that specific overseers who had not passed their accounts appear at petty sessions with their records. Most probably, the variation in notations recording the signature of poor rates, poor books, and overseers' accounts reflects both the idiosyncratic recording practices of the clerks and the idiosyncratic recording and accounting procedures of parish overseers. That these early minute books were compiled in such different manners is a reflection of the nature of petty sessional development. Petty sessions were institutions formed by and for the justices of areas within counties without guidance or direction from a central authority.

As table 7 reveals, eighteenth-century justices used their petty sessions to deal with a great amount and variety of administrative business. This concentration upon administration becomes even more evident upon consideration of the administrative tasks delegated to 'special' meetings and omitted from table 7. The justices held one meeting each year to appoint overseers and another annual meeting to license alehouses; they also held regular quarterly meetings to appoint surveyors of the highways and to hear their reports. Through these 'special' meetings, which were incorporated into the regular petty sessional calendar, the justices further extended their control of local government. Petty sessions was not merely an institution conveniently established to ratify the actions of parish officers. The justices in petty sessions acted to affect directly the administration of their divisions. They promulgated rules for licensing: Blackheath forbade the licensing of any new alehouses, and the licensing of those publicans who had been twice convicted for permitting skittles and other games in their establishments; Bromley demanded that the constables

21. Bromley, Bromley Central Library, Bromley vestry record book.

report all publicans who kept skittle grounds or gaming tables and required that all licensees who were not also victuallers be personally bound for the performance of their licences; Ashford made it a rule to suppress any alehouse as soon as complaint had been made against it.[22] Such control was effective. The number of alehouses in Kent increased by only 5 percent between the second and sixth decades of the century, and decreased by 10 percent after the new law of 1753 enabled the justices further to limit the grant of licences.[23] Similarly, in their surveillance of the surveyors of the highways the justices in petty sessions directly governed parish administration. The row entitled "Highway orders" in table 7 numerates those instances in which justices commanded surveyors to repair specified portions of specified roads, sometimes even instancing the manner in which they were to be repaired. As Sittingbourne's minute book reveals, the surveyors gave detailed reports at petty sessions of the state of the roads, and of the work that they intended to have done. At petty sessions too, overseers of the poor who had delayed passing their accounts were ordered to make haste or be fined. And, to insure that their edicts were effectual, the justices at petty sessions commanded the attendance of overseers, surveyors, and constables, and fined those who did not obey.[24]

Yet, perhaps the most impressive symbol of petty sessions' predominance in local administration was its absorption of supervision of the assessment and collection of the land and window taxes. Since justices were almost always commissioners of the land and window taxes, they arranged the meetings of tax commissioners commanded by statute to fit into their regular petty sessional calendar. Indeed, so united were the meetings of the tax commissioners and those of the justices that those few active tax commissioners who were not also justices are listed as presiding at Bromley and Malling petty sessions.

22. Greenwich Local History Library, Blackheath minute book, Sept. 21, 1747, and Sept. 27, 1748; Bromley, Bromley Central Library, Bromley minute book, Oct. 5, 1747, and Sept. 2, 1751; Kent A.O., U951/O4, pp. 3, 33.

23. This calculation is based on the licences for the Wingham, Tonbridge, Bearsted, Malling, Cranbrook, Sevenoaks, Dartford, Bromley, and Blackheath divisions in Kent A.O., Q/RLv1/39–52, Q/RLv3/12, Q/RLv3/20, and the Wingham and Sevenoaks minute books for the first two decades of the century. The figures for 1753 and thereafter are in Kent A.O., Q/RLv4/1.

24. For example: Maidstone, Maidstone Museum, Bearsted minute book, May 4, 1752; Greenwich Local History Library, Blackheath minute book, July 14, 1747, and Sept. 23, 1745; Wingham, Dog minute book, May 2, 8, 1710; Kent A.O., PS/W1, May 7, 1717; Bromley, Bromley Central Library, Bromley minute book, Sept. 12, 1751, May 4, 1752 and June 1, 1752.

Petty sessions minute books note the abatement of assessments to the land and window as well as to the poor taxes. Through its control of the machinery of taxation and the machinery of parish government, petty sessions effectively monopolized the powers of rule. By the 1730s, even Kent's newspaper was attesting the importance of petty sessions. So vital were these meetings to the administration of all activities of local government, and so routine had these meetings become that the petty sessions of east Kent placed advertisements in the *Kentish Post or Canterbury News-Letter* when the regular date or place of the meeting had to be changed.[25]

The presence of well-oiled governmental machinery, ready to be put to extraordinary uses, is revealed by the county's response to the cattle plague of the late 1740s. The government had first discovered the existence of plague in Essex in 1745, and in March of 1746 had promulgated Orders in Council as guidelines for the justices acting in their divisions in case plague should appear.[26] By the summer of 1746, plague had appeared in the Blackheath area. The justices summoned the parish officers to report on the state of the cattle; they endorsed certificates for the reimbursement of those whose cattle had been killed to prevent further contagion; they appointed a cattle inspector and even managed to persuade Quarter Sessions to pay the inspector a salary.[27] When plague appeared in the eastern division in October 1748, the clerks of petty sessions wrote to ask the clerk of the peace for the relevant Orders in Council, arranged special meetings for the petty sessions of the affected areas, advertised the meetings in the county newspaper, and subsequently returned the orders made by the justices to the clerk of the peace. The justices met, appointed inspectors, ordered that they report or be prosecuted, fixed the inspectors' salaries, prohibited the sale of cattle at local fairs, and soon began endorsing the certificates required to reimburse those whose cattle had been killed to prevent the spread of the plague.[28] That plague contin-

25. *The Kentish Post and Canterbury News-Letter,* Mar. 24–27, 1730/1731; Dec. 29–Jan. 2, 1739/1740; May 11–14, 1743; July 20–23, 1737; Kent A.O., PS/W3, July 5, 1737.

26. B.L., Add. MSS 32704, f. 151, John Milner to Duke of Newcastle, Great Russell Street, Apr. 9, 1745; P.R.O., PC 2/99, pp. 388ff.

27. Kent A.O., Q/SB 1747, William Radley to David Fuller, Greenwich, Jan. 12, 1747[8]; Greenwich Local History Library, Blackheath minute book, Dec. 8, 1747.

28. Kent A.O., Q/SB 1748, John Nethersole to Mr. Willard, Clerk to Mr. Fuller, Nov. 4, 1748; Same to Same, Oct. 26, 1748; John Nethersole to David Fuller, Nov. 30, 1748; James Hanson to David Fuller, Dec. 13, 1748; *Kentish Post,* Dec. 28–31, Nov. 5–9, Nov. 9–12, Oct. 2–29, 1748; Kent A.O., Q/SO E7, reports of meetings held at Ashford and Canterbury, Nov. 12 and Nov. 15, 1748; Q/SB 1749.

ued to wander through Kent during the 1750s is a reflection on eighteenth-century medical knowledge, not upon the machinery of petty sessions.

That the justices chose to construct an administrative machine controlled by petty sessions—that is, by the majority of justices in petty sessions—emphasizes the importance they assigned to administrative as distinct from criminal powers. Their administrative powers afforded them considerable opportunities for the use of judicious discretion, and a monopolistic petty sessions provided justices in the majority with a variety of occasions to display their might and deploy their patronage. In determining settlements, the justices in petty sessions apportioned the burdens of poor relief. Similarly, in granting certificates the justices used their discretionary authority to regulate migration and win adherents. The justices in petty sessions ordered parish officers to grant certificates to certain persons. When one potential migrant was refused a certificate, a future justice leased him sufficient land to prevent his removal, and so gained a follower.[29] In appointing parish officers, the majority of justices could flout the known wishes and the authority of resident gentlemen and even of justices. So the appointment of a surveyor marked a minor skirmish in the battle between Sir Edward Filmer, J.P., and Bowyer Hendley, J.P.[30] The signature of tax assessments and overseers' accounts also provided ample opportunity for the use of influence. Yet, perhaps the administrative power most obviously subject to judicial influence was that to license alehouses. The licensing of an alehouse could affect the pocket of a gentleman. At mid-century, one gentleman complained that a petty sessions had unreasonably refused to grant the tenant of his new inn a licence because the owner of the only other alehouse in the area had requested that his monopoly not be disturbed. The gentleman sought redress in the courts, but the courts declared that the decision to license was entirely within the discretion of the justices. As the gentleman protested, the justices in petty sessions wielded the power "to strip a man that has any property in a publick house whether Inn or otherwise and turn his tennant out a begging."[31] In giving petty

29. Sevenoaks, Sevenoaks Public Library, Sevenoaks minute book, Feb. 22, 1716[7]; Wingham, Dog minute book, Nov. 4, 1707 and Apr. 6, 1708; Kent A.O., U442/O45, Mar. 26, 1708.

30. Kent A.O., U120/C43, Hendley to Filmer, Jan. 18, 1735[6]; Filmer to Hendley, Jan. 18, 1735[6]; for the battle see chapter I, section 3.

31. B.L., Add. MSS 35604, ff. 329–330, Sir J. Astley to Hardwicke, Aug. 2, 1756; *Rex* v. *Young and Pitts,* 1 Burr. 557–564.

sessions the discretionary power allotted by law to two justices, the justices of Kent endowed the majority in petty sessions with the full terror of administrative authority.

The terror of the criminal law was less important to the maintenance of judicial interests. Kent's justices did not bestow upon their petty sessions similar exclusive and extra-legal jurisdiction in criminal matters, nor did their petty sessions deliver judgments on many criminal cases. Indeed, as table 8 reveals, the activity of Kent's petty sessions in matters of crime and quarrel was minimal.[32]

It might be argued that table 8 understates petty sessions' attention to crime because it does not enumerate criminal cases which the justices arbitrated, or quarrels which they arbitrated other than disputes between master and servant. The omission of arbitration reflects the limits of the record presented in petty sessions minute books. The minute books note only documents signed by the justices at petty sessions. While the settlement of a dispute between master and servant sometimes involved the issue of a document stating that the servant's contract was terminated or that the master owed the servant a specific amount in wages, arbitration of other disputes only infrequently demanded the issue of a document. Therefore, if fines or recognizances were not extracted from disputants who appeared before petty sessions, it is unlikely that the justices signed any document recording their decision, and so petty sessions minute books do not record their arbitration. Indeed, the minute books are not even adequate guides to the number of disputes brought to petty sessions' attention. Disputants could be directed to petty sessions by warrants issued by single justices, and these warrants would not be recorded in a petty sessions minute book. Nonetheless, table 8 demonstrates that petty sessions issued few warrants on complaints of crime and quarrel, and suggests that fewer warrants emanated from petty sessions at mid-century than in the early eighteenth century. Since single justices were also granting few warrants at mid-century, it is unlikely that the arbitration of disputes occupied so much of petty sessions' attention that its omission from table 8 grossly distorts petty sessions' concern with crime and quarrel.

The justices were not eager to use their punitive powers in criminal cases. When arbitrating quarrels, individual justices would occasionally order that a defendant pay a small sum, or that the defendant be

32. See n. 19 above.

mulcted on a charge of swearing. Otherwise, both in their justices' parlours and at petty sessions, they usually abstained from use of the power of judge and jury given them by statute.[33] According to their notebooks, the seven rural justices—the three Brockmans, Osborne, D'Aranda, Knatchbull, and Filmer—levied a fine about once every three or four years, and the justices were similarly chary of applications to use their criminal powers in petty sessions. When, in 1710, an informer appeared before the Rochester division's petty sessions to lay charges against persons who sold by weight rather than by measure, he received a cool reception. The law stipulated that there had to be two witnesses to this offence if the offender were to be prosecuted. The informer had one witness besides himself, and the question arose as to whether the informer could be accounted a witness. One justice decreed, correctly, that the informer could not and added that the information had not been properly drafted. The informer "objected that at other places before the Justices upon like occasions the Clerks were order[e]d to draw the Information." To which the justices austerely replied "we were not to find tools."[34]

Informers do not appear in the records of Hanoverian petty sessions, but the trade had not died. The self-employed were succeeded by His Majesty's officers of Customs and Excise—to whom the justices were equally antagonistic. Almost all the cases listed in table 8 involving evasion of excise duties and the illegal sale of ale or spirits were initiated by excisemen, who must have found Kent an unprofitable jurisdiction in which to labour. When an excise officer proved to the justices of the Rochester division that a tallow chandler had not observed the proper forms and paid the proper duties, and was therefore subject to a fine of £50, the justices reduced the fine to £12. It was their opinion that "no acts of Parliament were made to ruine the Subject and . . . the proportion of the fine to the offence depended very much upon the Circumstances of the persons [,]ability[,]etc."[35] The justices of other divisions held similar opinions. The justices of the Blackheath and Sevenoaks divisions frequently diminished the statutory fines on those convicted

33. P. Munsche, *Gentlemen and Poachers: The English Game Laws 1671–1831* (Cambridge, 1981), pp. 100–101 notes that the mid-century justices of Wiltshire used their powers of summary conviction to commit only a very few poachers to prison.

34. Hants. R.O., 18/M51/596, Sept. 29, 1710.

35. Hants. R.O., 18/M51/596, Oct. 30, 1710. See also S. Baxter, *The Development of the Treasury, 1660–1700* (Cambridge, Mass., 1957), pp. 80, 107–108, and Cockburn, "The Work of the North Riding Quarter Sessions in the Early Eighteenth Century," pp. 64–66.

TABLE 8 ACTIVITY OF KENT'S PETTY SESSIONS IN MATTERS OF CRIME AND QUARREL, AND IN ARBITRATION OF DISPUTES BETWEEN MASTERS AND SERVANTS

	Wingham 1706–1709	*Sevenoaks* 1716–1719	*Sittingbourne* 1722–1726	*Wingham* 1739–1742	*Blackheath* 1745–1748	*Malling* 1749–1752	*Bearsted* 1749–1752	*Bromley* 1749–1752	*Rochester* 1754–1757
Master/ servant[a]	10	3	8	4	3	0	7	0	0
Evasion of excise duty on malt, hops, mead, skins, candles[b]	0	10	2	14	3	0	0	0	0
Evasion of excise duty on tea, spirits[b]	0	0	0	8	2	0	0	0	0
Selling ale without licence[c]	2	3	4	18	7	1	0	0	2
Game laws[b]	0	8	0	1	0	1	1	0	0
Stealing wood, hedge-breaking[b]	0	18	0	0	1	0	0	1	0
Recognizances, crime or quarrel[d]	1	11	1	4	6	0	3	0	0
Warrants on complaint of crime or quarrel	9	36	9	2	14	1	0	1	0

Punished for stealing	0	1	1	0	0	0	0	0	2
Sent to House of Correction[e]	0	2	3	0	6	0	0	0	0
Other	0	1	0	1	3	1	0	1	2

[a]Numerates final decisions only, and does not include cases which resulted only in warrants to appear or in recognizances to appear at Quarter Sessions.

[b]Numerates only those cases on which petty sessions rendered judgment and so does not include cases for which only complaints or informations are noted.

[c]Includes selling spirits in amounts less than two gallons and allowing tippling. This row numerates only those cases on which petty sessions rendered judgment and so does not include cases for which only complaints or informations are noted.

[d]Not including recognizances issued in bastardy cases or in cases of dispute between masters and servants.

[e]Does not include vagrants or those punished for stealing. The latter are numerated in the row "punished for stealing."

before them by the excise officers. So did the justices of the Ashford division,[36] and persons convicted upon informations brought by excise officers in the Wingham division were regularly awarded reduced fines—in some cases reduced to less than 5 percent of the amount recommended by statute. It was their capacity to punish, not their frequent use of their criminal powers, which was the justices' major contribution to the maintenance of what peace there was in the Kentish countryside.

And so, despite the informer's contention that petty sessional clerks served their justices by preparing documents for criminal cases, the clerks' major function was that of assistant and executor in administrative matters. The clerks, at any rate, had no doubt as to which aspect of their duties was most important and remunerative. The clerks did not receive a salary. They obtained their income from the fees paid for the documents they issued, and the clerk of the Wingham division was well aware that documents relating to the division's administration provided the bulk of his income. In the first eighteen months following his appointment as Wingham's clerk, John Philips persuaded his masters to promulgate orders that their clerk receive one shilling for every warrant issued to constables and borsholders (including those for the licensing and highway sessions), one shilling for each warrant directing overseers of the poor to appear at the annual sessions for their appointment, six pence for every endorsement of the overseers' books, and five shillings for every pair of indentures of apprenticeship.[37] The clerks were administrative *bonnes à tout faire.* They drew up the warrants that brought parish officers before the justices; they provided the legal forms on which the decisions of petty sessions were transformed into legal orders; they placed notices of petty sessions' meetings in the newspapers; they recorded the proceedings of petty sessions in their minute books; before Quarter Sessions and Assizes met, they received from the individual justices lists of recognizances and drew up the formal recognizances. When the justices wanted a legal opinion on matters before them, they ordered their clerk to compose a statement of the case and present it to a barrister. Even in the conduct of criminal business, the clerk acted as the justices' administrative agent. When, in 1732, Wingham's justices decided to prosecute the poachers in their division, they commanded

36. Kent A.O., U951/O4, Sept. 13, 1737.
37. Wingham, Dog minute book, Mar. 28, 1706; Aug. 6, 1706; Mar. 5, 1705[6].

their clerk to present the miscreants at Quarter Sessions. When constables in the division proved negligent in executing warrants to bring vagrants and those out of service to petty sessions, Wingham's clerk was charged with the task of presenting the constables at Quarter Sessions. When Wingham's justices became disturbed at the number of unlicensed persons selling beer, ale, and brandy in their division, they commanded their clerk "to use means for detecting [and] convicting the said several offenders as shall be requisite" and promised to reimburse him for his pains.[38] By the reign of George II, the major executant officer at petty sessions was its clerk.

So, the office of clerk also reflects the development of petty sessions. In the 1680s, Sevenoaks petty sessions had revolved about the reports of the constables, and constables were officers of the parish and the hundred. The clerk, on the other hand, was the agent of the justices in petty sessions.[39] At some time between the late seventeenth- and the mid-eighteenth centuries, all of Kent's petty sessions acquired this symbol of divisional authority. Elham had a clerk in the 1690s and Wingham certainly had a clerk by 1703. Indeed, so profitable and permanent was the office of Wingham's clerk that the appointment of a new clerk in 1705 was accompanied by an order that the new clerk pay his predecessor £20 per annum for as long as his predecessor lived.[40] In some divisions, appointment of the clerk was a more recent phenomenon. A justice kept the minute book of the Sevenoaks division in 1708, but a permanent clerk had appeared by 1715.[41] In 1717, the clerk of the peace knew the names of the clerks to the Dartford, Bromley, Tonbridge, and Bearsted divisions, and had heard rumours of such a clerk in the Malling division. However, he addressed his letters to the Cranbrook division to "Mr. Tempest's Clerk"—Tempest was a justice—and his letter to the Rochester division to "Mr. Robert Brooke one of the Clerks to the Justices meeting at Rochester." Blackheath apparently had no clerk, and it is possible that the justices there also relied upon the services of a clerk employed privately by one of their justices.[42] Sir Snelling Thomas, the most active justice, had his

38. Kent A.O., PS/W2, Oct. 3, 1732, Dec. 7, 1731, Sept. 5, 1732, Apr. 5, 1727; U951/O3, July 14, 1738, and July 5, 1739.

39. For the supersession of the constables' independent authority in Nottinghamshire, see Chambers, *Nottinghamshire,* pp. 55–56.

40. B.L., Add. MSS 42598, ff. 45, 57; Wingham, Lion minute book, Aug. 3, 1703; Wingham, Dog minute book, May 15, 1705.

41. Kent A.O., U442/O45; Sevenoaks, Sevenoaks Public Library, Sevenoaks minute book, June 24, 1715.

42. Kent A.O., Q/AB/72, "Letter sent to the Justices Clk. March 22, 1716[7]."

own clerk.[43] Certainly, by 1753 every one of Kent's fourteen divisions had a clerk. Again, evidence of this development in petty sessions' structure is entirely unrelated to documents spawned by parliamentary or judicial action. In 1753, a new clerk of the peace assumed office in Kent and started to track his fees. In and after 1753, the clerk or his deputy recorded in the Quarter Sessions minute books the amount of money received as licensing fees from each division, noting the name of the payer and the payer's office—invariably clerk to the justices of the division.

In carrying shillings to Quarter Sessions, the divisional clerks were building a structure of administrative cooperation between the county's fourteen petty sessional divisions and the other administrative units in the county. The clerks were the principal means of communication between Quarter and petty sessions; indeed, in those divisions whose justices hardly ever attended Quarter Sessions, the divisional clerks may have been the only means of communication. When the clerk of the peace wished to send information or the orders of Quarter Sessions to the justices in their divisions, he addressed himself to the clerks of petty sessions. When the justices of the division desired information from the county's clerk, their clerk made their inquiries. When Quarter Sessions desired that the justices in their divisions inquire and report, the reporting agent was the clerk to the division.[44] Sir Wyndham Knatchbull and Sir Edward Filmer did not personally certify the recognizances they took into Quarter Sessions or Assizes; they gave them to their divisions' clerks.[45]

When not informing higher courts of the activities of justices in his division, the justices' clerk personally united diverse administrative activities of the county. All clerks to the land tax commissioners of the administrative county were also clerks to its petty sessional divisions—not a surprising development since the justices were also land tax commissioners and many so-called divisional meetings were joint meetings of commissioners of the peace, land, and window tax.[46]

43. Kent A.O., Q/SB 1716, agreement on settlement of Anne Perryman attested by J. Ruddock, clerk to Sir Snelling Thomas.

44. Kent A.O., Q/SO E6, Oct. 8, 1714; Q/SMa E1, July 15, 1712; Q/SO W8, Apr. 19, 1748; Q/SO E7, Oct. 8, 1756; Q/SB 1748, untitled list of justices; Q/SB 1748, John Nethersole to Mr. Willard, Clerk to Mr. Fuller, Oct. 26, 1748; Same to Same, Nov. 4, 1748.

45. Kent A.O., U951/O3, Dec. 7, 1734, July 14, 1738, July 5, 1739, Nov. 2, 1741; U120/O11, Thomas Punnet to Filmer, Mar. 16, 1748[9].

46. I am very grateful to Mr. Richard Grover for supplying information on the clerks to the land tax commissioners. The names of all the clerks to the commissioners of peace and land tax have not been discovered, but the pattern is indubitable.

David Penvold, clerk to the Elham division's commissioners of the peace and land tax prior to 1715, had also been treasurer of the division's militia money.[47] By 1723, John Philips was clerk to the justices and land tax commissioners of the Home and Wingham divisions and treasurer of the jail, house of correction, King's Bench and Marshalsea monies for the eastern half of the county.[48] Later in the century, a few of the justices' clerks were also clerks to towns in the county which were outside the jurisdiction of the justices.[49] Even when not acting in an official capacity, the justices' clerks knit together the administrative units of the county. Almost all were attorneys, and so they regularly attended Quarter Sessions, usually as legal representatives of the parishes in their divisions and frequently defending decisions made at petty sessions and appealed to Quarter Sessions.[50]

Yet, despite the clerk's legal expertise, Kent's justices considered him their servant, not their councillor. Though some eighteenth-century satirists depicted the clerk as the justices' ventriloquist, the only surviving record of debates over points of law at a Kentish petty sessions makes no reference to the opinions advanced by the clerk. John Nethersole was both an attorney and clerk of Ashford petty sessions when Sir Wyndham Knatchbull rode to the Saracen's Head in Ashford to meet with his brother justices. Knatchbull's diary rehearses legal debates—When should a land tax commissioner be disqualified from acting? Under what circumstances should a person be placed under bond to attend Quarter Sessions?—detailing the opinions of the justices. Those of the clerk, if solicited, he did not think worth mentioning. The clerk was, clearly, a subordinate officer of petty sessions.

Since the clerk was a subordinate officer of petty sessions, his office

47. Kent A.O., Q/SMa5, Apr. 28, 1704; Q/SO E5, Jan. 15, 1706.

48. Kent A.O., Q/SO E6, Apr. 26, 1723.

49. Mr. Burr, clerk of the Bearsted division in the 1790s was also town clerk of Maidstone, and Mr. Tappenden, clerk to the Sittingbourne division in the 1790s, was also town clerk of Faversham, as was Mr. Buck, clerk to the Sittingbourne division in the 1750s.

50. Lists of justices' clerks in the last quarter of the century were obtained from notations on a list of the 1776 commission (Kent A.O., Q/JL2), and a list of "Names and addresses of the Clerks to the Divisions of Justices in Kent" (Kent A.O., U269/O141). All but one of the justices' clerks active in the last quarter of the century are included in lists of attorneys resident in the counties—lists published for the first time in 1775. Those consulted were Browne's *General Law List* (London, 1777, 1782, 1785, 1787, 1798). Of the nine clerks whom records reveal as active in the fourth and fifth decades of the eighteenth century, six were listed as attorneys in 1730 (*Lists of Attornies and Solicitors . . . Presented to the House of Commons* [(London, 1729 (1730)]). For notes of attorneys involved in cases at Quarter Sessions, see marginal notations in Kent A.O., Q/SMa E5–7, Q/SMa W7–8.

and duties reflect the development of petty sessions as a corporate institution. When several persons decide to appoint officers or purchase property for the common service of the group, they are taking steps toward the formation of a corporate body. So, petty sessions' acquisition of property, placed in the custody of its clerk, is indicative of petty sessions' growth as an institution that was acquiring a character of its own. As early as 1706, the justices of Wingham ordered their clerk to obtain an abridgement of the statutes, a purchase financed by county funds. In 1717, the Wingham justices procured the *Statutes at Large,* "for the use of the Justices of the Peace of the Division at their monthly meetings," and the county again paid. By 1728, the Quarter Sessions of east Kent was ordering that the clerk of each of the five divisions in the eastern half of the county buy the legal books necessary for petty sessional business and submit their bills to east Kent's treasurer. Subsequent additions to the statute books were purchased by the clerk of the peace.[51] No such all-inclusive order appears in the Quarter Sessions books of west Kent. Yet, it is probable that the other half of the county was making similar provision piecemeal. In 1748, the treasurer of the western division was ordered to pay for the *Statutes at Large,* the latest edition of Nelson's *Justice of the Peace,* and an edition of the *Statutes at Large for the Provision of the Poor* purchased for the justices of the Bearsted division. Listed under the heading "Books Belonging to the Sitting at Bearsted" inscribed on the inside cover of the division's minute book are the three books plus *Instructions for Collectors of Excise.*[52] In 1797, Parliament decreed that copies of the statutes be provided for the justices in their divisions, but this parliamentary decree should not be interpreted as a major impetus for the establishment of petty sessions as a corporate entity. For Kent's petty sessions, at least, the 1797 statute was mere formal recognition of development which had taken place during the first half of the eighteenth century.

Similarly indicative of the development of petty sessions as a corporate entity were their minute books, kept by their clerks. Again, the minute books were the property of petty sessions and former clerks were ordered to surrender these books to their successors.[53] By insti-

51. Wingham, Dog minute book, Mar. 5, 1705[6]; Kent A.O., PS/W1, Sept. 3, 1717; Q/SMa E2, Jan. 14, 1717[8]; Q/SO E6, Jan. 9, 1727[8], and July 15, 1735.

52. Kent A.O., Q/SB 1748, order to pay Mr. Mercer for the books; Q/SO W8, Oct. 4, 1748; Maidstone Museum, Bearsted minute book.

53. Kent A.O., PS/W3, Oct. 7, 1735.

tuting this record of their proceedings, the justices in petty sessions acknowledged that their institution possessed a character and a history of its own. Several divisions had acquired this documentary evidence of petty sessions' personality during the reigns of the last two Stuarts. Elham's clerk was keeping a minute book in the 1690s, and in 1703 Wingham's clerk was ordered "to acquire a book in which to inscribe the proceedings of the Monthly Sessions."[54] By 1705, Wingham's first minute book had become the mere repository of scribbled rough drafts of the sessions' proceedings. Wingham now also had a formal minute book.

The introduction of form in its minute book heralded the introduction of a more formal order in petty sessions' proceedings. In 1709, shortly before their acquisition of a clerk who kept a minute book, the justices of the Sevenoaks division made it a standing rule, "That the first work at every meeting of the Justices of this Division be to Read over the Minutes of their Proceedings in the Two next preceeding Sittings, in order to the Perfecting Matters begun." Institutional structure was likewise defined by a contemporaneous order that each meeting of the sessions be guided by a chairman. At Sevenoaks in 1709, the office of chairman rotated among the justices. By 1743, the Blackheath division was appointing a permanent chairman.[55] Yet, the division which probably proceeded first and farthest along the path to definition of the structure and ceremony of petty sessions was that of Wingham. In 1706, shortly after they had acquired a new clerk and a more ornate minute book, the justices of Wingham set forth the rules which were to give order to their meetings: the justices would foregather alternately at the Red Lion and the Black Dog in Wingham; in the winter, when days were short, they would sit in the mornings as well as in the afternoons; their hosts were to provide a "Competent and well Ordered Dinner" set upon the table by one in the afternoon or forfeit their recompense; each justice was to pay two shillings for his dinner and deliver his money to the clerk of the division, or forfeit his share of the proceeds of the division's licensing session; and those awaiting audience with their worships of Wingham were to notify the clerk of their business and wait until duly called, upon pain of being the last admitted to the judicial presence. In a final statement of petty sessional grandeur, the Wingham justices authorized their clerk to

54. B.L., Add. MSS 42598, f. 57; Wingham, Lion minute book, Aug. 3, 1703.

55. Kent A.O., PS/SE1, p. 2; Greenwich Local History Library, Blackheath minute book, Aug. 9, 1743.

employ a doorkeeper, who was to certify the names of supplicants to the clerk, and who was to be paid by the clerk and furnished with a dinner.[56] Once an informal meeting of neighbouring justices, petty sessions was now a formal institution, possessing its own ceremonies and its own structure.

A structured petty sessions implied the definition of the members of petty sessions as well as of its procedure. Again, the clerk provided a touchstone for institutional definition. The office of petty sessional clerk was profitable and the appointment of a clerk therefore allowed the justices to display their powers of patronage. It followed that appointment of a clerk demanded identification of those who possessed the right to appoint, and this posed a problem. For, while the boundaries of the division were informally but clearly defined, the justices' rights to participation in the decisions of a petty sessions were not.[57] According to law, a justice could act anywhere in the county for which he was commissioned. In practice, justices sat in petty sessions which exercised jurisdiction over divisions in which they were not resident. As the title prefacing the record of each meeting of the Wingham division explained, the meeting was composed of "justices residing in or near the eastern division of the Lathe of St. Augustine." Since the division was not legally recognized, no law demanded that petty sessions more clearly define its membership. But the extra-legal activities of petty sessions—and particularly those involving the appointment of the officers of this extra-legal institution—would demand that the justices impose their own restrictions upon judicial power.

Both the evolution of petty sessions as a meeting of a discrete group of justices and the manner in which this evolution was related to the definition of petty sessions as a corporate entity are illustrated by the controversy over Elham's clerk. On October 6, 1718, the justices of the Elham division ousted David Penvold from the office of divisional clerk and appointed James Spillet. On April 6, 1719, the justices assembled to license the division's alehousekeepers when Penvold appeared, wishing to perform the clerical services associated with licensing and demanding part of the clerk's share of the fees. William Brockman, J.P., noted that the justices present were divided on the question:

56. Wingham, Dog minute book, Dec. 3, 1706.

57. The boundaries of the petty sessional divisions were those of the hundreds. Every petty sessional division contained two or more hundreds. Even the mutations of the Sittingbourne and Home divisions revolved around the translation of jurisdiction over the hundreds of Faversham and Boughton.

Sir William Hardres (Not being in the Division) Sir W. Honywood and his younger son Mr. E. Honywood (Not being in the Division) Taking part one way [,] Mr. David Papillon, Col. Marsh (Not being in the Division), Mr. Julius Deedes of Hythe and Myself Taking Another. . . .

Col. Marsh proposed at the Time, and before he offer'd to act, that if the other Gentlemen forbore to act, who did not live, or reside within the Division, neither would he act, or take any part at all.[58]

In the end, both clerks and all the justices acted, and no one knew how many licences had been granted or to whom. Lack of definition of the qualifications for membership in its petty sessions produced, for the moment, chaos in the administration of the Elham division. Yet, as both Brockman's parenthetical comments and Marsh's proposal reveal, the notion that justices could not determine the institutional arrangements of a petty sessions in a division in which they did not live or reside was already considered persuasive.

Though no law prevented justices from participating in decisions on the structure or officers of a division in which they did not normally act, it is probable that the justices developed an informal set of constitutional conventions which recognized the integrity of each petty sessional bench. Lack of such informal understandings would have produced chaos in administration, and Kent's petty sessions functioned quite efficiently. Certainly, when the successful applicant for the clerkship of the Bearsted division listed his supporters in 1742, he mentioned only those justices resident in the division.[59] In appointing their subordinate officers, the justices of a petty sessional division were defining judicial rights to membership in their corporation.

As the battle over Elham's clerk indicates, the self-definition of petty sessions was related to party conflict, and party struggle likewise contributed to the development of both the corporate identity and the administrative hegemony of petty sessions. Those who supported Spillet at Elham were all Whigs. The advocates of his rival were Sir William Hardres, a Tory M.P.; Sir William Honywood, who had plumped for a Tory at the last election; and Honywood's younger son, who was now following his father's lead. Sir William Honywood had not been present at petty sessions when the old clerk had been displaced, and it is probable that he had secured the attendance of both his son and Hardres at the licensing session in an effort to maintain Tory power. Because petty sessions had become so important in local

58. B.L., Add. MSS 42598, ff. 129, 148–149, 158.

59. Kent A.O., U120/O11, Thomas Punnett to Sir E. Filmer, Sept. 2, 1742.

administration, those with local power would endeavour to capture the institution for their interest and their party.

By the early eighteenth century, consideration of the power wielded by petty sessions dominated the political manipulation of the composition of Kent's bench. When, on the accession of George I, Kent's Lord Lieutenant reviewed the commission of the peace in order to nominate suitable candidates for appointment and dismissal, he scanned a list of those appointed and removed by the late Tory regime, organized according to petty sessional division.[60] Both his actions and those of the Tories further emphasize the importance of the division: between 1711 and 1713, the Tories arranged matters so that Tories were in the majority in all of Kent's fourteen divisions; by 1720 the Tories predominated in only two divisions.

There is, at the least, a striking coincidence in timing between the period of the most frantic political manipulation of the bench and that of petty sessions' attempts to monopolize the administrative powers allocated by law to any two justices of the county. It is not improbable that the fervent party conflict of the early eighteenth century was a major motive for these administrative innovations. Engrossment of administrative power by petty sessions enlarged the power of those in the majority at petty sessions and diminished the sway of those in the minority. In the early eighteenth century, alliances among justices were, to a large extent, based on party affiliation.

Party struggle may therefore have provided the impetus for the establishment of petty sessional hegemony. Yet, when party rivalry diminished, both the new administrative structure and the attitudes encouraged by its successful operation remained. The justices found themselves in possession of an administrative structure which insured that government would be controlled by the justices acting as a group. Similarly, party affiliation, extra-legal associations of justices, and the institutional structure of petty sessions would foster the growth of a corporate judicial identity at petty sessions.

Since, in the first three decades of Hanoverian rule, few Tories were justices and still fewer acted, meetings of petty sessions were local conferences of Whig governors.[61] Most probably, conflict between justices diminished, for justices were now allied with their associates on the bench. In 1738, it was argued that the appointment of justices of

60. Kent A.O., Q/JL1, "Justices Named and Alterations Since 1708 To 1713."
61. For judicial propensity to act, see chapters IX and X.

an opposing interest to a Herefordshire division would disturb "the good Harmony which subsists among those Gentlemen in the carrying on their Justices Affairs."[62] That this argument contains political apologetic is obvious. Equally revelatory are the assumptions that common political affiliation produced judicial amity, and that judicial amity was a necessity in local government. The same assumptions explain the terms in which mid-century justices objected to the appointment of Tories. Tories, they claimed, were "battling," "litigious," and "troublesome."[63] In other words, Tories would inject discord into judicial proceedings. Party hegemony aided the development of a common identity among justices, and when party waned, the desire for unity continued to influence judicial behaviour.

Judicial dining clubs provided another and probably more effective means of creating a united petty sessional bench. As early as 1706, the justices of Wingham had formed a dining club, and that club gave structure to their petty sessions. Justices who refused to pay their share of the club's dinners, or to ratify the set of resolutions establishing both the club and the procedure of petty sessions were to be excluded from their share of the licensing revenues—that is, they were not to be acknowledged as full members of petty sessions with rights to share in its profits.[64] By 1733, Bromley's justices also had a club which similarly shaped its members into a unified group. The justices contracted to meet at the Tiger on the first Monday of every month at 11 A.M., and to pay two shillings toward every dinner, whether in attendance or not.[65] By imposing upon themselves obligations which acknowledged their membership in a judicial group, the justices were forming themselves into a corporate body. In establishing these convivial gatherings, they also reinforced the sense of common identity among those who had just shared the divisional bench.

In turn, a sense of common identity springing from shared judicial and social activity produced new standards against which justices measured prospective colleagues. Justices would not want to work with those who impeded their proceedings, disrupted their meetings,

62. B.L., Add. MSS 35600, ff. 164–165, Duke of Chandos to Hardwicke, July 4, 1738.

63. B.L., Add. MSS 35604, ff. 274–275, Thomas Lane to Hardwicke; f. 234, Sir Francis Drake to Hardwicke, July 1754; f. 25, persons recommended by Sir Thomas Prendergast thought improper.

64. Wingham, Dog minute book, Dec. 3, 1706.

65. Bromley, Bromley Central Library, sheet of paper inserted in Bromley minute book.

and spoiled their dinners. So, the requirement that a prospective justice be able to enter into the collegial spirit of a petty sessions served to modify the model of a model justice. Behaviour suggesting that the nominee would use his powers in an uncooperative manner now constituted proof of unfitness for judicial office.

The emergence of new criteria for judicial behaviour was most evident in the assessment of nominees of lower status. In the seventeenth century, justices were gentlemen already preeminent in their neighbourhoods, and it was accepted that these powerful men would use their office to increase their power. By the mid-eighteenth century, there were many justices who gained more prestige from appointment to the commission than they brought to the office. It was thought unwarranted that such justices use their official powers to obtain complete dominance in their communities. At mid-century, one Hampshire justice explained why the temperament of a former captain in the East India service rendered him unfit for office:

> The objections I have to Captain Blake being of the Commission do not arise from my believing him capable of any dishonest or corrupt act, but from knowing by diverse facts that I have heard, and seen proofs of, that he is of an impetuous and litigious disposition, violent in his resentments, and so far blinded by them, even with very little provocation as to committ actions that are in every way improper; it is, by disputes of this sort in which he has threatened his parish with his future authority, that I became acquainted with his expectation: I shall add that his education, and the way of life he has been us'd to, no way qualify him for doing service in this office, and that his property in the County (a circumstance though which not a title is a pretence) is only a late purchase which cost him sixteen hundred pounds. . . . I shall act with him while it is possible, but such is the opinion of his impracticability, that every body will not have the same patience.[66]

In theory at least, the justice of modest status was not to be permitted those exhibitions of pride, temper, or dominance which had been accepted as marks of leadership among justices of earlier eras.

The new criteria for judicial behaviour were sometimes phrased so as to emphasize the proper conduct of a justice toward his inferiors. Yet, it is unlikely that a nominee's manner to his inferiors was as important in evaluation of his fitness for office as estimates of his probable conduct toward his brethren on the bench. A nominee's customary behaviour toward his equals was scrutinized: a man who always disagreed with his company would both be an unpleasant asso-

66. B.L., Add. MSS 35604, f. 254, Hans Stanley to Hardwicke, Oct. 17, 1754.

ciate and undermine the authority of petty sessions' decisions. By 1810, even the protegé of an aristocrat was denied elevation to Gloucestershire's bench because "his Temper was frequently so warm that other gentlemen might decline acting with him."[67] Gentlemen of subdued demeanour made more agreeable colleagues, and petty sessions was a collegial institution.

Of course, judgments of temperament and behaviour can easily become evaluations of status. Captain Blake's less than judicial conduct was attributed to his less than gentlemanly education and occupation. Insistence upon appropriate conduct was one means of excluding the increasingly numerous newly genteel from the later Hanoverian bench. By 1807, the Derbyshire bench could successfully remonstrate against the appointment of a nominee who, though possessed of "good sense and unexceptionable character," did not enjoy that "situation in life" which would "entitle him to a place in the commission of the peace of this county."[68] The early nineteenth-century bench may well have been more socially exclusive than its early eighteenth-century predecessor. Since in the early eighteenth century those with pretensions to gentility acquired landed estates, restriction of the commission to landowners would not have barred the newly eminent from the bench. And, in Kent at least, all early eighteenth-century justices were not landowners. When, in the early nineteenth century, membership in the commission of several counties was denied to those in trade and manufacture, many of the newly eminent were unable to obtain judicial office.[69] Nonetheless, in erecting new standards for judicial behaviour, in barring the bench to those in trade and manufacture, and in relating behaviour to status, the justices of the late eighteenth century were asserting both their common identity as members of a distinct social group and their corporate identity as members of a collegial institution able to judge the qualifications of prospective members.

By the early nineteenth century, the process of judicial appointment acknowledged the justices' corporate identity. Lords Lieutenant requested that the justices assess the qualifications of nominees, and

67. E. Moir, *Local Government in Gloucestershire*, p. 41.

68. J. C. Cox, *Three Centuries of Derbyshire Annals, as Illustrated by the Records of the County of Derby from Queen Elizabeth to Queen Victoria* (London and Derby, 1890), vol. 2, pp. 301–302.

69. D. Philips, "The Black Country Magistracy, 1835–1860," *Midland History* 3 (1975–1976): 166; J. R. Knipe, "The Justice of the Peace in Yorkshire, 1820–1914, A Social Study" (Ph.D. diss., University of Wisconsin, 1970), pp. 20–21.

even promised to abide by their recommendations.[70] In Kent, at least, the judicial group whose advice was most frequently requested was the bench of the petty sessional division in which the nominee resided. Kent's Lord Lieutenant would decline to state whether a nominee was acceptable until he had solicited the opinion of the justices of the division in which the nominee would act. Conversely, Kent's justices in petty sessions recommended as "the bench of the division" the appointment of those with whom they wished to be associated.[71] Again, their dining clubs enabled many petty sessions to make these corporate decisions. As some of these clubs admitted nonjustices on the nomination of a justice, eating the judicial dinner served as an audition for judicial office.[72] The peculiar institutional framework adopted by eighteenth-century justices bestowed upon their successors the ability to impress even the central government with their corporate identity.

Yet, probably the most impressive evidence of the emergence of the corporate identity of petty sessions were those actions which emphasized the involvement of every justice in the decisions taken by petty sessions. In the 1720s, the justices of the Wingham division were sharing the profits of the licensing session among all the justices of the division, making no distinction between those who had been present at that particular session and those who had not. Nonetheless, at mid-century petty sessions was not considered an institution whose decisions represented and bound all justices of the division. Appointments of petty sessions' clerks were signed by each justice of the division; resolutions passed at one meeting would be proferred again at the next, so that justices absent when the resolution was first discussed could express their views; and a justice had to sign a resolution of petty sessions before he could be considered bound by that resolution.[73] In contrast, the petty sessions of late eighteenth-century Kent was a representative institution, an institution whose decisions bound all the active justices of the division and spoke for all. In 1799, the justices of the Malling division resolved that "if in consequence of any

70. A. Brundage, "The Landed Interest and the New Poor Law: a reappraisal of the revolution in government," *English Historical Review* 87 (1972): 43; Knipe, "The Justice in Yorkshire," pp. 20–21.

71. Kent A.O., Q/JQc1–2.

72. P. Norman, "Notes on Bromley and the Neighbourhood," *Archaelogia Cantiana* 24 (1900): 151; Surrey R.O., PS3/1/1, Sept. 21, 1776 and June 30, 1781.

73. Bromley, Bromley Central Library, Bromley minute book, Sept. 2, 1765; Greenwich Local History Library, Blackheath minute book, Sept. 21 and Dec. 8, 1747; Wingham, Dog minute book, May 15, 1705 and Dec. 3, 1706.

Act done by the Magistrates assembled at their Monthly Meeting any Action or prosecution of any kind should be brought against the Magistrate or Magistrates who actually signed at such Meeting any Order or warrant or Commitment or Conviction . . . all the Magistrates of the Division who at any time have attended the Meeting whether present at the time or not shall proportionately pay the Expences which may be incurred by the Magistrate or Magistrates against whom such action or prosecution may be brought."[74] Administrative convenience and solidarity—social or political—may not be strange bedfellows. Yet, no parliamentary authority had sanctified their union, and their offspring was a thriving bastard.

Of course, the history of Kent is not that of England. Kent's justices had divided themselves into divisions decades before they were ordered to do so by the Privy Council in 1605, and these precocious beginnings may indicate that Kent's petty sessions also attained corporate definition before those of other counties. In some counties, new structures for Quarter Sessions may have substituted for the development of a petty sessions system. For example, in those counties where Quarter Sessions was adjourned from town to town throughout the county each quarter, the need for the local tribunal of petty sessions may have been less pressing. Yet, by the early nineteenth century, petty sessions was the "dynamic of local government" even in administratively retarded Wales.[75] Petty sessions—an institution made for and by the justices—encouraged England's governors to present a united front to those they governed.

74. Kent A.O., PS/Ma4, July 1, 1799.
75. D. L. V. Jones, "Law Enforcement and Popular Disturbances in Wales, 1795–1835," *Journal of Modern History* 42 (1970): 500–501.

CHAPTER EIGHT

Quarter Sessions

Almost since its establishment, Quarter Sessions has been acknowledged as the supreme institution of local government. Early eighteenth-century Quarter Sessions therefore presents a paradox, for in the first half of the eighteenth century the supreme institution of local government was not active in government. To the Webbs, Quarter Sessions' lassitude evidenced "the sullen torpor of the Jacobite sympathisers, and the cynical acquiescence in evil of the Walpolean Whigs."[1] But the Webbs were twentieth-century administrative reformers, imbued with modern notions of government. At their Quarter Sessions, Kent's justices enacted the early Hanoverian definition of government. For these justices, government did not necessarily entail continuous exercise of authority. Rather, government demanded a setting and a structure which convinced justices and populace alike that their rule was effective.

Fortunately for the historian, Kent had two Quarter Sessions. Fortunately, because comparison of these two courts allows for some distinction of idiosyncratic from typical behaviour. Kent's two Quarter Sessions acted independently. That for east Kent met at Canterbury and governed the area covered by the five petty sessional divisions of Sittingbourne, Wingham, Home, Ashford, and Elham, while that for the west met at Maidstone and ruled the area encompassing the remaining nine

1. S. and B. Webb, *English Local Government from the Revolution to the Municipal Corporations Act*, vol. 1, *The Parish and the County* (London, 1906), p. 364. For early seventeenth-century Quarter Sessions, see T. G. Barnes, *Somerset 1625–1640: A County's Government during the 'Personal Rule'* (Cambridge, Mass.: 1961), pp. 40–97.

petty sessional divisions. The bifurcation of the county was well established in the sixteenth century. In 1642, high constables were ordered to attend only that Quarter Sessions held in their half of the county, and by the eighteenth century each Quarter Sessions considered that it had no authority to deal with appeals from settlement cases arising in parishes governed by the other.[2] This division of jurisdiction had originally coincided with Quarter Sessions' perambulation: each year two meetings were held in the east and two in the west. In 1689, the justices of east Kent initiated the practice of meeting every quarter, and in 1732 an identical arrangement was adopted in the west. Though these two Quarter Sessions shared the same clerical staff, each elaborated its own procedure and rules. For instance, in determining appeals against assessments to the poor rates, the Quarter Sessions of east Kent did not allow clerics to deduct the cost of hiring a curate from the value of their livings while the Quarter Sessions of west Kent did.[3] Though these two Quarter Sessions developed independently, both displayed similar characteristics. Analysis of the activity of these two courts makes obvious the reason for the Webbs' condemnation of early Hanoverian Quarter Sessions; yet analysis of the courts' operation also reveals the early eighteenth-century foundations for the administratively active Quarter Sessions of the nineteenth century.

There were two modes of Quarter Sessional activity: the judicial and—for want of a better word—the administrative. In its most explicitly judicial guise, Quarter Sessions acted through juries. Complaints of crime and misdemeanour were presented to the grand jury, and if the grand jury found the complaints valid, offenders were tried before a petty jury. As table 9 demonstrates, Quarter Sessions' exercise of these judicial powers declined dramatically during the first half of the eighteenth century. Any table based on a few sample years is bound to contain distortions.[4] Nonetheless, table 9 reflects a trend apparent from just a glance at the indictment rolls: throughout the

2. P. Clarke, *English Provincial Society From the Reformation to the Revolution: Religion, Politics and Society in Kent 1500–1640* (Hassocks, Sussex, 1977), p. 114; R. D. Clarke, "West Kent Quarter-Sessions Orders in the Reign of Charles I," *Archaelogia Cantiana* 80 (1965): 228; Kent A.O., Q/SMa E2, July 10, 1716; Q/SMa W6, Oct. 7, 1740.

3. E. Hasted, *The History and Topographical Survey of the County of Kent*, 1st ed. (Canterbury, 1778–1799), vol. 4, p. 183r.

4. For the effect of war and high food prices on indictments for crime, see J. M. Beattie, "The Pattern of Crime in England 1660–1800," *Past and Present* 62 (1974): 84–95.

TABLE 9 BILLS PRESENTED TO THE GRAND JURY AT KENT'S QUARTER SESSIONS[a]

Category of offence	East Kent				West Kent			
	Mich. 1708–Mids. 1710	*1716–1717*	*1748–1749*	*1758–1759*	*1708–1709*	*1716–1717*	*1748–1749*	*1758–1759*
Criminal—attempted rape, riot, assault, theft, fraud, unlawful entry, leaving bastard in ditch	16	40	7	6	20	23	18	40
Offences against the game laws	1	2	0	0	5	9	1	0
Crime by words—seditious speech or publication, disrespect to justices	0	2	0	0	2	8	0	0
Practising a trade to which practitioner not apprenticed	1	1	1	1	3	4	2	11
Other economic—lodging vagabonds, permitting too many inmates, erecting cottage without a licence, selling on Sunday, engrossing, regrating, or selling without a licence, keeping a disorderly house, keeping an alehouse without a licence, using too many horses to pull a wagon	8	9	2	0	10	27	5	2
Neglect or improper conduct by parish officials or bailiffs	2	8	0	2	11	28	1	1

Individual placing nuisance in or failing to repair footpath or highway	33	6	2	0	26	15	1	8
Individual failing to keep watch or work in highway	0	0	0	0	20	10	1	0
Parish, hundred, or county failing to repair bridge or highway	21	13	0	3	11	16	19	16
Miscellaneous	4	1	0	0	10	6	1	0
Total cases in bills of indictment	86	82	12	12	118	146	49	78

[a]This table numerates cases, not the number of persons presented. All bills, whether found by the grand jury or not, are included in this table.

first half of the eighteenth century the number of indictments, and hence the size of the rolls, dwindled.

Though Quarter Sessions had originally been constituted as a court to try offenders against the laws and exercised jurisdiction over all offences but treason, the amplitude of its sway had been considerably reduced. By 1660, Kent's Quarter Sessions had surrendered to Assizes adjudication of all crimes for which the death penalty could be invoked, and in the first half of the eighteenth century its power to chastise minor criminals was applied to a diminishing number of complaints. Decline is most notable in east Kent, where it is probable that population remained stable or diminished slightly.[5] In the west—especially in the area near London—population increased and so there the maintenance of a stable level of indictments for minor crimes in the first half of the century masks diminution in the ratio of indictments to population.[6] Similarly, the increase in the number of minor crimes brought to the attention of west Kent's Quarter Sessions in the late 1750s camouflages the dwindling use of Quarter Sessions to correct minor offenders. By 1758, a few persons were being tried at Quarter Sessions for crimes which in the first half of the century would more usually have been sent to Assizes. As the number of cases heard at Assizes in 1748 through 1749 was almost precisely that heard at Assizes in 1758 through 1759, it is possible that in Kent as in Surrey increase in the business of Assizes impelled the justices to direct to Quarter Sessions cases that would formerly have merited the attention of the higher court.[7] It is quite likely that in the 1750s west Kent Quarter Sessions adjudicated a smaller proportion of minor assaults and thefts than the Quarter Sessions of the early eighteenth century.

Decline in Quarter Sessions' surveillance of minor offenders is more strikingly revealed by the recognizances returned to Quarter Sessions. In both the early and mid-century several persons were bound in

5. For decline in indictments for assault, see J. S. Cockburn, "The Work of the North Riding Quarter Sessions in the Early Eighteenth Century" (LL.M. thesis, Leeds University, 1961), p. 79. For decline in indictments for crime at Hertfordshire Quarter Sessions, see W. LeHardy, ed., *Hertfordshire County Records*, vol. 7 (Hertford, 1931), pp. xxxiii–xxxiv, and *Hertfordshire County Records*, vol. 8 (Hertford, 1935), p. xxxi. For decline in indictments for assault and crimes against property in Sussex in the first half of the century see Beattie, "The Pattern of Crime," pp. 69, 77.

6. P. Deane and W. A. Cole, *British Economic Growth 1688–1959* (Cambridge, 1962), pp. 101–103; see Beattie, "The Pattern of Crime," p. 60n. for the application of similar distinctions between rural and urban areas to determine the ratio of indictments to population in eighteenth-century Surrey.

7. J. M. Beattie, "Crime and the Courts in Surrey 1736–1753," in *Crime in England 1550–1800*, ed. J. S. Cockburn (London, 1977), pp. 175–176.

recognizances to attend the court, did attend the court, but were not charged before the grand jury. Over half of the cases resulting in such recognizances were minor assaults and quarrels. Sometimes Quarter Sessions ordered that the persons so bound enter again into a recognizance to attend the next Quarter Sessions. Much more frequently, persons bound in recognizances were simply dismissed—and perhaps admonished. In 1708 through 1709, persons involved in 113 cases so waited upon Quarter Sessions; in 1716 through 1717, the total number of cases producing such recognizances was 97. But the total number of cases delivering to Quarter Sessions persons who were not presented before the grand jury in 1748 through 1749 was 15, and that in 1758 through 1759 was 28.[8] In the early eighteenth century, Quarter Sessions kept the peace through suasion, exhortation, and the power to awe. By mid-century Quarter Sessions no longer executed this office.

Similarly expressive of the diminution of Quarter Sessions' interference with the ordinary concerns of the subject was its decreased surveillance of that conduct of the individual which affected the community's economy and the social relations of its inhabitants. The number of indictments for infringement of all economic regulations but one declined dramatically. The prosecution of the exception—practising a trade in which the practitioner had not been apprenticed—was undertaken by members of that trade. Prosecution of almost all other economic and administrative offences commenced with presentment by the constable. Individual self-interest therefore preserved prosecution of those not apprenticed, but the economic interest of the community ceased to concern either its constables or Quarter Sessions.[9] That indictment of individuals for failing to maintain or obstructing roads and footpaths similarly dwindled also represents decline in the court's supervision of the individual's communal responsibilities. Yet, perhaps most telling is the diminution of the "miscellaneous" indictments—a category which includes scolds, barrators, and those who let their hogs

8. This numeration excludes cases of bastardy, which did not lead to presentment before the grand jury, and those cases of dispute between master and servant in which the justices issued an order without reference to the grand jury. The numeration of recognizances not leading to indictment for 1708 through 1709 is based on the cases in east Kent's recognizance rolls for Mich. 1708 to Mids. 1710 and in west Kent's recognizance rolls for 1708 through 1709.

9. For decline of economic regulation and indictments for nuisance in Hertfordshire, see Le Hardy, ed., *Hertfordshire County Records,* vol. 7, pp. xxxiii–xxxiv, vol. 8, p. xxxi. For decline of economic regulation in the North Riding, see J. S. Cockburn, "The Work of the North Riding Quarter Sessions," pp. 218, 220.

injure their neighbours' property. By mid-century, indictments at Quarter Sessions can be classified into a few clear and distinct categories. Of the multiplicity of ills that could ail a community only a few of the most obvious were brought to the attention of the court.

By the beginning of the eighteenth century, a somewhat similar transformation had already begun to affect that portion of Quarter Sessions' business which was determined by the justices without reference to a jury. Here, too, Quarter Sessions had ceased to supervise the economy of the community. Despite a statute requiring that those who traded in grain (badgers) obtain a licence from Quarter Sessions, the numbers of badgers' licences issued by Kent's Quarter Sessions dwindled. In the days when the grain trade had actually been regulated, grain had been sold in market towns on market days. By the early eighteenth century, grain was sold by sample. Badgers might find it convenient to obtain a licence from Quarter Sessions, but it would have been rather difficult for the justices to insure that all badgers were licensed. The number of licences issued by Quarter Sessions suggests that the justices were not reluctant to acknowledge the new economic realities. Even in 1757, a year of extremely high prices, only eight badgers' licenses were issued by Kent's Quarter Sessions.[10]

Quarter Sessions' responsibility for the regulation of wages was similarly rendered obsolete by the vitality of the economy. At the end of the seventeenth century, maximum wage rates in the county exceeded those set by Quarter Sessions; in 1732, Quarter Sessions deleted all occupations other than agricultural labourers and household servants from the list of regulated wages; in 1767, Quarter Sessions ceased to assess any wages whatsoever; and there is no evidence in the official records of Quarter Sessions that the court acted to enforce its wage regulation.[11]

Yet reliance upon the official records of the court produces a distorted view of Quarter Sessions' importance and activity. That eighteenth-century Quarter Sessions did not act frequently in matters which had occupied the attention of its seventeenth-century predeces-

10. R. B. Westerfield, *Middlemen in English Business, Particularly Between 1660 and 1760,* Transactions of the Connecticut Academy of Arts and Sciences (New Haven, 1915), vol. 19, pp. 153–154; D. Baker, "The Marketing of Corn in the First Half of the Eighteenth Century: Northeast Kent," *Agricultural History Review* 18 (1970): 137–139, 149–150; see also Cockburn, "The Work of the North Riding Quarter Sessions," p. 215.

11. D. C. Coleman, "The Economy of Kent under the Later Stuarts" (Ph.D. thesis, University of London, 1966), pp. 355–363. See also Cockburn, "The Work of the North Riding Quarter Sessions," p. 212.

sor is not unequivocal evidence of judicial abandonment of administrative duties. Wage regulation is a case in point. The official record does not note that in the spring of 1732 the justices at east Kent's Quarter Sessions condemned the attempts of servants in husbandry to obtain "excessive" wages, and directed the justices in petty sessions to insure that the idle and those refusing to work for the wages sanctioned by Quarter Sessions be brought before them. Similarly, Quarter Sessions' records do not reveal that this ordinance inspired the justices of the Wingham division to renewed vigour in their surveillance of the idle and of those who offered wages higher than Quarter Sessions permitted.[12]

That petty sessions executed the task of wage supervision—a governmental responsibility heretofore considered unfulfilled in the early eighteenth century—is but a striking example of the extent to which matters formerly administered in Quarter Sessions now devolved upon petty sessions. In the seventeenth century, Quarter Sessions had frequently ordered that specific poor persons be relieved, adjudicated disputes between masters and servants, determined bastardy cases, and heard complaints against parish officials and their expenditures. As table 9 reveals, in the early eighteenth century Quarter Sessions heard complaints against individuals who had not performed their statutory labour on the highways or had allowed nuisances to obstruct highways and footways, and against parish officials who had neglected their duties. By mid-century, all these matters were the province of petty sessions. Most bastardy cases, disputes between master and servant, and requests for poor relief were settled at petty sessions or by the single justice. Petty sessions authorized the distraint of money from those who had not laboured on the highway and insured that surveyors maintain the highways. Petty sessions supervised the activity of constables, overseers, and surveyors, and even fined those who did not perform satisfactorily. By developing their petty sessions, the justices of Kent had relieved their Quarter Sessions of a large portion of that governmental business which involved the refusal of individuals to perform their obligations to the community.

In consequence, Quarter Sessions became even more obviously the apex of county administration. According to statute, the licensing of badgers, higglers, and Dissenters' places of worship and teachers, and

12. *The Kentish Post and Canterbury-Newsletter,* April 22–26, 1732; Kent A.O., PS/W2, Oct. 3, Oct. 10, Nov. 7, and Dec. 4, 1732, and April 3 and May 1, 1733.

the supervision of bridge maintenance had to take place in Quarter Sessions. In almost all other matters, Quarter Sessions was no longer the administrative body of first instance. Table 10 displays the major categories of business handled by the justices in Quarter Sessions without a jury. As table 10 reveals, aside from its activity in licensing and bridge maintenance, Quarter Sessions' main function was to supervise other courts: appeals, almost always in settlement cases, occupied most of its attention, and in west Kent the supremacy of Quarter Sessions was further emphasized when that court remedied the default of manor and hundred courts in the appointment of petty and high constables.

It is therefore not surprising that evidence of direct governmental action by Quarter Sessions declined. But this does not argue that judicial interest in government similarly diminished. Rather than exhibiting the lassitude of the justices, the lack of administrative activity in mid-eighteenth century Quarter Sessions reflects judicial interest in government. True, the total number of bills presented to the grand jury declined, but most presentments were made by constables or by aggrieved individuals. Though constables and even the community were increasingly disinclined to use the machinery of Quarter Sessions, the justices were not. Their interest is reflected in a category of indictments that did not dwindle: that of parishes, hundreds, and the county for failure to maintain roads and bridges. Many of these indictments were made by the justices themselves. According to law, a justice's presentment of a parish for neglect of its roads constituted an indictment of that parish, and justices found in this legal proceeding a useful device for their supervision of the highways. As Sir Wyndham Knatchbull noted, "Presented the road leading from Mersham to Ashford in the parish of Willesborough. The presentment only mention'd in general terms *a certain part of that road,* without specifying how much; so that by this means, it will never be taken off til the whole road is mended to satisfaction."[13] Similarly, administrative orders attest to judicial use of governmental powers. Parliament had granted justices in Quarter Sessions the power to levy a rate on any parish whose roads they deemed irreparable without considerable expenditure and, as table 10 reveals, the justices had no intention of abandoning this power. Judicial use of Quarter Sessions' machinery therefore reveals a sophisticated concept of governmental action and governmental struc-

13. Kent A.O., U951/O4, p. 7.

ture. The justices made Quarter Sessions a court which reviewed decisions of those bodies which immediately governed the county, and used the machinery of Quarter Sessions for direct action only when the law demanded that Quarter Sessions be the court of first instance. Similarly, the development of Quarter Sessions' structure revealed the judicial knack for administration.

Administrative developmment was most evident in Quarter Sessions' use of petty sessions. By the early eighteenth century, petty sessions had been made an indispensable cog in Quarter Sessions' machinery. Petty sessions now prepared Quarter Sessions' routine business. For example, the Quarter Sessions of east and west Kent ordered all constables to submit their lists of freeholders eligible for jury service to petty sessions, there to be inspected and corrected before presentation to Quarter Sessions. Before a constable in west Kent could be discharged from his office, he had to secure the signature of two justices—probably at petty sessions—to a list of two possible successors. If constables wished to be reimbursed for their expenses, they had to carry their bills to petty sessions; for without the imprimatur of petty sessions, their requests would not even be considered by Quarter Sessions.[14] Quarter Sessions likewise delegated to petty sessions responsibility for investigating and determining administrative disputes brought before Quarter Sessions. If a constable's, overseer's, or surveyor's account was queried, or if two parishes quarrelled over the share each was to pay for a common stock, the matter was referred to petty sessions. Sometimes, even an appeal from assessment to the poor rate might be referred back to the petty sessions which had originally authorized the assessment. Yet perhaps the assimilation of petty sessions in Quarter Sessions' administrative machinery is epitomized by its routine supervision of work ordered by Quarter Sessions. Even the formula for Quarter Sessions' orders acknowledges this new use of petty sessions. At the beginning of the century, when Quarter Sessions authorized the levy of a rate for the repair of roads or bridges upon a parish or a hundred, the order specified that assessments for the rate were to be confirmed by any two justices of the county and, in many instances, commanded the constables or surveyors receiving the monies to account before Quarter Sessions. By 1734, both east and west Kent had adopted a new formula: assessments were now to be

14. Kent A.O., Q/SO W7, Apr. 14, 1724, Apr. 17, 1730, Oct. 5, 1725, Oct. 8, 1717; Q/SO E6, July 10, 1733.

TABLE 10 MAJOR CATEGORIES OF ADMINISTRATIVE BUSINESS HANDLED AT KENT'S QUARTER SESSIONS, 1705–1754

	Removal Appeal[a] *Order Quash*	*Removal Appeal*[a] *Order Confirm*	*Highway*[b] *Rate*	*Bridge*[c]	*Constable Appointed*	*Apprentice Discharge Requested*	*Bastardy Cases*	*Jury-men Ex-cused*	*Badger Licence*	*Higgler Licence*	*Poor Rate Appeal*	*Licence Dissenting House*	*Licence Dissenting Teacher*	*Appeals vs. Vagrant Passes*
1705–1714														
W. Kent	73	51	7	21	173	6	25	13	7	0	10	20	6	0
E. Kent	111	72	7	6	23	11[d]	18+ 3 appeals	0	28	0	6	4	2	0
1715–1724														
W. Kent	86½	49½	6	35	196	8	10+ 3 appeals	11	22	8	17	26	4	0
E. Kent	105½	63½	2	6	29	10	11	0	34	0	15	4	1	0
1725–1734														
W. Kent	58½	24½	12	32	309	4	15+ 2 appeals	6	11	40	10	7	2	0
E. Kent	90	56	45	7	27	8	25+ 2 appeals	0	42	0	12	0	0	0
1735–1744														
W. Kent	60½	41½	14	47	443	16	22+ 4 appeals	1	2	82	4	4	1	6
E. Kent	67½	52½	12	8	32	13	22	0	9	7	10	1	0	0

1745–1754														
W. Kent	70½	44½	43	36	379	11[d]	11+ 1 appeal	0	0	142	6	3	0	9
E. Kent	64½	20½	12	14	21	3	13	0	0	0	13	0	0	0

[a]Some removal appeals were respited and no final decision ever recorded. These are not included in the table. "½" signifies part of an order confirmed or quashed.

[b]This does not include orders to reimburse surveyors for repairs already made.

[c]This column includes orders to pay justices or constables for repairs already made, taxes imposed for the same purpose, presentation of the bridge by the grand jury, and reference of repairs to justices. If more than one order or if several varieties of order, reference, etc., seem to refer to the same repair, the repair is counted only once. This column tabulates the number of bridge repair initiatives receiving Quartor Sessions' attention.

[d]Including one not discharged.

confirmed by two justices of the division in which the parish or hundred lay, and the recipient of the proceeds was to account before the justices of the division at their "monthly meeting."

Since petty sessions now prepared the routine business of Quarter Sessions and supervised the execution of its routine orders, it was only natural that petty sessions also be constituted as Quarter Sessions' agents for more specialized administrative tasks. Parliament might declare that supervision of the turnpike from Rochester to Gravesend and the turnpike between Chatham and Canterbury was the duty of Quarter Sessions, but the justices delegated administration of the first to the justices of the Rochester division and that of the second to the justices of the Home division.[15] The county jails were Quarter Sessions' responsibility. But as the jail for the west was in the Bearsted division and that for the east in the Home division, the justices of these divisions were routinely entrusted with the tasks of supervising repairs to the buildings and of approving payments for maintenance of the fabric and sustenance of the inmates. The justices of the Blackheath and Dartford divisions likewise administered the houses of correction at Deptford and Dartford.[16] Indeed, it is probable that the Blackheath justices were responsible for the erection of a house of correction at Deptford. The new house was west Kent Quarter Sessions' major venture into new building in the first quarter of the eighteenth century, and it was initially funded by a tax not on the county, but on just the hundred of Blackheath.[17] Not only were petty sessions performing Quarter Sessions' administrative functions, but they might also have been seizing the administrative initiative usually associated with Quarter Sessions.

For a time, some west Kent petty sessions even assumed responsibility for supervision of Quarter Sessions' officers. During the first two

15. Kent A. O., Q/SO E6, July 14, 1730, July 11, 1732; Q/SMa W6, Jan. 11, 1737[8]; Q/SO W8, June 6, 1747, Sept. 21, 1748, and Jan. 11, 1749[50].

16. Kent A.O., Q/SMa W3, April 22, 1718; Q/SO W6, Oct. 8, 1706; Q/SO W7, Oct. 2, 1716, April 30, 1717, April 7, 1719, Oct. 5, 1725, Oct. 6, 1730; Q/SMa E2, April 29, 1715; Q/SO E6, Jan. 9, 1727[8]. Some orders consign these matters to the justices of the division; others consign them to specified justices who are, in fact, the justices acting in one division. In early Hanoverian Norfolk, Quarter Sessions also assigned tasks to the justices of a division (J. Rosenheim, "The Gentry of Restoration Norfolk, 1660–1720" [Ph.D. diss., Princeton University, 1981], p. 132, n. 58).

17. Kent A.O., Q/SO W5, Apr. 14, 1702, Apr. 21, 1704. Quarter Sessions' order was appealed to Queen's Bench, which declared that the tax for the house of correction had to be levied on the county and not just on the hundred (1 Salkeld 362, The Case of the Hundred of Blackheath. I want to thank Joanna Innes for this reference.).

decades of the century, annual inspection of the accounts of the treasurer of the western division's bridge money was conducted by the justices of the Malling division. The treasurers of the county stock, jail and vagrant monies for the west accounted before the justices of the Bearsted division, and it was not until the mid-1720s that audit of all county monies was vested in a committee of Quarter Sessions comprising justices of more than one petty sessional division.[18] Clearly, petty sessions were used as standing committees of Quarter Sessions. By incorporating petty sessions into the structure of Kent's Quarter Sessions, Kent's justices made their governmental machinery more effective and efficient.

At the same time, the justices were reinforcing the structure of Quarter Sessions itself. Even before the Glorious Revolution, the informal conventions of Kent's Quarter Sessions had provided the *sine qua non* of effective judicial control: a permanent chairman. He was a redoubtable figure, as even the minutes of petty sessions attest. Let Thomas Hill but appear at Wingham petty sessions, and the clerk would inscribe his name among the list of attendants, adding the title "Chairman of Quarter Sessions."[19] In the early eighteenth century, the powers and duties of this personage were elaborated. The chairman supervised the conduct of Sessions' business in the period between its meetings. The chairman of west Kent Sessions would on his own authority instruct the clerk of the peace to discover which taxes had not been collected and to direct the justices in petty sessions to insure their collection.[20] By the 1730s, the chairman of east Kent was regularly examining the minutes of his court.[21] Yet, the evolution of such informal conventions was insufficient for west Kent's justices. These dignitaries elevated their chairman and their Sessions in a formal definition of the chairman's powers in court. By order of Quarter Sessions: the sheriff was to provide the chairman with a list of all summoned to serve on the Sessions' juries; the clerk of the peace was to deliver to the chairman a list of all recognizances returned to the court

18. Kent A.O., Q/SO W6, May 3, 1709, Apr. 14, 1713; Q/SMa W2, Apr. 10, 1711, Apr. 14, 1713; Q/SO W7, Oct. 4, 1715, Jan. 13, 1715[6]; Q/AB/72, D. Fuller to the justices of the Cranbrook division; Q/AB/70, treasurer of bridge money accounts from 1729.

19. Kent A.O., PS/W3, Jan. 7, 1734[5].

20. Kent A.O., Q/AB/72, John Brewer to David Fuller, Feb. 26, 1711[2].

21. Kent A.O., Q/SMa E4, Apr. 6, July 16, 1734 and Jan. 14, Apr. 18, 1735 and *passim;* Q/SMa E5, *passim.*

and of the offences specified therein, a list of all recognizances which had been respited, a copy of the sheriff's process for taking all accused of offences or misdemeanours, specifying the offences or misdemeanours, and at the conclusion of each Sessions, the minutes of the court. And, in a final self-denying ordinance, the justices disclosed their belief that Sessional grandeur would be enhanced through their obeisance: justices themselves could not speak in court without the permission of the chair.[22]

Efficiency and courtroom etiquette were also promoted by the promulgation of rules arranging the business of the court. In west Kent, the licensing of badgers occurred only on the second day of Sessions and upon motion in open court. In east Kent, the court ordered that all those who persuaded the grand jury to declare their presentments valid be given due notice if the indictment was to be contested in a trial. The Sessions of both divisions of the county established rules to insure fair and orderly procedure in appeals against settlement orders: the courts allotted a special day of each Sessions for hearing these appeals, set a schedule for notifying both court and defendant of the appeal, and tried to prevent vexatious appeals and delaying tactics.[23] Procedural orders could also enhance the dignity and status of the court. Some Quarter Sessions engaged in the congenial practice of making orders when the justices gathered in their chambers after the Sessions had been formally adjourned. In 1741, the Quarter Sessions of east Kent forthrightly declared against this illegal practice: henceforth orders must needs follow upon "Motion made in open Court."[24] West Kent's justices apparently felt no need to insure the publicity of their proceedings. What entranced these magistrates were devices which publicly marked these proceedings as august and perhaps even efficient. In 1729, to promote "the better regularity of proceedings" the justices of west Kent forbade attorneys, solicitors, and justices' clerks from making any motion to the court. Henceforth,

22. Kent A.O., Q/SO W7, Oct. 8, 1723; Q/SMa W4, Oct. 8, 1723. Rosenheim, "The Gentry of Restoration Norfolk," pp. 121–122, notes that in the second decade of the eighteenth century Norfolk's Quarter Sessions also established rules governing procedure on appeals, and demanded that all recognizances be listed with the clerk of the peace on the first day of Quarter Sessions.

23. Kent A.O., Q/SMa W2, May 3, 1709; Q/SO E5, Apr. 25, 1707; Q/SMa W3, Oct. 7, 1718; Q/SO W7, Apr. 29, 1726, Apr. 15, 1729, Apr. 7, 1730; Q/SO W8, Apr. 27, 1742, Apr. 19, 1748; Q/SMa E2, July 13, 1714, Apr. 29, 1720; Q/SO E6, Apr. 23, 1723, July 31, 1731.

24. Kent A.O., Q/SO E7, Jan. 13, 1740[1]; G. Jacob, *An Appendix to the Modern Justice: containing the particular Business of the Quarter Sessions* (London, 1718), p. 14.

in theory, only barristers could address their worships formally assembled in Quarter Sessions.[25]

Undoubtedly more effective in the foundation of an efficient administration—though less likely to inspire awe among the multitudes—was Quarter Sessions' elaboration of controls over its subordinate officers. Those most in need of restraint were the treasurers. At the beginning of the eighteenth century there were three treasurers in west Kent: one for the bridge money, one for the jail and vagrant monies, and one for the county stock. The treasurers of the last two funds exchanged offices annually, thereby presumably insuring an annual accounting and county solvency. Alas, it was not so. The office of treasurer was unpaid, but it was nonetheless an office of profit. The treasurers had the right to invest the monies of their funds as they pleased. So long as they were able to meet calls upon their funds from their own resources, the system worked well. That in 1704 the court had to order the jailkeeper to bring before it Mr. John Maplesden, late treasurer of the county stock, "to answer the Court concerning his office of Treasurer" argues financial ill fortune for Maplesden and county alike.[26] The court attempted to prevent such defalcation immediately by requiring the treasurers of the jail and vagrant monies and the county stock to keep account of their receipts and expenditures, which would be duplicated by books kept by the clerk of the peace. Any expense not entered into the clerk's books would not be credited to the treasurers, who were to produce their account books annually before the Quarter Sessions.[27] Obviously, this method of control might not be entirely efficacious during the period (1705–1712) when the clerk of the peace was one of the treasurers. Yet, a mere thirteen years after the defalcation of a treasurer, the treasurers[28] of the division's funds were ordered to give security acceptable to the justices for the monies in their hands. Quarter Sessions delegation to petty sessions of the inspection of the treasurers' accounts ceased; they were to account to Quarter Sessions annually, give security annually, and lodge their accounts with the court. No expenses would be allowed unless they

25. Kent A.O., Q/SO W7, Apr. 15, 1729; see also J. C. Cox, *Three Centuries of Derbyshire Annals, as Illustrated by the Records of the County of Derby from Queen Elizabeth to Queen Victoria* (London, 1890), vol. 1, p. 12. Rosenheim, "The Gentry of Restoration Norfolk," p. 121, notes that in 1710 one of Norfolk's Quarter Sessions ordered that all counsel appear in their legal gowns.

26. Kent A.O., Q/SMa5, July 24, 1704.

27. Kent A.O., Q/SO W5, Apr. 21, 1704; Q/SO W6, Apr. 17, 1705.

28. As of April 6, 1716, the bridge money fund was being supervised by one of the other two treasurers.

produced their bills on the first day of Sessions, and no bills would be allowed unless they were for expenditures authorized by the court.[29]

East Kent's financial misadventures were less spectacular than those of west Kent. The death of Edmund Hardres, treasurer of all eastern county funds for over two decades, in 1723 left the county £36.14.2 in the red. Two years earlier, Hardres had had to persuade two justices to stand as security for passing his accounts—both his justice sureties were surnamed Hardres—and a year later he was removed from office.[30] His successor, clerk to the petty sessions of Home and Wingham, had been ordered to give security, and in turn his successor, appointed in 1752, had to enter into a bond of £500.[31] In 1718, east Kent's Quarter Sessions attempted to insure that no one person—be he treasurer or justice—could authorize expenditure of county funds; all such orders had to be approved by Quarter Sessions. These ordinances evidently placed too great a strain on east Kent's officers and justices alike. In 1748, Quarter Sessions conceded by forbidding their treasurer from paying sums in excess of sixpence without an order for payment signed by at least one justice.[32] Nonetheless, east Kent Quarter Sessions had rendered its treasurer, if not its justices, into an object of administrative control.

Meanwhile, the clerk of the peace was busily engaged in expanding his profits. Private vice was public gain. As the clerk augmented his income by increasing the number and variety of his duties, the clerk's pursuit of wealth laid the foundation of a county bureaucracy. In Anne's reign, the clerk was defending his county in actions involving county bridges and taxes at Assizes, and also on occasion prosecuting disorderly persons and other minor malefactors. By 1719, Quarter Sessions had decided to appoint their clerk as solicitor and attorney in the prosecution of constables who had not collected county taxes and "in all other matters for this county."[33] So it was only natural that Quarter Sessions would appoint their clerk as their solicitor to obtain

29. Kent A.O., Q/SMa W3, Oct. 8, 1717; Q/SMa W4, Apr. 26, 1720; Q/SO W7, Oct. 6, 1719; Q/SO W7, Apr. 29, 1726.

30. Kent A. O., Q/SO E6, July 16, 1723; Q/SMa E2, Apr. 21, 1721; Q/SO E6, Apr. 13, 1722.

31. Kent A.O., Q/SO E7, Jan. 14, 1752.

32. Kent A.O., Q/SMa E1, July 15, 1712; Q/SMa E2, July 15, 1718; Q/SO E6, Oct. 8, 1725; Q/SO E7, Apr. 22, 1748.

33. Kent A.O., Q/SO E4, Oct. 6, 1704; Q/SO W6, Apr. 13, 1708, Apr. 18, 1710; Q/SMa W4, Oct. 6, 1719; Q/SMa W5, Apr. 11, 1727; Q/SMa W7, Apr. 4, 1749; see also J. Hurstfield, "County Government 1530–1660," in *Victoria History of the County of Wiltshire,* ed. R. B. Pugh (London, 1957), pp. 173–174.

those acts of Parliament necessary for the conduct of county business.[34] On all these occasions the clerk noted that he was to be reimbursed for his pains. The clerk also obtained fees for distributing orders of Quarter Sessions to petty sessions' clerks and to constables. Whether he was similarly paid for other of his extra-sessional activities cannot be determined. He searched the county's records to determine its legal responsibilities in the maintenance of bridges. He kept duplicates of the assessments made on each parish and noted, for the benefit of Quarter Sessions, those parishes which had neglected to contribute to county rates. He acquired information to satisfy Quarter Sessions' curiosity, and collected returns from divisional clerks and constables. He received and coordinated recognizances and letters instructing him about the presentment of persons or parishes. Eventually such labour, too, yielded profits. In the 1730s, the clerk's proceeds from just the administrative business conducted at each of Kent's quarterly Sessions amounted to between £4 and £8.[35]

Undoubtedly ordinary administrative business provided but a small portion of the income of the clerk's office. In the 1730s, the clerk of the peace for Middlesex was netting between £550 and £730 per annum.[36] Middlesex was probably the most profitable clerkship in the kingdom, but David Fuller, attorney and clerk of the peace from 1702 to 1753, prospered sufficiently to buy Chillingdon manor and its house in Maidstone. His successor, Francis Austen, agent to the Duke of Dorset, founded a county and administrative dynasty. In 1773, his son succeeded both to the county's clerkship and to a considerable landed estate, which he further enlarged. Such affluence argues for flourishing and prosperous business in the clerkship and consequently for growing staff.

In the first decade of the eighteenth century, the clerk had at least one assistant. By the fourth decade he had a minimum of two, both of whom noted the orders and verdicts of Quarter Sessions. Only one of these underlings can be identified, and he was an attorney. By the fifth decade, the clerk was employing James Willard, who was officially recognized as his deputy, and at least one other subordinate, Samuel Eastchurch. Eastchurch's career marks the appearance of a structured hierarchy of professional posts in the county's service. As

34. Kent A.O., Q/SO W8, Oct. 7, 1735.

35. Kent A.O., Q/SMa W5, Apr. 15, 1729, Apr. 27, 1731, Apr. 8, 1732, Apr. 15, 1735, Oct. 17, 1735; Q/SMa W6, Oct. 4, 1743.

36. B.L., Add. MSS 35586, f. 200.

an attorney, Eastchurch was in the early 1740s employed by Quarter Sessions to defend its decisions at Assizes. In 1747, he appeared as administrative officer to the committee of Quarter Sessions entrusted with the task of constructing a new jail. By 1753, Eastchurch was deputy clerk.[37] At mid-century, Kent possessed a staff of professional administrators who gained experience in county government as they mounted a ladder of increasingly remunerative and responsible posts. Even the county's clerk was not unaffected. Though Francis Austen became clerk in 1753 because he was a client of the custos, his appointment could be justified even by the standards of a modern civil service. Austen was well acquainted with county business: in the 1730s he was Kent's undersheriff. Like Austen, other of the county's officers served in several capacities; many were administrative pluralists. In the second decade of the century, William Henman, attorney, was undersheriff and clerk to the Bearsted division. In the 1740s, John Mason, attorney, noted the orders of Quarter Sessions for the benefit of the clerk and also served as one of west Kent's treasurers.[38] His associate as treasurer, the attorney Samuel Fullager, became clerk of the Bearsted division in the 1760s. Comparison of west Kent's treasurers with those of east Kent emphasizes the significance of their careers. In 1752, the newly appointed treasurer of east Kent was a bookseller. In west Kent, the office of treasurer had been the perquisite of attorneys since at least 1716. That west Kent boasted a professional staff while some of east Kent's business was conducted by amateurs reveals the influence of the clerk. The clerk of the peace lived in Maidstone. As he executed his office, he trained candidates for less eminent county posts and simultaneously sketched the framework for a county bureaucracy.

Equipped with a knowledgeable staff, a defined procedure for the conduct of its business, and a flotilla of standing committees to insure the performance of its commands, the Quarter Sessions of the mid-eighteenth century was an impressive organ of government. And at mid-century west Kent's Quarter Sessions determined to engrave its grandeur in the very stone of the county. Like many another Quarter Sessions of the 1750s, 1760s, and 1770s, that of west Kent was moved

37. Kent A.O., Q/SO W8, Apr. 7, 1741, Jan. 14, 1741[2], Oct. 6, 1747; Sir E. Stephens, compiler, *The Clerks of the Counties 1360–1960,* Society of Clerks of the Peace of Counties and of Clerks of County Councils (1961), p. 111.

38. Kent A.O., Q/SMa W6, Oct. 4, 1743.

to erect a new courthouse.[39] The project was completed with remarkable expedition. The corporation of Maidstone first suggested that the courthouse it shared with west Kent Quarter Sessions be remodelled in January 1756. In April, the clerk of the peace laid plans of the courthouses in Derby, Leicester, Northampton, Warwick, Worcester, and Nottingham before Quarter Sessions; the justices decided upon a building replete with court hall, convenient rooms for justices and jury, and a pound for prisoners; and Quarter Sessions delegated further superintendance of the work to a committee of justices. In April 1758, the justices chose a design featuring an octagonal propylaeum, specified that arches and piers be built of Kentish hewn stone, and allocated £500 to the project. By 1759, construction had begun.[40] Their new courthouse epitomized the justices' concept of government: an administrative system which enabled the justices to execute those tasks they considered necessary in a setting which conveyed to the governed the power of their rulers.

And yet, despite its administrative staff and its administrative system, its courtroom procedure and its new courthouse, the Quarter Sessions of George II's Kent would still, to a modern observer, lack some of the usual attributes of government. For in the second quarter of the eighteenth century Quarter Sessions neither introduced innovations in government nor assumed new administrative burdens nor even obviously and actively directed the activities of the justices.

The records of east Kent's Quarter Sessions for 1705 to 1761 do not contain a single general directive designed to guide the conduct of justices out of Quarter Sessions. The Quarter Sessions of west Kent was slightly more active. It issued three such exhortations: one, in 1717, instructing justices in petty sessions to insure that all those receiving poor relief wear a badge flaunting the letter "P"; one, in 1719, enjoining justices to enforce the game laws, and, to that end, to issue warrants for the apprehension and punishment of the idle and disorderly; and one, in 1723, ordaining that petty sessions set their licensing days between Epiphany and Easter Quarter Sessions so that

39. R. B. Pugh, *Itinerant Justices in English History* (Exeter, 1967), pp. 27–28; *A Descriptive Report on the Quarter Sessions, Other Official, and Ecclesiastical Records in the Custody of the County Councils of East and West Sussex*, East Sussex County Council Record Publication, no. 2 (1954); J. Godber, *History of Bedfordshire 1066–1888* (Luton, Bedfordshire, 1969), p. 370; 20 George II c. 21.

40. Kent A.O., Q/SO W9, Jan. 15, 1756, Apr. 27, 1756; Q/SMa W8, Apr. 27, 1756, Apr. 27, 1758, May 12, 1758; Q/SO W10, Apr. 24, 1759.

appeals against refusals to grant licences could be heard at Quarter Sessions.[41] It is symptomatic of Quarter Sessions' debility as the agency nominally controlling county government that no such appeals are recorded from 1723 to 1761—the terminal date of this study.

Only in a very few varieties of business did Quarter Sessions dominate justices out of Sessions through its power to review their orders and judgments. Appeals to Quarter Sessions were expensive, and so the most frequent appellants were parishes—requesting review of settlement decisions and in the 1740s and 1750s of vagrant passes. Of the 103 appeals against assessments to the poor and highway rates heard by Quarter Sessions between 1705 and 1754, 50 were brought by persons denominated baronet, esquire, gentleman or cleric, and twelve by groups of two or more persons. In the half century from 1705 to 1754, only twenty-four individuals appealed to Quarter Sessions against orders and judgments of two or more justices. (Fifteen of these appeals were against orders in bastardy cases.) And Quarter Sessions did not entertain any appeals against convictions by single justices out of Quarter Sessions. Even the supervision of parish officers did not engage Quarter Sessions' attention. Between 1705 and 1754, the records of Quarter Sessions note its determination of only four appeals against the accounts of overseers and surveyors, and indicate that Quarter Sessions took some action in only five more such cases. Surveillance over parish officers was now the province of petty sessions, but few of the activities of petty sessions or the single justice were scrutinized by the supreme court of the county.

Having spared or divested itself of the surveillance of parish officials and justices out of Sessions implicit in its appellate jurisdiction, Quarter Sessions might have turned its energies to projects which were truly county concerns, projects such as the new courthouse. And west Kent's Quarter Sessions did embark on another county project. It built a new jail. But comparison of its performance in the construction of these two county edifices points to the difference between modern and mid-eighteenth century concepts of effective government. Just three years lapsed between the proposal for and the construction of a new courthouse. In the matter of the jail, west Kent's administrative procedure was somewhat less expeditious. In 1725, Quarter Sessions ordered that a committee of justices of the Bearsted division locate a site for the new jail and arrange for the presentment of the present jail

41. Kent A.O., Q/SO W7, Oct. 8, 1717, Oct. 6, 1719, Apr. 23, 1723.

as inadequate by the grand jury at Assizes. The jail was duly presented (in 1729), and the court thereupon ordered the clerk of the peace and undersheriff to solicit the county's members of Parliament for an act authorizing purchase of land. The act was secured in 1736 and construction of the jail was initiated, under the supervision of the justices of the Bearsted division, in 1746.[42]

For the justices of west Kent, good government did not necessarily entail expansion of governmental facilities, speedy execution of new projects, assumption of new administrative burdens, institution of new arrangements to improve the lives or increase the security of those they governed, or reform of the structure of government. West Kent's new courthouse may have embodied the administrative efficiency and potential for administrative innovation of its Quarter Sessions, but at mid-century west Kent's justices did not regard administrative innovation as a necessary component of Quarter Sessions' role. For these justices, Quarter Session's role was that of efficient and impressive maintenance of the *status quo*.

Efficient and impressive maintenance of the *status quo* can be an extremely useful function. But, unless the *status quo* is seriously threatened, its maintenance is rarely exciting. "Mostly settlement appeals and other Poor Law business (nothing interesting)," wrote the Webbs after examining the order book of east Kent's Quarter Sessions.[43] Many of Kent's justices were of the Webbs' opinion. During the first half of the eighteenth century, Kent's justices became increasingly disinclined to attend Quarter Sessions.

In the first five years of the seventeenth century, over 75 percent of Kent's active justices regularly rode to Quarter Sessions, and it is possible that similar enthusiasm for Quarter Sessional proceedings crowded the later Stuart bench.[44] Unfortunately, the number of justices attending the Quarter Sessions of later Stuart and early Hanoverian Kent cannot be precisely determined, for the clerk considered a list of twelve justices sufficient to dignify the records of his court and ceased recording attendants once he had reached that magic number.

42. Kent A.O., Q/SO W7, Oct. 5, 1725, Apr. 15, 1729, Oct. 7, 1729, Oct. 6, 1730; Q/SO W8, Oct. 7, 1735, Jan. 16, 1745[6].

43. London School of Economics, Webb Collection on Local Government, vol. 136, comment on 1740 to 1763 order book.

44. J. Gleason, *The Justices of the Peace in England, 1558 to 1640* (Oxford, 1969), p. 105; S. C. Ratcliff and H. C. Johnson, eds., *Warwick County Records*, vol. 7 (Warwick, 1946), p. xlii; A. Fletcher, *A County Community in Peace and War* (London, 1975), p. 358; Kent A.O., Q/SO W3, Apr. 8, 1673, list of twenty-three justices signing a brief at Quarter Sessions.

Other evidence reveals the presence of justices not listed in the clerk's official returns.[45] By the 1750s, it was a rare meeting of Quarter Sessions that convened as many as a dozen magistrates. On average, eight or nine justices now presided at Quarter Sessions. As the number of active justices in the sixth decade of the century was only slightly smaller than that in the first decade, it is obvious that the propensity of active justices to attend Quarter Sessions had declined, and declined by some proportion greater then 25 percent. In the 1740s, 41 percent of Kent's active justices never attended Quarter Sessions.[46]

The distribution of non-attendants hints at the reasons for this decline. The character and location of a petty sessional division's bench together determined the likelihood that Quarter Sessions would attract its members. Those petty sessional divisions which were both distant from Canterbury and Maidstone—Kent's Quarter Sessional towns—and ruled by justices of less than average status and landed wealth sent few justices to the county's Sessions. In the 1740s, justices of the Blackheath, Bromley, Tonbridge, Rochester, and Sittingbourne divisions—justices who were almost uniformly mere gentlemen—almost never appeared at Quarter Sessions. But the justices of Cranbrook, Elham, and Ashford—equally distant from Quarter Sessions and possessed of large estates—attended, as did minor gentry in divisions near Maidstone and Canterbury. Lesser justices in outlying areas saw no reason to journey to Quarter Sessions, there to join a county elite with whom they were unacquainted by virtue of neighbourhood or social status. In the later Stuart era these justices had occasionally found reason to grace the bench. Then parties had battled for dominance at Quarter Sessions; sedition or the licensing of Dissenting places of worship or other matters of political import occupied the court's attention; and Quarter Sessions exerted control over malefactors and adjudicated as court of first instance matters affecting parish government. By mid-century such matters no longer disturbed the peace of Quarter Sessions. No longer need a justice maintain his

45. For example, signatures to the accounts of west Kent's bridge treasurer for 1729–1741 (Kent A.O., Q/AB/70) indicate the presence of justices not listed in Quarter Sessions minute or order books or in the clerk's returns to the national government.

46. Similarly, of twenty-nine Cambridgeshire justices who took out a dedimus between 1740 and 1760, eleven attended Quarter Sessions three times or less. The numeration of Cambridgeshire justices excludes mayors of Cambridge and vice-chancellors of the university. For the list of attendants at Cambridgeshire's Quarter Sessions, see C. Howard, "The Justices of the Peace and County Government: Northamptonshire, Cambridgeshire, and the West Riding, 1730–95" (Ph.D. diss., Johns Hopkins University, 1975), pp. 299–312.

power or that of his party at the county's premier court. Whig hegemony preserved a proper political imbalance at Quarter Sessions, while lesser justices rested their power on collective action at petty sessions. Possessed of relatively minimal prestige and little wealth, the mere gentleman could not have hoped to use his office to obtain political advancement or to expand his interest. Not so the greater gentry, who therefore found occasional appearance at Quarter Sessions useful. As the justices had made their Sessions a theatre of power, it was an ideal setting for those who wished to advertise their might.

Yet, even the greater gentry's estimate of the importance of their county's premier court had altered, and the change in their attitude is best presented through their elected representative—the chairman of Quarter Sessions. During the first half of the eighteenth century, the power to direct Quarter Sessions was gradually let fall from the hands of the county elite. Under the later Stuarts, Kent's chairmen had been barristers who were members of Parliament; their eloquence and learning, exhibited in their charges, endowed the court with the mystical authority of ancient and fundamental law. Under George I and in the first decade of George II's reign, Kent's chairmen were members of Parliament; their parliamentary offices reminded both justices and the governed of the court's power. In 1768, the chairman of east Kent was John Carter of Deal, a substantial and undoubtedly worthy member of the gentry, but by no means to be numbered among the county great. In 1774, the office of chairman of west Kent's Sessions devolved upon Pierrepont Cromp, cleric. The elite of mid-century Kent evidently thought that the office of chairman was more trouble than it was worth. Since immediate power over neighbourhoods was wielded through petty sessions, the office of chairman could safely be lodged with a respectable gentleman willing to perform its minor but increasingly numerous administrative chores. Since Quarter Sessions had divested itself of much of its power, even regular attendance at its meetings was no longer incumbent on the greater gentry. At mid-century the greater gentry considered Quarter Sessions an institution appropriate for occasional display of their prestige, but not an institution which would greatly augment the power of its director.

When, at the close of the eighteenth century, administrative power was seen to be an instrument of innovative leadership, when Quarter Sessions met to consider proposals for the reform of the poor laws and the relief of the poor, when Quarter Sessions gave guidance to petty sessions on the licensing of alehouses, when Quarter Sessions expanded its administrative machinery for the construction of roads and bridges, when Quarter Sessions undertook reform of the jails and informed itself of the punishment of prisoners, and when Quarter Sessions collected, controlled, and expended ever increasing local rates, then attendance at Quarter Sessions grew and attendants included even the nobility. In the nineteenth century, the chairman of Quarter Sessions might well be an aristocrat. To this later incarnation of itself the Quarter Sessions of the mid-century bequeathed the administrative machinery on which the Quarter Sessions of the future was to be based—the practice of delegating local matters to petty sessions, control over county finances, a developed procedure in court. To some extent mid-century Quarter Sessions even nourished the concept of government which would animate its successor. West Kent's new courthouse and its dilatory procedures in the erection of its new jail symbolize early Hanoverian emphasis on government by display, but both structures also represent an interest in the use of Quarter Sessions for administrative development which would become more predominant later in the century. The jail produced a small flurry of orders for its ventilation and enlargement.[47] Both courthouse and jail necessitated increased county expenditure, and so in the late 1740s west Kent Quarter Sessions began to levy larger county rates.[48] In the late 1750s, orders for county rates suddenly reappear in the order books of east Kent's Quarter Sessions—an innovation that may have been related to its decision in 1757 to repair its jail.[49] By the accession of George III, Kent's justices had glimpsed the potential for administrative innovation and its concomitant expenditure inherent in Quarter Sessions' powers, and Quarter Sessions itself had begun to attract

47. Kent A.O., Q/SO W9, Oct. 3, 1752, Jan. 11, 1753, July 12, 1753, Jan. 17, 1754.

48. Before 1743, west Kent levied four different rates. Three rates—those for the county stock, the jail, and the vagrant monies—were levied each year. Every few years, west Kent levied a fourth rate for repair of county bridges, and on a couple of occasions it also levied an extraordinary rate for repair of the jail. In 1743, all rates were consolidated, as permitted by 12 George II c. 29, and a general county rate was levied thereafter. In the first four decades of the century, west Kent's rates amounted to about £600 per annum. (For the annual yield of the first three rates, see the treasurers' accounts in Kent A.O., Q/SB, 1717, 1718, and 1737. For the bridge monies, see Q/AB/70.) By the 1750s, west Kent's Quarter Sessions was mulcting west Kent of more than £900 per annum.

49. Kent A.O., Q/SO E7, July 12, 1757. In the 1720s and 1730s east Kent order books had frequently contained a note that the "usual assessments and rates" were to be continued. By the late 1760s, the expenditure of east Kent's Quarter Sessions was 50 percent greater than that of the late 1740s (Kent A.O., Q/FAe1, Q/FAe2).

those justices who involved themselves in the work of magistracy. When, in the 1760s, chairmen were chosen not to awe but to administer, the unusually active lesser justices in outlying areas began to appear at Kent's Quarter Sessions. In divesting itself of responsibility for adjudication of individual complaints, by acknowledging that Quarter Sessions was no longer the cockpit of political struggle, and by constructing machinery that could be used to disseminate its commands, early Hanoverian Quarter Sessions had spawned a governmental structure and setting which by the accession of George III attracted those fascinated by administration. And, while later Hanoverian justices are distinguished by their zeal for administrative innovation, they did not disdain the government precepts of their predecessors. Public display of grandeur was the aristocrats' forte, and they found in Quarter Sessions a highly developed theatre for those who wished to strut the public stage.[50]

50. J. M. Lee, *Social Leaders and Public Persons: A Study of County Government in Cheshire Since 1888* (Oxford, 1963), p. 16; R. Shorthouse, "Justices of the Peace in Northamptonshire, 1830–1845, Part II the Work of the County Magistrates," *Northamptonshire Past and Present* 5 (1975): 244.

PART FOUR

The Image of the Bench

CHAPTER NINE

By the Company they Keep

Public Opinion and Judicial Behaviour

In 1709 and 1710, Gabriel Walters, justice of the peace for the county of Kent, sat on the county's grand jury at Assizes. At or after the first Assizes, he wrote short notes about two of the cases brought to the attention of the grand jury. At or after the second Assizes, he recorded information about none of the cases. On both occasions he did record, in his justice's notebook, the name of each and every member of the grand jury with whom he had been associated in full and public view of the county, carefully placing a check against the names of those with whom he had been similarly joined in former years. Paul D'Aranda, justice of the peace for the county of Kent, also kept a justice's notebook in which he recorded the names of all the members of the grand jury on which he sat in 1708. In 1709, D'Aranda sat on a special jury impanelled to determine a dispute over rights to the oyster fishery in the Medway. In the course of the case the jury went out in two boats to take soundings of the river, and D'Aranda recorded the names of those on the jury, carefully distinguishing those who sat in the same boat as he from those in the other boat.[1] When gentlemen associated themselves with other gentlemen in view of the county, they were aware that public estimation of their status and power would be affected by the company they were seen to keep.

Only in an age when rigid distinctions separate the abstract concept of legitimate power from the individual who holds that power, only

1. Hants. R.O., 18/M51/595, pp. 45, 49; Kent A.O., U442/O45, Mar. 8, 1707[8], and unpaginated, last page but one.

when legitimate power is not personified, does form become mere formality. Eighteenth-century government rested on the symbiosis of personal and official power. Bestowal of public office acknowledged a gentleman's power as a private individual, and the manner in which a gentleman was presented in public calibrated his private status. For the eighteenth century, public form was considered and therefore was a reflection of private reality, and the forms of government were as important as its content.

The dominant form of rule imposed by the commission of the peace was the association of gentlemen in public. Even the seemingly innocuous recital of the commission at every Assizes proclaimed the justices as members of a group, while at Quarter and petty sessions justices publicly consorted upon the bench. A justice's colleagues symbolized his status; the manner in which he was treated portrayed his power. Great, therefore, was the justice's need to shape the image presented by his fellows, for the justice's company told the governed whether he was important or not. So eighteenth-century justices adopted forms for association designed to advertise their power. At the beginning of the century these forms protected the prestige of the majority of justices. By mid-century concepts of judicial association were moulding the justices into a unified group.

If gentlemen were known by the company they kept, then a gentleman had better insure that he kept good company. Justices therefore insisted that their colleagues boast wealth or birth or power—or preferably all three. The modern observer might deplore this judicial snobbery, but the justification of opposition to the appointment of men of marginal status recognized the importance of public opinion for a government based on rule by display. As the Duke of Bolton explained when he objected to the elevation of clerics to Glamorganshire's bench, "Gentlemen of estates don't care to be put on a level with these people." In law, on the bench at Quarter Sessions, in the inn at petty sessions, every justice was the equal of his fellow justice, or as the eighteenth century would say, his "brother justice." If a gentleman publicly consorted with his social inferiors in circumstances implying equality of status, the public might well interpret his action as a proclamation of derogation. So in 1754, when Hardwicke was casting about for nominees to the Cambridgeshire commission, he was advised to consider whether the appointment of a Dissenter in the matting trade, a former servant in the wine trade, and a poorly beneficed cleric would "give Disgust . . . to Gentlemen of higher rank nominated to act with them." Even the justices of Westminster, men hardly advanced in the ranks of gentility, recoiled at the suggestion that their parish organist join them on the bench, and the Lord Chancellor thought their objection reasonable.[2] England's justices had no need of Versailles to instruct them in the niceties of social distinctions. Englishmen might rejoice in a society which lacked rigid caste barriers, but the absence of automatically accorded rank rendered Englishmen all the more sensitive to the nuances of social status. Ruling a society which based both status and government on public association, justices were doubly aware of the importance of the impression conveyed by public appearance.

Therefore justices found public appearance with their opponents as obnoxious as public association with their inferiors. It was the nature of opponents to oppose; judicial enemies publicly challenged each other's interest. As one justice explained, it was preferable if his colleagues were those to whom he was privately allied for "then there will be no jarring." Yet there was even a better reason to avoid public appearance with one's opponents. Since public form reflected private reality, public association implied private connection, and judicial service in the company of one's opponents conveyed the unfortunate impression that a justice supported the activities of colleagues he abhorred. Justices had no wish so to confuse the public. They preferred that their inferiors know by which interest they were governed. In 1705, one group of justices reported that they "were forced to be irregular" in their proceedings "for want of people of the quorum." The only justice of the quorum in their vicinity was "Tom Eyre, whose company we affect not."[3] Exclusion of an opponent constituted a public statement of dissociation. If this statement could be presented in a manner which announced the impotence of one's opponent, so much the better.

Such is the setting for the tale of Thomas Floyer, J.P. of Hertfordshire in the hundreds of Odsey and Edwinstree. When in April 1738, Floyer appeared in the justices' room of a local inn to sit with his colleagues at petty sessions, his colleagues declared that they "would do the business by themselves" for they "were Determined not to act

2. B.L., Add. MSS 35604, f. 98, Duke of Bolton to Hardwicke, May 24, 1753; Add. MSS 35679, f. 129, Edward Leeds to Hardwicke, July 23, 1754; W. Coxe, ed., *Memoirs of the Life and Administration of Sir Robert Walpole, Earl of Orford* (London, 1798), vol. 3, p. 601, Hardwicke to Orford, Aug. 4, 1744.

3. *HMC, Cowper*, 12th Report, App., Part III, vol. 3, p. 57, J. Beresford to T. Coke, Jan. 21, 1704[5]; p. 11, R. Hardinge to T. Coke, June 19, 1702.

with him." Floyer insisted on joining their company, whereupon the justices adjourned to another room, whither Floyer pursued them, and so to another room and round the inn till the end of the day. The actions of Floyer's colleagues may seem farcical; in actuality they were making a public proclamation of their power. By denying Floyer their company the justices were announcing their refusal to recognize Floyer as a legitimate associate. By declining either to sit with Floyer or append their signatures to any order he had signed, the justices were depriving Floyer of the powers of his judicial office, for the law accorded very few administrative powers to a justice acting without colleagues. Ultimately Floyer's colleagues engineered his removal from the bench.

It is not known what charges Floyer's enemies advanced to justify his removal. The only documents relating to the case in Hardwicke's papers are a series of affidavits assembled by Floyer charging his colleagues with malfeasance, and even these indicate that Floyer did not tell all that he might. According to Floyer, his tribulations sprang from a personal quarrel with Pulter Forester, J.P., but Floyer did not describe this particular dispute. Nonetheless, Floyer's submissions do document other personal disputes which were enlivening the justices' conduct of their public office, and in so doing these submissions make explicit the manner in which justices used public association to inform the governed of the might of their private alliances.

Floyer and his opponents were engaged in a battle over the profits of alehouses. In 1737, Floyer convicted one Thomas Wynniat of brewing and selling gin and other spiritous liquors illegally. Wynniat's patron was William Calvert, J.P., who rented an alehouse to Wynniat, in whose chaff house Wynniat concealed his utensils from the excisemen, and whose influence prevented several witnesses from testifying against Wynniat. The conviction was but one blow in a battle which Calvert and Floyer had been waging for the past year.

Eight months earlier, at the annual licensing session for the hundreds of Odsey and Edwinstree, Calvert had objected to renewing the licence of William Baines. Baines was the most considerable victualler in the neighbourhood, and he suspected that Calvert wanted him to move to another public house so that one of Calvert's clients could assume Baines's flourishing business. Baines soon found a patron—Thomas Floyer. Since Baines had been refused a licence, Floyer had given him a blank licence, and declared that if Baines could find another justice who would sign the licence, he would also sign.

Baines's licence soon became the centre of Hertfordshire's judicial storms.

Calvert and his confederates would declare that the licence had never been signed. But Floyer testified that, after considerable disputation among the three justices present, Baines was called back to the justices' table and offered a licence if he could find sureties who agreed to be bound to twice the usual amount. According to Baines's sureties, Baines then obtained his licence. Others disputed this assertion. Mr. Heton, an agent of a justice absent from the session, and William Moor, innkeeper, seemed to remember that Baines had not been licensed. However, Floyer's witnesses recalled that Heton had been walking and talking near the window at the end of the room opposite from the justices' table while the session had been in progress. Baines and others testified that Baines had put the five shillings for his licence in the pewter bowl on the justices' table. True, at the end of the session Calvert and Freeman, the third justice present, had refused to accept their share of Baines's licensing money. Yet Heton had accepted his master's share. As for William Moor, it was deposed that he had tricked a labourer into signing a release protecting justice Freeman from the consequences of sentencing that labourer to the house of correction without a hearing. Moor might state that he remembered the occasion when Baines's license had been considered and refused. But others crowding round the door to the justices' room would swear that they saw Baines licensed.

Whether Baines was licensed or not became the question of fact at the nub of a series of legal proceedings. In November, Calvert forced an excise officer to charge Baines with selling liquor without a licence. Baines claimed that he had lost that precious licence, but he brought one of his sureties to the hearing to testify that his trade in spirits was legal. The two justices at the hearing were Baines's nemesis: Calvert and Freeman. Their worships refused to hear Baines's evidence; indeed "the door was shut upon" his surety, and Baines was fined £1 and forbidden from continuing in his trade. Shortly before this last persecution Calvert had told Baines that "he had no manner of ill will against him . . . but that . . . Mr. Floyer was the Person he . . . had a mind to get the better of." Accordingly, Baines now consulted Floyer.

It was Floyer's advice that Baines seek the help of a London lawyer. Fortunately, Floyer knew one and gave Baines a letter of introduction; and later, as legal costs mounted, Floyer contributed ten guineas to the costs of proceeding with the case. In the meantime, Floyer also took over the lease on Baines's alehouse, in case Baines was permanently barred from continuing in his trade. Baines's lawyer appealed his conviction to King's Bench, to which court Calvert and Freeman falsely returned that Baines had confessed. So Baines's lawyer moved for an information against Baines's two persecutors. The two justices, in turn, tried to suborn witnesses, offering a labourer money to buy turnips and a joiner work from the neighbourhood's gentlemen if they would testify against Baines. Both rejected the offers, the labourer declaring that he could always get credit to buy turnips. (Floyer had previously lent the labourer turnip money.) By the summer of 1737, the case reached Hertfordshire Assizes where the two justices were tried, convicted, and directed to give Baines satisfaction. They refused. And so in Easter 1738 they were fined £200. Meanwhile excerpts from the charges in the case mysteriously blossomed on the garden walls in surrounding villages and even on the gateposts of Floyer's own house. Floyer denied that he was responsible for the publication, but somebody saw to it that Floyer's world was informed of the iniquity and impotence of Floyer's enemies.

Defeated at law Calvert and Freeman may have been, but they had not irredeemably lost their power and they determined that their world take notice of their might. Their power rested upon both office and private connection: the alliance of Calvert and Freeman was bolstered by the adherence of Calvert's son, also a J.P., and Pulter Forester, Floyer's personal enemy. These four justices constituted the overwhelming majority of the justices active in the government of the hundreds of Odsey and Edwinstree. Since judicial office entailed public association, Floyer's enemies could transform the joint public appearance of justices mandated by law into exhibitions of the might of their private alliance. By standing together against Floyer they could at once deprive him of power and inform the neighbourhood of his impotence.

The first intimation of Floyer's vulnerability was communicated shortly after the conviction of Calvert and Freeman, at the December meeting of petty sessions for the hundreds of Odsey and Edwinstree. When Floyer tendered certificates that some excise officers had taken their oaths to his colleagues, Calvert and Freeman refused to sign their names next to his. When Floyer began to sign warrants summoning the surveyors to the January highway sessions, Forester "at the instigation" of Calvert and Freeman snatched the warrants from his hand and tore them to bits, declaring that the justices were resolved to exclude Floyer from the government of the hundreds of Odsey and Edwinstree. And that is just what they did. They refused to be associated with him, whether the association involved adding their signatures to his, informing him of the meetings of petty sessions, or admitting him to their company in public.[4] Whether the justices had just cause to ostracize Floyer, Floyer's own submissions obviously do not reveal. Yet the documents which present his case, revolving about the competition of gentlemen to patronize and be seen to patronize alehousekeepers, reveal justices conscious of the gaze of the community which knew of their warrants, heard of their plans and flocked round the door to the justices' room in Hertfordshire inns. When justices gathered to govern their neighbourhoods, their prime concern was the lesson on the location of power which their association communicated to the governed.

Though justices were associated by the sovereign's commission, it was judicial groups and not the central government which determined the image of power presented to the governed. Judicial groups could even impose their will upon the central government, and they could do so because judicial service was voluntary. Since justices neither received material profit from their service nor hoped to use judicial office to advance to more lucrative positions, the Lord Chancellor had minimal ability to regulate their patterns of assocation. The Lord Chancellor could use the powers of the courts against justices who acted illegally, but the only sanction he could bring against justices whose actions were legal but inconvenient was removal from the commission. When all the justices but one in a division were allied in a conspiracy to defeat not so much the law as the will of the central government, that sanction was ineffective.

Floyer's case exposes the Lord Chancellor's impotence. Take Floyer's presentation of the dispute over Brent Pelham's poor rate. Once Floyer had signed the rate, the other justices refused to append their signatures. Brent Pelham's overseer had to apply to King's Bench for a *mandamus* ordering one of Floyer's enemies to sign. As the overseer noted, the application for a *mandamus* was "attended by great Expence . . . to the parishioners." The strategy adopted by

4. B.L., Add. MSS 35600, ff. 130–133, petition of Thomas Floyer; ff. 135–163, affidavits of William Baines, Thomas Heneage, Pell Margetson, Thomas Crew, Thomas Floyer, Thomas Judd, William Rayment, James Fletcher, John Chipperfield, Thomas Shepherd, Henry Kensey, sworn June 14, 15, 16, 22, 26, July 4 and 7, 1738; P.R.O., Index 6658, Mich. 11 George II and Easter 11 George II; C234/16, Aug. 2, 1738; *Kentish Post or Canterbury News-Letter,* July 20–23, 1737.

Floyer's enemies allowed the Lord Chancellor but three options: to allow every one of Floyer's judicial actions to produce a lawsuit expensive to the governed; to dismiss all the justices of the division except Floyer; or to dismiss Floyer. The legal system could not process nor the Lord Chancellor countenance an unending series of lawsuits engendered by the ostracism of one justice; it was unlikely that the Lord Chancellor could find replacements for an entire petty sessional bench possessed of both suitable status and political colouration; and therefore Floyer had to be dismissed. When the overwhelming majority of otherwise acceptable justices in a division resolved not to acknowledge the legitimacy of the Lord Chancellor's appointment of a justice, the Lord Chancellor had little choice but to bow to their will.

While it is not possible to determine if party enmity played a part in Floyer's quarrel, it is unlikely that purely personal disputes among justices frequently forced the hand of the Lord Chancellor. Only the threat of chaos in government could compel the Lord Chancellor to alter a county's commission. Chaos ensued when justices joined together in a group whose activities disrupted local government. The threat of chaos likewise appeared when justices joined together and jointly declared that they would not act unless their wishes were heeded. Therefore, if justices were to impose their will on the national government they had to find a framework of association which enabled them to stand united—united in refusal to act with their opponents, or in refusal to act at all. Party provided that framework, and the rise of party enabled justices to assume greater control of the composition of the commission of the peace.

In a political system structured by interests, the quarrels of one gentleman need not become those of his colleagues. A justice could choose not to support any of the disputants. Party increased the ramifications of disputes. As more gentlemen chose to adhere to a party, it was more probable that both personal quarrels and conflicts over judicial decisions which affected gentlemen's interests would assume party colourations, for gentlemen not directly involved in a quarrel or immediately affected by a judicial decision would nonetheless consider it their concern. Addison's Sir Roger de Coverley put it this way: parties "spoil good Neighbourhood, and make honest Gentlemen hate one another; besides that they manifestly tend to the Prejudice of the Land-Tax, and the Destruction of the Game."[5] Sir Roger was a fic-

5. [J. Addison] *The Spectator,* ed. by D. Bond, vol. 1 (Oxford, 1965), p. 509.

tion, but the justices of Sussex were real. In 1719, their actions exemplified the tie that now bound disputes between persons and interests to party conflict. In 1719, Sir Harry Goring claimed that an attempt to oust him from the Sussex commission was instigated by Sir Henry Peachey because Goring "had supported a Cause He had at Quarter Sessions against Sir H. Peachey." Yet Newcastle was advised to request that Goring be removed on the grounds that "it is the unanimous request of the Whig Gentlemen and that you are informed his behaviour is such that no quiet country gentleman can act with him." The Sussex Whigs had good reason to object to association with Goring. Sir Harry Goring was no Whig; in 1722, he had to flee to France to escape prosecution for his involvement in a Jacobite plot.[6] Even if a justice of one party was not entangled in a dispute with a justice of the other, his party affiliation alone was sufficient incentive for justices of the opposing party to request his removal. Party therefore meant that justices had more cause to protest against judicial appointments because they considered increasing numbers of gentlemen their enemies.

Indeed it is likely that justices were more eager to rid the bench of their party antagonists than was the central government. While Lord Chancellors had no wish to place political enemies on the bench, they also considered it politic to abstain from wholesale removal of all possible opponents: it was preferable to win friends than to add to the ranks of the opposing party. Local gentlemen faced with the prospect of public appearance with an opponent were less sanguine about toleration of the enemy. Within a year of his resumption of office Lord Chancellor Cowper was being charged with insufficient assiduity in the dismissal of Tories. His reply illuminates the unity and power which party bestowed upon judicial groups. According to the Lord Chancellor, many Whig justices were refusing to act and justifying their abdication of duty by declaring "that they don't care to act while such or such (perhaps some of the most considerable in the county), are in; which Humour, if it be yielded to, will make the Com[mission]s in a manner Elective, and betray the Power and Dignity of the Crown."[7] Early eighteenth-century Lord Chancellors, Cowper included, yielded to this judicial humour. They had little choice. Early eighteenth-century Lord Chancellors had to insure that their party's

6. B.L., Add. MSS 32686, f. 53, Newcastle to [?], Cockpitt, Sept. 29, 1719; f. 147, Henry Pelham to Newcastle, Sept. 17, 1719; G. V. Bennett, *The Tory Crisis in Church and State* (Oxford, 1975), p. 256.

7. Herts. R.O., Panshanger MSS, D/EP/F152, Cowper Memorial.

judicial adherents would continue to act, and to act in support of their party. When their judicial adherents stood united, they could press their demands upon the Lord Chancellor, for no Lord Chancellor wished to estrange a large and locally powerful group of party supporters. Party had enabled national politicians to enlist the aid of local gentlemen, but party also enabled the justices to act as a group and so dictate to the central government. In the 1730s and 1740s, Lord Chancellor Hardwicke was still being informed that the appointment of "such or such" was "disagreeable" to the justices of the neighbourhood, many of whom would refuse to act if the obnoxious nominee were associated with them in the commission.

Confrontation with the central government was the supreme test of the might of local party. Even in the early eighteenth century, Lord Chancellors by no means surrendered their powers to regulate the composition of the commission. When Cheshire's Tory members of Parliament demanded that ten ardent Whigs be erased from their county's commission, Lord Chancellor Harcourt so far acknowledged their grievance as to remove six.[8] As justices always possessed more power to shape their institutions than to influence the central government, it was party's effect upon the manner in which justices presented themselves to the governed that was its most impressive contribution to the development of a unified bench.

Party was an association of gentlemen. Since justices staged their pageant of rule so as to inform their inferiors of the might of their private alliances, justices would naturally use their public appearances to display the power of their party. As Floyer's enemies realized, the most effective advertisement of an alliance's power was a proclamation of the alliance's hegemony over a judicial institution. If a petty or Quarter Sessions appeared as the embodiment of a party, then the sessions' powers would convince the governed that the party's judicial adherents were mighty, while the sessions' status as an institution of ancient and impartial law persuaded the governed that the party's judicial adherents were their lawful and natural rulers. Therefore their party affiliation encouraged justices in a majority at sessions to camouflage the dissent of the minority by presenting their sessions as cohesive entities.

In this they were abetted by the law, for the law gave unique status

8. B.L., Loan 29/196, ff. 134, 135, G. Warburton and C. Cholmondely to [Harley], 1710; P.R.O., C234/5, Mar. 10, 1710 [11].

to joint judicial activity. Two justices had more and different powers than one, and justices assembled in Quarter Sessions had more and different powers than justices acting out of Quarter Sessions. When justices foregathered in their judicial institutions they collectively represented something other and more than the sum of their powers as individual justices. The law therefore implied that justices acting as a group comprised a distinct and discrete entity. According to contemporary opinion, justices acting as a group embodied the will of the county. When Charles II wished to question the validity of a petition for the convocation of Parliament he asked whether the petition "came from the Sessions? No. If from the Grand Jury? No. Then his Majesty . . . [declared] that he did not take it from the county."[9]

While the seventeenth-century public recognized judicial sessions as a corporate body, that body did not possess a clearly identifiable political personality. The justices represented the will of the county because in both their private and public capacities they wielded power over the county's inhabitants. Though as a group the justices personified the might of land, law, and sovereign, and though individual justices were obviously adherents of political interests, the politics of interest could not sustain the presentation of a sessions as a unified political entity. Almost every justice symbolized the power of a distinct and different interest. In imposing unity on a multitude of interests, party divided justices into two fairly cohesive and mutually antagonistic groups. Until the Lord Chancellor altered the composition of the bench by the issue of a new commission, justices in one of these groups could reasonably expect to be in a majority at sessions, and justices in a permanent majority would wish that the power of the majority be constantly evident to the governed. Justices in the majority therefore needed a symbol, a symbol which both expressed their party affiliation and the unity of the institution which they dominated. They found their symbol in the chairman of Quarter Sessions.

In theory, Quarter Sessions was chaired by the custos; in fact, chairmen of early seventeenth-century Quarter Sessions were deputies of the custos, appointed by the central government. By the early eighteenth century, the chairman of Quarter Sessions was elected by the justices in Quarter Sessions. Gloucestershire's Quarter Sessions had probably had chairmen in the seventeenth century, but it was not until

9. R. W. Blencowe, ed., *Diary of the Times of Charles the Second by the Honourable Henry Sidney* (London, 1843), vol. 1, p. 252, Dowager Countess of Sunderland to Mr. Sidney, Jan. 23 [1679/80].

1710 that the list of attendants at Quarter Sessions invariably began with the name of the chairman—an innovation undoubtedly related to the formal evolution of the Sessions. The chairman of the Kent Quarter Sessions that petitioned Parliament in 1701—himself a petitioner and jailed for it—was elected; in fact, he was elected even though he was not present at the election, and the justices kept the chair vacant for several hours in expectation of his arrival. In 1709, the Quarter Sessions of the West Riding of Yorkshire resolved to elect a chairman; by Anne's reign the Quarter Sessions of Wiltshire and Shropshire were both electing chairmen and electing the same person as chairman for a number of years.[10]

Obviously, election expressed the will of the majority and by the early eighteenth century majorities at Quarter Sessions were structured by party. Evidence on election to the chair is both rare and fragmentary, but fortunately someone scribbled on the back of a Sessions paper a list of the vote on the election of west Kent's chairman at the first Quarter Sessions of the reign of George I.[11] The former and defeated chairman, a Tory member of Anne's Parliaments, had the voices of ten fellow justices. Nine of the ten supported the Tories at either or both of the elections of 1713 and 1715.[12] The new chairman, a future Whig knight of the shire, had the support of seventeen judicial brethren, fifteen of whom voted for the Whigs at either or both of the elections of 1713 and 1715.[13] At the election of west Kent's chairman

10. T. G. Barnes, *Somerset 1625–1640, A County's Government During the 'Personal Rule'* (Cambridge, Mass., 1961), pp. 70–72; *Cobbett's Parliamentary History of England from the Norman Conquest to the Year 1803,* vol. 5 (London, 1809), Appendix xvii, "The History of the Kentish Petition," p. clxvii; S. and B. Webb, *English Local Government from the Revolution to the Municipal Corporations Act,* vol. 1, *The Parish and the County,* pp. 433–434; I. E. Gray and E. T. Graydon, *Gloucestershire Quarter Sessions Archives 1660–1889 and Other Official Records* (Gloucester, 1958), p. 86; J. Montagu, *The Charge of James Montagu, Esq., to the Grand Jury . . . of the County of Wilts: At the General Quarter-Sessions of the Peace, held at the Devizes, April 26, 1720* (London, 1720), p. 7; Herts. R.O., Panshanger MSS D/EP/F154, Earl of Bradford to [Cowper], Dec. 27, 1714. This last reference reveals that the Webbs' assertion that Shropshire did not elect a chairman in this period is erroneous. The Webbs were primarily interested in evidence of the election of permanent chairmen as the outward sign of administrative grace. It is therefore probable that their notices of the election of chairmen considerably postdate the initiation of the practice of election.

11. Kent A.O., Q/SB 1715; see also Lady Margaret Maria Verney, *Verney Letters of the Eighteenth Century from the Manuscripts at Claydon House* (London, 1930), vol. 1, p. 243, Lord Fermanagh to Ralph Verney, Oct. 16, 1712.

12. The remaining justice voted for the Whigs. He was removed from the commission in 1719, possibly because he supported his Tory colleagues.

13. Neither of the two remaining justices voted at either election.

a host of Whigs confronted a phalanx of Tories and the central government had considered the skirmish sufficiently important to determine its outcome. The new Whig chairman would not have been elected had not the new Whig Lord Chancellor sealed a new commission shortly before Quarter Sessions met. The new commission elevated both the new chairman and twelve of his supporters to the bench. West Kent's chairman personified party power, and change in the chairman notified the governed that they had new leaders whom it would be wise to follow.

Fortunately for the party in the majority, the chairman symbolized the institution of Quarter Sessions as well as the might of those who had elected him. Whigs and Tories might struggle at Quarter Sessions, but after the battle Quarter Sessions could speak with just one voice. Quarter Sessions could deliver but a single decision on any case; the decision was that of the majority and it was pronounced by the chairman. By insuring that one of their number was chairman, justices in the majority at Quarter Sessions annexed to their party the mystique of the institution which epitomized rule by the county's natural leaders according to the dictates of law.

The deposition of a chairman therefore proclaimed that the electorate had been deceived; the power of the chairman's supporters was less than his election implied, while the legal imprimatur which his reign bestowed upon his party's authority distorted the true intent of the law. When, in 1742, justices and gentlemen of the West Riding of Yorkshire charged William Wrightson with malfeasance and requested that he be removed from the commission, Wrightson replied that the justices acting with him had so far approved his conduct as generally to choose him chairman of Quarter Sessions. Most probably it was because Wrightson was chairman that he was attacked.

Such an interpretation appears all the more likely when the circumstances which gave rise to the charges against Wrightson are examined. Wrightson had committed his alleged offence during an election. Wrightson supported the Opposition candidate. The sponsor of the petition against Wrightson was Sir Rowland Winn, a leading Yorkshire Whig. The majority of the affidavits against Wrightson were taken by the Dean of York, who added electioneering in the Whig interest to his clerical duties, and by the Lord Viscount Irwin, chief supporter of the victorious Whig candidate. As Wrightson noted, the petition for his removal was not signed by the majority of justices active in the West Riding; as Wrightson was too politic to declare, the signators included a number of politically active Whigs, several of whom were in the Irwin interest.[14]

According to the Whigs, Wrightson had committed an offence so heinous that his presence on the bench made a mockery of English justice. Specifically, his treatment of one John Flint had flouted English law. John Flint, ship's carpenter, had led a riot in the Castle Yard at York designed to carry voters from the booth recording votes for the Whig candidate to that numbering supporters of the Opposition's candidate, and Flint had therefore been committed to jail until he could find men willing to stand surety both for his appearance at Assizes and for his good behaviour. Wrightson had not only released Flint—undoubtedly an impolitic act—but, it was alleged, had released him without consulting either the justice who had committed him or the gentleman on whose charge he was imprisoned, had allowed men of insufficient property to stand as Flint's sureties, and had not bound Flint to his good behaviour. So, as soon as Flint was released he appeared at the head of a mob which threw mud at the Whig candidate and his entourage when the Whigs were making their triumphal march through the city.[15]

Wrightson had no intention of letting such allegations go unanswered. According to his memorial, his West Riding opponents had fabricated their charges out of whole cloth. Wrightson denied and proved his denial of the allegation that he had not bound Flint to his good behaviour. Wrightson's witnesses swore that Wrightson had inquired whether Flint's guarantors possessed sufficient property to stand surety. Since, Wrightson stated, the warrant committing Flint had not instanced any "particular or aggravating Circumstances" he had not considered it necessary to consult with the justice who committed Flint, and since the warrant did not name the complainant it was impossible to consult with the gentleman on whose complaint Flint had been committed. Nor should Wrightson have been aware of the charges against Flint. He had not knowingly bailed a rioter who

14. C. Collyer, "The Yorkshire Election of 1734," *Proceedings of the Leeds Philosophical and Literary Society* 7: part 1 (1952): 59; C. Collyer, "The Yorkshire Election of 1741", *Proceedings of the Leeds Philosophical and Literary Society* 7: 2 (1953): 143, 145; R. Sedgwick, *The House of Commons 1715–1754* (New York, 1970), vol. 2, *sub* Sir Lionel Pilkington, Arthur Ingram.

15. For other instances of judicial aid to ringleaders of election riots, see N. Rogers, "Aristocratic Clientage, Trade and Independency: Popular Politics in Pre-Radical Westminster," *Past and Present* 61 (1973): 81.

was preventing the king's subjects from exercising their right to vote because as far as he could recall there had not been any riot. Indeed, if in fact there had been a riot, why was Flint not prosecuted when he appeared on his recognizance at the Assizes?

The Lord Chancellor to whom both Wrightson's replies and his opponents' charges were sent would probably guess at an answer to that question. Among the documents he perused were two affidavits signed by John Flint himself. The first supported the tale of Wrightson's misdeeds. The second told a different story. After the second riot, Flint had discovered that Thomas Pulleyn, a member of the Whig candidate's entourage, intended to swear a warrant against him. So, Flint had gone to ask Pulleyn's pardon, and Pulleyn had demanded that Flint also tender his apologies to other Whigs whom his conduct had offended. Pulleyn first took Flint to Viscount Irwin's residence, and then, because Irwin was not at home, Pulleyn accompanied Flint to see the Dean of York. As Flint told his crony, when he entered the dean's residence and "the great doors were shutt upon him," Flint became apprehensive that he would be committed to the jail of the Liberty of St. Peters "from whence he knew they wou'd not easily allow him to be bayled"; and so Flint agreed to "Sign and say any thing to get out of their liberty."[16]

Flint may indeed have been the hapless prisoner of St. Peters', but it is more likely that he did a deal. A statement impugning Wrightson's judicial character would seem a fair exchange for a promise not to prosecute Flint at Assizes. As Yorkshire's Whigs had managed to wrest one of the county seats from the Opposition they would naturally seek to mark their resurgence by procuring the dismissal of the symbol of Opposition power in the county—the chairman of Quarter Sessions. Since the chairman endowed his party with the mystique of legal authority, the Whigs' partisan attack would paradoxically be based on a strategy of framing evidence to prove that the chairman was not impartial.

As Wrightson retained his place on the West Riding's commission, Hardwicke evidently decided that the chairman had not used his power in an illegally partisan manner. Whether Hardwicke would have considered irrefutable proof of an inappropriate release of an Opposition rioter behaviour so illegally partisan that it necessitated

16. B.L., Add. MSS 35601, f. 3, Sir Rowland Winn to Lord Malton, Feb. 24, 1741 [2]; ff. 5–6, 7–9, 11–18, documents and affidavits submitted by Wrightson's opponents; f. 21, W. Wrightson to Gabriel Mallet, May 8, 1742; ff. 23–26, 29, 31–34, documents and affidavits submitted by Wrightson.

removal cannot be determined. Certainly, the chairman had ample opportunity to use the power of his office in a manner simultaneously legal and partisan. The chairman was no mere figurehead. He gave the charge to the grand jury, and the chairman's charge could be a statement of party doctrine. The chairman declared the rules of procedure, directed the orders, summed up evidence, and pronounced judgment, and these functions too enabled the chairman to aid his party.[17] In 1683, the Whig chairman of Northumberland's Quarter Sessions refused to accept both an information laid against a conventicle of five hundred persons and presentments of the grand jury calling for the suppression of "faction," i.e., of the Whigs. Oldmixon even averred that the chairman wrote the presentments of the grand jury "because he cou'd then make it speak as he pleas'd."[18]

Oldmixon exaggerated. He was attempting to impugn those presentments of later Stuart grand juries which were statements of Tory ideology—presentments demanding that the laws against popery, schism, and conventicles and other "unlawful meetings" be enforced. While it is unlikely that the chairman wrote routine presentments, it is quite probable that the chairman did guide the grand jury's political reflections. Certainly William Colepeper did.

Colepeper was chairman of west Kent's Quarter Sessions in 1701 when its grand jury decided to petition the House of Commons to transform its loyal addresses into bills of supply so that William III could defend his title in war. According to the Tories, Colepeper had with malice aforethought obtained the imprimatur of the grand jury on a document which had been sent to him by the Whig politicians in London. The Tory dominated House of Commons adjudged the petition seditious and consigned Colepeper and four of his judicial colleagues to the care of its sergeant at arms. Both Colepeper and the petition found their defender in Daniel Defoe, who wrote a pamphlet to prove that the petition, emanating from the grand jury, was indeed the voice of the county. According to Defoe, the chairman merely and dutifully expressed the opinion of the court of Quarter Sessions.

While Quarter Sessions was being held, wrote Defoe, several principal freeholders informed the chairman that "it was their desire that

17. *Office of the Clerk of Assize . . . Together with the Office of the Clerk of the Peace*, 2nd ed. (London, 1682), pp. 117, 156.

18. M. Child, "Prelude to Revolution: Politics in County Durham, 1678–1688" (Ph.D. diss., University of Maryland, 1972), pp. 78–80; J. Oldmixon, *The History of Addresses,* 2 vols. (London, 1709–1711), vol. 1, p. 40.

the bench would consider of makeing some application to the parliament, to acquaint them with the apprehensions of the people. The Chairman replied 'It was the proper work of the grand-jury to present the Grievances of the country, and therefore he referred them to the said grand-jury who were sitting.' " The grand jury consulted, accepted the proposal, and requested that the justices join with them. Colepeper as chairman communicated the jury's sentiments to the justices; the justices applauded their endeavour and desired that Colepeper compose the petition, which he did. The grand jury and justices then signed.[19]

Twenty-five years later, Colepeper recounted a different version of the event. As he remembered it, he had carefully arranged to meet the jurymen by accident in the street, where he persuaded the jury to join with the justices in a petition. Then, after the justices' dinner, where "there was nothing but Mirth and Kindness," Colepeper informed the justices of the grand jury's desire and was asked to draw the petition. The chairman refused "to dictate" to the justices, but first heard their views and then framed them into a petition. As Colepeper's reminiscence is embedded in a pamphlet designed to justify himself and vilify his brother-in-law—another of the five petitioners—it may be that his account exaggerates his own role.[20] Yet the difference between the two stories does seem that which would distinguish the ideal—the chairman acting at the behest of the greycoats of Kent—from the actual—the chairman instructing the grand jury in the part it was to play, using his office to dominate the court. Colepeper's own tale emphasizes another ideal which party may have made real: the chairman as spokesman of the bench, and preferably, a unanimous bench.

When justices used their party majority to elect a partisan chairman, to hinder or promote petitions and addresses, to order the grand jury to present all those "making scandalous reflections on the present government" or to make orders against Dissenters;[21] when they allowed their fellows to use the court to persecute personal enemies;[22]

19. *The History of the Kentish Petition Answer'd* (London, 1701), p. 11; *Parliamentary History,* vol. 5, app. xvii, "The History of the Kentish Petition," pp. clxxvi–clxxvii.

20. "The Case between the King and Richard Biggs alias Blue Dick . . . , " quoted in R. Goodsall, *Stede Hill* (London, 1950), pp. 131–133.

21. N. Luttrell, *A Brief Historical Relation of State Affairs from September 1678 to April 1714,* 6 vols. (Oxford, 1857), vol. 2, p. 212, Apr. 1691; vol. 1, p. 140, Oct., 1681.

22. Herts. R.O., Panshanger MSS D/EP/F152, "Other Informations touching upon several Irregularities and Oppressions committed by the said Justices in the execution of their Office," informations of Dandle Hughes, David Williams, and Richard Lewis.

when they based decisions on administrative matters on the political affiliation of those affected, by their actions they made evident and effective the political beliefs and powers of the majority of the bench. Justices seen as a group sitting at Quarter Sessions were the collective and visible embodiment of power in the county. They saw their group and chose that those they ruled see their group as a symbol and weapon of political power. So, when a political agent of the Duke of Dorset reported on the progress of the campaign to elect Dorset's candidates as the county's knights he rejoiced that, at the last Quarter Sessions "there was a handsome appearance of Friends, and none of the Opp[o]s[ition] but Sir P. Boteler."[23]

As the agent's report suggests, when justices in the majority used their power to impart a partisan identity to Quarter Sessions, justices in the minority decided not to attend Quarter Sessions—and thereby further emphasized both Quarter Sessions' partisan image and its unity. Again, a justice's decision to abstain from parading his office was based on his assessment of the effect his public appearance would have on his public image. Justices in the majority might dislike public association with their opponents, but justices in the minority shrank from advertisement of their impotence. As Edmund Bohun explained when he resolved to leave Norfolk for London in 1684: "I had been extremely ill used by my fellow justices, in the execution of my office; and by one Capt. Hall, three several times in publick; and though I demanded justice against him, yet I could get no redress; but their unkindness daily encreased so that the country became extremely uneasy to me."[24] Few justices felt obliged to condemn themselves to exile because they had been publicly insulted. Many more would simply resolve to avoid giving their opponents opportunity for triumphal display. So in the 1630s, when a Puritan caucus ruled in east Sussex, the justices of the west ceased attending the summer Quarter Sessions at which justices of both sections of the county had together graced the bench. Likewise, in 1753 Tory justices preferred not to appear at west Kent's Quarter Sessions, and when Oxfordshire's Tories sought to promote the election of their candidate by unwonted attendance at Quarter Sessions they quickly retired when confronted with a hostile Whig majority.[25]

23. Kent A.O., U269/C149/10, T. Curteis to [Sackville Bale], Oct. 7, 1753.

24. S. W. Rix, ed., *The Diary and Autobiography of Edmund Bohun, Esq.* (Eccles, 1853), p. 64.

25. A. Fletcher, *A County Community in Peace and War* (London, 1975), p. 243; R. Robson, *The Oxfordshire Election of 1754* (London, 1949), p. 61.

The lot of the minority at petty sessions was equally invidious, for by the early eighteenth century some of the decisions which most explicitly conveyed the power of party were being made at petty sessions, in full view of the neighbourhood. It was at petty sessions that the oaths of allegiance were tendered, and justices decided whether the oath-taker need enunciate loudly and clearly or simply mumble a few words with hand shielding lips.[26] The recruiting acts of Anne's reign, acts repugnant to the Tories and supported by the Whigs, were administered by the justices in petty sessions. Recruitment proved a double-edged political sword. Not only could the justices in petty sessions announce the political sympathies of the majority by their policy in enforcing the act, but they could also reveal their political sympathies through their choice of victims for the armed forces. If one had to recruit an Englishman, then it was preferable to enlist the supporter of one's opponents. Though only four charges of misuse of judicial power survive among the papers Cowper received as Queen Anne's Lord Chancellor, three revolve about the enforcement of the recruiting acts.[27] Even prosecutions for sedition at Quarter Sessions or Assizes may have been considered exemplary exercises of power, power that was regularly being wielded in petty sessions. After one petty sessions Gabriel Walters noted: "A person bound in a Bond of £400 to his Good-Behaviour, He desired to know his Crimes and Accusers, but was told 'twas only to secure the Government against suspected Persons—The Recorder was the Person that laid the whole scheme of the Business, and patchd up the Indictment in Terms suited to his known Abilities."[28] The Recorder was Francis Barrell of Rochester, a noted Tory. Walters was a Whig.

Since the decisions of justices in petty sessions could affect a gentleman's interest or signal party dominance, justices attempted to capture this institution for their party. In Queen Anne's reign, Kent's Lord Lieutenant reported, two Tory justices had "Sett up a separate meeting from the other Justices in Eyhorn Division to encourage the Torys."

26. Herts. R.O., Panshanger MSS D/EP/F153, "From Lord W. Lancashire"; D/EP/F154, deposition of Richard Scofield.

27. Herts. R.O., Panshanger MSS D/EP/F154, William Blathwayt to Cowper, Mar. 13, 1708[9]; D/EP/F153, Sunderland to Cowper, Jan. 20, 1708/1709; affidavit of Walter Carwardine, July 20, 1706; B.L., Blenheim Loan, C1–36, affidavit of Wm. Pryour, Mar. 27, 1708; Sunderland to Cowper, Whitehall, Jan. 28, 1708/1709; P. Whichcote, Tho. Bendyshe and Will. Worts to [Sunderland], Oct. 16, 1708; C1–52, Jas. Montague and R. Eyre to the Queen, July 2, 1709; Luttrell, *Brief Relation,* vol. 5, p. 429, May 30, 1704.

28. Hants. R.O., 18/M51/595, pp. 54–55.

Other justices in the minority simply abandoned the contest. In Wiltshire, a considerable proportion of the justices who had attended Quarter Sessions in 1710 ceased to appear after the Tories added their supporters to the commission and purged some of their opponents. In 1715, Lord Cowper was informed that the few "honest" justices in Lancashire "cannot act because the majority are against them." To prove his point, Cowper's informant listed Lancashire's active justices by petty sessional division and showed that Tories were in the majority in every division. The situation could be remedied if the more virulent Tories in each division were removed and Whigs added, for then Lancashire's currently inactive Whig justices would act "on purpose to be an overbalance."[29] Whig justices would emerge from retirement if they could be assured that they would not be outvoted and so publicly humiliated at petty sessions.

Likewise, Tories would withdraw from public life if they were fated to be members of a permanent minority. By 1715, the effects of Hanoverian rule and manipulation of the commission by Whig Lord Chancellors were already evident. In Kent, a dispirited clergyman who refused to take the oaths was observing that "the Whigs govern us with an absolute sway, and the honest Church-men tho' in equal commissio with them dare not to shew their faces." At the same time another Tory justice was luxuriating in the depression caused by Whig reinstatement and Tory banishment. Shorn of his deputy lieutenancy and reduced to a "Puny Justice of Quorum," Sir Thomas Cave, M.P. for Leicestershire, urged the future and Tory Lord Verney: "Ah hang it, Leave thy Justice Trade, and come and hunt in my open Air, enjoying Dryden's blessed Retirement—

> Felix qui procul ex negotiis
> Paterna rura bobus exercet suis."[30]

Solaced by an ideology which transformed withdrawal to the private joys of a country house into a virtuous response to the corruption of public life, early Hanoverian Tories shielded their dignity and sup-

29. Herts. R.O., Panshanger MSS D/EP/F153, "List of justices to be left out . . . from Earl of Rockinghams hand, 1715"; "From Lord W. Lancashire"; "1715. The names and characters of all the Justices of Peace in Lancashire who now act"; "1715 Justices of Peace for Lancashire, the names of those who are desired to be put in." L.K.J. Glassey, *Politics and The Appointment of Justices of the Peace 1675–1720* (Oxford, 1979), pp. 267–268.

30. Bodleian Library, Ballard MSS, vol. 15, f. 118, Rev. [John Johnson] to Dr. Charlett, Aug. 22, 1715; *Verney Letters,* vol. 1, pp. 341–342, Sir Thomas Cave to Ralph Verney, Oct. 24, 1715.

ported their party by abdication from office. As late as the 1750s it was noted that the Tory justices of Oxfordshire were less likely to act than the Whigs,[31] while in 1754 two-thirds of Kent's Whig justices but less than half the Tories assumed the burdens of their commission. In only one Kentish petty sessional division were Tories more assiduous than their opponents, and even this exception illustrates the rule: justices in the political minority, be it Whig or Tory, were less likely to act than justices in the political majority. In the Ashford division, home of Kent's sole Tory candidate in 1754, all the active justices who voted were Tories, and all the justices who voted for the Whigs, a minority of the division's justices, were inactive. Since justices realized that their power and status would be assessed by their ability to influence the decisions of petty and Quarter Sessions, and since early Hanoverian Lord Chancellors insured that the Whigs dominated most petty and Quarter Sessions, many Tories decided to absent themselves from the bench. So, in the reigns of the first two Hanoverians both petty and Quarter Sessions acquired a party identity and a unity based on party affiliation.

Both the relation between public association and private connection and that between party adherence and judicial majorities would influence the behaviour of nineteenth-century justices. In early nineteenth-century Yorkshire, Michael Stocks, J.P., was the anti-hero of an episode that had its early Hanoverian analogue in the tale of Thomas Floyer. Stocks, a man of humble origins who had risen to the station of tavern and colliery owner, became a justice of the West Riding in 1807—an honour many attributed to his efforts to obtain the election of the Lord Lieutenant's son. Stocks was a Whig. The justices with whom he was associated were Tory, and they had for some time held a public petty sessions at a local inn. When Stocks arrived to take his place at the justices' table, the justices refused to appear with him and adjourned the sessions. Stocks appealed to the Lord Lieutenant, who declared that the meeting was open to all. The justices took legal counsel and changed the site of their petty sessions to the clerk's house. Likewise, they initiated an extended campaign to have Stocks removed from the bench. After a number of unsuccessful attempts to prove Stocks guilty of illegal activity, they had their revenge. In 1830, Stocks was removed from the commission pending his trial on a charge of perjury. Stocks was acquitted, but he was not reinstated. By

31. Robson, *Oxfordshire Election,* pp. 41–42.

1830, the West Riding had a Tory Lord Lieutenant who refused to recommend that Stocks be reappointed. Though the Whig Lord Chancellor had initially determined to restore Stocks to the commission, he finally decided to honour the Lord Lieutenant's wishes.[32]

It would be simplistic to conclude that the resemblance between the tales of Thomas Floyer and Michael Stocks proves that either the behaviour of justices or the concept of behaviour appropriate to justices remained unchanged during the course of the eighteenth century. Stocks's case reveals that the political implications of judicial association would be exploited when national parties reemerged under the later Hanoverians, just as they had been realized when party battled party in the first decades of the eighteenth century. At mid-century, party was fragmenting and judicial assessments of appropriate public associates altered accordingly. In 1745, the Earl of Coventry informed Hardwicke that "the appearance of the Principal Gentlemen of the County in my Son's Interest" had induced him "To Act with Em, which I have declin'd ever since Sir Richard Lane and His Son were restor'd, being struck out by L[or]d Macclesfield, takeing exorbitant Fear, but I believe the Country will never be troubled by 'em any more. . . ."[33] Politics may make strange bedfellows, but lack of a clearly defined opposing party vastly increases the number of acceptable mates. Gentlemen need no longer abstain from judicial activity for fear of the partisan signals conveyed by public association. Disintegration of party made the partisan character of judicial institutions both less discernible and less necessary. So, during the first decade of George III's reign the chairmen of Kent's Quarter Sessions ceased to be leading gentry known to the county as prominent supporters of a party. In the 1790s, Thomas Gisborne could declare that a justice's refusal to act "with one of his brethren from political or personal prejudice" was "reprehensible."[34] By the accession of George III, party allegiance no longer guaranteed that justices would present a united front to the governed.

That does not mean that judicial unity was perceived as any the less necessary. Judicial unity once achieved for partisan purposes was by no means abandoned when party strife no longer divided gentry society. Instead of presenting themselves as a united party group, justices

32. J. R. Knipe, "The Justice of the Peace in Yorkshire, 1820–1914" (Ph.D. diss., University of Wisconsin, 1970), pp. 59–77.

33. B.L., Add. MSS 35586, f. 364, Earl of Coventry to Hardwicke, June 8, 1745.

34. T. Gisborne, *An Enquiry into the Duties of Men in the Higher and Middle Classes of Society* (London, 1795), vol. 1, p. 449.

of the mid-century began to emphasize the value of unity among all governors. Especially was the need for solidarity evident when justices confronted groups of discontented among the governed.

The governed were numerous; the justices were not. When a justice acted to preserve the peace of the realm from the threat of riot and insurrection he acted as an individual, and however golden-tongued that individual, he possessed insufficient force and prestige to quell a mob determined to express its grievances. When the poor of Dartford rioted to protest the loss of their employment to Irishmen, and one justice committed four of the rioters, the remainder of the mob assembled round the justice's house threatening to pull it down, and did not disperse until the justice released those he had imprisoned.[35] At mid-century the Lord Lieutenant of Sussex discovered that his county's justices would not take action against the smuggling gangs who terrified the coast: they were afraid that their houses or barns might be set on fire.[36] In 1757, Yorkshire's justices were stymied by a similar choice between public anarchy and private misfortune. The high price of corn and the Militia Act had together fomented rebellion among the populace. It was possible, explained one justice, to discourage rioters by arming reliable inhabitants "when Gentlemen live in an area near to a Market Town, but it is Impracticable when Gentlemen live at a distance from each other or from a great Town which is the Case of many Gentlemen in this County where a Mobb may come and pull down your House and other Mischief before you can get any assistance but your servants who cannot be supposed to be of a sufficient Number to put a stop to a Mobb of 200 or 300 People . . . . " The justice could think of but one solution: "to desire all the Gentlemen that are in the Commission of the Peace to take out their dedimus to attend the assizes and sessions to keep up the dignity of the Courts and act with Spirit and Resolution . . . and then whatever steps were taken it would be the Act of the whole and not that of any private Person and when the Country People saw that the Gentlemen acted with spirit and unanimously and were determined not to be governed by a Mobb they would submit. . . ." One justice, acting with spirit, was defenceless. But if all the justices displayed their readiness to defend the constitution, the vulgar would realize that their cause was

35. *The Kentish Post or Canterbury News-Letter,* July 28–31, July 31–August 4, 1736.

36. C. Winslow, "Sussex Smugglers" in *Albion's Fatal Tree,* ed. D. Hay et al. (New York, 1975), pp. 123, 158.

unjust and their power ephemeral.[37] Besides, the odds against attack on any individual justice increased in proportion to the number of justices who acted with spirit.

By the late 1750s, justices were facing the mob as a group. When Richmond in Yorkshire was threatened by a mob in 1757, the mayor dispatched expresses to the leading gentlemen of the neighbourhood who arrived to protect the town with "700 Horse and 200 Foot, well arm'd and accoutered." The mob decided not to appear. In 1759, when riot disrupted meetings for the recruitment of the militia at Ashford and Elham in Kent, the justices did not act as individuals or even as members of a petty sessions. Instead, they convened a special meeting of east Kent's Quarter Sessions at the Sessions House in Canterbury where they attempted to discover the instigators of the riots, issued warrants and a reward for the apprehension of two of the ringleaders, committed sixteen rioters to jail to await trial, and bound over several more to appear at Assizes to answer an indictment. For one full week the justices sat upon their bench, morning and evening, jointly embodying the will of the law and the unity of the magistracy of east Kent, Whig and Tory alike. At Assizes a bipartisan grand jury, numbering seventeen justices among its members and headed by the Whig and Tory candidates for the county seats at the last election, fined and imprisoned those who had disturbed the peace of the county by rioting against the implementation of an act of Parliament.[38]

When mid-century justices maintained the peace, they emphasized the authority of the magistracy as a group and they insured that that group be on display as a group. No longer could a justice rely on his individual authority as patriarchal leader of a village community. Justices suspected that the village community was not a cohesive body with the justice as its head. The justices of both Kent and Yorkshire thought the mobs had rioted with the consent and connivance of substantial farmers,[39] and their impressive appearance as a magisterial group was a reminder to the labourer that authority greater and a group distinct from farmers ruled the land. As their pageant also emphasized, neither riot nor government was a merely communal con-

37. B.L., Add. MSS 32874, ff. 425–426, Sir Rowland Winn to Newcastle, Oct. 3, 1757; see also E. P. Thompson, "Patrician Society, Plebian Culture," *Journal of Social History* 7 (1974): 404–405.

38. *Kentish Post or Canterbury News-Letter,* Dec. 17–21, 1757; July 18–21, 25–28, 28–Aug. 1, Aug. 4–8, 1759; P.R.O., Ass 35/199.

39. Kent A.O., U269/C147/20, Lewis Watson et al. to Duke of Dorset, July 18, 1759.

cern; both were matters with which the county's rulers dealt as a nonpartisan group.

Before the mid-eighteenth century it is unlikely that justices could have depended on the cooperation of their colleagues to suppress a disturbance, especially a disturbance associated with a party programme, and the Militia Act was considered a Tory measure. When, in the late seventeenth and early eighteenth centuries, party warred with party, offenders against the king's peace found partisan supporters in the courts. Even murderers, if of the proper party, might be excused their crimes—or so it was rumoured.[40] At mid-century a miscreant might solicit aid from prominent gentlemen, but he could no longer rely upon the sympathy of a partisan group of governors. In theory always nonpartisan, government was in fact becoming less partisan as the disintegration of party enabled governors to distinguish between the needs of party and the dictates of law. The decline of party struggle therefore enabled justices to shift emphases in their concept of judicial service. By the mid-century, justices who assumed the burdens of the commission were praised not as servants of the monarch or supporters of a partisan interpretation of the settlement in Church and state, but as defenders of a constitution esteemed by all members of England's elite. The appearance of governors as a united group therefore made concrete the concept of judicial impartiality, while decline in the proportion of justices who acted suggested that those justices who did choose to execute the charge of their commission were inspired by a desire to serve the public.

Justices of the seventeenth century had appeared before the governed as an assortment of eminent community leaders. Justices of the early eighteenth century, impelled by party struggle to inform the governed of the party affiliation of the majority at their sessions, had presented themselves as a united partisan group. At mid-century, when party struggle ceased to divide the county's rulers, the unity of party was transformed into the unanimity of the entire group of governors. By the end of the century, England's elite perceived its judicial service as a means of displaying the might, unanimity, and altruism of its social stratum to a potentially revolutionary populace. The elite's response to the radicalism engendered by the French Revolution was a radical increase in the number of justices who declared themselves

40. J. Pruett, "The Clergy of Leicestershire, 1660–1714" (Ph.D. diss., Princeton University, 1973), p. 264.

willing to assume the burdens of judicial office.[41] And, just as change in the justices' behaviour intimated a new concept of relations between local governors, so by mid-century change in the composition of the bench symbolized a new definition of the relation between the rulers and the ruled.

41. See appendix E, figure 1.

CHAPTER TEN

The Bench of Kent

Politics, Status, and the Rewards of Office

When in 1714 Kent's Lord Lieutenant and custos rotulorum wished to survey the state of the county's bench, he had laid before him two lists of justices arrayed according to petty sessional division: the first list noted those whom Lord Chancellor Harcourt had removed from the commission, and the second noted those whom Harcourt had appointed. In 1775, Kent's Lord Lieutenant and custos was again examining the composition of the county's bench as displayed by a list of justices arranged according to petty sessional division. This list divided the county's justices into two categories: those who acted and those who did not.[1] That in 1714 Kent's highest official viewed the commission in the light of party politics, while six decades later his successor emphasized the needs of administration is obvious. Less immediately apparent is the effect of both considerations upon the composition of Kent's bench. Persuaded by the demands of politics and administration to alter its criteria for the selection of justices, the central government issued commissions of the peace which proclaimed an altered definition of appropriate local governors. As Kent's justices possessed views and powers of their own, their interpretation of judicial office was also disseminated to the public. In choosing whether to act or not, Kent's justices revealed their assessment of the rewards of judicial office, while those who acted altered the image of the county's rulers.

In 1679 Celia Fiennes, on tour in the Weald of Kent, was moved to

1. Kent A.O., Q/JL1, U269/O96.

observe: "the old proverb was a Yeoman of Kent could buy out a Gentleman of Wales and Knight of Scales and a Lord of the North Country, his Estate was so much the better."[2] The prosperity of the Kentish yeoman was so well known, so often stressed, that it had become proverbial, and the proverb was understood to have implications other than simply economic. Wealth meant independence, and independence meant freedom from tyrannous rule. At the end of the eighteenth century, one commentator explained that the intermingling of the lands of yeoman and gentry and the prevalence of freehold tenure resulted in "a state of freedom . . . productive of good will" between governed and governors, "there being no part of the kingdom where the people are more quietly governed, or submit with more pleasure to the laws and magistracy of the county."[3] According to another proverb, government reflects the governed. And so, the independence of the Kentish yeoman was taken as symbolic of the freedom and independence of the entire county. Most especially did the freedom of the yeomen magnify the glory of their governors. Like the yeomen, the gentry of Kent were independent.

No aristocrat had estates so widespread throughout the ninth largest county in the land as to claim to dictate to its inhabitants. Even the estates of the greatest peers in the county—those chosen as its Lords Lieutenant and custodes rotulorum—are illustrative of the limits of aristocratic sway. The earls of Winchilsea might be Lords Lieutenant and custodes rotulorum of the county from 1660 to 1662, 1668 to 1687, 1689 to 1693, and 1704 to 1705, but their lands extended only to estates about Eastwell in the Ashford division, and their fortunes were so limited that, in Anne's reign, the fourth earl was known to be a "poor lord."[4] Henry Sidney, Earl of Romney, Lord Lieutenant and custos rotulorum from 1689 to 1704, owed his fortune, title, and office to his intimate friendship with King William. Lands he had few. Instead, his claim to office in the county rested upon the possessions of his elder brother, whose son, the sixth Earl of Leicester, was Lord Warden of the Cinque Ports from 1717 to 1728 and Lord Lieutenant of the county from 1727 to 1737. Leicester ruled from the mediaeval mansion of Penshurst near the Sussex border, surrounded by estates in

2. C. Morris, ed., *The Journeys of Celia Fiennes* (London, 1949), p. 136. Morris explains that "Scales" is Cadiz.

3. E. Hasted, *The History and Topographical Survey of the County of Kent*, 2nd ed. (Canterbury, 1797–1801), vol. 1, p. 301.

4. G. Holmes, *British Politics in the Age of Anne* (London, 1967), p. 433.

the divisions of Sevenoaks and Tonbridge. In 1747, the house of Sidney's history in Kent ended with the death of the seventh earl, allegedly insane.[5] The power of Lionel Cranfield, Duke of Dorset, radiated from the Renaissance palace of Knole, high on a hill above the market town of Sevenoaks. He held land in nine parishes, all in the Sevenoaks division,[6] and the offices of Lord Warden of the Cinque Ports from 1708 to 1712, 1714 to 1717, and 1728 to 1765, of Lord Lieutenant from 1724 to 1727 and 1746 to 1765, and of custos rotulorum from 1724 to 1765. Yet the duke's power was insufficient to secure the election of his eldest son as knight of the shire in 1734.

The earls of Rockingham, Lords Lieutenant and custodes rotulorum from 1705 to 1724, and Lords Lieutenant from 1737 to 1745, were the greatest landholders in the county during the first half of the eighteenth century. Their power reached its height in 1736 with the marriage of the second earl to the Kentish heiress, Katherine Furnese. The second earl and countess rented lands in thirty-eight parishes spread over four divisions to over 140 persons.[7] Yet even this vast accumulation may have been insufficient to overawe a county of 413 parishes divided among fourteen divisions and inhabited by some 8,000 voters. When the second earl died childless in 1745, the Rockingham lands were split, and their threat to the county's independence—if threat it was—was at an end. As the proverb indicated, Kent was too large, too prosperous, and too populous to be captured by an aristocratic raid on its territory. Especially was it populous in its gentry.

In no county in seventeenth-century England were there more gentry per acre than in Kent. Approximately one thousand families formed a community of gentry knit together by ties of neighbourhood, landownership, and marriage. Over two-thirds of the gentry of mid-seventeenth-century Kent chose Kentish brides, and the propensity to marry a country-woman increased as one moved further along the Dover Road from London's outskirts to the Kentish coast. The bond between the gentry and their county was emphasized physically and metaphysically by the pattern of their landownership. Compared to mid-seventeenth-century gentry of other counties, the gentry of Kent

5. E. Hasted, *The History and Topographical Survey of the County of Kent,* 1st ed. (Canterbury, 1778–1799), vol. 1, pp. 401, 413–414.

6. K. von den Steinen, "The Fabric of an Interest: The First Duke of Dorset and Kentish and Sussex Politics, 1705–1765" (Ph.D. diss., U.C.L.A., 1969), p. 152.

7. Kent A.O., U471/A3, Rental of the Countess of Rockingham's estate, 1746; Rockingham Castle, Rental of Lewis Watson's Kentish Estates, 1753; Rental of the Earl of Rockingham's Paternal Estates in Kent, 1742.

had a relatively low proportion of their total estates in other counties; and a remarkably high proportion of those whose Kentish estates entitled them to gentry status resided in the county, on their estates. Land bestowed eminence, but duration of landownership entailed additional local status. Three-quarters of the gentry of 1640 had been settled in Kent before the Tudors ascended the throne. Outstanding among these gentry and representative of the values of their community were the twenty to thirty families accorded leadership in the county.[8]

Though it has not been possible to make a detailed and systematic study of the extent to which the marriage and landownership patterns of Kent's eighteenth-century gentry differed from that of their seventeenth-century predecessors, evidence does point to the persistence of at least some elements of the seventeenth-century patterns. If the peers of eighteenth-century Kent were not distinguished from the greater gentry by possession of vastly larger Kentish estates, they were differentiated by greater wealth, derived from possession of large estates in several counties. Of the twenty English and Irish peers inhabiting Kentish seats in 1761, sixteen had seats in other counties.[9] Such diversity of landholding could not be rivalled by the gentry whose leadership was, paradoxically, maintained by the concentration of their attention upon their neighbourhoods. The sense of identification with county and Kentish community also survived the Civil War. Beneath the white marble bust of Miss Anne Milles in Canterbury Cathedral is an inscription recording both her death at age twenty in 1714 and her title—"The Beauty of Kent."[10] While the sense of community among gentry persisted into the eighteenth century, as did the tradition of gentry leadership, the nature of Kent's rulers and of their leadership subtly changed. A study of the personnel of the commission of the peace becomes an inquiry into changes in the composition and modes of leadership in the upper ranks of Kentish society.

1. THE COMPOSITION OF KENT'S COMMISSION OF THE PEACE

Naturally, the structure of Kent's 'natural governors'—the gentry—was reflected in its actual government, the commission of the peace. In

8. A. M. Everitt, *The Community of Kent and the Great Rebellion 1640–60* (Leicester, 1966), pp. 33–36, 42–43.

9. *The Court and City Register* (London, 1761).

10. Hasted, *History of Kent,* 2nd ed., vol. 12, p. 378.

1586, there were more justices of the peace in Kent than in any county in England,[11] and in 1679 Kent's commission was second only to that of Middlesex. The commission of the early seventeenth century was composed of representatives of the twenty to thirty major gentry families, associated with an equal number of lesser gentry and gentlemen of the law. The barristers brought legal expertise and the authority of the hallowed and ancient laws of the land to the commission of the county. As a group the gentry lent the luster and prestige of time-honoured and accepted leadership to the commission of the peace.

Though the county's commission in 1679 numbered more than twice that of 1636, it is clear that the later commission was the direct heir of the social traditions of the earlier. Eighteen of the fifty-six gentry families on the commission of 1636 were represented in the commission of 1679. As the size of the 1679 commission indicates, the definition of gentry community may have been extended; yet it was not changed. The justices of 1679 may have been divided by political allegiance, but they were united by common status. All but one of those on the commissions of March and July 1679 can be identified through published genealogies and histories of the county. Possessors of landed wealth, members of families which had long been acknowledged as the county's natural rulers, residents of a county free from aristocratic dominance, Kent's justices were independent, and an independent bench was the ideal of local government. Justices of lesser status would be "creatures of their superiors, or . . . influenced by the Fees they can get, or by Animosity to greater Men,"[12] but an eminent bench could administer the law impartially, affected by neither fear nor envy nor favour. Though the justices on Kent's bench at the accession of George III could likewise claim impartiality, their understanding of the connotations of 'independence' differed from that of the justices of 1679. Change in the status of those elevated to Kent's bench would subtly transform perceptions of the social standing necessary to guarantee appropriate judicial conduct, and alter the justices' assessment of the rewards and responsibilities of their office. The status of the justices of 1679 was higher than that of any group of justices placed upon the bench in the next nine decades.

Status is a quality and therefore not easily measured. An inhabitant

11. E. Moir, *The Justice of the Peace* (Harmondsworth, Middx., 1969), p. 30.

12. B.L., Add. MSS 38446, f. 333, T. Russell to Lord Hawkesbury, Sept. 17, 1789; see also Herts. R.O., Panshanger MSS D/EP/F155, Sir H. Mackworth to [Cowper], Oct. 6, 1714.

of seventeenth-century Kent would have had little difficulty in estimating the social status of his governors, but the intuition of the seventeenth-century Kentishman is both deficient in and insufficient for the historian. Unlike the seventeenth-century Kentishman, the historian cannot judge the justice by his attire, cannot hear the rumours circulating in the county, and cannot be influenced by the justice's demeanour. It is only by chance that the historian learns that "Sir John [Hales] labors under the most unhappy character of any Gentleman, that has an Estate in our County, not so much for his Religio as for the address of his temper."[13] Similarly, while his judgment of status served the Kentishman's need, the historian must be able to back judgment with proof, and proof of the status of groups of persons must rest upon evidence which is both accessible and quantifiable.

It seems reasonable that, if a justice is not mentioned in the published pedigrees of Kent's gentry; if his residence, lands, memorial plaque, or charitable donations are not mentioned in an exhaustive twelve-volume history of the country published at the end of the eighteenth century and later enlarged to cover the Blackheath division in even greater detail; if he again escapes mention in local histories of those parishes near London or the Thames subject to the most change, or in a compendious account of the church monuments in the less distinguished diocese of the county;[14] if he was not a member of Parliament, sheriff of the county, or mayor of a Kentish borough; if his name cannot be found in lists of those holding office under the central government; if he is listed neither in the university registers nor in those of the Inns of Court—then he must have been a comparative nonentity, not obviously a member of the community of county gentry by virtue of birth, marriage, wealth, connection, estate, or education.

13. Bodleian Lib., Ballard MSS, vol. 15, f. 103, Rev. Jo[hn] Johnson to [Dr. Charlett], June 5, 1711.

14. Hasted, *The History of Kent,* 2nd ed.; H. H. Drake, ed. *Hasted's History of Kent, Corrected, Enlarged and Continued to the Present Time, Part I, The Hundred of Blackheath* (London, 1886); W. T. Vincent, *The Records of the Woolwich District,* 2 vols. (London, [n.d.]); J. Dunkin, *The History and Antiquities of Dartford with Topographical Notes of the Neighbourhood* (London, 1845); E. L. S. Horsburgh, *Bromley, Kent from the earliest times to the present century . . . with a New Introduction and Appendix to the 1971 Edition* (Wakefield, Yorkshire, 1971); C. Freeman, *The History, Antiquities, Improvements, etc. of the parish of Bromley, Kent* (Bromley, 1832); R. Borrowman, *Beckenham Past and Present* (Beckenham, 1910); N. Dews, *The History of Deptford* (London, 1884); E. A. Webb, G. W. Miller, and J. Beckwith, *The History of Chislehurst* (London, 1899); W. Shrubsole and S. Denne, *The History and Antiquities of Rochester and its Environs* (Rochester, 1772); J. Thorpe, *Registrum Roffense: or, A Collection of Antient Records . . . of the Diocese and Cathedral Church of Rochester* (London, 1769).

Three categories were chosen to determine the relative status of the justices who do meet one or more of the above criteria. It is assumed that possession of the office of justice accrued honour to its possessor and his family. In demonstrating that it was able to perpetuate honour and power by obtaining the appointment of descendants to the commission, the family both enhanced and revealed its status. Therefore, that a justice had his father or paternal grandfather on the commission is taken as one indicator of status, and that he was able to pass the honour of appointment to the next generation is taken as another. The third indicator of status to be examined is education. Since it was usual for a member of the gentry to be registered at the Inns of Court in the seventeenth century and rather unusual in the eighteenth century, attendance at an Inn cannot be used to measure the relative status of groups of justices appointed at intervals separated by several decades. The total number of attendants at the universities also declined throughout the reigns of the later Stuarts and the first two Hanoverians. Yet the decrease in the tendency of the gentry to educate their sons at the universities was not as drastic as that in the population as a whole. There was no perceptible diminution in the tendency of the baronets on Kent's commission to claim the prestige of university attendance and in 1743 there was a clear relationship between university attendance and the social status of Kent's justices.[15] Those justices who had attended university had greater estates and were more likely to have both forbears and descendants on the commission than justices who had not attended university. University attendance was still a symbol of status. Therefore, though an argument as to status based on comparison of the university attendance of one group of justices with that of another appointed several decades later is not totally persuasive, neither is it entirely vitiated by the decline in the gentry's patronage of the universities.

Education and the hereditability of a place on the commission are crude indicators of status, bound to distort the actual rank of some justices. William Perry, custos rotulorum of the county of Radnor, son-in-law of the sixth Earl of Leicester and, through his wife, master of the Sidney's Penshurst estates, appears in the tables as a justice who had neither descendant nor forbear upon the commission, but simply attended university. The purpose of the following examination is to determine the social status of the 1,098 gentlemen named in Kent's

15. Appendix C, table C-4.

commissions between 1679 and 1761. The justices are arrayed in groups, no group numbering less than forty-five. When individuals are merged in groups of this size, distortions of individual status induced by the inflexible nature of the categories chosen to determine status have little significance. Fortunately, an opportunity to test the application of these criteria is close at hand.

It has been claimed that James II's selection of justices was an affront to the gentry of England. According to the criteria chosen to measure status, it was. Of the total of ninety-seven justices appointed by James, eighty-five had not sat upon the bench before—and deservedly so. While 35 percent of the commission in 1679 could proclaim that father or paternal grandfather had graced the bench, only 23 percent of James's new appointees could claim such prestige. Thirty-five percent of the commission in 1679 had attended university, but only 14 percent of the new justices. Forty percent of the justices in 1679 had been registered at the Inns of Court, but only 26 percent of the new rulers of the county. Even omission from the calculation of those identified as Dissenters or Catholics—unlikely aspirants for the benefits of an Anglican education or for judicial honours in Restoration England—does not endow the remainder with greater prestige.[16] Of the sixty-eight justices first placed on the commission by James II who were neither Catholics nor Dissenters, 22 percent cannot even be identified. Clearly, James's nominees for county leadership were marginal members, if members at all, of the community of those who ought to rule Kent. Such certainly was the opinion of succeeding regimes. While 43 percent of the justices of 1679 would be followed upon the bench by their immediate descendants, only 19 percent of the justices first advanced to the commission by James were so able to perpetuate their glory. James's appointment of justices who would adhere to his policies had flouted the tradition of rule in Kent.[17]

Similarly, James's manipulation of the commission had produced

16. The calculation of the number of Catholics and Dissenters among James's appointees is based on: the return for Kent in Sir G. Duckett, *Penal Laws and Test Act 1687–1688,* 2 vols. (London, 1882); a list of Popish recusants in Kent, House of Lords MSS, Main Papers no. 321 (c52), Dec. 4, 1680; a list of those under prosecution for recusancy in 1685, *CSPD, James II,* vol. 1, no. 1874, Nov. 9, 1685; a list of those receiving a dispensation from taking the oaths, *CSPD, James II,* vol. 2, no. 1414, Feb. 4, 1687. It is likely that this enumeration includes almost all the Catholics who were justices, but misses some Dissenters. On the other hand, the omission of Dissenters should not drastically affect the argument about status, as some Dissenters sat on Kent's commission after 1689 and had graced Kent's bench during the Interregnum.

17. For tables revealing the status of the justices of 1679–1761, see appendix B.

unwonted instability in the composition of Kent's bench. Even when compared to Charles II's removal of judicial opponents, James's measures seem excessive. While Charles had expunged the names of twenty-five justices from the commission between 1680 and 1685, James eliminated fifty-one, and the treatment of James's justices after the revolution was equally draconian. James's purge was followed by a purge of those whom James had considered acceptable. In 1689, 73 percent of those whom James had elevated to the bench and 78 percent of those whom he had allowed to remain on the bench were excised from the commission. Of the 112 justices on Kent's bench in September 1685, only eight enjoyed uninterrupted tenure of their office during the next four years.[18]

Though three-quarters of those whom James had removed and half of those dismissed by Charles were once more on Kent's bench by 1689, neither political manipulation of the commission nor the concomitant erosion of the status of appointees ceased after the Glorious Revolution. As it was expected and perhaps administratively necessary that the number on Kent's bench approximate that in the early 1680s, and as several eminent justices were dismissed in the purge of 1689, those regulating the commission at William's accession looked favourably upon gentlemen slightly lower in the social scale than the justices of 1679. Yet, that party warfare at Westminster would be reflected in the commissions became apparent only when Somers became Lord Keeper in 1693. Contemporaries could not mistake the party bias in his appointments. When the Tories obtained power, they removed three-quarters of those appointed during Somers' first year in office. The status of those appointed during Somers' tenure of office is slightly lower than that of the justices of 1679. Conversely, the status of those appointed by the Tories between July 1700 and 1704[19] is markedly higher than that of Somers' appointees, indicating that those who would have been appointed to the commission between 1693 and 1700 if the selection had not been politically biased had been ex-

18. This and all succeeding numerations of justices do not include justices in the honourary clause or those who are the sons of peers. The figures of those removed are minimal, including only those who are known to have been alive at the date of removal. The figure for those removed by James does not include the nine justices he first removed and then reappointed.

19. In Kent, the group of Tory appointees does not include those added in the summer of 1705. Though Wright remained Lord Keeper until the autumn of 1705, Kent's Tory Lord Lieutenant and custos was replaced in April 1705 by the Whig Lord Rockingham, and the first commission issued under Rockingham, in July 1705, restored several of the Whigs who had been purged by the Tories.

cluded. Nonetheless there is a disturbing note even in this seemingly socially impeccable group. Eleven percent of the Tory appointees cannot be identified, and so the elevation of those who in 1679 would have possessed a legitimate claim to a seat on the bench was accompanied by the appointment of several who were honoured simply because the Tories, like the Whigs before them, were seeking political supporters. During Cowper's first term of office, Kent's Whigs chose to rely upon appointees of a status only slightly lower than that of Kent's traditional rulers, and so it was left to Anne's last Lord Chancellor and the first two Lord Chancellors of the first Hanoverian to decrease decisively the social standing considered requisite for elevation to Kent's bench. Between 1711 and 1719, the Lord Chancellors scoured Kent's commission of opponents and embellished it with allies. Harcourt removed thirty-six and appointed ninety-three; Cowper eliminated fifty-three and honoured eighty-nine; and in 1719 Macclesfield dismissed thirty justices and raised twenty-one to Kent's bench.[20] The groups of justices who were first awarded a place upon the bench between 1711 and 1723 could boast a status only marginally higher than that of those appointed by James II, but by the 1720s marginal gentlemen were no longer considered unsuitable for the government of Kent.

Horrified protests against the appointment of unfit governors fill both contemporary and historians' accounts of the reign of James II. Few if any such aspersions were cast upon the bench at the accession of George III. And yet a large proportion of the justices at mid-century were just as undistinguished as James's appointees. Though the average status of the justices appointed between 1724 and 1761 was higher than that of their immediate predecessors, Kent's bench at mid-century was still less illustrious than that of 1679. Since the commission of 1761 listed almost twice as many justices as those of the last years of Charles II's reign, it endowed a much greater number of minor gentry and gentlemen with the power to rule Kent and so placed a greater proportion of the marginal members of Kent's elite upon its bench. The parties' manipulation of the commission had accustomed the county to the justice of lesser degree.

Packing of the bench by party politicians was more acceptable than James's manipulation of the commission because party politicians, un-

20. The figures for removals do not include those removed and restored by the same Lord Chancellor. The figures for appointments do include those removed by one Lord Chancellor and reappointed by another.

like James, were able to produce and reflect the increasing party identification of Kent's gentry and gentlemen. Unlike either Charles II or James II, the politicians in the half century after the Glorious Revolution were increasingly able to identify their allies and opponents in the county. While Charles II had expunged the names of some of the county's prominent Whigs from its commission, it is not evident that he succeeded in discovering appointees who would be any more prone to support his policies than those he permitted to remain upon the bench. When, in 1687, Kent's Lord Lieutenant asked the justices whether they would agree to repeal of the Test and Penal acts and vote for those pledged to repeal, the justices appointed between 1680 and 1685 were no more and no less inclined to support James's policies than those who had been on the bench since 1679. James in his turn had attempted to impose unnatural alliances on Kent's elite. By reinstating a fifth of those whom his brother had removed and simultaneously appointing Dissenters and Catholics to the commission, James was trying to secure an alliance of the extremes against the middle. He was unsuccessful. Even though Sir Edward Dering was reinserted in the commission by James, who thereby hoped to expunge the insult of Dering's omission in 1680, Dering combined with seven other of the county's leading gentry (five of whom had been dismissed from the bench by James) to declare for the Prince of Orange.[21] Likewise, the removal of justices immediately after the Glorious Revolution reveals the absence of a connection between the alliances of justices as perceived by James and those which actually formed in the county. Of those removed after the Revolution, an almost identical proportion would be reappointed by Whigs and Tories in the reigns of the last Stuarts. Since James's analysis of political affiliation had not accorded with that of the justices, and since in 1689 a considerable number of justices had not yet committed themselves to a party, the central government's manipulation of the commission in the 1680s does not reflect the political divisions among Kent's elite.

In contrast, after the Glorious Revolution manipulation of the commission's composition resulted in a growing sense of party identification among the justices, an identification increasingly made by the national government and increasingly acknowledged by the justices themselves. That during the first two decades of the eighteenth century successive administrations exhibited an increasing tendency to label

21. B.L., Add. MSS 52924, unpaginated.

those appointed by the preceding administration as political enemies is indicative both of the growth of the national government's assumption of connection between local political groups and national political party, and of the development from somewhat fluid local politics of increasingly rigid local political parties. As table 11(a) reveals, the Tory administration of 1700 to 1704 was suspicious of those appointed under Somers; the Tory administration of 1711 to 1713 regarded appointment under the Whigs of 1705 to 1710 as presumptive grounds for removal; the Whig administration of 1714 to 1719 held similar views about those appointed during the first Tory regime and apparently viewed appointment under the second Tory government as a virtual declaration of political and perhaps treasonous opposition. Similarly, successive national governments developed an increasingly accurate memory of the insults paid their local supporters. As table 11(b) reveals, the probability that a justice removed under one administration would be reappointed by the next administration increased with the intensification of party strife and the emergence of more clear-cut political parties.

And the justices' actions indicated that the emergence of party identification among members of the commission was not merely a mirage tantalizing the politicians at Westminster. The pattern of party in Kent emerges with startling clarity from the pollbooks of 1713 and 1715.[22] Table 12 shows that when the county went to the polls, the majority of those justices who voted who had been appointed between 1700 and 1710 voted for the party which had honoured them, but a minority voted for their presumptive enemies. Though the presence of party in Kent before 1711 is obvious, it is also apparent that between 1700 and 1710, the national government had not been exclusively partisan in its policy of appointment, and that the gentlemen of Kent had not allowed themselves to be totally governed by rigid and mutually exclusive political allegiance. After 1710, the situation changed. The pollbooks reveal both an overwhelmingly partisan policy of appointment on the part of the government and an equally strong party identification among those appointed to the bench. Even the Whig preference of the appointees of July 1711 reveals the strength of party. The removal of thirty justices in February 1711 had immediately been followed by the restoration of five of these justices in July 1711. The list of ten appointees of July 1711 is overwhelmingly Whig—quite possibly representative of the pressure of

22. Kent A.O., Q/RPe1/1713; Bodleian Lib., Rawlinson MSS B338.

TABLE 11 GROWTH IN PARTY AFFILIATION OF KENT'S JUSTICES AS PERCEIVED BY THE NATIONAL GOVERNMENT[a]

(a) APPOINTMENT AND ELIMINATION

Justices on Commission	Appointees: Total	Eliminated: Number	Eliminated: Percent	Remainder: Total	Eliminated: Number	Eliminated: Percent
Justices on Feb. 1700 Commission	Appointees of July 1693-Feb. 1700 on 1700 Commission: Total	Eliminated 1700–1704 Number	Percent	Remainder of Feb. 1700 Commission: Total	Eliminated 1700–1704 Number	Percent
134	49	18	37%	85	17	20%
Justices on 1710 Commission	Appointees of 1705–1710 on 1710 Commission: Total	Eliminated 1711–1713 Number	Percent	Remainder of 1710 Commission: Total	Eliminated 1711–1713 Number	Percent
181	61	22	36%	120	11	9%
Justices on 1713 Commission	Appointees of 1700–1704 on 1713 Commission: Total	Eliminated 1714–1719 Number	Percent	Remainder of 1713 Commission: Total	Eliminated 1714–1719 Number	Percent
206	35	16	46%	97	13	13%
	Appointees of Feb. 1711 and 1713 on 1713 Commission: Total	Eliminated 1714–1719 Number	Percent			
	74	48	65%			

TABLE 11 *Continued*

(b) REAPPOINTMENT

Justices Eliminated		Eliminated Justices Who Were Reappointed		
Year Eliminated	Number	Year reappointed	Number	Percent reappointed
1693–1700	9	1700–1704	4	44%
1700–1704	42	1705–1710	17	40
1711–1713	36	1714–1719	27	75

[a]In both parts (a) and (b) only those known to have been alive at the time of omission from the commission are noted. As the date of death of some justices cannot be ascertained, the figures for those eliminated are minimal ones. For the same reason, it was impossible to determine how many of those eliminated died before a new government could restore them to the bench. Therefore, this consideration is not reflected in (b). It should be noted that neither (a) nor (b) includes among the group of justices who were eliminated those justices who were subsequently restored by the same Lord Chancellor who removed them from the bench. It should also be noted that the number of justices removed from Kent's bench in 1700–1704 in this table differs from the number given in table 1. Table 1 presents the number of justices which House of Lords, Main Papers, MSS no. 2011, March 20, 1703[4] states were removed. For the inaccuracies of the House of Lords list, see chapter III, n. 36. Table 11 also includes the two justices removed from Kent's bench after the House of Lords list was compiled.

TABLE 12 THE PARTY AFFILIATIONS OF KENT'S JUSTICES: THE ELECTIONS OF 1713 AND 1715

	Total in group	*Number of Justices voting*	*Whig in 1713 and/or 1715*	*Percent of those voting*	*Tory in 1713 and/or 1715*	*Percent of those voting*	*Split vote or change in party allegiance*	*Percent of those voting*
Added July 1700–1704 and alive 1713[a]	41	22	9	41%	13	59%	0	0%
Added 1705–1710 and alive 1713	59	43	31	72	7	16	5	12
Added Feb. 1711 and 1713 and alive 1713	80	64	3	5	58	90	3	5
Added July 1711 and alive 1713	8	7	5	71	1	14	1	14
Added Oct. 1714	54	39	38	97	0	0	1	3
Added 1715–1719	58	30	27	90	0	0	3	10

[a]The size of judicial groups in this table differs from that of the groups in table 11(a). Unlike table 11(a) this table numbers in the group of those appointed during a period all those appointed in that period, including those who had been appointed and removed in an earlier period. Unlike table 11(a), this table also includes those who had been removed from the commission but were still alive.

the county's Whig Lord Lieutenant and custos rotulorum upon the Lord Chancellor. Of the eight appointees of July 1711, alive in 1713, four were left out of the 1713 commission, and all four voted for the Whig candidates. The appointees of July 1711, like those of February 1711, of 1713, and of 1714–1719, are symbolic of the political polarization of the county. In using appointment to the bench to win adherents, the national politicians had drawn Kent's rulers into party politics, and the appointment of lesser justices had increased both the political participation and local power of families formerly on the periphery of both politics and local government.

In the reigns of the first two Hanoverians, party struggle continued to give a distinctive cast to Kent's bench. Whig hegemony at Westminster meant Whig rulers for the county. Compare the status, landholdings, and judicial fate of the Tories appointed by Harcourt between 1711 and 1713 with those of the Whigs appointed by Cowper between 1714 and 1718. The Tories were as landed as the Whigs. An identical proportion of each group cannot be identified. An identical proportion of each group had attended university, and had a father or paternal grandfather on Kent's commission. But the proportion of Whigs who perpetuated their lineage upon the bench was double that of the Tories.[23] The same tale is told by the pollbooks for the elections of 1734 and 1754. As table 13 indicates, those Tories whom the poll clerks considered worthy of the title *Esquire* were less likely to be justices than Whigs of similar status.[24]

As these pollbooks reveal, Whig hegemony did not translate into Whig monopoly. A few Tories were being reinstated in Kent's commission before the accession of George II. It was the replacement of the Earl of Rockingham by the Duke of Dorset as Lord Lieutenant and custos on Rockingham's death in 1724 that occasioned the new policy of reconciliation. Shortly after assuming office Dorset perused a list of those removed from Kent's bench since 1714,[25] and then reappointed seven former justices. Dorset's action by no means signalled the disintegration of party in Kent. At the election of 1727, 44 percent of the voters among the duke's appointees chose the Tories, while 94 percent of the voters among those elevated to the bench between 1714 and 1723 supported the Whigs.[26] Nor did Dorset's early appointments foreshadow a nonpartisan policy of appointment to the bench. In the first three decades of Hanoverian rule, only the most distinguished of Kent's Tories were allowed to rule the county. As Dorset honoured a large proportion of the eminent Tories in the mid-1720s, only a few more Tories were allowed to clamber upon the bench in the 1730s and 1740s. For instance, only one of the nineteen new justices of 1734 had voted for the Tories in the election of that year. It would have been difficult to justify the exclusion of this obdurate appointee. James Des Bouverie was one of the wealthiest gentlemen in the county. In 1747, he would be elevated to the peerage as Viscount Folkestone upon payment of £12,000.

23. See appendix B tables B-1 through B-4 and appendix C, table C-1.

24. *The Poll for Knights of the Shire to Represent the County of Kent . . . Taken the 15th and 16th of May 1734* (London, 1734); *The Poll for Knights of the Shire to Represent the County of Kent . . . Taken . . . the 1st and 2d of May 1754* (London, 1754).

25. Kent A.O., Q/JL1

26. The pollbook for 1727 is Kent A.O., Q/RPe1/1727.

TABLE 13 JUDICIAL APPOINTMENT AND PARTY AFFILIATION AT KENT'S ELECTIONS OF 1734 AND 1754

		Whig		*Tory*		*Split*	
	Total	*Number*	*Percent*	*Number*	*Percent*	*Number*	*Percent*
1734							
Esquires who are J.P.s:	47	24	51%	17	36%	6	13%
Esquires who are not J.P.s:	36	11	31	22	61	3	8
1754							
Esquires who are J.P.s:	91	73	80	15	17	3	3
Esquires who are not J.P.s	84	47	56	35	42	2	2

It was not until mid-century that the composition of Kent's bench forecast the end of party strife.[27] When the county went to the polls in 1754, 29 percent of those justices appointed in 1751 who voted plumped for the sole Tory candidate, while a further 9 percent split their vote. In contrast, of those appointed before 1751 who voted, only 14 percent opted for the Tory and only 3 percent split their vote. Since Kent's Tories were so debilitated in 1754 that only one Tory candidate stood for election, the remarkable support given the Tory candidate by those recently appointed to Kent's bench indicates a policy of appointment which was only slightly partisan. By 1751, the composition of Kent's commission presaged the political truce which would characterize the county's politics from the accession of George III until the French Revolution.

As would be expected, gradual modification in the policy of partisan exclusion was reflected in the status of those appointed to Kent's bench. Readmission of the more prominent Tories resulted in an increase in the average status of appointees: the appointees of 1724 to 1743 were more eminent than the justices of 1711 to 1723, and the

27. At the election of 1734, 16 percent of the justices who had voted in 1727 either completely or partially altered their party allegiance. This is a remarkable switch of party support. Of the justices who voted in 1727 and also had voted at one or both of the elections of 1713 and 1715, only 6 percent chose one or more candidates of a party different from that for which they had opted when they last voted. It was the Whig party which suffered most from the change of judicial allegiance in 1734, but the repugnance of some Whigs for Walpole and the excise is indicative neither of a decline in party struggle nor even of a fragmentation of party. In 1754, only 3 percent of those justices who voted a straight party ticket in 1734 altered their allegiance, while the six justices who split their vote in 1734 and voted in 1754 voted a party ticket. As Kent's voters were fairly evenly divided between the Whig and Tory camps, the justices' alteration of allegiance in 1734 reveals the shift in political alignment which enabled Kent's Tories to prolong the period of party warfare into mid-century.

appointees of 1751 to 1761 more illustrious than those of 1724 to 1743. Nonetheless, the commission of the mid-century never attained the distinction of Kent's bench in 1679, for reinstatement of more eminent families was not accompanied by restraint in the appointment of the less illustrious. In the half century after the Glorious Revolution, political strife had allowed lesser gentry and gentlemen access to the bench in numbers undreamed of in the reign of Charles II. At mid-century, political considerations still demanded the appointment of sufficient Whigs to counter the Tories, and withdrawal of the privilege of government from the minor gentry would have been impolitic.

Inevitably, recognition of the claims of less eminent nominees to a place in the commission involved acknowledgment of the entitlement of the more illustrious to a seat upon the bench. By 1743, the greater landowners virtually entailed judicial office upon their heirs.[28] The number of justices appointed between 1751 and 1761 who represented families which graced the bench for three successive generations was 60 percent greater than the number of justices in 1679 who were similarly members of a three-generational judicial lineage. Either the group of greater landholders had expanded since 1679, or the social definition of the greater gentry had been broadened to include those who in 1679 had been marginal to the group, or the national government of the mid-eighteenth century exercised less discretion in the choice of justices than the government of 1679. Most probably the entrenchment of the greater gentry in the commission was the product of all three. The image of the greater gentry as inevitable justices was manufactured in the eighteenth century.

Both the increase in the number of justices and the entrenchment of the greater gentry on the bench can be seen as the result first of party strife, and then of the diminution of that strife. So clearly did party politics affect the appointment of justices between 1693 and 1723, so clearly do the tables reveal variation in status between groups of justices appointed by successive administrations that the differences between these groups of justices in themselves indicate the existence of a *deus ex machina*—in this case a Lord Chancellor furthering the cause of his party. No similarly clear-cut division between groups of appointees appears on examination of the status of those appointed to the commission after 1723. Nonetheless, a motif first apparent in the

28. See appendix C, table C-3. The judicial prerogatives of the greater gentry would be even more evident if families which failed in the male line were excluded from the table.

judicial appointments of the age of party strife continued to affect the pattern of judicial rule. Marginal justices, justices whose claim to gentility was questionable, were still placed upon the commission. Even though the status of the average mid-century appointee was greater than that of the justices appointed under Anne and George I, a considerable proportion of mid-century justices were barely gentlemen.[29] So much at least is indicated by the fact that 11 percent of those appointed between 1724 and 1761 cannot even be identified. These marginal justices had even less prestige and local power than the minor gentry, and so it might be expected that decline in the parties' frantic search for adherents would virtually eliminate these mere or near gentlemen from the bench. Their continued presence on the commission indicates that, during the late seventeenth and early eighteenth centuries, demands other than those of politics were also affecting judicial appointment. In the reign of George II the demands of administration, demands earlier obscured by political strife, placed an increasingly obvious stamp upon the image of Kent's government.

Both new administrative demands and increasing acknowledgment of these demands are most clearly seen in the change in the pattern of distribution of justices.[30] In 1680, 54 percent of the justices resident in the county lived in five of the county's petty sessional divisions: Bearsted, Malling, Ashford, Home, and Wingham. In these divisions, clustered round Maidstone and Canterbury and scattered across the hills bordering the Weald, lived the greater proportion of Kent's

29. Both the increasing entrenchment of the greater gentry and the increasing presence of minor gentry and gentlemen are indicated by increase in the disparity between the status of groups of appointees and the status of justices on any one commission. From the 1720s onwards, the status of the justices on any one commission was always markedly higher than the status of the justices in any one group of appointees. Obviously, the less eminent justices were older than the more eminent when they ascended the bench, and died sooner after their appointment. So, any group of appointees contained a greater proportion of the less eminent than the commission as a whole. That by mid-century judicial office became virtually hereditary among the greater gentry resulted in commissions which seem in some ways more illustrious than those of Restoration England. Only 35 percent of the justices of 1679 were preceded on the bench by a father or paternal grandfather, but 41 percent of the justices in the commission of 1743 and 45 percent of the justices in the commission of 1761 descended from a judicial father or paternal grandfather. Nonetheless, two indicators of status reveal that this enhancement of judicial eminence reflects the entrenchment of the greater gentry rather than a marked rise in the eminence of most justices. Only 30 percent of the justices in the 1743 commission and 29 percent of the justices in the 1761 commission were able to endow their heirs with judicial office; in contrast, 43 percent of the justices of 1679 were succeeded on the bench by their heirs. Likewise, 11 percent of the commission of 1743 and 10 percent of the commission of 1761 cannot be identified, while only one of the 1679 justices cannot be traced in Kent's histories and published genealogies.

30. See appendix D, table D-1.

gentry.[31] The number of justices on Kent's commission almost doubled between 1680 and 1761. Yet, the areas that received the greatest increase in justices were not those most noted for the prestige of their residents.

The remarkable increase in the number of justices in the Sevenoaks division, a pleasant land of green hills and valleys, may be in part attributed to the power of its most illustrious resident—the Duke of Dorset, who, as Lord Lieutenant from 1724 to 1727 and 1746 to 1765, and custos rotulorum from 1724 to 1765, naturally used his office to win friends and influence neighbours—almost all of whom were in the division of Sevenoaks. The increase in the number of justices in other divisions demands different explanations. Four of these divisions were those portions of Kent whose economy and population expanded most rapidly during the eighteenth century. The Blackheath division bordering London, and fated to be annexed by the metropolitan colossus in the nineteenth century, was becoming both suburb of villa and minor mansion and repository of the labourers flocking to the Deptford docks and Woolwich artillery.[32] Its development affected those divisions adjacent to it—Bromley, a division of farms, market town and minor social centre;[33] and Dartford, an area of market gardens near the Thames, with farms and minor industries along its inland rivers.[34] Contiguous to Dartford was the Rochester division, expanding under the influence of the dockyards at Chatham and Queenborough and the growth of the ports of Rochester and Gravesend.[35] And, in all probability, the Sittingbourne division was also one of the areas in the county growing more rapidly in the early eighteenth century. By 1700, Faversham, the major town in the area, was "an example of urban prosperity," prosperity nourished in the

31. Everitt, *Community of Kent,* pp. 19, 27; Hasted, *History of Kent,* 1st ed., vol. 3, p. 670.

32. D. C. Coleman, "Naval Dockyards Under the Later Stuarts," *Economic History Review,* 2nd ser. 6 (1953–1954): 139, 141; D. C. Coleman, "The Economy of Kent Under the Later Stuarts, 1660–1714" (Ph.D. thesis, University of London, 1951), pp. 15–16, 310–311.

33. B. Taylor, "Bromley, Beckenham and Penge, Kent, Since 1750: A Comparative Study of the Changing Geography of Three Towns on the Southern Fringe of the Metropolis" (Ph.D. thesis, University of London, 1966), p. 136.

34. J. Boys, *A General View of the Agriculture of the County of Kent* (London, 1796), pp. 17–18; Coleman, "The Economy of Kent," pp. 202–206, 208; Hasted, *History of Kent,* 2nd ed., vol. 1, p. 270.

35. Coleman, "Naval Dockyards Under the Later Stuarts," pp. 139, 141; Coleman, "The Economy of Kent," pp. 138f., 236–239; H. Rees, "The Medway Towns—Their Settlement, Growth and Economic Development" (Ph.D. thesis, University of London, 1954), p. 314.

eighteenth century by its breweries, gunpowder factories, and coastal trade.[36] And the Dover road, turnpiked during the first half of the eighteenth century, traversed four of these five divisions, bringing trade, coaches, and passengers.[37] So, in four divisions, and perhaps a fifth—Sittingbourne—the need to serve more rapidly growing populations may account for the more rapid rate of expansion of these divisions' complement of justices.

Another set of administrative pressures may also explain the comparatively rapid rate of growth in the number of justices in the Dartford and Sittingbourne divisions as well as that in Cranbrook and Tonbridge. In 1680, there were only three justices in the Dartford division and four in that of Sittingbourne. Neither division was small—the Sittingbourne division was one of the largest in the county—and the sparse scattering of justices would have made access to a justice difficult to all but those in the neighbourhoods of these few justices. Similar difficulties would attend the efforts of the inhabitants of the Kentish Weald to obtain speedy justice. The Weald was a land of heavy clay soil, nourishing sheep, cattle, and great oak trees—the home of prosperous yeomen and clothiers, the "greycoats of Kent."[38] In the eighteenth century, the greater part of the Weald was divided among two petty sessional divisions. Cranbrook, a division encompassing about 90 square miles, possessed but six justices in 1680, and in the area that would become the Tonbridge division there were only two commissioners of the peace.

Administrative need might provide a reason for the more rapid expansion of the commission in the divisions of Blackheath, Bromley, Dartford, Rochester, Sittingbourne, Tonbridge, and Cranbrook than in the other areas of the county. Yet, the timing of the expansion is as significant in understanding the phenomenon as the fact of expansion itself. The major period of expansion in the Rochester, Cranbrook, and Tonbridge divisions, and that of continued rapid growth in the Blackheath, Bromley and Sittingbourne divisions was 1704 to 1713.[39] Political and administrative exigency united in the search for justices

36. Coleman, "The Economy of Kent," pp. 220–222.

37. The effect of the Dover road on the parish and town of Sittingbourne is noted in Hasted, *History of Kent,* 2nd ed., vol. 6, pp. 150f.

38. Boys, *General View . . . of Kent,* pp. 19, 111; Coleman, "The Economy of Kent," pp. 61, 66; A. Everitt, "Nonconformity in Country Parishes," in *Land, Church, and People, Essays Presented to Professor H. P. R. Finberg,* ed. J. Thirsk, *Agricultural History Review,* supp. 18 (1970): 191.

39. Appendix D, table D-1.

to perform the administrative tasks necessary to the county and exercise political influence helpful to the national government. When, from 1714 to 1720, the Whig policy of exclusion reduced the size of the commission to that of 1708, it was these divisions that suffered the greatest loss of justices. Political tools were disposable when no longer useful. It was less easy to displace an established member of the Kentish gentry. Yet, between 1720 and 1743, expansion once again occurred, and once again occurred most markedly in these same divisions. Administrative needs could not long be ignored.

Administrative need therefore established the lesser justice as a permanent and numerically impressive fixture on the bench. In 1743, the average landed wealth of the justices of the Blackheath, Bromley, Sittingbourne, Rochester, Cranbrook, and Tonbridge divisions was notably lower than that of the justices in the rest of the county. So, too, was the likelihood that the justices of these divisions had been preceded on the commission by father or grandfather, would be succeeded on the commission by their sons, or had attended university. And the justices appointed to rule these divisions between 1751 and 1761 perpetuated this dichotomy.[40]

The alteration of the judicial stereotype represented by these new justices was not simply a modification of the old model. True, the justices of the late seventeenth century were selected from among the more eminent landholders, while the new appointees in the Tonbridge and Cranbrook divisions were lesser landholders, as were some of those in the Rochester and Sittingbourne divisions. But the justices of the Blackheath division could not be regarded as gentry of any variety. Isaac Loader, former ironsmith and by 1700 major supplier of iron to the navy, may have had a house in Greenwich "with gardens, orangeries, and other magnificence," but it is not recorded that he was possessed of a landed estate.[41] Sir Ambrose Crowley, justice from 1711 to 1713, was head of the largest iron works in the nation. He had a wharf, warehouses, and a fine Jacobean house in Greenwich, but no estate in Kent.[42] And these were among the more distinguished appointees to the Blackheath bench. Twelve of the twenty-five justices in the Blackheath division in 1743 are not even listed as inhabitants of noteworthy residences. The justices of the Blackheath division ob-

40. Appendix C, tables C-1 and C-2; appendix D, tables D-2 and D-3.

41. M. W. Flinn, *Men of Iron* (Edinburgh, 1962), pp. 149, 173–174; Drake, *Hasted's History of Kent*, pp. 34, 44, 31n.6.

42. *Ibid.*, pp. 79n, 81n.

tained their substance in occupations other than that of landowner, occupations which might not sustain a close scrutiny of their practitioners' pretensions to gentility. In 1835, when twenty-five justices were acting on their commission to maintain the peace in the Blackheath division, the clerk of Blackheath's petty sessions indicated that he preferred not to report on "the Trade or profession of the Justices in this Division." He did not feel that he "ought to be called upon to perform the invidious task of making the Inquiries requisite for arriving at the desired Result unless peremptorily ordered to do so."[43] By the mid-eighteenth century, the precedent for appointing such men as justices of Blackheath was well established. That by 1743 the justices of Blackheath comprised 10 percent of the commission and 13 percent of those who acted on their commission affected the standards for the selection of Kent's justices. Other such men in other parts of the county could now be considered suitable nominees to the bench. In 1751, the Duke of Dorset supported the nomination of Samuel Shepherd of Faversham: "he is zealous and active on all occasions, when the interest of the Government is concern'd [,] he is a man of great substance, and I believe a very honest one, we want justices of this sort, in that part of the County. . . . Shepherd 'tis true is a Brewer, but there are some of that profession about Deptford, that are in the Commission and make very good justices. . . ."[44] Shepherd was appointed, and his brewery still flourishes.

The justices of the Blackheath division stood as an emblem of the changes in the values and gradations of the social hierarchy occurring during the eighteenth century. In the commission as in social consciousness, nonlanded gentlemen were loosely associated with the governing elite. If a gentleman wished to enhance his position and appear a member of the gentry, he might buy a country estate. Unlike the estates of the landed gentry, his estate was not intended to maintain the wealth of his family. Money was expected to flow from other pursuits. Therefore, he bought a small estate—a fine house and a few hundred acres—sufficient to support the appearance of a landed gentleman,[45] but insufficient to maintain the reality of a member of the governing elite, closely involved by economic and personal

43. Kent A.O., Q/CR5, C. A. Smith to H. A. Wildes [deputy clerk of the peace], Greenwich, May 16, 1835.

44. B.L., Add. MSS 35603, f. 307, Duke of Dorset to Hardwicke, July 12, 1751.

45. H. J. Habbakuk, "English Landownership, 1680–1740," *Economic History Review*, 10 (1940): 5.

ties with those he governed. In the seventeenth century, those appointed to the commission were possessed of sufficient wealth and prestige within their communities to command the deference of their inferiors. By the mid-eighteenth century, judicial office was no longer a guarantee that its tenant could as a private individual claim the leadership of his neighbourhood. Nor could the mid-eighteenth-century commission base its claim to deference upon professional association with the mysteries of the law. In 1679, one of every six justices was a barrister, but only one in ten of Kent's mid-century justices illumined his colleagues with the reflected brilliance of legal expertise. No longer was the bench an unadulterated symbol of natural authority.

Inevitably, change in both the number and status of justices altered the image of the commission. In 1679, the commission was a selection from among the landed elite, and the governed could see that their justices had been singled out from among the eminent for a special trust. In contrast, the commission of 1761 included a roll call of the landed elite, and so the entrenchment of the greater gentry justices on the bench transformed these justices from signally honoured individuals into the embodiment of an eminent social stratum. That by 1761 the greater gentry were joined in the commission by increasing numbers of mere gentlemen, individuals not obviously tied to their communities by family background, a tradition of local leadership, or landed estate, emphasized the distance between the governors and the communities they governed. No longer was judicial office a guarantee that its possessor wielded 'natural' authority within a small rural community. Within a few decades, the justice could symbolize the monopoly of the increasing powers of formal government by an elite only tenuously related to their communities.

2. KENT'S BENCH: ACTIVE AND INACTIVE JUSTICES

Though the national government expected that the new commission would act as had its predecessors, alteration in the composition of the commission could not but alter judicial behaviour. By appointing eminent individuals to the bench, the national government conscripted to its service the justices' powers as private individuals, while the justices had volunteered their services because their official powers complemented their roles as unofficial leaders of their communities. As the composition of the commission altered, so would the justices' concept of their responsibilities. In deciding whether they cared to act, the justices of the mid-eighteenth century enacted their analysis of the rewards of their office.

As seventeenth-century justices were both members and leaders of their communities, appointment to the commission reinforced that influence over their neighbours which they already possessed. It was expected and normal that these justices would choose to exercise the powers of their office. The new justices of the mid-eighteenth century—mere gentlemen, gentlemen who had acquired country villas for their summer retreats, minor gentry—stood in a different relation to those they governed. Nonlanded gentlemen possessed wealth and prestige insufficient for the establishment of an interest. It is quite likely that the gentlemen justices were not the obvious leaders of their communities but instead a selection among the more wealthy in urban and semi-urban areas. The majority of the minor gentry lived in areas already captured by the wealthier members of their group. The new pseudo-gentry, those gentlemen who had purchased small estates in order to acquire prestige and a pleasant retreat, were but tenuously tied to their communities. While they attempted to ape the style of gentry life, it is questionable whether they wanted or were able to imitate the substance of gentry power. They might well consider that their time, energy, and wealth could be spent in ways more profitable and enjoyable than involvement in the petty affairs of a rural parish. Gentlemen, minor gentry, and pseudo-gentry wielded relatively little influence before they were appointed to the commission, and it is improbable that exercise of the powers of judicial office would greatly increase that influence. Indeed, it is unlikely that they craved increased influence. When Richard Stratton, director of the Bank of England and resident of a comparatively rural parish in the Blackheath division, was nominated to the commission, the Lord Lieutenant had but one fear: that he would not find the time to act.[46] The Lord Lieutenant's fears were realized; Stratton did not act.

In this, Stratton was typical of his judicial generation. By the mid-eighteenth century, an increasingly large proportion of justices was refusing to assume the burdens of their office. It is difficult to measure this decline in judicial activity exactly. There is no one set of records which completely documents judicial activity for the period 1679 to

46. B.L., Add. MSS 35603, ff. 307–308, Duke of Dorset to Hardwicke, July 12, 1751.

1761. Four types of record do indicate decline in the justices' propensity to act, and to a limited degree measure its extent. First, the records of Assizes hint that in the 1670s almost all justices acted. The documents produced at each Assizes include a list of the commission, the *nomina ministrorum,* and in the 1670s the clerk of Assizes would scribble a notation beside the names of those justices who had not taken the oaths of office. Rarely are more than two or three justices so labelled, and these justices are almost always men who had been appointed to the commission less than two years before that particular Assizes. By Anne's reign the clerk of Assizes was no longer keeping a record of those justices who had not taken their oaths, but the central government both kept and preserved a record of those who chose to act. Justices had to obtain an authorization to take the oaths. The authorization—the writ dedimus—was issued from Chancery through the Crown Office, and there is a book listing justices who obtained a dedimus during Anne's reign.[47] Comparison of the book's list to Kent's judicial records reveals that this book does not note all the justices appointed between 1702 and 1705 who acted. Application for the dedimus could be made to the Crown Office or to the Lord Chancellor's secretary of commissions, and it is possible that this book records only those writs granted through the Crown Office. Therefore, though all the justices appointed during the remainder of Anne's reign whom surviving records show as active are listed in this book, it may still underestimate the justices' desire to serve their sovereign. Even so, this record can be compared with another similar record to reveal decline in judicial activity. There are Crown Office books recording the issue of the dedimus from 1738 to 1786, and books of the Petty Bag Office (whose clerks received two shillings and sixpence of the fee for the dedimus) from 1763 to 1838.[48] These Hanoverian records do list all justices who obtained their dedimus. Of those appointed to Kent's commission between 1706 and 1713, at least 53 percent took the oaths of office within five years of appointment. Of those appointed to Kent's commission between 1743 and 1758, only 35 percent obtained a dedimus within five years.[49] As several of those appointed during Anne's reign were dismissed from office less than five years after their appointment, and as the dedimus book for her reign does not list those justices appointed less than five years before her

47. P.R.O., C193/43.
48. P.R.O., C193/44–45, C220/9/8–9.
49. Peers and peers' sons are excluded from this calculation.

death who obtained a dedimus after her death, the evidence of the dedimus books minimizes the decline in judicial activity.

While his acquisition of a dedimus signalled a justice's intention that he not appear inactive, it is possible that some justices who obtained a dedimus did not act, and very probable that those who obtained a dedimus and remained in the commission for several decades were inactive during some of the period in which they held office. Another source—lists of active justices made by the clerk of the peace or for the Lord Lieutenant—allows estimation both of the percentage of the commission obtaining a dedimus and of the percentage of the commission actually active at a specific date. In 1719, one of the judges riding the Home Circuit ordered the clerk to provide the Lord Chancellor with a list of all justices who resided in the county and refused to act. That list survives. Being conscientious, Kent's clerk listed all justices, whether resident in the county or not. According to his report, 74 percent of all justices and 83 percent of those resident in the county acted on their commission.[50] It is quite possible that the clerk categorized as active justices who rarely acted. However, the next surviving list—which was scribbled by the clerk as he conducted his business in 1737—is restricted to justices actually active, though it does not list all justices whom other records prove were active.[51] At least fifteen faithful servants of the Crown were omitted. Inclusion of the fifteen would mean that a minimum of 62 percent of Kent's justices were assuming the burdens of office. When, in 1775, the Lord Lieutenant obtained a list of all justices resident in the county who acted, he could see that only forty-five magistrates were ruling the county.[52] Though this list again omits some active justices, it is unlikely that more than one-third of Kent's resident justices were actively maintaining the peace. In 1780, the Lord Lieutenant was scanning a list of those justices who had obtained a dedimus; only eighty-two (about 40 percent of the justices then alive) had cared to take the oaths of office.[53]

As the lists of active justices compiled during the eighteenth century are not entirely accurate, recourse must be had to a final method of calculating the number of active justices: compilation of lists of active

50. Kent A.O., Q/JL1; T. B. Howell, ed., *State Trials* (London, 1812), vol. 15, col. 1422, Sir Littleton Powys to Lord Chancellor Parker, Aug. 4, 1719.

51. This list is in Kent A.O., Q/SB 1748.

52. Kent A.O., U269/O96.

53. Kent A.O., Q/JL2.

justices from the documents produced by active justices. There are records of attendants at Quarter Sessions and petty sessions, and sometimes of attendants at licensing sessions; recognizances returned to Quarter Sessions bear judicial signatures, as do settlement orders submitted to Quarter Sessions on appeal; Quarter Sessions order books contain (probably incomplete) lists of the justices who qualified as directed by the act of 1745, and the jail calendars of both Quarter Sessions and Assizes sometimes note the names of the justices who committed the prisoners. To these lists were added those justices who obtained a dedimus less than five years before the date at which activity is being examined.[54] As all these records are much more complete for the 1740s and 1750s than for the first two decades of the century, one would therefore suspect they would suggest that a greater proportion of George II's justices acted than did their predecessors. However, these records yield table 14. Whichever way one calculates it, the propensity of justices to serve their sovereign had declined. By the accession of George III, less than half of the justices obtained a dedimus; at the accession of his great-grandfather, three-quarters of the commission took the oaths of office. By the accession of George III, about 40 percent of the entire commission were actively maintaining the peace; at the accession of his great-grandfather, at least two-thirds of the entire commission accepted the responsibilities of office.

Most negligent were the peers and their offspring, but even in the early eighteenth century these aristocrats had found judicial activity unrewarding. Only one of the seven peers and peers' sons appointed to Kent's commission between 1706 and 1713 took the oaths of office. Of the forty-two peers and peers' sons with estates in the county appointed to the commission between 1743 and 1761, only seven obtained a dedimus. Lack of aristocratic dominance of local government therefore encouraged Kent's greater gentry to seize governmental power.

Analysis of the estates possessed by the non-aristocratic justices in Kent's commission in 1743 reveals one law of judicial behaviour: the larger a justice's estate, the more likely it is that he will act. Of the select group of landowners from which the overwhelming majority of

54. Quarter Sessions papers and Quarter Sessions recognizance rolls at the Kent A.O., and Kent's petty sessions minute books reveal that at least 90 percent of the justices who took out a dedimus at mid-century acted as justices soon after they took out their dedimus. It is very probable that most of the remaining 10 percent also acted, though loss of petty sessions minute books and these justices' failure to sign orders which were appealed to Quarter Sessions have left their activity unrecorded.

TABLE 14 PROPORTION OF KENT'S JUSTICES WHO ACTED[a]

Years	*Number of active justices*	*Number of justices in commission*	*Percent active*
1708–1709	99	(in 1708) 174	57%
1716–1717	117	(in 1716) 206	57
1748–1749	104	(in 1748)[b] 183	57
1758–1759	97	(in 1758) 243	40

[a]Peers and peers' sons are excluded from this table.
[b]Adjusted to exclude ⅝ of those who died between the issue of the commission in 1743 and the issue of the next commission in 1751.

deputy lieutenants were drawn in the 1740s,[55] 76 percent acted in the 1740s. Only 61 percent of the lesser resident justices on Kent's commission in 1743 were similarly inclined. Not only did the greater landowners enthusiastically accept office, but analysis of the relative landed wealth of the justices within each petty sessional division reveals that the two or three justices who possessed the greatest estates in each division—whatever the size of their estates—almost invariably acted. In only four cases did the justice possessed of the greatest landed wealth not act. Sir John Hales, Bart., the greatest landed magnate in the Home division, was a recluse. Having passed the first part of his life as a rake, he spent the last as a hermit. His food was passed up to his window in a basket, and it was only after he had not appeared at his window for two weeks that his house was entered and his dead body discovered.[56] Sir Thomas Dyke, Bart., the greatest magnate of the Dartford division, had estates and residences in both Kent and Sussex. When in Kent, Tory Dyke may have declined association with the acting justices of his division, all of whom had voted for Whig candidates in 1734 and would again vote the Whig ticket in 1754. James Blackmore of Cranbrook, a leading Dissenter,[57] very probably abstained from the Sacraments and thereby disqualified himself for office.[58]

55. Those possessing estates which rate "Hasted points" of five or above. See the introduction to appendix C.
56. Hasted, *History of Kent,* 1st ed., vol. 2, p. 578w.
57. Kent A.O., U269/C148/27, petition to Duke of Dorset, Cranbrook, Nov. 3, 1733.
58. N. C. Hunt, *Two Early Political Associations* (Oxford, 1961), pp. 122–127 explains that even though indemnity acts protecting office holders who had not taken the Sacraments were passed in the first half of the century, indemnity acts were not yet a

The fourth inactive justice and leading landowner of his division was Sir Gregory Page, Bart., of Blackheath. Sir Gregory, heir of an extremely wealthy shipowner, resided in the elegant district of Greenwich bordering Greenwich park, hospital, and observatory. Sir Gregory was no mere merchant. His mansion, ornamented outside by a handsome front with Ionic portico and inside with pictures by Giordano, Battoni, Van Huysum, and Rubens, was one of the landmarks of the area.[59] Perhaps Sir Gregory disdained association with the less exalted brethren of the Blackheath bench, the least distinguished in the county. For, in the Blackheath division, the pattern of leadership prevalent elsewhere in the county was reversed. There, the least landed justices were more likely to act than those possessed of greater estates.

The exception illustrates the rule. The lack of enthusiasm for judicial activity manifested by the Blackheath justices of greater estates is a clue to motives that drove gentry magnates elsewhere in the county to obtain a dedimus. It may well be that the Blackheath landowners simply found the duties of semi-urban magistracy distasteful. It is also possible that Sir Gregory Page, like Richard Stratton, director of the Bank of England and another justice of the Blackheath division, was too busy to act. In other words, rewards that greater gentry derived from judicial activity in other areas were not forthcoming to the Blackheath justice. Constant attention to the quarrels of the poor neither enhanced prestige nor resulted in political power.

Unlike the Blackheath justices, the justices of the other divisions were brought by their office most frequently into contact with substantial members of the community—surveyors, overseers of the poor, churchwardens: voters all. The judicial activities in which the justices of other divisions were most frequently involved were administrative decisions which affected the purses of the voters they governed. Administrative decisions were sufficiently infrequent and the communities sufficiently small that each decision could be seen to have an

---

regular annual event. No such acts were passed between 1714 and 1727, and there were no indemnity acts in 1730, 1732, and 1744. Even when annual indemnity acts were passed in the first half of the century, there were still gaps between the final date allowed for taking the Sacraments in one act and the date when the next act came into effect. A Dissenter holding office without taking the Sacraments and not under the protection of an Indemnity Act was liable to prosecution, as were all who held office without taking the Sacraments during their first year of activity in office.

59. [A. Young], *A Six Week Tour Through the Southern Counties of England and Wales . . . by the Author of the Farmer's Letters,* 2nd ed., corrected and enlarged (London, 1769), pp. 98f.

impact upon the voters' income. The relatively small size of rural communities also prevented the administration of justice from assuming the characteristics of anonymous government. Voters knew who the leading magistrates were; perhaps they were even acquainted with the magistrates and the magistrates with them. That the justices appreciated the potential for political power inherent in their office is revealed by their voting record. At the election of 1734, 80 percent of the active justices voted, but only 53 percent of the inactive. At the election of 1754, 78 percent of the active justices voted, but only 57 percent of the inactive.[60] The greater gentry in rural divisions used their office to enhance the political influence they possessed as private persons. In the age of the first two Hanoverians almost every member of the commission who attempted to become a knight of the shire took care to be an active justice.[61]

Since the lesser gentry were insufficiently wealthy and eminent to use their office to acquire appreciable political power, the enticements of interest could not tempt them to undertake judicial service. Nor could they expect other more material benefits to flow from their service. As the roll of those who received a *supersedeas* reveals, there were few opportunities for the English rural justice to use his office to line his pockets. Of the thirty-six justices superseded between 1737 and 1800, three had dishonoured the commissions of Scots counties, eleven the commissions of Westminster and Middlesex, three those of other English boroughs and liberties, seven the commissions of Wales, and only twelve the commissions of English counties other than Middlesex. In the metropolis, justices could profit from their office by methods which were regarded as corrupt. The disproportionate representation of Welsh justices on this list of the nefarious may indicate that Welsh gentry customarily exercised more power over their inferiors than their English counterparts, and so judicial office tempted several to uses of their powers considered injudicious by the governors of England. By the mid-eighteenth century, an English country gentleman could expect that judicial office would enhance whatever natural authority he already possessed; he could not entertain hopes of gain, material or immaterial, not already inherent in his station in private life.

60. Justices not resident in the county are excluded from these calculations.

61. It can not be determined if William, Viscount Vane acted as a justice. The Hon. Mildmay Fane and Sir Wyndham Knatchbull Wyndham died less than five years after appointment to the commission.

By the mid-eighteenth century, a Kentish justice might find that office did not allow him even to satisfy an ambition limited to rule of his own neighbourhood. Petty sessions' monopoly of administrative powers limited an individual justice's freedom of action, and though the greater gentry could use petty sessions to extend their dominions, the lesser justice possessed authority insufficient to persuade his colleagues to grant him a realm of his own. Even in his own parish the rule of an individual justice might not be unchallenged. As the number of justices increased, so did the chances that more than one justice might reside in any parish. All the more populous parishes of the Blackheath division boasted at least two justices. Unable to reign supreme in their own parishes, and asked to serve an unusually large and demanding population containing an unusually large proportion of nonvoters, the more prominent justices of Blackheath found little reward in their office. So, too, the lesser gentry throughout the county considered the powers of office less enticing than had their predecessors.

Likewise, mid-eighteenth century lesser gentry might have calculated that they derived less prestige from judicial activity than had their predecessors. In the seventeenth century, lesser justices had acquired honour through their judicial association with the greater gentry, but by the mid-eighteenth century only about 40 percent of the active justices were greater gentry.

By mid-century more altruistic motives for activity had also diminished. When, in the early eighteenth century, the vote of any justice might be crucial in the struggle for party dominance at petty and Quarter Sessions, every justice might be impressed by the need for his action. If he considered that the dominance of his party would further the national interest—and there was no reason why he should not—judicial activity could be regarded as an urgent public duty. In contrast, early Hanoverian Tories might calculate that they best served their party by abstaining from judicial activity. If a Tory acted in his party's interests, he would be outvoted. It might be less injurious to refrain from inflicting humiliation upon himself and his party. So, in 1754, 66 percent of the justices who voted for the Whig candidates were active, but only 46 percent of the Tory justices acted on their commission. It is likely that several decades of Whig hegemony had likewise weakened the impetus for activity among Whig justices. Secure in the knowledge that Whig domination was a fact of both national politics and the composition of Kent's bench, a Whig might conclude that his service was not essential for protection of his party or his constitution. When party conflict all but disappeared, and Englishmen were united in agreement that theirs was the best of constitutions, there was even less political impetus for activity. In Kent, there was not even a contest for the county seats between 1754 and 1790. In such a stable political environment, few justices could pretend that the state of the county's politics required their judicial service.

Expansion of the commission, diminution of the status of the average appointee, diminution of the honour of appointment, loss of opportunity for local dominance and of political impetus for activity—each can be interpreted as a cause for decline in propensity to act. But plausibility is not proof. Since one or more of these effects occurred in varying degrees in every division but one, the best strategy for revealing that these plausible causes of decline in propensity to act were actual causes is to let the exception prove the rule. The exception is the Elham division, the one division of Kent whose bench was not affected by the changes investigated in this chapter. In the area of Kent farthest from London, farthest from the incursions of the new pseudo-gentry, far away from urban centres and even major county towns, isolated among the Downs and high bluffs of England's southeast coast, the justices of the Elham division surveyed the spreading acres essential for the sheep that were the area's only (legitimate)[62] product, and acted much as their predecessors had done. Six of the eight justices in the division named in the commission of 1743 were active in the maintenance of the peace. So were both of the justices elevated to the bench between 1751 and 1761. The status of the justices appointed to the Elham bench was among the highest in the county; so were their landholdings; the division's complement of justices was the smallest in the county, and the Elham contingent of justices was the least affected by the expansion of the commission. No one party dominated the bench of the Elham division. In the elections of 1734 and 1754, the votes of the division's active justices were evenly divided among Whig and Tory. The record of only one other divisional bench could rival Elham's devotion to duty. In the Malling division, sparsely inhabited in the seventeenth century, where expansion of the commission was limited—especially before 1751, where judicial status was high and landholdings great, where the Tory cause was served by the

62. Smuggling was the division's other major industry.

two baronet families of Twisden and Twysden, justices again exhibited an abnormal inclination to serve their sovereign.[63]

Undoubtedly forces other than those examined in this study affected the decline in the justices' propensity to act. Foremost among them may have been change in the concept of both the gentleman and his role. When manner rather than birth and landed estate defined gentility, and when ability to participate in the London season defined manner, both the gentleman and his role were only tenuously related to the life of the rural community. That gentlemen and pseudo-gentry were appointed to Kent's commission and so acknowledged as members of the governing elite, and that these justices declined to assume the burdens of government suggests subtle transformation of the concepts of leadership on which English government was based. An elite whose power was based on control of the communities living on its lands was connecting itself to a new elite less tied to the communities of their inferiors. While the pseudo-gentry aped the older elite by acquiring county seats, some of the older gentry also imitated the manners and detachment of the new gentlemen.

At the same time, the zeal for activity exhibited by the justices of greater estates and status serves as a warning not to exaggerate change in the eighteenth-century image of the countryside's leaders. Both their personal prestige and their judicial activity made these justices living exemplars of what a justice should be—and the emphasis is on living. Change in the judicial image did not occur by displacement of one model by another, but rather by accretion of new values round a model already value-laden. The greater gentry's lands and status bound them to their communities. Indeed, their acceptance of judicial duty was simultaneously an acknowledgment of their ties to their communities and a display of power within those communities. So, their activity alone insured the continuity of the image of patriarchal paternalism, and the greater gentry justices comprised a large portion of the active bench. Many of the greater gentry justices may have assumed roles quite similar to those of their seventeenth-century predecessors. Others illustrate the manner in which new concepts of local leadership were grafted to the older paternal image. Consider, for example, the dynasty of Toke justices. In the 1730s, John Toke, like his father before him, was a justice in Kent's Ashford division. Toke maintained his interest and supported his party by protecting his ad-

63. Appendix E, table E-1.

herents from taxation, but neither John nor his son—also an active justice in the Ashford division—left evidence that they were interested in reforming the structure or operations of local government. In 1769, John's grandson was appointed to the Ashford bench. Within a year he had both taken out his dedimus and published *Five Letters on the State of the Poor in the County of Kent,* a pamphlet which set forth a plan for the supervision and conduct of workhouses, and advocated the appointment of inspectors to superintend parish poor relief and report to petty sessions.[64] His interest in reform of local administration and his emphasis on petty sessions might have marked grandson Toke as a patrician paternalist; but his lineage, his lands, and his belief that gentlemen should devote more time to the charitable concerns of their parishes declared his patriarchal inheritance. Concern for the condition of the governed could denote both patriarchal and patrician paternalism, and grandson Toke symbolizes the assimilation of a new role to the older image.

Even as the greater gentry's greater service preserved the image of patriarchal rule, so it also affected the manner in which the justices remodelled that image so as to make it more attractive to a populace less subject to patriarchal domination. In the seventeenth century, judicial activity had been normal and therefore expected. By the mid-eighteenth century, the decision to act was more extraordinary, and therefore both notable and praiseworthy. So, in 1759, Kent's newspaper considered noteworthy the appearance of some newly appointed justices at Quarter Sessions to take their oaths of office. The Oxfordshire election of 1754 likewise illustrates the new emphasis on judicial activity. There, the candidate who was an active magistrate was advertised as one of the few who so cared for the public welfare that he assumed the burdens of the commission. Judicial service was now an unusual and altruistic act of public service. As Blackstone explained, judicial office had become so onerous that many gentlemen abstained from judicial activity. Therefore, "the country is greatly indebted to any gentleman of figure who will undertake to perform that duty, which in consequence of his rank in life he owes more peculiarly to his country." Freedom, Blackstone declared, depended upon independent governors. Only if the independent served their country would the populace be spared the "selfish ambition, avarice, or personal resent-

64. J. Toke, *Five Letters on the State of the Poor in the County of Kent as First Printed in the Year 1770* (Canterbury, 1808).

ment" of justices of low degree.[65] Since the greater gentry acted, once again the greater gentry—the epitome of the independent Englishman—preserved the nation from arbitrary rule.

Though the greater gentry of both the seventeenth and mid-eighteenth centuries personified their eras' definition of independence, by the mid-eighteenth century 'independence' had acquired new connotations. In the seventeenth century, an independent country gentleman might well have been unallied to the great and so relatively independent of the alliances which shaped national politics. In the early eighteenth century, few justices were unconnected to party. By mid-century, 'independent' had become a euphemism for Tory; and when party struggle ceased to structure English politics the label 'independent' camouflaged engagement in the political struggles that determined access to the spoils of national politics.[66] Nonetheless, country gentlemen managed to persuade contemporaries and latter-day observers alike that they were independent. That service as a justice is a component of the image of the independent country gentleman suggests that judicial activity allowed the greater gentry to mask their political involvement in a guise at once attractive and deceptive. Judicial activity became proof of the country gentleman's independence. Since his judicial activity demanded that he prefer service in the countryside to metropolitan pleasures, the rural justice was untainted by the corruption of Court and city.[67] Since judicial service was unrewarded, the rural justice's activity demonstrated his determination to serve his community in an office free from the temptations of favour. True, judicial service allowed the greater gentry to maintain their interests; but since the less powerful found judicial service unenticing, the greater gentry could cloak the benefits they derived from office in the hairshirt of public service. It was only natural that the greater gentry congratulate themselves on their paternal concern for their communities, a concern that was proved by their judicial service, a service that was in turn evidence of their independence.

65. Sir W. Blackstone, *Commentaries on the Laws of England* (Philadelphia, 1771–1772), vol. 4, pp. 278–279 and vol. 1, p. 354; *The Kentish Post and Canterbury News-letter,* Jan. 10–13, 1759; R. Robson, *The Oxfordshire Election of 1754* (London, 1949), pp. 42–43.

66. D. Jarrett, "The Myth of 'Patriotism' in Eighteenth-Century English Politics," in *Britain and the Netherlands,* vol. 5, ed. J. S. Bromley and E. H. Kossman (The Hague, 1975), vol. 5, pp. 120–140; L. Colley, *In Defiance of Oligarchy: The Tory Party 1714–1760* (Cambridge, 1982), pp. 95–96.

67. See, for example, W. Langhorne, *The Country Justice* (London, 1774–1777), esp. part I, pp. 11–13, part II, pp. 19, 21–23.

Emphasis on judicial service as a hallmark of independence also served another useful function. It allowed the new members of the elite—gentlemen and pseudo-gentry—to claim the status appropriate to local governors. Provided that these lesser justices did not benefit from office, so long as they were neither trading justices nor obviously lackeys of the aristocracy, these justices too could be presented as impartial and so independent rulers. In the seventeenth century, it was assumed that the power which enabled a gentleman to be independent was based on his lands and so on his leadership in his neighbourhood. For the elite as a group, the equation of activity with independence circumvented awkward questions about the new justices' relation to their communities. So the subtle alteration of the meaning of independence as applied to a justice fitted nicely into new social definitions of independence. By the mid-eighteenth century, the term 'independent gentleman' could denote a man of leisure, a man sufficiently disengaged from the pursuit of wealth to have time for other concerns. And what concern was more laudable than that for the public good? For the lesser justice too, judicial activity could be proof of status, a proof all the more desirable if his status was suspect. In Kent's Blackheath division, the division inhabited by the least eminent group of justices in the county, the least illustrious members of the group were those most eager to maintain the peace.

It is easy to be cynical about the ideals of rule propagated by encomiums on the paternal service of the eighteenth-century justice. Ideals can be self-serving, but they can also inspire men to action. It is likely that many of the greater gentry and a large proportion of the lesser gentlemen on Kent's commission who acted did so because they desired good governance for their neighbourhoods, and it is even more probable that the justices of later Hanoverian England were attempting to enact the ideal of altruistic public service. Though the early Hanoverian justice had to invest relatively little time in judicial pursuits in order to establish a reputation as a paternal ruler, the later Hanoverian justice found that judicial service had become more onerous. New attention to controlling poor relief, to building roads and jails, to licensing alehouses and regulating public morality all added to the justices' administrative chores. At the same time the justices' responsibility for maintenance of the peace assumed a new importance. Crime was now a possible precursor to insurrection and so a threat to the social order. It is very probable that early nineteenth-century justices conducted a great deal more business than did their mid-eighteenth century predecessors,[68] but greater activity did not necessarily imply ever increasing influence. Those administrative powers which enabled a justice to affect voters diminished from the 1790s on—one could instance the reform of the settlement laws and the introduction of the income tax—and were even more diluted by the reforms of the 1830s. That early nineteenth-century gentlemen accepted the duties of a more bothersome and less rewarding judicial office may, in part, be a tribute to the self-congratulation of the mid-eighteenth-century greater gentry. It may well have been the mid-eighteenth-century's emphasis on the justice's unselfish concern for the public which impelled many a nineteenth-century justice to serve his county.

68. For instance, Samuel Whitbread acted as a justice about once every day (*Samuel Whitbread's Notebooks, 1810–1811, 1813–1814,* Bedfordshire Historical Record Society, vol. 50 [1971]).

CHAPTER ELEVEN

Models of the Model Justice

Ye shall do no unrighteousness in judgment;
thou shalt not respect the person of the Poor,
nor honour the person of the Mighty;
but in righteousness shalt thou judge thy Neighbour.
Lev. 19:15

What more fitting a motto for a guide to justices? So thought Edmund Bohun when he emblazoned it on the title page of his *The Justice of Peace, His Calling and Qualifications,* first published in 1684. Bohun's book was a moral counsel to the justice. The reader was admonished to remember that as a commissioner of the peace he was both instrument of divine justice and defender of the state. Both Bohun's biblical epigraph and evocative title capture the essence of the image of the justice emitted from the literature written for justices in the sixteenth and seventeenth centuries. Both also emphasize precisely those qualities omitted from this literature in the reigns of the first two Hanoverians. Eighteenth-century justices' manuals presented the justice within a different framework, a framework which assumed that the justice stood in no need of exhortation to do right.

To writers of eighteenth-century manuals, the justice was a component of the legal system. Since the law controlled the justice's actions, since the justice's eminence depended upon the law, the legal system provided all the dignity and counsel that a justice could need. So, eighteenth-century manuals eschewed comment on the glory of the justice's office. Subordinating the justice to the legal system, they minimized the importance of the individual justice, and did not strive to imbue justices with the moral qualities usually associated with those who hold high and responsible office.

Earlier manuals had presented a striking image of the model justice—a paternal ruler governing his community in the interest of God and sovereign. Despite the absence of such an easily discernible moral ideal in eighteenth-century manuals, these manuals too depict a model justice. The eighteenth-century model was a triumphant reconciliation of contradictions: England's justices were amateur volunteers; their rule was nearly autonomous; but despite their lack of legal training and their autonomy, their government accorded with the principles of English law. Even parliamentary statutes and pronouncements of the judges which restricted the justices' powers paid due homage to this ideal, an ideal whose evolution is most evident in the manuals written for and by the justices themselves.

1. THE JUSTICE IN JUSTICES' MANUALS

The *locus classicus* of guides for Elizabethan and early Stuart justices is William Lambard's *Eirenarcha: or of the Office of the Justices of Peace,* first published in 1581. Lambard's manual was published at least fifteen times, the last printing and edition being that of 1619, when it was ousted by Dalton's *The Countrey Justice,* a manual frequently acknowledging the *Eirenarcha* as its source, and even more frequently paraphrasing Lambard without acknowledgment. *The Countrey Justice* was republished throughout the seventeenth century and the first half of the eighteenth century, when it was gradually replaced by the predecessors of the Reverend Richard Burn's *The Office of Justice of the Peace and Parish Officer.*

The *Eirenarcha* focused upon the justice. Lambard begins with a consideration of the etymology of the justice's title. Chapter 1 informs the reader of the significance of the title 'justice', a title derived from that originally given the Chief Justice of the realm. The sovereign's judges, states Lambard, were called justices "to the ende, that the mention of their name, should put them in minde of their office, and should continually (as it were) sollicite them to administer Justice. . . ."[1] Chapter 2 proceeds logically to an analysis of the significance of 'peace,' a word upon whose manifold meanings Lambard dwells. As Lambard proves, that definition of peace which it is the justice's duty to maintain is the definition based on English law: peace emanating from the protection of rights and the suppression of violence. Having established the justice's task through examination of his title, Lambard moves to a history of the justice's office, noting statutes

1. W. Lambarde, *Eirenarcha: or of the Office of the Justices of Peace* (London, 1581), pp. 3–4.

which insure that those appointed justice are equal to their task. Parliament intended that a justice be an able judge and therefore required "that he come furnished with three of the principall ornamentes of a Judge, that is to saye, with Justice, Wisdome, and Fortitude. . . . And above all, that he love and feare God aright, without whiche he can not bee accounted Good at all."[2] So Parliament prohibited the appointment of barrators, of those who endeavour to buy the office, and of those of small substance "whose povertie made them both covetous and contemptible."[3] Likewise, Parliament has rightly required that justices take oaths of office:

> Such as doe occupie Judicial places, ought to take heede what they doe: knowing (as Jehosaphat saide) that they exercise not the judgements of Men onelie, but of God himselfe, whose power, as they doe participate: So he also is present on the Bench with them. And therefore, it hath alwayes been the policie of Christian lawes, to appoint meete forms of Religious attestations (or Othes) for such Officers to take: meaning thereby, not onlie to set God continually before their eyes . . . but also to threate them (as it were) with temporall paines provided against corrupt dealings, and withall, to strengthen their minds, and arm their courages, against the force of humaine affections, which otherwise might allure them and draw them out of the way.[4]

As one seventeenth-century manual put it, the intention of this commission was either to find good men or make them so.[5]

Himself a barrister and an increasingly wealthy and landed member of the gentry, Lambard was confident that his colleagues were endowed with the status and abilities adequate for virtuous execution of their office. Indeed, Lambard was sure that his colleagues were even more qualified than the letter of the law demanded. Fifteenth-century statute stipulated that justices be possessed of lands yielding £20 per annum, "And I do not doubt, but as the rate of all things is greatlye risen since that time, so is there also good care taken, that none be nowe placed in the Commission, whose livings have not increased according to the same proportion."[6]

Lambard might have been hesitant about endorsing the qualifications of Edmund Bohun. Though Bohun wrote with ease in both Latin and Greek and was so admired for his articulate expression that he

2. *Ibid.*, p. 35.
3. *Ibid.*, pp. 32–34.
4. *Ibid.*, pp. 57–58.
5. J. Keble, *An Assistance to Justices of the Peace, For the Easier Performance of their Duty* (London, 1683), *sub* "To the Reader."
6. *Eirenarcha* (London, 1581), p. 35.

was on occasion asked to take the chair and give the charge to the grand jury, Bohun did not possess social status sufficient to evoke automatic deference. Bohun was a member of the minor gentry. His estate yielded him but a modest competence, and in 1684 he rented his ancestral acres and decamped to London, there to win the office of licenser of the press which he soon lost in the fray of parliamentary party politics.[7] As Bohun himself believed, the appointment of the justice of lesser degree was a comparatively recent phenomenon.[8] Bohun represented a new variety of justice—the minor gentry and gentlemen who became even more prominent on the bench in the era of party warfare. Bohun's ruminations on judicial office reflected the effect of both the new politics and the new justice on the model of the model commissioner of the peace.

Despite the temporal and social distance dividing Bohun and Lambard, the stereotype of the justice produced by Bohun is in many ways a culmination of that found in the *Eirenarcha*. Bohun lays even more stress than Lambard on the moral and mental qualities requisite in a member of His Majesty's commission. He explains why a justice should be patient, meek, calm, sober, chaste, industrious, honest, and humble; why he needs a good mind, judgment, and memory; why it is necessary that he understand the character of the English, their government, and their politics. And, like Lambard and the statutes of the realm, he requires that a justice be valiant, of good reputation, and of competent estate. Like Lambard again, he insists that a justice honour God—an attitude Bohun interprets as desire for the salvation of those in the justice's care. This last reflection leads Bohun onto paths foreign to his predecessors, for to Bohun preservation of the Church and monarchy against the attack of republicans, Catholics, and Puritans ought to be a major preoccupation of the justice. By enforcing the laws against conventicles and recusants, and by doing justice to all so that none can be discontented, the justice is a bulwark of Church and state, a "minister of God" and a "representative of the King"—phrases which in Bohun assume a rather different meaning than in Lambard.[9]

Obviously, Bohun was a Tory propagandist, and the combination of his status with his politics explains why his justice is even more of a

7. S. W. Rix, ed., *The Diary and Autobiography of Edmund Bohun, Esq.* (Eccles, 1853), pp. xxiv, 64, 70(c), 92, 120.

8. E. Bohun, *The Justice of Peace, His Calling and Qualifications* (London, 1693), pp. 18ff.

9. *Ibid.*, pp. 172–173.

moral paragon than the justice of the *Eirenarcha*. As Bohun noted, party had invaded the bench. Justices "combine in Parties one against another" and endeavour to wreck their opponents' estates and reputations.[10] Most vulnerable were the minor gentry among the justices, and it was the Tory minor gentry who were being elevated to the bench even as Bohun wrote. So, Bohun's tract is a paean to the justices of competent but modest estate, a plea for their succour, and a counsel for their activity. Great need had they of moral courage as they contemplate affronting the great. Morality, Bohun noted, is both necessary and profitable. Concern for the religion and constitution of England should inspire justices to feats of judicial valour. Moral behaviour will also reconcile their superiors to their presence on the bench. Likewise, constant display of public and private morality will entitle the justice to the veneration of his neighbours[11]—an end most necessary to the new justice who had, aside from office, meager claim to honour.

Bohun's description of conduct befitting a justice is therefore in the tradition of Lambard, but his emphasis upon morality should be attributed to the exigencies of the new justice—of men like himself. Bohun was not the natural governor of the community assumed by Lambard and Dalton; virtue and civility were even more requisite for the new justice than the old. So Bohun reiterated that the preeminent duty of the justice was to set a good example. Dalton had stated that justices were "God's Lieutenants."[12] In a phrase rather distant from Dalton's magisterial metaphor, Bohun urged the justices to "set up as lights upon a hill."[13]

The admonition that justices should serve as models for the conduct of their inferiors was repeated in the literature of the eighteenth century, though not, be it noted, in literature written specifically for justices. If the idea was identical, the context was not. Lambard, Dalton, and Bohun all showed justices what they should be. Eighteenth-century writers showed justices what they ought not to be and warned of the dire effects of poor example.

> No Wonder if the sheep do miss the Way
> When those who ought to guide 'em run astray:

10. *Ibid.*, Preface, pp. 15–16, 107.
11. *Ibid.*, Preface, pp. 18ff., 48–51.
12. M. Dalton, *The Country Justice* (London, 1705), p. 17.
13. *The Justice of Peace* (1693), p. 22.

If Vice you would correct, this Maxim know,
Your self should first a good Example shew.

So ended a satire on the trading justice.[14]

Justices too condemned the conduct of their colleagues, and worried that the elevation of lesser gentlemen tarnished the reputation of the bench. So thought William Nelson, Chancery reporter, chairman of the Sussex bench, and author of one of the most widely used justices' manuals of the early eighteenth century. "This Court of Justices of Peace, which was once, as my Lord *Coke* observes, such a Form of subordinate Government for the Quiet of the Realm, that if duly executed, no part of the Christian World had the like, hath been composed of such an unsuitable Mixture of Men, that 'tis become a Subject in Plays, and a Jest in Comedies." Nelson suggested that the commission be reformed so as to insure both its honour and its utility. In every county, "there should be eight Honorary Justices constituted of Men of the best Quality therein, who should not be obliged constantly to attend the Service any farther than their Zeal for Justice and Love for their Country shall incline them," and eight stipendiary magistrates who would act constantly or be penalized.[15] Likewise, Edward Hasted, sometime chairman of east Kent Quarter Sessions, historian of Kent, and Fellow of the Royal Society, regretted that despite the qualification acts men of "small substance and low rank had crept into the commission."[16]

When Hasted first published his remarks in 1778, he would only barely have met the qualifications demanded by those who pressed for the exclusion of justices of mean degree in the age of Anne. The 1701 bill for the qualification of justices had demanded an annual income from land of £400 per annum. Hasted enjoyed less than £500 per annum,[17] and he was well on his way to dissipating his inheritance.

14. [C. Bullock] *The Per-Juror, As it is Acted at the Theatre in Lincoln's Inn Fields* (London, 1717), p. 32; see also T. Gisborne, *An Enquiry into the Duties of Men in the Higher and Middle Classes of Society* (London, 1795), vol. 1, p. 407.

15. W. Nelson, *The Office and Authority of a Justice of Peace,* 6th ed. (London, 1718), p. 388.

16. E. Hasted, *The History and Topographical Survey of the County of Kent,* 2nd ed. (Canterbury, 1797–1801), vol. 1, p. 218.

17. "Anecdotes of the Hasted Family," *Archaelogia Cantiana* 26 (1904): 278. The above sum was obtained by subtracting from the Hasted family income that income which was due Hasted's mother. For an examination of Hasted, see A. Everitt, "Kentish Family Portrait" in *Rural Change and Urban Growth,* ed. C. W. Chalklin and M. A. Havinden (London, 1974), and A. Everitt's "Introduction" to E. Hasted, *The History and Topographical Survey of the County of Kent* (Canterbury, 1797–1801, reprinted in 1972).

When the second edition of his *History* was published in 1798, he was a debtor residing in King's Bench prison. Expenses attributed by some to extravagance, by others to the cost of publishing his *History,* and by others to the cost of maintaining his mistress had resulted in his downfall.[18] Nor was Hasted's family of any great antiquity among the landowners of the county. His grandfather, chief painter to the royal navy at Chatham, had begun the purchase of the family estates in 1718. His father, an attorney and barrister, had retired to a merely rented country house in the county,[19] and Edward Hasted was the first of his lineage to sit upon the Kentish bench. Obviously, Hasted had no intention of impugning his own qualifications for judicial service, but even Bohun's argument would have provided little justification for the elevation of so minor a gentleman to the Kentish bench.

Fortunately for Hasted, he became a justice at a time when the justices' self-image had accommodated to the appointment of gentlemen of his ilk. Acceptance of the minor justice—indeed of all justices—is the hallmark of the Reverend Richard Burn's *The Justice of the Peace and Parish Officer,* first published in 1755. Burn's manual was rapidly acknowledged as the *summa* of judicial office. A plethora of justices' manuals had appeared in the first half of the eighteenth century, but few authors cared to compete with Burn. His manual remained the standard work until well into the nineteenth century; the thirtieth and last edition was published in 1869. From 1755 on, when justices wished to be instructed in their office, they read Burn, and from Burn all justices could derive a heartening view of their abilities. Consider his reflections on the quorum. Following Lambard, Burn explained that the quorum was originally devised so that judicial proceedings could be conducted in the presence of those learned in the law. However, "learning being now greatly advanced and improved since the first institution of this office, this distinction is not usually made in the commissions of late years, but all the justices are equally assigned to be of the quorum." Quite a compliment to the 80 percent of the bench who had never even attended the Inns of Court. Hasted would write that "every gentlemen of rank and property in a county" considered himself "slighted" if he were not made a justice.[20] In Burn's opinion, any gentleman would make a good justice.

18. *Ibid.,* p. 293.
19. *Ibid.,* pp. 271–277.
20. R. Burn, *The Justice of the Peace and Parish Officer,* 3rd ed. (London, 1756), p. 428, *sub* "Justices of the peace"; Hasted, *History of Kent,* 2nd ed., vol. 1, p. 218.

Significantly, Burn did not define what a good justice was. Lambard, Dalton, and Bohun had presented an explicit stereotype of the justice. They had labelled the justice a representative of the king and a servant of God. Not so the Reverend Richard Burn. Burn confined his consideration of judicial office to a brief history, straight out of Lambard and Dalton, and to recitation of the laws governing judicial appointment, the rituals accompanying elevation to the bench, and the legal precedents determining the extent of judicial power. His only attempt to generalize about the office are the following observations which begin his section on justices and which, as he acknowledges, he took from Lambard and Dalton:

> Justices of the peace are judges of record, appointed by the king. . . .
>
> Dalton c.2

> And a record of a memorial made by a justice of the peace, of things done before him judicially in the execution of his office, shall be of such credit, that it shall not be gainsaid. . . . Great cause therefore have the justices to take heed that they abuse not this credit, either to the oppressing of the subject by making an untrue record, or the defrauding of the king by suppressing the record that is true and lawful.
>
> Lambard 63–66[21]

Burn chose to quote those of Lambard's and Dalton's apothegms which emphasized the justices' role as officers of the law, and emphasis upon the justices' encasement in the framework of law provided a sufficient substitute for an explicit stereotype of the model justice. Unlike Lambard and Dalton, Burn felt no need to exhort his colleagues to virtuous and moral behaviour. Lambard and Dalton had assumed that the rule of their colleagues was to a great extent based on their power as individuals. Since these justices acted as individuals, their manuals sought to influence the conduct of the individual justice. To Burn, such moral counsel was irrelevant. The rule of mid-eighteenth-century justices was enshrined within English law; law and law alone provided sufficient definition, counsel, and dignity for the English justice.

Even the structure of Burn's manual implicitly reminded the justice that he was preeminently a part of the English legal system. Lambard and Dalton had begun their manuals with lengthy treatises on judicial office. Burn, like his early eighteenth-century predecessors, ordered his

21. Burn, *The Justice of the Peace,* 3rd ed. (1756), p. 420, *sub* "Justices of the peace."

manual alphabetically, beginning with 'Accessary' and ending on 'Wreck.' His description of the justice is allocated to a section entitled 'Justices of the Peace,' a section which in alphabetic logic immediately followed 'Jurors' and immediately preceded 'Land Tax.' No longer is the justice a unique individual, tenant of an office which impels him to extraordinarily virtuous conduct, or the foundation of both this kingdom and the next. The justice is merely a part of the legal apparatus, like the writ of *certiorari* and the overseers of the poor. So, any gentleman could be a satisfactory justice. He need not be the "natural" leader of his community, nor did he need extraordinary moral counsel to fulfill the demands of a uniquely important office. All that he needed was instruction in the legal rules governing the exercise of his powers.

It was because Burn provided lucid, comprehensive, and accurate instruction that his manual became a classic. Burn defined every legal term that the justice would encounter. He described every task the justice might perform and carefully outlined, in chronological order, every step in every judicial procedure. For instance, in his section on settlement Burn begins by defining settlement, proceeds to an examination of the legal requirements for obtaining a settlement, then turns to orders for removal back to a place of settlement—giving examples of the correct forms for orders of removal, and concludes by outlining the proper procedure in appeals against decisions on settlement. Every law and every decision of the judges which applied to any aspect of settlement appears in its logical place. The justice who possessed this manual did not need to be learned in the law in order to execute his office. The justice could just open his Burn and follow instructions.

While the justice using manuals written before Burn would be advised—and sometimes was advised—to consult other legal works, any justice could feel confident in acting as Burn directed. So complete and so respected was this manual that even the king's judges acknowledged its authority. In 1787, the judges of King's Bench were of the opinion that the record of one justice's conviction of a defendant for using a gun contrary to the game laws gave insufficient evidence of the offence. Yet, since the conviction followed the model provided in Burn's manual, the judges decided to consider the conviction as valid in law.[22] In Burn, the justice at last had a complete and virtually

22. 2 T.R. 24, *Rex* v. *Thompson.*

indisputable guide to the rules controlling the procedures of his office. With Burn, the justice could be an administrator of the law.

It is arguable that, when justices thought of themselves as legal administrators, they became less inclined to act as the patriarchal voice of their communities. Both Lambard and Bohun had advised the justice to settle the disputes of his community without recourse to formal legal proceedings, but the justice as mediator of his neighbourhood makes no appearance in Burn. In the late eighteenth century, some would decry the attenuation of ties between the justice and his community. Gone was the justice from his ancestral hall, gone benevolence from rule, gone charity from government. In days of yore, "the Poor at Hand their natural Patrons saw," but now justices allowed the parish overseer to harry the poor to their graves.[23] Inflexible and disinterested administration had superseded the personal involvement of the patriarch.

While the new concept of rule distanced the justice from his community, it did not demand that the justice abandon his paternal role. Instead, it altered that role. Mindful that they were public servants of the law, the new model justices might be more inclined to risk acting in ways that offended voters. So in the late eighteenth century farmers and shopkeepers complained that justices were too liberal in their administration of poor relief. Early eighteenth-century justices were not reputed to act in a manner which hindered them from acquiring a political interest. Despite lamentations on the disappearance of paternalism, the old emphasis on paternal rule was incorporated into the new model of the justice. Serving the law, acting as a public servant, he served all of the public—not just the yeomen of his village. But unlike the older model of the justice, the new served from a distance. Most frequently, diatribes against the justice who too freely distributed poor relief noted that the justice did not live in the community whose poor rates he was dispensing.[24]

Perhaps the relative disinclination of some later eighteenth-century justices to use their office to acquire a political interest can be attributed to the greater proportion of justices who were lesser gentlemen, possessed of insufficient influence to lead their communities. Many of the new justices could not realistically aspire to the role of patriarchal

23. W. Langhorne, *The Country Justice* (London, 1774–1777), esp. part II, p. 19.
24. S. and B. Webb, *English Local Government from the Revolution to the Municipal Corporations Act*, vol. 1, *The Parish and the County* (London, 1906), pp. 589–590; A. Brundage, *The Making of the New Poor Law* (New Brunswick, N. J., 1978), p. 22.

paternalist. They could assume the more 'patrician' role of legal administrator—of a gentleman cognizant of the culture and governmental forms which guaranteed England's peculiar freedom. By grafting the attribute of legal administrator to the older paternal image, England's rulers insured that the lesser justice would receive the deference accorded his more illustrious predecessors. No longer did the justice have to assume the majesty of king or God to awe his community. The new justice was hallowed by the mystery of the law which he administered.

2. THE JUSTICE AND ENGLISH LAW

Since the propriety of judicial rule now depended so entirely upon its encasement by the framework of law, it was of the first importance that judicial rule not contravene the principles upon which the legal system was based. Subordination of the image of the justice to that of the legal system therefore induced analysis of the powers of the justice within that system. Burn was not alone in finding these powers anomalous.

Most disturbing was the disparity between the justices' powers of summary conviction and the law's veneration of trial by jury. Wrote Burn:

> The power of a justice of the peace is in restraint of the common law, and in abundance of instances is a tacit repeal of that famous clause in the great charter, that a man should be tried by his equals; which also was the common law of the land long before the great charter, even from time immemorial beyond the date of histories and records.[25]

Burn was participating in a debate which had begun to enliven justices' manuals in the late seventeenth century. A preface to the 1677 edition of Dalton's *The Countrey Justice* had damned summary conviction through a brief history of its origins. It was Henry VII who had first granted justices summary powers, and the pernicious effects of those powers are sufficiently indicated by the names Empson and Dudley. As the preface noted, abrogation of the right to trial by jury "may tend to the subversion of both liberty and property."[26] In 1745, the preface to Barlow's *The Justice of Peace: A Treatise Containing*

25. Burn, *The Justice of the Peace*, 3rd ed. (1756), p. 159, *sub* "Conviction."
26. M. Dalton, *The Countrey Justice* (London, 1677), *sub* "To the Reader." This preface first appears in this edition and is reprinted in later editions.

the Power and Duty of that Magistrate issued a rejoinder. "It is in the *English* Constitution alone that the Security of the Peace is committed by the Prince to Men of ample Fortunes in the respective Neighbourhoods; not to venal Magistrates, but to Gentlemen who serve their Country most commonly at their own Charges; not to Strangers, who can ill distinguish between the Oath of the Honest Man and the Knave, but to such whose Knowledge of their Neighbours enables them to make a proper Judgment of the Testimony produced before them; and thus, as far as their Jurisdiction reaches, the Subject has the same Advantage in his judge of Fact, as he enjoys in Matters of more Moment, in the Trial by Juries; that is, he is tried by his Country, within the Meaning of that legal Adage."[27]

A much more influential legal authority disagreed. William Blackstone's *Commentaries on the Laws of England,* first delivered as lectures at Oxford in the 1750s and then published in 1765, stated unequivocally that summary conviction was "fundamentally opposed to the spirit of our constitution." In a series of passages which echo Tory elegies on the elected justice, Tory denunciation of the growth of government, and Tory depiction of the justices of mean degree as "tools of office," Blackstone knit legal criticism of summary conviction to more wide-ranging reflections on decline in the quality of the sovereign's justices. Summary jurisdiction, wrote Blackstone, had so increased the burden of judicial office that many "gentlemen of rank and character" abstain from acting as justices. In discouraging the activity of the honourable, summary jurisdiction had delivered England's local government into the hands of those who sought gain from office.[28]

As Blackstone's argument indicates, consideration of summary jurisdiction led not only to analysis of the powers appropriate to justices within the legal system. It also entailed consideration of the justice's role, unique in Europe, as a voluntary and unpaid officer of government. What should be the limits of the justices' powers, and how could their powers be limited without destroying an autonomous system of local government? What censures were appropriate for controlling those who altruistically served the law? How could a system of local government based on the rule of a community by its

27. T. Barlow, *The Justice of Peace: A Treatise Containing the Power and Duty of that Magistrate* (London, 1745), pp. vii–viii.
28. Sir W. Blackstone, *Commentaries on the Laws of England* (Philadelphia, 1771–1772), vol. 4, pp. 278–279, 343–344, 421; vol. 1, pp. 334–336; see also vol. 3, p. 82.

resident gentlemen be attuned to the principles of English law? Eighteenth-century judges and Parliaments had to confront these questions because the growth of the justices' powers out of Quarter Sessions and the new emphasis upon the justice as part of the legal system forced them to reconcile the justices' role with English law. In answering these questions, both judges and Parliament sketched their own portraits of the ideal justice of the peace.

The judges had constantly to define the limits of the justices' powers for, by the late seventeenth century, the judges had invented a means to review the justices' judgments and orders. In the seventeenth century, the judges of King's Bench had instituted a new system for review by expansion of the use of the writ of *certiorari.*[29] Before the seventeenth century the writ had been used to bring before King's Bench the record of indictments initiated before inferior courts; by 1680, the judges were quashing justices' judgments and administrative orders brought before them by *certiorari. Certiorari* therefore demonstrated the supremacy of the judges and so of the law. By the early eighteenth century, the judges were determined to insist on the supremacy of the law and of their courts. They insisted on their right to review judgments and orders made by any inferior jurisdiction. Not only did the judges determine whether an inferior jurisdiction had the power to make a judgment or order; by the early eighteenth century, the judges had also endowed themselves with the power to determine whether inferior authorities had made "a wrong judgment in a matter within the limits of their jurisdiction."[30]

29. Justices' actions could also be reviewed through use of two other prerogative writs: *habeas corpus* and *mandamus. Mandamus* issued to compel a justice to perform a "ministerial act," i.e., an act in which he did not exercise any discretion. It is unlikely that many judicial actions, or failures to act, were reviewed by *mandamus.* Though Burn states that "the most usual way" of compelling justices "to exercise their office is by a writ of mandamus out of the king's bench" (Burn, *Justice of the Peace,* 3rd ed. [1756], p. 435, *sub* "Justices of the peace"), he does not even devote a section to *mandamus* in his manual. Certainly, the number of writs of *mandamus* issued to justices recorded in the mid-eighteenth-century Great Dogget Books of King's Bench (P.R.O., Index 6658, 6659) is very much less than the number of writs of *certiorari. Habeas corpus* issued to review imprisonment upon a warrant either before or after conviction. If there were errors in law on the warrant—as, for example, a warrant committing a prisoner until he pay a fine whose amount was not stated on the warrant—the judges would quash the warrant and free the prisoner. But, if the plaintiff averred that his conviction was defective, though the defect did not appear on the warrant of committal, the conviction had to be quashed through *certiorari* before the plaintiff could be released through *habeas corpus* (W. Paley, *The Law and Practice of Summary Convictions on Penal Statutes by Justices of the Peace* [London, 1814], pp. 210–211).

30. E. Henderson, *Foundations of English Administrative Law* (Cambridge, Mass., 1963), pp. 95, 114; S. A. de Smith, *Judicial Review of Administrative Action,* 3rd

At the same time, increase in the powers assigned to the justices, especially those exercised out of Quarter Sessions, meant that the judges were more frequently requested to review the justices' judgments and orders. Parliament continually added to the offences which could be adjudged summarily by the justices: in 1663, only some seventy offences were subject to the justices' summary jurisdiction; by 1776, the number of such offences had risen to over two hundred.[31] In the late seventeenth century, Parliament likewise extended the justices' administrative powers. In particular, the Settlement Act of 1662 gave justices power to make decisions which England's parishes were eager to appeal.

The conjoint rise of King's Bench as a court for the review of the activities of inferior jurisdictions and the expansion of the justices' powers therefore posed a recurring problem: To what extent should the judges regulate the justices' activities? If the judges habitually allowed full review of all the justices' judgments and orders, then both the justices' autonomy and their ability to rule effectively would be threatened. Local government would be thrown into chaos, for no judgment or order could be made or enforced until heard by the judges, and the judges would in practice be the rulers of the countryside. Further, the judges themselves might not have welcomed an ever increasing load of relatively unprofitable appeals. On the other hand, if the judges did not permit themselves to scrutinize the justices' activities, Englishmen could not be assured that the actions of their local governors accorded with English law. The judges therefore had to establish a set of rules for reviewing the justices' activities which simultaneously maintained the justices' image as autonomous rulers and allowed the judges to overturn their judgments and orders. This they did in the definition of legal principles to govern the use of the writ of *certiorari*.

Most apparent in the decisions on *certiorari* of late seventeenth-century judges is their determination to restrict the scope of their review. In the mid-seventeenth century, cases involving at least some

---

ed. (London, 1973), pp. 95, 512–513; A. Rubinstein, *Jurisdiction and Illegality* (Oxford, 1965), p. 68.

31. W. Young, *A Vade Mecum, or Table, containing the Substance of such Statutes; wherein any one, or more Justices of the Peace are enabled to Act*, 7th ed., corrected and amended (London, 1663); F. Frankfurter and T. G. Corcoran, "Petty Federal Offenses and the Constitutional Guarantee of Trial by Jury," *Harvard Law Review* 29 (1926): 928, 933.

of the justices' administrative orders obtained a hearing *de novo* before the judges on *certiorari*. By the late seventeenth century, trial of fact could not be had on *certiorari*. The judges now limited their review to the written record of the justices' judgments and orders set before them, and that record need not include the evidence on which the justices had based their determination. The judges declared: "there is no Necessity for setting out the Reason of their judgment. We never do it in this Court." The judges also allowed omission from the record of other matters, matters which it usually contained. In some instances, the judges even decided that the record need not prove that the justices had followed the procedure specified by the statute which had empowered the justices to make their order. In restricting their review to the "face of the record" and thereby prohibiting any account or even summary of the evidence, the judges promulgated a self-denying ordinance: there were now many aspects of the justices' judgments and orders which the judges declared themselves incompetent to review.

By the 1720s, the judges were formulating a legal theory which purported to define and justify the limits of their review. Those aspects of the justices' judgment or order which had to be included in the record so that they could be reviewed were labelled 'jurisdictional.' The label implied that the judges' review was limited to insuring that the justices had the legal authority to consider the case which was being appealed. In theory, this was a neat definition which safeguarded the justices' autonomy while insuring that they did not exceed the limits of their authority.

In practice, the distinction between jurisdictional and nonjurisdictional matters was less than clear. If, for example, a statute endowed justices with certain powers, did the procedures which the statute specified that the justices follow constitute part of the definition of the justices' jurisdiction? Neither the judges' decisions nor parliamentary statute clearly differentiated what in the justices' judgments and orders was 'jurisdictional' from what was not. During the course of the eighteenth century the judges used the lack of clarity in their theory of jurisdiction to justify review of matters which some might not deem 'jurisdictional.' On occasion, the judges even labelled as 'jurisdictional' evidence necessary to a fair hearing, so that in some instances they did review the justices' assessment of fact.[32] To insure that their considera-

32. Henderson, *Foundations of English Administrative Law*, pp. 6, 109–110, 143–159.

tion of the justices' decisions not be obstructed by their "face of the record" rule, mid-eighteenth-century judges introduced new refinements into the rules governing presentation of evidence on *certiorari.* At some time between 1736 and 1757, the judges began to allow the submission of affidavits to supplement the official record, if the affidavits went to the justices' jurisdiction or lack thereof.[33]

So, by the mid-eighteenth century the judges had developed a satisfactory legal framework for the review of the justices' judgments and orders. The legal theory on which they based the rules governing their review was sufficiently flexible to allow them to intervene whenever they considered such intervention necessary to justice. At the same time, the judges' decisions bolstered the justices' authority. According to the judges' own theory, the justices and only the justices adjudged the facts of a case; the justices ruled the counties. That the judges allowed certain aspects of the justices' judgments and orders to be reviewed only reinforced the justices' image as resident representatives of the law. According to the judges' pronouncements, the justices were ideal governors—autonomous rulers whose decisions happily accorded with the principles of English law.

Enhancement of the justices' image by reconciliation of their powers with the principles of English law is most strikingly illustrated by the judges' decisions on review of the justices' summary convictions. Summary convictions are a subset of those of the justices' judgments which could be brought to the attention of King's Bench by *certiorari.* But, unlike the precedents governing the review of the justices' administrative decisions, those governing review of their summary convictions spring almost entirely from the cases brought before eighteenth-century judges. Before the mid-seventeenth century, the justices wielded relatively few powers of summary conviction, but in the late seventeenth and eighteenth centuries the number of offences for which they could convict summarily increased enormously.[34] So, it was in the eighteenth century that the judges determined the limits of their review. So new were these powers and the effect of the judges' review upon their use that the first guide devoted exclusively to summary conviction was published as late as 1792. As its author noted, summary conviction was the only "defective and unsatisfactory title" in Burn's mid-eighteenth-century

33. L. J. Jaffe, "Judicial Review: Constitutional Fact and Jurisdictional Fact," *Harvard Law Review* 70 (1957): 960.
34. See note 31 above.

manual.[35] Of the precedents cited in this guide, only three date from before 1700; thirty arise from decisions delivered by the judges between 1701 and 1730; twelve from decisions of 1731 to 1760, and twenty-one from decisions of 1761 to 1790. As the history of *certiorari* would hint, the precedents are contradictory.

Central to the justices' powers of summary conviction was the notion that Parliament had intended that the justices and only the justices judge the facts of cases which they could determine summarily. Though early eighteenth-century judges disliked the abrogation of trial by jury,[36] they nonetheless felt bound to respect Parliament's intent. When hearing an appeal against a summary conviction, they demanded that the record of the conviction prove that the justice had jurisdiction, but they declined to review the justice's assessment of the evidence. Therefore, in the early eighteenth century the judges declared that the record of a summary conviction presented to the judges on *certiorari* need not detail the evidence.[37] By 1735, the judges had begun to reverse themselves. It now appeared to the judges that the judgment must set out the evidence so that the judges could determine whether the justice had exceeded his jurisdiction: the law did not allow an informer, who would profit from a conviction, to be counted as one of the witnesses required by statute.[38] At mid-century, the judges were stating that justices must submit the evidence so that the judges could determine whether the justices had done right.[39] As in their other decisions on *certiorari*, the judges had first emphasized both in their theory and practice the principle of the justices' autonomy, and the judges had then qualified their practice through expansion of the concept of jurisdiction so as to allow a thorough review of the justices' convictions when they considered it necessary.

So, by the early nineteenth century the law on summary convictions was a confusing combination of early eighteenth-century precedents underlining the justices' autonomy and later precedents which allowed the judges to infringe upon the justices' autonomy in practice without negating the justices' theoretical autonomy. The confusion was en-

35. W. Boscawen, *A Treatise on Convictions on Penal Statutes* (London, 1792), p. 3.
36. Paley, *Summary Convictions* (1814), p. 50.
37. 1 Salkeld 369, *Regina* v. *Pullen*.
38. 2 Stra. 997–999, *Rex* v. *Lloyd*. Orders need not detail the evidence, and the distinction between orders and convictions was simple: those judgments which before 1732 were recorded in Latin were convictions; those which before 1732 were recorded in English were orders.
39. Sayer 304, *Rex* v. *Bissex;* 4 Burr. 2063, *Rex* v. *Killett, Clk.*

shrined in William Paley's classic, *The Law and Practice of Summary Convictions,* first published in 1814. Consider, for example, Paley's attempt to enunciate a general rule defining the justices' autonomy in assessing evidence. Paley begins by stating, "As to the degree and sufficiency of the Evidence, and credit due to the witnesses, the Magistrates alone are the judges." His axiom is immediately qualified: in making summary convictions, justices assume the role of the jury; "therefore whatever the Court of King's Bench upon an inspection of the proceedings would deem sufficient to be left to a Jury on a trial, will be considered by them adequate to sustain the conclusion drawn by the convicting Magistrates." As Paley—wisely—did not explain what evidence was sufficient to be left to a jury, his rule is not notable for its clarity. Further opacity is introduced in his more detailed discussion, where he notes that the judges have quashed convictions when they considered that the evidence on which the convictions were based was insufficient.[40] Paley did not even try to discover a general principle determining the degree of freedom allowed justices in their procedure on summary convictions. By the end of the eighteenth century, the judges required a strict accounting of some procedures; of others they did not. So Paley wrote: "The safest rule perhaps that can be laid down upon the subject, is in the words of Lord Ellenborough, 'that the court will intend nothing in favour of convictions, and will intend nothing against them.' "[41]

Clarity of legal principle reflected in unambiguously clear legal practice had not been achieved because clarity of principle and practice was not the judges' primary *desideratum.* What Paley and the judges did attain was a series of legal axioms which simultaneously reconciled the justices' power to convict summarily with the law's respect for trial by jury, allowed the judges to review the justices' exercise of their summary powers, and reinforced the justices' image as autonomous rulers of the countryside. As a result, the judges' evaluation of the justices' powers and role changed. In the early eighteenth century, the judges considered the justices' power to convict summarily legal but suspect. Said Lord Chief Justice Holt: "the defendant is put to a summary trial different from magna charta, for it is a fundamental privilege of an Englishman to be tried by a jury."[42] In contrast, by 1787 Judge Ashurst was opining that, in whatever light

40. Paley, *Summary Convictions* (1814), pp. 141–144.
41. *Ibid.,* pp. 52–53.
42. Quoted *ibid.,* p. 50.

summary conviction "may formerly have been viewed, yet the country are now convinced that they derive considerable advantage from the exercise of the powers delegated to the justices of the peace."[43] Because by the late eighteenth century the judges had reconciled the irreconcilable, they could look with complacency upon their handiwork: the legal image of the ideal justice, a justice whose autonomous rule accorded with the principles of law.

While Parliament agreed with the judges that the justices should be both autonomous and imbued with the spirit of English law, Parliament was not enthusiastic about the judges' efforts to attain the ideal through the use of *certiorari*. Judicial review restricted the justices' autonomy, and so Parliament endeavoured to restrict the use of *certiorari*. In a series of later Stuart and early Hanoverian statutes, Parliament ordered that those who obtained a *certiorari* must post bond to prosecute their appeals, that those whose appeals proved unsuccessful pay the defendants' costs, and that the time allowed for obtaining the writ be limited to six months after the justices' judgment or order.[44] As the judges had noted that some applications for the writ were actually attempts to postpone indefinitely consideration of alleged offences,[45] it is probable that the judges agreed with the intent of these statutes. The judges were less sympathetic to another parliamentary maneuver. Parliament decreed that *certiorari* not be available for appeal against some summary convictions. Insisting on their duty to maintain the rule of law, the judges out-maneuvered Parliament. By 1760, King's Bench was asserting that, notwithstanding parliamentary decrees denying the judges the right to issue *certiorari*, it had the responsibility of insuring that the justices did not exceed their jurisdiction.[46] To the extent that parliamentary clauses depriving the plaintiff of *certiorari* restricted the judges' review, Parliament increased the justices' autonomy. Certainly, those statutes which attached conditions to the grant of *certiorari* better enabled justices to insure that their judgments and orders took effect and limited appeals.

Nonetheless, Parliament, too, was unwilling to allow each justice to become the tyrant of his parish. At the same time that it began restrict-

43. 2 T.R. 23, *Rex* v. *Thompson*.

44. 5 William III c. 11; 8 and 9 William III c. 33; 5 George II c. 19; 13 George II c. 18.

45. de Smith, *Judicial Review of Administrative Action*, 2nd ed. (London, 1968), p. 371.

46. Paley, *Summary Convictions* (1814), pp. 212–215; de Smith, *Judicial Review*, 2nd ed., p. 345; Rubinstein, *Jurisdiction and Illegality*, pp. 72–73.

ing *certiorari,* Parliament invented a new structure for review of summary convictions. Beginning in the reign of Charles II, and increasingly throughout the eighteenth century, Parliament appended to statutes authorizing summary conviction a clause permitting those so convicted to appeal to the justices in Quarter Sessions.[47] In the first half of the eighteenth century, defendants rarely took advantage of this new and cheaper avenue for appeal. But by the early nineteenth century, one justice found such appeals sufficiently frequent to protest against Quarter Sessions' procedure upon appeals. It seems that some Quarter Sessions allowed the introduction of evidence which did not appear upon the record of the conviction, evidence which presumably had not been presented before the convicting justice.[48] By substituting appeal to Quarter Sessions for *certiorari,* Parliament had limited the authority of justices acting singly or in pairs by expanding the authority of justices acting as a group in Quarter Sessions. Like the judges, Parliament had invented a legal structure which exonerated each individual justice from the imputation of tyranny. Even more than the judges', Parliament's legal invention reinforced the justices' autonomy.

Restriction of appeal aided in the solution of yet another problem—a problem which, like the justices' autonomy, was rooted in an implicit conflict between English law and the justices' role. On the one hand, the law permitted the prosecution of justices for misuse of their official powers; on the other, English government rested upon the justices, and justices were both amateurs and volunteers. As the overwhelming majority of justices had no training in the law which they administered, it was quite likely that from time to time a justice would make a mistake. Indeed, as a succession of statutes and judges' decisions made the law of local government into an ever more complicated maze, it would be amazing if justices did not err. If erring justices were fined or jailed, as the law permitted, gentlemen might refuse to offer their services to the state. Surely the justices should not be penalized for their public service.

In limiting *certiorari* and directing appeals from justices out of sessions to their colleagues in Quarter Sessions, both judges and Parliament shielded the nation's amateur rulers. A plaintiff could not

47. Paley, *Summary Convictions* (1814), p. 196.
48. J. Nares, *A Summary of The Law on Penal Convictions* (London, 1814), pp. 106–107.

usually bring a civil action against a justice until the judgment or order of which he complained had been quashed.[49] As limitation of *certiorari* diminished the subject's ability to appeal against the justices' judgments and orders, and as appeal to Quarter Sessions allowed justices to reinforce their colleagues' authority,[50] both devices protected the justices from civil suits.

They did not, in Parliament's opinion, protect the justices enough. In 1751 and 1804, Parliament passed acts which further enabled justices to avoid civil liability.[51] The act of 1751 decreed that a plaintiff must give a justice one month's notice before initiating a civil suit; in that month the justice could tender amends to the plaintiff; if the plaintiff refused the amends tendered by the justice and brought suit, and if the jury found that the amends were sufficient, the plaintiff would both lose his case and have to pay the justice's costs. Erring justices who admitted their error were to be spared the trouble of legal proceedings. The act of 1804 further shielded justices from inconveniences which might arise from their activities in office. According to this act, plaintiffs who wished to bring civil suits against justices for convictions which had been quashed could recover only the fine which had been levied—if a fine had been levied—and the additional sum of twopence. A plaintiff could profit by more than twopence only by proving that the justice had acted maliciously or without probable cause.[52] As a future Lord Chan-

49. Paley, *Summary Convictions,* pp. 239–246. In the seventeenth century, a justice's order or conviction made "without jurisdiction" could be attacked in a civil suit without first obtaining a verdict quashing the order or conviction. When, in the eighteenth century, the judges expanded the concept of jurisdiction in *certiorari* cases, they also expanded the concept of acts done without jurisdiction in civil suits against justices. Therefore, during the course of the eighteenth century, it became easier to attack a justice's judgment or order in a civil suit without first obtaining a verdict quashing that judgment or order. Nonetheless, it remains probable that during most of the eighteenth century orders and convictions were more likely to be challenged successfully on *certiorari* than in a civil suit. So those who did not have an airtight case that a justice had acted without jurisdiction may have preferred to obtain a verdict quashing the justice's judgment or order first and then bring a civil suit against the justice (Rubinstein, *Jurisdiction and Illegality,* pp. 46–47, 68–85, 112, 172–183, 224; de Smith, *Judicial Review,* 2nd ed., p. 83).

50. Nares, *Penal Convictions,* pp. 106–107.

51. 24 George II c. 44; 43 George III c. 141.

52. D. Thompson, "Judicial Immunity and the Protection of Justices," *Modern Law Review* 21 (1958): 529, argues that the 1804 act made justices liable in tort where they had not been liable before. Thompson relies on legal writers' frequent citation of the maxim that justices, like judges, could not be sued by a private party for those of their actions which were "judicial," but that they could be so sued for their "ministerial" acts (see, for example, Burn, *Justice of the Peace,* 3rd ed. [1756], p. 434, *sub* "Justices of the peace"). It is probable that the judges' inflation of the concept of acts done without

cellor later observed, proof of malice was difficult both to obtain and to sustain at law.[53]

That Parliament found it necessary to pass both statutes might indicate that justices were likely to face civil suits for acts committed in the performance of their official duties. Such a surmise would be unduly pessimistic. It is difficult to determine the number of civil suits brought against justices. But, since it is probable that in the first half of the century most of those judgments and orders which eventually produced civil suits against justices had to be quashed by the judges before civil suits could be initiated, the number of justices' actions brought before the judges by *certiorari* provides a rough index to the frequency of threat of civil suit. Between 1743 and 1748, no summary conviction made by Kent's justices, no indictment at Kent's Quarter Sessions, and only one order made by Kent's justices—a settlement order—was brought before the judges by *certiorari.*[54]

It is possible that the justices of Westminster and Middlesex more frequently braved the terrors of the higher civil courts. A 1730 manual for metropolitan justices cautioned against lax observance of the law's requirements. Gentlemen of "Fortunes and Figure in their Counties" might not fear the consequences of their irregular administration: they can permit their servants to draw up judicial orders, and if one of these documents is adjudged illegal, the servant bears the blame; "*his Honour* is not presum'd to be at Leisure to attend to such trifling Concerns; But though Men of commanding Fortunes may be above the Laws, we have Instances of some others, in the Commission, who have had Actions brought against them and have paid very dear for their Mistakes." As London's premier trading justice noted, the attorneys who swarmed round the Old Bailey were only too eager to "entangle" the justice in difficulties, so that he could later be sued before the judges.[55] It is possible that in the late eighteenth-century

jurisdiction deprived the justices of this defence when they were sued in tort for their "judicial" acts. The judges did not distinguish between judgments and orders which the justices had the power to make but which were not made in the proper fashion, and judgments and orders which justices had no authority to make: both were acts done without jurisdiction. So the justice who erred in a case which he had the authority to consider might be sued in tort (Rubinstein, *Jurisdiction and Illegality,* pp. 58, 82, 172–174).

53. Hansard, *Parliamentary Debates,* new series, vol. 18 (1828), pp. 165–166, Feb. 7, 1828.

54. P.R.O., Index 6659.

55. J. Harvey, *A Collection of Precedents Relating to the Office of a Justice of Peace* (London, 1730), pp. iv–v; Sir T. DeVeil, *Observations on the Practice of a Justice of the*

justices found themselves more vulnerable to both *certiorari* and civil suits than had their predecessors. In 1799, the justices of Kent's Malling division considered it necessary to pass a resolution committing all magistrates of the division who had at any time attended its petty sessions to contribute to the legal expenses of defending the petty sessions' decisions.[56] Whether the acts of 1751 and 1804 were intended as shields for metropolitan or rural magistrates cannot be determined. Clearly, both acts were inspired by a vision of the ideal justice—of the squire who deserved better from his country than a mulct for ignorance of the law.

The judges shared Parliament's vision. They found their opportunity to pronounce on the discipline appropriate to a voluntary magistracy when they deliberated on criminal suits brought against justices. In theory, justices could be confronted with the might of the criminal law either by an indictment at Quarter Sessions or Assizes or by an application for an information against a justice to King's Bench. In fact, those who wished to prosecute justices by a criminal action applied to King's Bench for an information. By the mid-eighteenth century, the judges were not eager to grant such informations. Said Judge Ashurst, even if justices had not "strictly speaking, acted legally, we will not grant an information against them unless they have acted corruptly. When magistrates act uprightly and honestly, even though they mistake the law, no information ought to be granted against them." Lord Chief Justice Mansfield was more vehement: if the justices' "judgement is wrong, yet their heart and intention pure, God forbid that they should be punished!"[57]

It is debatable whether the King's Bench of earlier eras had been more receptive to complaints against justices. On the one hand, the dicta of mid-eighteenth-century judges simply elaborated an opinion which Lambard believed prevalent among some sixteenth-century judges: "if a Justice of Peace do anything of Recorde ignorantly, and for want of knowedge, he should not be punished for it."[58] On the other hand, early eighteenth-century manuals gave no guide whatsoever to the principles governing the judges' discipline of the voluntary

Peace: Intended for such Gentlemen as design to act for Middlesex or Westminster (London, 1747), pp. 3–4, 8–9, 12–13.

56. Kent A.O., PS/Ma4, July 1, 1799.

57. 1 T.R. 653, *Rex* v. *Jackson;* 1 Burr. 562, *Rex* v. *Young and Pitts;* see also 2 Burr. 1162, *Rex* v. *Palmer and Baines,* and 2 Burr. 787, *Rex* v. *Cox.*

58. Lambarde, *Eirenarcha* (1581), pp. 506–507.

magistracy, and later manuals cited as precedents cases which had arisen in the 1750s to the 1780s. Again, by mid-century the judges had constructed a framework for supervision of the justices which allowed the justices' violation of law to be reviewed while protecting the justices' position as autonomous, voluntary, and nonprofessional rulers. Like their decisions on appeals from the justices' summary jurisdiction and administrative orders, the judges' pronouncements on prosecution of justices under criminal law for offences committed in office added to the mystique of the justice's role. Far be it from the judges to condemn the gentlemen who volunteered to rule England under law. The justices' rule was praiseworthy, even when "strictly speaking" it happened to be illegal.

Examination of the justices' role within the legal system had caused both Parliament and judges to define the justices' powers more precisely. The justices' summary jurisdiction, their administrative autonomy, their amateur and volunteer status—all had to be accommodated within the framework of English law, and all could be so accommodated without flagrant violation of the law's principles. However, there was one aspect of the justices' rule which was in direct contradiction with one of the fundamental principles of English law: that no man should be judge of his own cause. The justices' rule violated this axiom. Gentlemen were made justices so that they would govern their own neighbourhoods, and they were made justices because they had property and influence—property and influence in their own neighbourhoods. In governing his neighbourhood, it was not unlikely that a justice would make judgments and orders affecting his interest, that he would be a judge in his own cause.

The possibility that a justice might be judge in his own cause had long been recognized by England's rulers. The problem first and most clearly presented itself to Parliament in the form of summary jurisdiction. As Paley noted, the earliest statute endowing justices with the powers of summary conviction forbade justices from using their powers in a case involving their own property. A justice could penalize those who stole apples from an orchard, so long as the orchard was not his own. By the late seventeenth century, and increasingly in the eighteenth century, Parliament was inclined to insist that those justices who pursued occupations other than that of country gentleman not exercise those powers which would affect their profits. So, brewers were forbidden from sitting at licensing sessions; bakers were forbidden from enforcing laws regulating the sale of bread; and practicing attorneys were forbidden from being justices at all.[59] As early as 1683, Edmund Bohun had noted that when an attorney who was a justice was paid for advice on a case which he would later adjudicate, there were grounds for assuming that the justice's decision was not completely impartial.[60] Very possibly, both Parliament's establishment of Quarter Sessions as an appellate tribunal for summary convictions and its passage of acts which gave summary powers to two justices rather than one were efforts to enhance the image of the justice as a disinterested judge. Considerations which led to the use of both devices are reflected in the deliberations of the 1749 Parliament over a bill to punish theft by workmen from manufacturers. The new act was to supersede a statute which gave jurisdiction to one justice. Horatio Walpole's constituents lobbied unsuccessfully for jurisdiction to be lodged in two—their reasoning being countered by the argument that in distant country districts it was sometimes difficult to secure the presence of two justices. On the other hand, the parliamentary committee decided that, as the penalty of £50 "is a pretty high one and the conviction may be made by one justice, who in great city[s] may be a manufacturer; . . . there is to be a clause of Appeal."[61] By the mid-eighteenth century, one aristocrat even believed it plausible to argue for the elevation of a clergyman resident on his estate to the bench on the grounds that "it would be improper in mee, who does act sometimes, to be trying my own causes. . . ."[62] Increasingly aware that their rule depended upon the reverence accorded English law, England's rulers took care that their image accord with that law's basic axiom.[63]

The judges, too, safeguarded the principle that no man should be judge in his own cause. Because they were judges, and because they were entrusted with preserving the law, their definition of the limits of the justices' power was more stringent. By 1742, the judges were attempting to refashion the justices in their own image. If the definition of the justices' powers which the judges then proclaimed was allowed to prevail, the justices would have become truly disinterested. The judges promulgated their new definition of the prohibited degrees

59. Paley, *Summary Convictions* (1814), pp. 10–11; 5 George II c. 18; 18 George II c. 20.

60. Bohun, *The Justice of Peace* (1693), p. 120.

61. B.L., Add. MSS 35590, ff. 267–268, H. Walpole to Hardwicke, Mar. 25, 1748/1749.

62. B.L., Add. MSS 35601, f. 201, Earl of Ailesbury to Hardwicke, June 3, 1743.

63. For reflections on the manner in which the eighteenth-century elite's emphasis on the rule of law affected their behaviour see E. P. Thompson, *Whigs and Hunters* (New York, 1975), pp. 258–269.

of a justice's activity in their decision on an appeal from a settlement case. John Toke, justice of the county of Kent, had signed a settlement order commanding that a pauper be moved from a parish in which Toke paid poor rates to another parish which the order declared was the pauper's parish of settlement. The judges quashed the order: Toke, they stated, had acted as a judge in his own cause.[64] By removing the pauper from the parish in which he was rated, Toke had decreased the parish's expenses and so lowered his own taxes.

Earlier in the century the judges had treated the justices' personal involvement in administrative cases in a more cavalier fashion. In Anne's reign, an overseer of the poor had complained to the judges that several justices had refused to sign an order to remove a pauper to the parish in which he was legally settled. According to one judge, the justices had refused to sign the order because they were inhabitants of the parish to which the pauper was to be removed. The judges nevertheless refused to interfere: "the Court will not presume that the justices would act contrary to their duty; besides there are justices enough in the county who are of neither party."[65] By the 1740s, emphasis upon the justices' role as part of the law had awakened the judges to the inherent conflict between the justice as officer of the law and the older image of the justice as patriarchal governor of his community. As the judges' decision in the Toke case would have prevented a justice from making any administrative order which might affect the expenses of any parish where that justice paid rates, their decision would have abolished a system of local government based on gentlemen's administration of their own neighbourhoods. In effect, according to the judges, the justice as judge had superseded the justice as patriarchal ruler.

Parliament quickly passed an act which appeared to harmonize the justices' rule with English law. Justices could continue to determine settlement and bastardy cases and to authorize highway and poor rates; but if a justice made an order or judgment affecting a parish in which he paid rates, and that order or judgment was appealed to Quarter Sessions, the justice could not vote on the appeal.[66] Again, Parliament attempted to prevent conflict between law and the justices' powers by limiting the authority of justices acting singly or in pairs and enlarging the authority of justices as a group in Quarter

64. Sir J. Burrow, *Decisions of the Court of King's Bench upon settlement cases . . . from March 1732 to June 1776, inclusive,* 2nd ed. (London, 1786), pp. 194–198, *Rex* v. *Great Chart.*

65. Sess. Cas. 5, *Plimpton St. Maurice* v. *Plimpton Morris.*

66. 16 George II c. 18.

Sessions. The routine administrative activities of any individual justice just might violate the spirit of English law, but the local bench collectively personified the law and its principles. Composed of gentlemen, who were by definition cognizant of the virtues of England's constitution, of volunteers and therefore of altruistic public servants, and of amateurs who therefore represented freedom based on self-government, the bench of justices collectively embodied the ideals of English government.

During the reigns of the later Stuarts and early Hanoverians, the governmental ideals personified by the justices had subtly been modified. The ideal justice was less a 'patriarch' and more a 'patrician.' He was less the voice of a community and more its disinterested judge. He was less the 'natural leader' of his neighbourhood and more its administrator. Both patriarchal and patrician justices were undoubtedly eminent, but the bases for their eminence were somewhat different. The patriarchal justice embodied the prestige of a locally powerful individual: he wielded considerable influence as a private person; he frequently acted as a single justice in his official capacity; he might be regarded as the local miniature of the sovereign. In contrast, the patrician model had a greater tendency to present the justice as a member of a group. The patrician justice need not be a major landowner or head of an interest; instead he was a representative of the upper strata of English society, of its gentry and gentlemen. The patrician was also a member of a group of justices: he frequently acted at petty sessions with his judicial brethren; and eighteenth-century legislation assumed that the assembly of justices at Quarter Sessions represented the law and its principles. While patriarchal and patrician justices symbolized both England's sovereign and its law, the more explicitly legal framework of the patrician model emphasized the justices' affiliation with the law. Less a miniature of the sovereign than the patriarch, the patrician was more a representative of that higher English culture which had promoted and preserved England's peculiar freedoms. Indeed, the patrician's judicial service constituted a *tableau vivant* of the virtues of that culture, for by assuming the duties of his office he paid homage to the concept of voluntary self-government under law. In contrast, the patriarchal model assumed that the justice's service was the natural corollary of his private power, a power which the central government had acknowledged in appointing him to office.

As both patrician and patriarchal models assumed that the justice occupied a station in society superior to that of those he governed, many of the differences between the models derive from the ways in which each sketched his relation to his inferiors. The patriarchal justice was the leader of his neighbourhood, and his leadership was based on his prestige and power as a private individual in that neighbourhood. The patrician justice was more distanced from the specific local community which he governed. Ideally, he was disinterested and therefore unaffected by the judgments and administrative decisions he made. In comparison to the patriarchal model, the patrician model placed less emphasis on the private ties which bound the justice to his local community and more emphasis on the institutional and cultural ties which bound him to his fellow justices. The patriarchal ideal enabled the justice to think of his judicial service in the context of specific local demands—indeed of the demands of specific individuals in his locality—and of his relation to specific individuals. But the patrician ideal encouraged the justice to regard his official activity as service to a wider and less limited public. So the evolution of patriarchal to patrician model governor entailed greater definition of the nature of governmental power. Local government became less an extension of the myriad varieties of authority wielded by powerful private individuals and less a rather vaguely defined control of specific and unique neighbourhoods. Instead, local government became more the execution of tasks, tasks which involved giving directions to parish officers, and tasks whose execution might lead the justice to conclude that alterations in the county's administrative system and expansion of its facilities would benefit the county's inhabitants.

As the justices' manuals indicate, the process of transformation from patriarchal to patrician rule had begun before the later Stuart era. It also undoubtedly continued into the Victorian era. Nonetheless, this evolution in the style of rule had been encouraged by changes in the politics and local administration of later Stuart and early Hanoverian England. The rise of party made England's political nation more sensitive to partiality in local government. Before the rise of party, justices had undoubtedly acted so as to further their interests, but a gentleman did not have to assume that any one interest would always dominate the bench. Several interests might have influence in a county, and if a plaintiff found that justices in one interest were reluctant to act on his plaint, he might appeal to justices in other interests. Before the rise of party, local power had been structured by a number of interests arrayed in alliances of varying patterns. But party divided the interests into two opposing groups, and Whig hegemony subordinated one group to the other. Under the later Stuarts and early Hanoverians, partiality in local government became more obvious. Likewise, since later Stuart and early Hanoverian justices wielded more administrative powers than their Tudor predecessors and wielded them in a petty sessional structure which enabled the majority of justices to control the administration of an entire division, they had greater opportunity to enhance their interests through administrative decision. At the same time as administrative and political change increased the range and visibility of judicial partiality, the concept of government enshrined by the Glorious Revolution discouraged partial rule. Law was to reign supreme in this land. By the mid-eighteenth century, the potential for partial rule inherent in judicial office was regarded as implicitly antithetical to the principles of English government. So early Hanoverian Tories argued that justices, like judges, should be disinterested; and Lord Chancellor Hardwicke thought it reasonable to adopt a policy of dismissal from the bench which attenuated the tie between the justices and party.

Alterations in both politics and local administration likewise worked to emphasize the bond between justices as they weakened those between justices and their neighbourhoods. Both party and the consolidation of petty sessions encouraged the justices to present themselves to the governed as a unified group. Cohesion among the justices enabled them further to develop their administrative institutions, and when party strife diminished they found themselves equipped with structures for government which could be used to extend the scope and efficiency of local administration. Yet the mere presence of social problems or administrative machinery which allowed justices to deal with these problems is insufficient explanation for later eighteenth-century justices' increased attempts to adopt administrative solutions for social problems. When justices embarked on these new administrative initiatives, they were adopting an altered concept of administrative decision, a concept which regarded administrative decision as a product of general concerns about local government rather than as a verdict on battles between interests. To some extent, the new approach to administration was fostered by decline in party and political strife. To some extent, it was also fostered by the appointment of increasing numbers of mere gentry and gentlemen to the bench. The needs of both party and administration persuaded Lord Chancellors to appoint these lesser justices. As the lesser justices possessed insufficient influence as private persons to claim an interest, they might be more apt to regard administrative decision as a disinterested response to the problems of government.

Nonetheless, however much the new justices may have modified the model of the model justice, they displayed characteristics common to both the partician and the patriarchal ideals. They emanated from the upper ranks of society and therefore had sufficient leisure to serve as volunteer rulers, as amateur nonprofessional governors, as personifications of the principle of the self-government of a community through the service of its more prominent citizens. It was in the last decade of the eighteenth century that Parliament turned, with regret, to consideration of justices modelled according to specifications differing from those which made the eighteenth-century ideal so laudable. The service proferred voluntarily by gentlemen resident in London and its environs had proved insufficient. New magistrates were needed, magistrates who would constantly and conscientiously administer the criminal law. And so, in 1792 Parliament passed an act appointing the first stipendiary magistrates in England.[67] Stipendiary magistrates were professionals, and so they would be expected to possess more intimate knowledge of the law than their amateur colleagues. In 1835, five years at the bar was made a minimum qualification for the stipendiary magistracy.[68] Yet, however well qualified the stipendiaries, they lacked the major attributes of both models of the eighteenth-century model justice. They were not volunteers; gentlemen who had to be paid to rule could not claim to be the natural leaders of their communities; neither could they present themselves as altruistic governors of their neighbourhoods. To such rulers, Parliament would not extend the informal prerogatives of judicial office. The act creating stipendiary magistrates prohibited these magistrates from sitting as members of Parliament, from voting for a member of Parliament in the area of their jurisdiction, and from influencing the votes of those they governed. Even in creating a living repudiation of both models of the eighteenth-century justice, the act honoured those models and their paradoxes. The ideal and privileged justice was still the gentleman volunteer, the administrator of the law who ruled under law though he knew not the law, the leader of his community who served for no reward other than considerable autonomy in leading his community. Perhaps the act establishing stipendiary magistracy was the last statement of a century less squeamish than its successors in acknowledging the connection between justice, administration, and political power—a connection it viewed as natural.

67. 32 George III c. 53.

68. A. Harding, *A Social History of English Law* (Harmondsworth, Middx., 1966), p. 346.

Appendices

General Introduction to Appendices

The establishment of any criteria requires certain rather arbitrary definitions. The following explanation and the introductions to appendices B, C, and D are intended to clarify the criteria adopted.

A general problem applicable to all of the tables was the definition of the scope of the term "commission of the peace." The tables are intended to trace changes in the composition of the bench, and so are focused on the part of the commission following the honourary clause. The honourary clause lists all members of the Privy Council, all titled aristocrats appointed to the commission and sons of titled aristocrats, the judges who rode the circuit and those judges resident in the county, and the solicitor- and attorney-general. While there was some change in the composition of the honourary clause—notably an increased tendency to appoint the sons of aristocrats toward the end of the period—I decided that, since very few of those named in the honourary clause ever acted as justices, the persons named in that clause were either peripheral or irrelevant to my inquiry. Therefore, they are not included in the tables. John Campbell of Sundridge, who succeeded to the dukedom of Argyle in 1761, was listed in the nonhonourary portion of Kent's commission before he succeeded to his title. As I have excluded all other heirs of aristocrats, I also excluded Campbell from those tables in appendices B through E which examine Kent's bench.

It will be seen that some of the tables in appendices B, C, D, and E indicate that the number of justices on Kent's commission at a certain date differs slightly from the number stated to be in Kent's commission in appendix A. Appendix A lists the number of names in the counties' commissions of the peace. Occasionally, a justice is named twice. Since Appendices B, C, D, and E chart the status and activity of those who were actually justices of Kent, their tables do not include the fictional justice created when the same person was listed twice in a commission.

APPENDIX A.

The Number of Justices in the Commissions of England and Wales

THE NUMBER OF JUSTICES IN THE COMMISSIONS OF ENGLAND AND WALES[a]

	1680	*1702*											*1761*			
Bedfordshire	39	60	1705[b]/56	1714/70									60	1769/108		
Berkshire	39	75	1706[b]/80										245			1792/221
Buckinghamshire	51	80	1705[b]/111	1714/136	1715/121							1755/167	239			
Cambridgeshire	37	62	1705[b]/60	1714/75		1721/59			1731/79				67			
Cheshire	43	48	1705[b]/95	1714/105				1727/79					145			
Cornwall	41	108	1705[b]/107					1727/90							1786/195	
Cumberland	32	36	1705[b]/34				1726/36						62			
Derbyshire	27	53	1705[b]/58	1714/70									128			1792/165
Devonshire	77	115	1706/109			1723/129				1737/155			197			1795/298
Dorset	42	72	1705[b]/68			1722/82							109			1795/187
Durham	40	57	1705[b]/59		1716[c]/46											
Essex	86	117	1706/140	1714/188									317			

Gloucestershire	54		134	1706/120								196			
Hampshire	63		97		1714/152							229			
Herefordshire	57		58							1736[e]/107		139			1792/187
Hertfordshire	49		88	1706/108	1714/123							197			
Huntingdonshire	19		31		1714/35							61	1783/70		
Kent	129	1688[f]/137	153	1706[f]/165	1714[f]/240	1715[f]/202	1720[f]/175	1729[f]/215	1733[f]/239		1758[f]/243	254		1791/280	
Lancashire	64														
Leicestershire	38		64			1716/62		1730/81				144			1792/163
Lincoln Holland	22		37									134			
Lincoln Kesteven	38	1698[g]/44	53		1712[g]/74		1720[g]/75					196			1793/259
Lincoln Lindsey	34		62									197			
Middlesex	129		212									499[h]			
Monmouthshire	28		53		1714/70		1722/54			1741[i]/66		116			

APPENDIX A. *Continued*

	1680	*1702*										*1761*		
Norfolk	96		111			1714/131					1747/135	172		
Northamptonshire	41	1687/44	66	1706/62		1714/84	1715/76	1725/64				163		1794/364
Northumberland	41		42									107	1790/201	
Nottinghamshire	27[d]		38		1711[k]/64							67	1786/137	
Oxfordshire	47		96			1715/110	1721/86					155	1791/208	
Rutland	11		14			1715/32			1731/30			31		
Shropshire	56		68				1721/109					234		1793/394
Somerset	52		81			1714/112		1722/100		1739[l]/157		268		
Staffordshire	41		60			1715/64						172	1792/189	
Suffolk	80		112	1706/119				1724/131				154	1791/205	
Surrey	87		118	1706/149		1714/202					1742/345	488		1796/435
Sussex	73		88			1714/103	1715/115		1731/98			163		

Warwickshire	35		57								151			
Westmorland	23		23				1727/29				46			
Wiltshire	74		98								212			1797/191
Worcestershire	35		62			1714/82					137			
E. Yorkshire	24		44	1705[b]/62			1725/78				109		1792/101	
N. Yorkshire	42		75	1705[b]/66							1762/233			
W. Yorkshire	56	1696/91	104	1705[b]/106		1714/126				1748/228		1762/341	1792/449	
Anglesey	13		31	1707/26		1715/39				1748/56	59		1789/85	
Brecknockshire	28		45	1707/38			1724/40				98			
Caernarvonshire	22		26			1714/44		1729/45	1739/38	1754/62	67			
Cardiganshire	24		22	1706/34				1727/51			100	1785/99		
Carmarthenshire	41		35	1706/38		1715/60					85			
Denbighshire	41		41		1710/39					1740/67	85		1790/100	

APPENDIX A. *Continued*

	1680	1702							1761		
Flintshire	34	49			1723/50			1756/56	120		
Glamorgan	25	38				1726/44			115		1793/181
Merioneth	24	30	1707/24				1733/41	1748/61	64	1792/208	
Montgomeryshire	39	36							76		
Pembrokeshire	38	38	1704/43	1714[m]/52		1727[n]/69		1742/76	138		
Radnorshire	22	27					1734/52	1755/48	61		1793/151

[a]This numeration excludes peers, their sons, and all others in the honourary list introducing the commission. The column for 1680 is based on the number in the commissions after the remodelling of 1679/1680 as shown in House of Lords R.O., House of Lords MSS no. 275, Main Papers, Nov. 9, 1680. That for 1702 is based on B.L., Harleian MSS 7512. Unless otherwise noted, the other numerations are based on P.R.O., C234.

[b]P.R.O., C193/43.

[c]Herts. R.O., Panshanger MSS D/EP/F153.

[d]S. N. Esquire, *A Catalogue of All His Majesties Justices of the Peace* . . . (London, 1680).

[e]B.L., Add MSS 35602, f. 100.

[f]Kent A.O., Q/JC

[g]Lincolnshire A.O., Q/JC

[h]Greater London R.O., MJP/L11a

[i]B.L., Add MSS 35600, ff. 283–284.

[k]Herts. R.O., Panshanger MSS D/EP/F154

[l]Somerset R.O., Q/JC110

[m]Herts. R.O., Panshanger MSS D/EP/F155

[n]B.L., Add. MSS 35601, ff. 57–58.

APPENDIX B

The Status and Education of Kent's Justices

INTRODUCTION

Appendix B charts the status and education of Kent's justices by displaying the proportion of justices who could not be identified, the proportion of justices who succeeded their father or paternal grandfather on Kent's bench, the proportion of justices who were succeeded on Kent's bench by their sons, and the proportion of justices who attended the universities or the Inns of Court. Some justices were appointed, removed, and reappointed—and possibly again removed and reappointed. The tables in appendix B list the justice who was removed and reappointed one time only: at the date of first appointment.

All Kent's commissions of the peace issued between 1679 and 1800, except that of October 2, 1688, have been reconstructed through the commissions deposited at the Kent Archives Office, the *nomina ministrorum* in the Assize records and the fiats ordering the issue of new commissions—both at the Public Record Office, books of the peace for 1680–1683, 1685, 1702,[1] and lists of justices in February 1688 in Sir G. Duckett's *Penal Laws and Test Act.*[2] Information on appointment to the commission before 1679 is based on: (1) the commissions of August 17, 1670, and April 19, 1671, deposited at the Kent Archives Office; (2) books of the peace for 1660–1664, 1657–1658, and March 1652;[3] (3) *Justices of the Peace, 1642–1700,* which is a computer printout of changes in the commissions noted in the Crown Office Docquet Books compiled by B. Crook and deposited at the Public Record Office; and (4) lists of Kent's commission in 1608, 1626, and 1636 in J. H. Gleason's *The Justices of the Peace in England, 1558 to 1640.*[4] It is possible that some justices who were both appointed to and removed from Kent's commission before 1679 do not appear in the lists of justices obtained from these sources. All justices appointed after 1679, who do not appear in the two commis-

1. House of Lords R.O., House of Lords MSS no. 275, Main Papers, 9 Nov., 1680; P.R.O., C193/12/4–5; B.L., Harleian MSS 7512.
2. Sir G. Duckett, *Penal Laws and Test Act, 1687–1688,* 2 vols. (London, 1882).
3. P.R.O., C220/9/4, C193/12/3, C193/13/5; B.L., Stowe MSS 577.
4. J. H. Gleason, *The Justices of the Peace in England, 1558 to 1640* (Oxford, 1960).

sions issued in 1679, are treated as if the date of their appointment after 1679 is the date of their first appointment. Since my information on the composition of Kent's commissions before 1679 is less complete than that for 1679 to 1800, it is likely that table B–2 slightly understates the proportion of late seventeenth-century justices who could boast paternal predecessors on Kent's bench. Likewise, since registers of admissions to the universities before 1660 do not note all those admitted, table B–4 may slightly understate the proportion of late seventeenth-century justices who had attended university.[5]

Tables B–2 and B–3 focus on the ability of families to entail judicial office to the next generation. Occasionally, a justice might be the heir of a relative who was neither his father nor his grandfather. If this justice bore the same last name as the gentleman from whom he inherited, his succession to the gentleman's lands represented the continuity of that gentleman's family's local power. Since tables B–2 and B–3 trace the ability of families to pass judicial honours on to the next generation, and since categories classifying justices' judicial predecessors have to be kept simple for the sake of clarity, I have adopted the following rules: a gentleman who inherited from a Kentish justice who both bore the same last name as himself and was of an older generation is considered to have had a "father" or "paternal grandfather" on Kent's commission; conversely, a justice whose estates and judicial office pass to a gentleman of the next generation bearing the same last name as himself is considered to have been succeeded in his office by a "son." In order to clarify my use of "generation": (1) inheritance by a brother or first cousin is not counted as passing office to a "son"; (2) inheritance by a nephew or first cousin once removed is.

It will be noticed that the size of some groups of appointees in table B–3, which traces the proportion of justices succeeded in office by their sons, is slightly lower than the size of the same groups in other tables. Occasionally, a justice was elevated to the peerage some time after he had been appointed to the commission. Since the aim of this table is to investigate the extent to which gentry and gentlemen were able to perpetuate their family's judicial status, and since elevation to the peerage raised the new peer considerably above his former fellows and made appointment to the bench virtually automatic, those who were so elevated have been excluded from table B–3.

5. L. Stone, "The Size and Composition of the Oxford Student Body 1580–1910," in *The University in Society*, ed. L. Stone, vol. 1 (Princeton, 1974), pp. 12, 83.

TABLE B-1. PROPORTION OF KENT'S JUSTICES WHO COULD NOT BE IDENTIFIED

Justice Group	*Number in Group*	*Number not Identified*	*Percent not Identified*
Commissions of Mar. and July 1679	148	1	1%
Appointed Jan. 1680 –Jan. 1685	45	3	7
Appointed Feb. 1685 –Aug. 1688	85	21	25
Appointed 1689 –Mar. 1693	70	4	6
Appointed July 1693 –Feb. 1700	46	5	11
Appointed July 1700 –July 1704	54	6	11
Appointed July 1705 –June 1710	53	1	2
Appointed Feb. 1711 –1713	90	13	14
Appointed Oct. 1714 –1718	62	9	14
Appointed 1719–1723	61	10	16
Appointed 1724–1743	191	23	12
Appointed 1751–1761	193	19	10

Table B-1 charts those not identified in county histories and genealogies, in the records of the universities and Inns of Court, in the lists of those probably appointed to the commission by virtue of other office, and in the lists of the mayors of Kent's boroughs.

TABLE B-2. JUSTICES PRECEDED BY PATERNAL ANCESTOR ON KENT'S BENCH

Justice Group	*Number in Group*	*Paternal Grandfather on Commission*	*Father on Commission*	*Father or Paternal Grandfather on Commission*	*Percent Father or Paternal Grandfather on Commission*
Commissions of Mar. and July 1679	148	21	44	52	35%
Excluding clerics	147	21	44	52	35
Appointed Jan. 1680–Jan. 1685	45	6	10	12	27
Appointed Feb. 1685–Aug. 1688	85	8	19	20	23
Appointed 1689–Mar. 1693	70	9	16	21	30
Excluding clerics	69	9	16	21	30
Appointed July 1693–Feb. 1700	46	6	12	15	33
Appointed July 1700–July 1704	54	9	21	24	44
Excluding clerics	52	9	21	24	46
Appointed July 1705–June 1710	53	7	16	17	32
Excluding clerics	52	7	16	17	33
Appointed Feb. 1711–1713	90	9	21	23	25
Excluding clerics	86	9	20	22	26
Appointed Oct. 1714–1718	62	6	13	16	26
Excluding clerics	61	6	13	16	26
Appointed 1719–1723	61	9	15	16	26
Appointed 1724–1743	191	35	59	67	35
Excluding clerics	181	35	56	64	35
Appointed 1751–1761	193	44	76	79	41
Excluding clerics	175	43	71	74	42

TABLE B-3. JUSTICES SUCCEEDED BY THEIR SONS ON KENT'S BENCH

Justice Group	*Number in Group*	*Those with Son on Commission*	*Percent succeeded by Son on Commission*
Commissions of Mar. and July 1679	148	63	43%
Excluding clerics	147	63	43
Appointed Jan. 1680–Jan. 1685	45	16	35
Appointed Feb. 1685–Aug. 1688	84	16	19
Appointed 1689–Feb. 1693	70	19	27
Excluding clerics	69	19	27
Appointed July 1693–Feb. 1700	45	14	31
Appointed July 1700–July 1704	53	18	34
Excluding clerics	51	18	35
Appointed July 1705–June 1710	52	16	31
Excluding clerics	51	16	31
Appointed Feb. 1711–1713	90	16	18
Excluding clerics	86	16	19
Appointed Oct. 1714–1718	62	21	34
Excluding clerics	61	21	34
Appointed 1719–1723	60	12	20
Appointed 1724–1743	188	49	26
Excluding clerics	178	46	26
Appointed 1751–1761	191	49	26
Excluding clerics	173	45	26

TABLE B-4. UNIVERSITY EDUCATION OF KENT'S JUSTICES

Justice Group	*Number in Group*	*Number attending University*	*Percent attending University*
Commissions of Mar. and July 1679	148	50	34%
Excluding clerics	147	49	33
Appointed Jan. 1680 –Jan. 1685	45	20	44
Appointed Feb. 1685 —Aug. 1688	85	12	14
Appointed 1689– Mar. 1693	70	27	39
Excluding clerics	69	27	39
Appointed July 1693 –Feb. 1700	45	8	18
Appointed July 1700 –July 1704	54	17	31
Excluding clerics	52	15	29
Appointed July 1705 –June 1710	53	19	36
Excluding clerics	52	18	35
Appointed Feb. 1711 –1713	90	23	25
Excluding clerics	86	19	22
Appointed Oct. 1714 –1718	62	14	23
Excluding clerics	61	14	23
Appointed 1719 –1723	61	9	15
Appointed 1724 –1743	191	52	27
Excluding clerics	181	43	24
Appointed 1751 –1761	193	69	36
Excluding clerics	175	52	30

TABLES B-5. ATTENDANCE AT INNS OF COURT BY KENT'S JUSTICES

Justice Group	*Number in Group*	*Number attending Inns*	*Percent attending Inns*
Commissions of Mar. and July 1679	148	59	40%
Excluding clerics	147	59	40
Appointed Jan. 1680–Jan. 1685	45	17	38
Appointed Feb. 1685–Aug. 1688	85	22	26
Appointed 1689–March 1693	70	24	34
Excluding clerics	69	24	35
Appointed July 1693–Feb. 1700	46	13	28
Appointed July 1700–July 1704	54	11	20
Excluding clerics	52	11	21
Appointed July 1705–June 1710	53	8	15
Excluding clerics	52	8	15
Appointed Feb. 1711–1713	90	19	21
Excluding clerics	86	18	21
Appointed Oct. 1714–1718	62	10	16
Excluding clerics	61	10	16
Appointed 1719–1723	61	10	16
Appointed 1724–1743	191	39	20
Excluding clerics	181	39	22
Appointed 1751–1761	193	34	18
Excluding clerics	175	33	19

APPENDIX C

The Landholdings of Kent's Justices

INTRODUCTION

It is difficult to determine the landed wealth of gentry families. Usually the estate records of these families have not survived. In order to discover whether one group of justices controlled more lands and more tenants than another, I have adopted an admittedly simplistic expedient. During the last quarter of the eighteenth century, Edward Hasted wrote a *History and Topographical Survey of the County of Kent* in which he described the descent of the manors, advowsons, and eminent houses of the county, recorded the holders of the properties leased from the Church, detailed the more notable monuments and plaques in the parish churches, and listed the donors of all charitable bequests. In the late nineteenth century, the section dealing with Blackheath hundred, that area nearest London and subject to the most frequent changes in ownership and the most extensive new building, was revised by H. H. Drake. I decided to give every justice mentioned in Hasted or Drake a "point," to give an additional "point" for record of possession of eminent house, seat, or seat and adjacent manor, and to give another point every time the justice was listed as in possession of another piece of property. As the pattern which emerged from this system indicated that justices in the Blackheath, Bromley, Rochester, and Tonbridge divisions were less eminent than their brethren elsewhere in the county, I attempted to compensate for possible gaps in Hasted's knowledge and Drake's elaborations by giving "points" to those noted in parish and town histories of the first three of these divisions and in an account of plaques and monuments in the churches of the diocese of Rochester, which encompassed most of west Kent.[1] This "point" system is disturbingly similar to the "counting of manors" now discounted by historians. Since Hasted and Drake note possessions of farms and woods, and of properties leased from the Church, the record compiled from their works is somewhat different from that obtained by counting manors. Of course, the method is entirely open to the objections that one property may not be of comparable value to another, though they are given identical point value,

1. For these sources see chapter X, n. 14.

and that Hasted's and Drake's record of nonmanorial property is quite probably incomplete.[2] It should be stressed that the landholding "data" derived by the "Hasted point system" is based on fundamentally incomplete evidence. Yet, it should also be noted that this system does seem to yield results that accord with other evidence on the relative status of Kent's gentry. As table C-3 indicates, the greater a justice's "points," the more likely it is that he boasts both predecessors and successors on the commission, and that he has been to a university and an Inn of Court. Likewise, comparison of the deputy lieutenants to the élite as defined by these "points" indicates that the point system does distinguish between the greater and the lesser justices. The deputy lieutenants were chosen primarily from among the greater gentry. Sixty percent of the justices with "points" of five or above were deputy lieutenants in the 1740s. Only 15 percent of the remaining justices were so honoured.[3] While the evidence derived from this "point system" is by no means conclusive, it does deserve to be rated as suggestive. When such evidence is used in conjunction with other data and agrees with conclusions drawn from other data, it is probably indicative of an historical fact.

It will be noted that the following tables do not evaluate the landed estates of those justices who were heir to other justices and were on the same commission as those to whom they were heir. If the lands these heirs would eventually inherit were accredited to them, these lands would be counted twice. If the heirs are not credited with any lands, their status in landed society is undervalued. Therefore, heirs have been excluded from the calculation, and the presence of an heir in the judicial complement of a division is simply noted in the column headed "heirs." It should be noted that the heirs on the 1743 commission appear most prominently in the divisions characterized as the gentry heartland.

There is, of course, no reason for a county boundary to limit a gentleman's desire to acquire property, but the limits of county histories are those of county boundaries. Therefore, it has not been possible to trace the gentry's landholdings in counties other than Kent. The divisions of Blackheath, Bromley, Tonbridge, Sevenoaks, and Cran-

2. Hasted does distinguish between possession of manorial rights and manorial lands.

3. For a list of those appointed deputy lieutenants in 1738, see P.R.O., SP 44/181, pp. 416–417. For a list of those appointed deputy lieutenants in 1746, see P.R.O., SP 44/186, pp. 404–405.

brook bordered upon one or both of the counties of Surrey and Sussex, and a very few of the justices in these divisions were also on the Surrey or Sussex commission. It might be argued that the following tables undervalue the landholdings of these divisions' justices and that this undervaluation accounts for the relatively small estates credited to the justices of the first three of these divisions.

On the other hand, it might be argued that restriction of the extension of the survey of landholdings to Surrey and Sussex would distort the tables to the disadvantage of the greater landholders. Even in the mid-seventeenth century, Kent's baronets were much more likely to take their brides from counties other than Kent, Sussex, or Surrey than the untitled gentry. In acquiring a wealthy and distinguished bride, a baronet may well have acquired a wealthy and distinguished estate in a distant county. Indeed the more eminent a landholder, the more likely it is that he could acquire another notable estate by marriage. In the mid-eighteenth century, the baronets in Kent's commission were concentrated in divisions which did not border Surrey and Sussex, and the divisions in which they resided boasted a number of untitled gentry who were as distinguished as Kent's baronets. Cursory examination of the commissions of other counties reveals that some of these baronets were justices of distant regions—of Oxfordshire, Bedfordshire, Gloucestershire, Somerset, and Brecknockshire, for example. It is therefore likely that the slight undervaluation of the landholdings of justices in divisions bordering Surrey and Sussex is balanced by undervaluation of the landholdings of the justices in the gentry heartland.

TABLE C-1. LANDHOLDINGS OF THOSE FIRST APPOINTED TO KENT'S COMMISSION, 1711–1713 AND 1714–1718

Petty Sessional Division	*Number appointed 1711–1713 who are heir to J.P.s then sitting on the bench*	*Number of remaining J.P.s appointed 1711–1713*	*Landholdings: Hasted Points*		*Number appointed 1714–1718 who are heir to J.P.s then sitting on the bench*	*Number of remaining J.P.s appointed 1714–1718*	*Landholdings: Hasted Points*	
			Total	*Average*			*Total*	*Average*
Wingham	0	3	7	2.3	0	5	26	5.2
Home	0	5	16	3.2	0	3	6	2.0
Elham	0	0	0		0	1	6	6.0
Ashford	0	0	0		0	3	9	3.0
Sittingbourne	0	6	11	1.8	0	3	9	3.0
Rochester	0	7	20	2.9	0	3	8	2.7
Cranbrook	0	11	26	2.4	1	6	19	3.2
Tonbridge	0	5	9	1.8	0	1	2	2.0
Bearsted	1	6	24	4.0	2	6	14	2.3
Malling	0	6	34	5.7	0	1	4	4.0
Sevenoaks	0	6	28	4.7	0	5	17	3.4
Dartford	0	5	13	2.6	0	1	3	3.0
Bromley	0	12	23	1.9	0	5	11	2.2
Blackheath	1	10	6	0.6	0	9	11	1.2
Subtotal	2	82	217	2.6	3	52	145	2.8
Residence Unknown	0	2	0	0	0	3	0	0
Out of County	0	4	12	3.0	0	4	7	1.7
Total	2	88	229	2.6	3	59	152	2.6

TABLE C-2. RELATION BETWEEN PETTY SESSIONAL DIVISION AND LANDHOLDINGS OF THE JUSTICES IN KENT'S COMMISSION OF 1743

Petty Sessional Division	Number of justices who are heir to those who are also justices in 1743	Number of remaining justices	Landholdings: Total Hasted Points	Average Hasted Points
Wingham	2	18	83	4.6
Home	1	14	69	4.9
Elham	1	7	58	8.3
Ashford	1	8	78	9.8
Sittingbourne	0	10	33	3.3
Rochester	0	10	19	1.9
Cranbrook	0	15	56	3.7
Tonbridge	1	5	12	2.4
Bearsted	4	20	97	4.9
Malling	1	6	62	10.3
Sevenoaks	1	19	85	4.5
Dartford	0	8	31	3.9
Bromley	0	20	45	2.3
Blackheath	0	25	39	1.6
Total	12	185	767	4.1
Residence Unknown		10	4	
Total	—	195	771	4.0
Out of County		16	24	
Total	—	211	795	3.8

TABLE C-3. LANDHOLDING, STATUS, AND ACTIVITY AS A JUSTICE, KENT'S COMMISSION OF 1743

Landholding: Hasted Points	*0*	*1*	*2*	*3*	*4*	*5*	*6*	*7–8*	*9–13*	*14–22*
Deputy Lieutenant in the 1740s	0%	20%	12%	17%	25%	40%	64%	54%	78%	67%
Paternal Grandfather J.P.	0%	10%	6%	26%	29%	10%	57%	31%	44%	78%
Father J.P.	5%	0%	21%	52%	38%	30%	64%	54%	56%	67%
Son J.P.	5%	10%	18%	26%	38%	50%	50%	54%	89%	78%
Attends University	14%	10%	21%	22%	21%	30%	43%	31%	56%	67%
Attends Inn of Court	14%	5%	18%	26%	21%	30%	36%	23%	11%	33%
Barrister	9%	0%	15%	9%	13%	10%	21%	8%	0%	11%
Acts as J.P., 1737–1750	55%	55%	64%	61%	71%	80%	57%	77%	100%	78%
Total number of J.P.s	22	20	33	23	24	10	14	13	9	9

This table excludes those justices in the 1743 commission who were subsequently ennobled, those who were clerics, those who were heir to lands possessed by other justices named in the 1743 commission, those whose county of residence is not known, and those who did not reside in Kent.

TABLE C-4. UNIVERSITY ATTENDANCE AND SOCIAL STATUS: KENT'S COMMISSION OF 1743

J.P.s	*J.P.s attending university Total 46*		*J.P.s not attending university Total 131*	
Paternal grandfather J.P.	24	52%	17	13%
Father J.P.	26	57%	33	25%
Son J.P.	24	52%	34	26%
Attended Inn of Court	20	43%	16	12%
Barrister	11	24%	7	5%
Landholding:				
Total Hasted points	298—average 6.5		462—average 3.5	

This table excludes those justices on the 1743 commission who were subsequently ennobled, those who were clerics, those who were heir to lands possessed by other justices named in the 1743 commission, those whose county of residence is not known, and those who did not reside in Kent.

APPENDIX D

Petty Sessional Division and Status in Kent's Commission

INTRODUCTION

As shown in chapter VII, the Tonbridge division was nonexistent before 1706, and the Home and Sittingbourne divisions may not have assumed their final forms until the early 1740s. As that chapter also demonstrates, justices near the border of divisions may have chosen to act in the neighbouring division in which they were not resident. Tables D-1 to D-3 place justices according to their residence within the borders of the divisions as deduced from the licensing registers of 1753.

TABLE D-1. DISTRIBUTION OF KENT'S JUSTICES

Petty Sessional Division	*Number of Justices* 1680	1704	1713	1720	1743	1761	*1680 as percent of 1761*
Wingham	14	27 (Wingham and Home)	15	14	20	21	67%
Home	12		18	14	15	18	67
Elham	5	4	7	8	8	6	83
Ashford	9	9	6	5	9	16	56
Sittingbourne	4	6	9	8	10	14	28
Rochester	7	8	18	9	10	14	50
Cranbrook	6	6	18	10	15	15	40
Tonbridge	2	4	8	5	6	7	28
Bearsted	17	11	16	18	24	29	59
Malling	10	13	14	11	7	15	67
Sevenoaks	6	5	8	14	20	24	25
Dartford	3	5	7	7	8	10	30
Bromley	5	9	16	13	20	21	24
Blackheath	9	15	22	21	25	25	36
Total	109	122	182	157	197	235	
Residence Unknown	6	2	2	5	10	5	
Total	115	124	184	162	207	240	
Out of County	18	20	21	13	16	12	
Total	133	144	205	175	223	252	

TABLE D-2. STATUS AND PETTY SESSIONAL DIVISION: KENT'S COMMISSION OF 1743

Petty sessional division	Number of justices	*Percent of Justices:* Preceded on commission by paternal grandfather	Preceded on commission by father	Succeeded on commission by son	Attending university	At Inn of Court
Wingham	19	21%	32%	32%	32%	11%
Home	15	60	33	33	53	40
Elham	8	63	63	63	13	13
Ashford	9	33	56	78	56	11
Sittingbourne	10	0	20	50	10	0
Rochester	10	0	10	0	20	0
Cranbrook	15	33	47	20	27	27
Tonbridge	6	17	17	0	17	33
Bearsted	24	29	54	50	38	25
Malling	7	86	100	57	57	14
Sevenoaks	20	30	60	65	35	65
Dartford	8	13	13	25	25	38
Bromley	20	10	25	20	10	15
Blackheath	25	0	8	12	8	4
Residence Unknown	10	0	20	0	0	10
Out of County	15	7	13	7	13	7
Total	221	23%	34%	32%	25%	20%

This table excludes the two justices on the 1743 commission who were subsequently ennobled.

TABLE D-3. STATUS AND PETTY SESSIONAL DIVISION: JUSTICES APPOINTED TO KENT'S BENCH BETWEEN 1751 AND 1761

		Percent of Justices				
Petty sessional division	*Number of justices appointed*	*Preceded on commission by paternal grandfather*	*Preceded on commission by father*	*Succeeded on commission by son*	*Attending university*	*At Inn of Court*
Wingham	12	33%	42%	58%	50%	25%
Home	14	43	64	43	79	36
Elham	2	100	100	100	0	50
Ashford	12	50	75	50	58	25
Sittingbourne	12	25	33	17	50	17
Rochester	15	0	7	7	7	0
Cranbrook	7	14	43	14	29	29
Tonbridge	7	0	14	29	43	14
Bearsted	19	32	47	21	32	11
Malling	10	30	60	40	10	20
Sevenoaks	17	24	47	24	35	18
Dartford	10	10	40	40	50	20
Bromley	22	23	32	9	32	18
Blackheath	15	7	27	27	20	7
Residence Unknown	5	0	0	0	20	0
Out of County	12	8	33	0	33	25
Total	191	23%	39%	26%	36%	18%

This table excludes the two justices who were subsequently ennobled.

APPENDIX E

Propensity of Justices to Act

TABLE E-1. ACTIVITY OF KENT JUSTICES BY DIVISION

Division	*Total in 1743*	*Total Acting 1737–1750*		*Number in 1743 Commission Obtaining Dedimus after 1750*	*Number Appointed 1751–1761*	*Obtaining Dedimus*	
		Number	*Percent*			*Number*	*Percent*
Wingham	20	15	75%	2	12	5	42%
Home	15	9	60		14	7	50
Elham	8	6	75		2	2	100
Ashford	9	8	89		12	5	42
Sittingbourne	10	6	60		12	7	58
Cranbrook	15	6	40	2	7	3	43
Rochester	10	3	30		15	13	87
Tonbridge	6	5	83		7	4	57
Bearsted	24	18	75	1	19	8	42
Malling	7	7	100		10	7	70
Sevenoaks	20	14	70		18	11	61
Dartford	8	5	63		11	4	36
Bromley	20	11	55		22	9	41
Blackheath	25	16	64		15	5	33
Residence Unknown	10	1	10		5	2	40
Out of County	16				12		
Total	223	130	58%	5	193	92	48%

TABLE E-2. PROPENSITY OF KENT JUSTICES TO OBTAIN DEDIMUSES

Commission	*Number Appointed*	*Obtaining Dedimus in Five Years*		*Number Obtaining Dedimus Later*	*Total Obtaining Dedimus*	*Percent Obtaining Dedimus*
		Number	*Percent*			
1743 Commission						
Laymen	59	20		6		
Clerics	2	0		0		
	61	20	33%	6	26	43%
1751 Commission						
Laymen	81	30		6		
Clerics	6	3		0		
	87	33	38	6	39	45
1758 Commission						
Laymen	59	17		4		
Clerics	9	7		1		
	68	24	35	5	29	43
1761 Commission						
Laymen	35	21		0		
Clerics	3	3		0		
	38	24	63	0	24	63
Little fiat,[a] 1768						
Cleric	1	1	100		1	100
1769 Commission						
Laymen	124	21		13		
Clerics	22	9		1		
	146	30	21	14	44	30
Little fiat, 1770						
Laymen	4	1	25	1	2	50
Little fiat, 1774						
Laymen	2	1	50	0	1	50
Little fiat, 1775						
Laymen	1	1	100		1	100
1776 Commission						
Laymen	36	14		3		
Clerics	11	5		1		
	47	19	40	4	23	49
Little fiat, 1776						
Cleric	1	0	0	0	0	0
Little fiat, 1780						
Laymen	6	5	83	0	5	83
Little fiat, 1784						
Laymen	1	1	100		1	100

TABLE E-2. *Continued*

Commission	*Number Appointed*	*Obtaining Dedimus in Five Years*		*Number Obtaining Dedimus Later*	*Total Obtaining Dedimus*	*Percent Obtaining Dedimus*
		Number	*Percent*			
1791 Commission						
Laymen	92	40		8		
Clerics	11	3		1		
	103	43	42	9	52	50

[a]From mid-century, Lord Chancellors used the little fiat to add justices to the commission without renewing the entire commission. See L. Glassey and N. Landau, "The Commission of the Peace in the Eighteenth Century: A New Source," *B.I.H.R.* 45 (1972): 253, 255–258.

FIG. E-1. NUMBER OF DEDIMUSES OBTAINED ANNUALLY BY J.P.S. OF ENGLAND AND WALES (FIVE-YEAR MOVING AVERAGE) 1728–1833

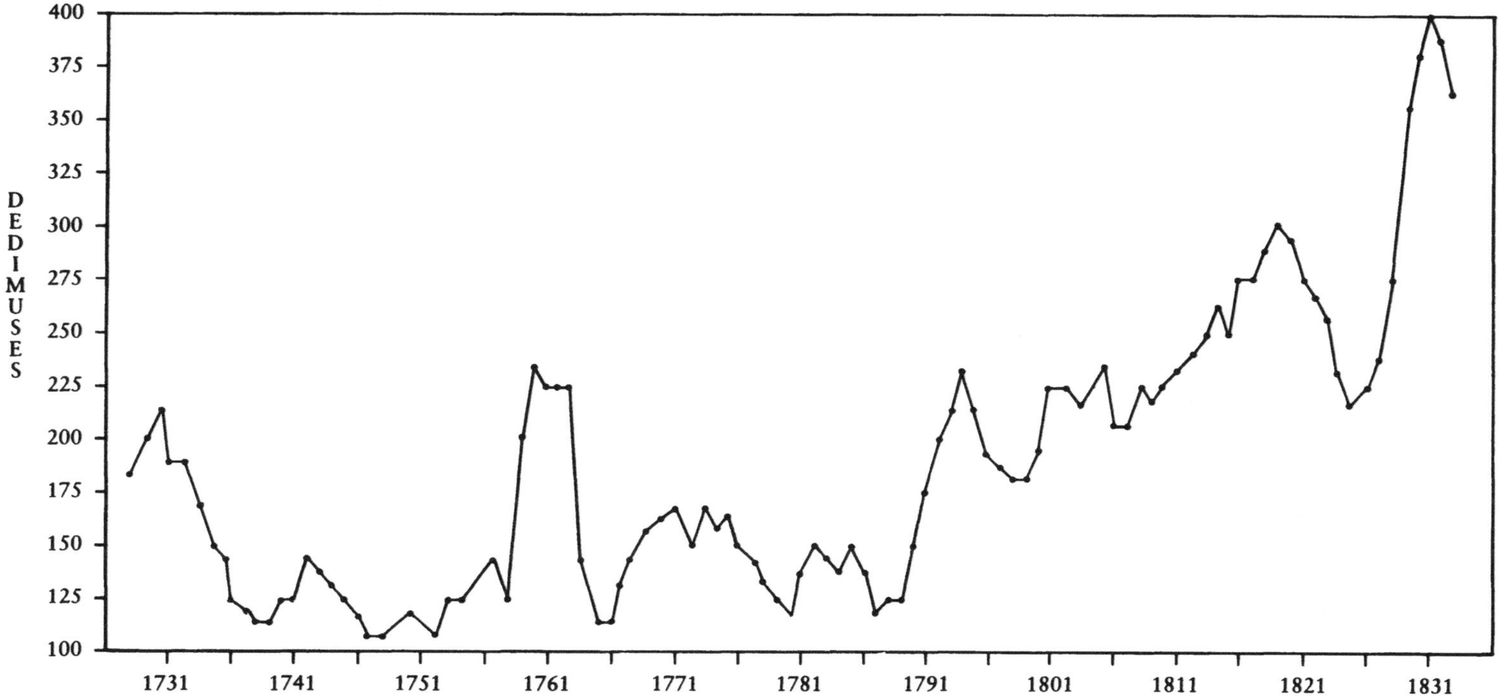

Sources: P.R.O., C193/66, C193/44–45, C220/9/8–9. Each county received a new commission shortly following the accession of a new monarch, and this accounts in part for the increase in the number of dedimuses obtained in the five years surrounding the dates of the accession of new monarchs (1727, 1760, 1820, and 1830).

Bibliography of Manuscript Sources

BODLEIAN LIBRARY, OXFORD

Ballard MSS, vol. 15, miscellaneous letters to Dr. Charlett
Rawlinson MSS B338, copy of the pollbook for the election of Kent's knights of the shire, Feb., 1715

BRITISH LIBRARY, LONDON

Newcastle papers:
Add. MSS 32686, General correspondence, 1697–1723
Add. MSS 32687, Home correspondence, 1724–1732
Add. MSS 32704, Home correspondence, Jan.–Aug., 1745
Add. MSS 32804, Diplomatic correspondence, 1745
Add. MSS 32993, Memoranda to June 1748
Add. MSS 32874, General correspondence, Sept.–Oct. 1757

Hardwicke papers:
Add. MSS 35351, Correspondence of the first Earl of Hardwicke with his son, Viscount Royston, 1731–1757
Add. MSS 35585–35590, Hardwicke's personal correspondence, 1725–1749
Add. MSS 35600–35604, Hardwicke correspondence on the appointment of sheriffs and justices of the peace, 1737–1756
Add. MSS 35679, Hardwicke papers relating to Cambridgeshire, 1741–1763
Add. MSS 35870, Minutes of the Cabinet and Privy Council, 1733–1766

Liverpool papers:
Add. MSS 38446–7, Papers relating to the Duchy of Lancaster, 1609–1794

Brockman papers:

Add. MSS 42586–42590, Correspondence, 1600–1843

Add. MSS 42592–3, Political and parliamentary papers

Add. MSS 42596–7, Family papers, including notes by William Brockman on his activity as a J.P. in the 1690s

Add. MSS 42598–42600, Justice's diaries of William, James, and Ralph Drake Brockman

Add. MSS 52924, Diary of Sir John Knatchbull, 1688–1690

Egerton MSS 2985, Heath and Verney Papers, VIII, Miscellaneous papers relating to administrative work in late seventeenth-century Kent performed by Sir John Heath

Harleian MSS 7512, Book of the Peace [1702]

Stowe MSS 577, Book of the Peace, Mar. 1. 1651[2]

Loans:

Blenheim MSS, c1–36, Legal papers of the third Earl of Sunderland, 1708–1709

Portland Loan, Loan 29/27, Miscellaneous papers relating to Herefordshire

Loan 29/50, nos. 70–79, Harley papers relating to Herefordshire

Loan 29/131, Harley correspondence, including that with Henry Compton, Bishop of London

Loan 29/196, Harley papers, general correspondence, 1710

BROMLEY CENTRAL LIBRARY, BROMLEY

Bromley petty sessions minute books, 1747–1787

Bromley vestry record book

CUMBRIA COUNTY RECORD OFFICE, CARLISLE

Lonsdale MSS, no. 76, James Lowther to Sir John Lowther, Jan. 9 (I wish to thank Professor Henry Horwitz for giving me a transcript of this letter.)

DR. WILLIAMS' LIBRARY, LONDON

Morrice MSS Q, Entering book, 1686–1689

DOG INN, WINGHAM, KENT

Wingham petty sessions minute book, 1705–1715 (A xerox copy of this book is deposited at the Kent A.O.)

GLOUCESTERSHIRE RECORD OFFICE, GLOUCESTER

Sherborne MSS D678, Fam Set 57/D, Dutton correspondence, 1733–1742

GREATER LONDON RECORD OFFICE, LONDON

MJP/L11a, Middlesex commission of the peace, 1761

GREENWICH LOCAL HISTORY LIBRARY, WOODLANDS, BLACKHEATH, LONDON

Blackheath petty sessions minute books, 1743–1749, 1795–1809

HAMPSHIRE RECORD OFFICE, WINCHESTER

18/M51/595–6, Shelley-Rolls MSS, notebooks of Gabriel Walters, including notes on his activities as justice of Kent in the early eighteenth century

HEREFORDSHIRE RECORD OFFICE, HERTFORD

Panshanger MSS, letters and papers of Lord Chancellor Cowper

HOUSE OF LORDS RECORD OFFICE, LONDON

House of Lords, Main Papers, no. 321(c52), list of Popish recusants in Kent, Dec. 4, 1680

no. 274, minute book of the committee of the House of Lords considering the commissions of the peace, Nov. $\frac{9}{22}$, 1680

no. 275, book of the peace, Nov. 9, 1680

no. 2011, list of those removed from the commissions of the peace since Midsummer, 1700, delivered Mar. 20, 1703[4]

no. 2117, list of those appointed to the commissions of the peace since the last Parliament, delivered Feb. 16, 1704[5]

HUNTINGTON LIBRARY, SAN MARINO, CALIFORNIA

ST 57, vols. 16–30, Chandos correspondence, out-letters, 1718–1727

KENT ARCHIVES OFFICE, MAIDSTONE

Petty Sessions

PS/A1, Ashford petty sessions minute book, 1773–1793

PS/Ma1–4, Malling petty sessions minute books, 1747–1800

PS/NA1, North Aylesford (Rochester division) petty sessions minute book, 1754–1767

PS/Se1, Sevenoaks petty sessions minute book, 1709–1710

PS/T, Tonbridge petty sessions minute book, 1767–1784

PS/US1, Upper Scray (Sittingbourne division) petty sessions minute book, 1722–1729

PS/US4–6, Upper Scray (Sittingbourne division) "sitting books," 1760–1765, 1776–1794

PS/W1–3a, Wingham petty sessions minute books, 1715–1744, 1756–1769

Quarter Sessions

Q/AB 70–72, Bridge Treasurer's accounts, papers, and correspondence

Q/SB, Quarter Sessions papers. A collection of the "miscellaneous" papers that arise in the conduct of Quarter Sessions' business, including the original of settlement orders returned to Quarter Sessions, some records of convictions before justices acting out of Quarter Sessions, and letters to the clerk of the peace and the chairman of Quarter Sessions.

Q/FAe1,2, East Kent Treasurers' accounts

Q/SI, indictment rolls. After 1730 the east Kent rolls and after 1732 the west Kent rolls include recognizances.

Q/SPi, process books of indictments

Q/SMa, Quarter Sessions minute books

Q/SO, Quarter Sessions order books

Q/SRc, recognizance rolls

Returns to Quarter Sessions

Q/RLv, returns of licensing sessions and register of licences granted in the county.

Q/RSj, returns of convictions for swearing profane oaths

Q/RSr, returns from petty sessions on recruitment, 1708

Justices of the Peace and Clerk of the Peace

Q/CR 5–6, returns to parliamentary queries on justices' clerks and the justices, 1830s

Q/JC 12–57, Kent commissions of the peace, 1670–1761

Q/JL 1–2, lists of justices, 1705–1777

Q/JQc 1–2, correspondence on the appointment of justices, 1817–1829

Q/JQw, writs of dedimus potestatem, 1705–1771

Papers of Kent's justices, Lords Lieutenant and custodes rotulorum

Wykham Martin MSS: U23/O1, Ralph Buffkin's justice's diary, 1689–1713

Filmer MSS: U120/C43, Sir Edward Filmer's correspondence, 1733–1743

U120/O11, Sir Edward Filmer's papers as justice of the peace

U120/O22, Sir Edward Filmer's justice's diary, 1750–1754

Sackville of Knole MSS: U269, letters and papers of the eighteenth-century Dukes of Dorset, including lists of justices and deputy lieutenants
Norman MSS: U310/O14, William Emmett's and George Norman's justice's diaries
Gordon Ward Collection: U442/O45, Paul D'Aranda's justice's diary and minutes of Sevenoaks petty sessions, 1708
Waldershare Park MSS: U471/A3, Countess of Rockingham's rental book of estates in Kent, 1746–1758
Dering MSS (Surrenden Estate): U570/O1, Sir Edward Dering's justice's diary, 1626–1635
Osborne MSS: U771/A14, Thomas Osborne's justice's diary
Knatchbull MSS: U951/O2, Sir Wyndham Knatchbull's precedent book
U951/O3, Sir Wyndham Knatchbull's justice's diary
U951/O4, Sir Wyndham Knatchbull's "Account of such Sessions and Sittings as I have been at, since my acting as a Justice of the Peace, A. 1734"

Pollbooks

Q/RPe1/1713, copy of the poll for the election of Kent's knights of the shire, 1713
Q/RPe1/1727, pollbook for the election of Kent's knights of the shire, 1727

Miscellaneous

NR/Z27, list of town clerks, bailiffs, and mayors of New Romney
U820/Z1, petition of the grand jury at Assizes, 1710

LINCOLNSHIRE ARCHIVES OFFICE, LINCOLN

Lincoln Kesteven Q/JC, Lincoln Kesteven commissions of the peace
Massingberd MSS 20/93, William Massingberd at Gunby to Burrell Massingberd in London, April 1, 1711
Monson MSS 28B/14/1–4, papers relating to the family of the earls of Rockingham

LONDON SCHOOL OF ECONOMICS, LONDON

Webb Collection on Local Government, vols. 136–140, extracts from Kent Quarter Sessions order books and notes on Kentish courts with authority concurrent with or exclusive of the county's justices

LONGLEAT HOUSE, WILTSHIRE

Coventry Papers vi, f.230, Sir Thomas Peyton to Coventry, Jan. 23, 1679/1680

MAIDSTONE MUSEUM, MAIDSTONE

Bearsted petty sessions minute book, 1748–1764

UNIVERSITY OF NOTTINGHAM LIBRARY, NOTTINGHAM

Portland Collection, Pw A 1171–2, letters from Somers to the first Earl of Portland, 1693

Pw 2 Hy929, papers of Robert Harley, letter from the first Earl of Oxford, 1721

PUBLIC RECORD OFFICE, LONDON

Assizes

Ass 24/23–24, Order Books, Western Circuit, 1677–1687, 1725–1743

Ass 31/1–2, Agenda Books, Home Circuit, 1735–1752

Ass 35/114–200, indictment rolls, Home Circuit, 1673–1760, includes grand jury lists and *nomina ministrorum*

Chancery

Index 4214–4220, Crown Office Docquet Books, 1660–1810 (now C231/7–13)

C193/12/3–5, Entry books for commissions of the peace, May 1662–Mar. 1664, May 1680–July 1683, and ca. Oct., 1685

C193/13/5, Entry for commissions of the peace, Mar. 1657–Mar. 1658

C193/43, Dedimus book from 1701 to 1710 [actually goes to 1714]

C193/44–45, Justices Dedimus Books, Clerk of the Crown's Account with the Secretary of Commissions, 1738–1786

C193/66, Crown Office Cash Book, 1725–1745

C202, Petty Bag Chancery writs

C220/9/4, Entry book for commissions of the peace, Oct. 1660–Dec. 1662

C220/9/8–9, Petty Bag Office, Account Books of Money received from the Clerk of the Crown for Justices' Dedimus Potestatem, 1763–1838

C234, Fiats appointing justices of the peace, 1705–1929

Exchequer

E137/18/7–10, King's Remembrancer's Estreats of Fines, Charles II–George II

E362/3–60, Lord Treasurer's Remembrancer's Estreats of Fines, 1681–1731. Both estreats contain lists of justices present at Quarter Sessions

King's Bench

Index 6658–6659, Great Doggett Books, reign of George II

KB 10/25, indictments, King's Bench, Crown Side, 1740–1741

KB 28/159, Plea Roll, King's Bench, Crown Side, Mich. 15 George II

Privy Council

PC2, Privy Council Registers

State Papers, Domestic

SP 44/82–85, Secretaries of State, correspondence on criminal matters, 1728–1756

SP 44/106, Domestic Secretaries' Letter Book, Sunderland, 1706–1709

SP 44/116–134, Domestic Secretaries' Letter Books, 1714–1758

SP 44/171–187, Military entry books, 1704–1754, includes appointments of deputy lieutenants

SP 44/283–285, Minutes and correspondence of the Lords Justices, June–Nov., 1720

PUBLIC RECORD OFFICE OF NORTHERN IRELAND, BELFAST

De Ros MSS D638/85/1, Earl of Macclesfield to Lord Coningsby, July 28, 1720

T1135/18, Lord Coningsby to the Earl of Macclesfield, Jan. 7, 1720–1721

RED LION HOTEL, WINGHAM, KENT

Wingham petty sessions minute book, 1703–1712

ROCKINGHAM CASTLE, NORTHAMPTONSHIRE

Rockingham MSS, rentals of the estates of the second Earl of Rockingham, and rental of Lewis Watson's estates in Kent, 1753

SEVENOAKS PUBLIC LIBRARY, SEVENOAKS, KENT

Sevenoaks petty sessions minute book, 1715–1726

SOMERSET RECORD OFFICE, TAUNTON

Q/JC/110, commission of the peace for Somerset, 1739

SOUTH CARLTON, LINCOLNSHIRE

Monson MSS, including estate papers, wills, and settlements of the Rockingham and Monson families

SURREY RECORD OFFICE, KINGSTON UPON THAMES

PS3/1/1, Kingston petty sessions minute book, 1752–1794

WILTSHIRE RECORD OFFICE, TROWBRIDGE

Justice's diary of William Hunt, 1744–1749

INFORMATION RECEIVED, DERIVED FROM THE RECORDS OF KENT'S TOWNS

Information on the Town Clerks of Canterbury received from A. Oakley, Cathedral Librarian, Canterbury

Information on the Town Clerks of Faversham received from R. Lawrie, Town Clerk

Information on the Town Clerks and Recorders of Folkestone received from K. C. Sussams, Borough Librarian

Information on the Mayors of Hythe received from A. Roper, Honorary Archivist

Information on the Bailiffs of Lydd received by C. L. Winfield, Town Clerk

Information on the Mayors of Queensborough received from D. A. Clarke, Town Clerk

Information on the Town Clerks and Recorders of Rochester received from J. A. McGhee, Town Clerk

Information on the Town Clerks, "Councillors," and Mayors of Tenterden received from G. A. Saunders, Town Clerk.

Index

Designer: Lisa Mirski / Bonnie Smetts
Compositor: Huron Valley Graphics
Printer: McNaughton & Gunn, Inc.
Binder: John H. Dekker & Sons
Text: 10/13 Sabon
Display: Sabon and Garamond Old Style

www.ingramcontent.com/pod-product-compliance
Ingram Content Group UK Ltd.
Pitfield, Milton Keynes, MK11 3LW, UK
UKHW040233290926
15471UKWH00002B/175

9 780520 307636